FORGOTTEN STARS

Forgotten Stars

Rediscovering Manilius' Astronomica

Edited by
STEVEN J. GREEN AND KATHARINA VOLK

OXFORD
UNIVERSITY PRESS

OXFORD

UNIVERSITY PRESS

Great Clarendon Street, Oxford OX2 6DP

Oxford University Press is a department of the University of Oxford.
It furthers the University's objective of excellence in research, scholarship,
and education by publishing worldwide in

Oxford New York

Auckland Cape Town Dar es Salaam Hong Kong Karachi
Kuala Lumpur Madrid Melbourne Mexico City Nairobi
New Delhi Shanghai Taipei Toronto

With offices in

Argentina Austria Brazil Chile Czech Republic France Greece
Guatemala Hungary Italy Japan Poland Portugal Singapore
South Korea Switzerland Thailand Turkey Ukraine Vietnam

Oxford is a registered trade mark of Oxford University Press
in the UK and in certain other countries

Published in the United States
by Oxford University Press Inc., New York

© Oxford University Press 2011

The moral rights of the author have been asserted
Database right Oxford University Press (maker)

First published 2011

British Library Cataloguing in Publication Data

Data available

Library of Congress Cataloging in Publication Data

Data available

Typeset by SPI Publisher Services, Pondicherry, India
Printed in Great Britain
on acid-free paper by
MPG Books Group, Bodmin and King's Lynn

ISBN 978-0-19-958646-2

3 5 7 9 10 8 6 4 2

To the Memory of
Josèphe-Henriette Abry

Preface

The *Astronomica* of Manilius: a five-book didactic poem at least partly written under Augustus. General first impressions might lead one to think that Manilius has much to attract critical attention from the Anglophone world. For the classical scholar, both the Augustan age and the 'golden' nature of its literary production are of course central to research and teaching. For the more general enthusiast, Manilius claims to be—and the extant literary record would support him—the first Roman to set out the workings of natal (or genethlialogical) astrology, a topic to whose enduring popular interest any daily western newspaper will testify.

As is often the case, however, first impressions can be misleading, and Manilius' *Astronomica* remains a work much understudied and underrated in the Anglophone world. A major contributing factor to this neglect is the significant difference one must observe between the ancient and (popular) modern definitions of natal astrology. In the western world, astrology is typically depicted as inclusive and accessible to all classes, vague on detail and psychologically comforting in nature; its practitioners are deemed to have little recourse to proper scientific calculation; such predictions are therefore felt to be harmless, and certainly apolitical (in spite of some notorious anecdotes about the use of astrology by political figures such as Hitler and Ronald Reagan; see Barton 1994*a*: 4).

Ancient Roman astrology, particularly at the time in which Manilius was writing, could not be more different, as Tamsyn Barton's important works have shown us. To be sure, echoes of the modern-day popular astrologer can be found in the charlatans that peddled their unsophisticated trade to the masses in the Circus Maximus of ancient Rome. But proper astrology was, for the Romans, a serious science: it was fact. The complex calculations required to cast a horoscope rendered astrology an art exclusive to a small number of (foreign) experts. Moreover, particularly under Augustus, astrology became an intensely political affair, as the emperor manipulated the potential of astrology for positive political discourse whilst at the same time fashioning legislation to curtail its use among his rivals.

Consistent with the serious scientific nature of astrology under the Roman Empire, Manilius' serious astrological poem has proven to be very difficult for Anglophone readers—classicists and general enthusiasts alike—to master. Housman's infamously harsh verdict on the poem—that its only saving grace was its author's 'eminent aptitude for doing sums in verse' (1903–30: 2.xiii)—has been allowed to rule for too long, and yet it might seem to be a fair assessment to the reader who is stuck in the mathematical mire of the calculation of the ascendant in book 3. Nor does Manilius appear to help himself in this matter: books 4 and 5 are far more accessible to the lay reader, and yet one wonders how many readers can steel themselves to get this far. Goold's 1977 Loeb edition, with its extensive explanatory notes and diagrams, marked a significant development in the accessibility of Manilius to a larger audience. It is surprising, therefore, that Goold's masterly production has not generated the critical attention from Anglophone scholars that it deserved. (The most noteworthy pieces on Manilius in English since 1977 have typically come along approximately every ten years: see especially Wilson 1985; Neuburg 1993; Volk 2001, 2002.) It is with a similar (but reinforced) desire to put this neglected poet firmly back on the scholarly map that the present volume is offered. (Katharina Volk has recently published the first major monograph on Manilius to appear in English (Oxford, 2009). Our conference, however, can claim no credit for inspiring this particular piece of scholarship.)

The current collection of essays started its life as a major conference on Manilius, co-organized by the editors of this volume and held at Columbia University, New York, in October 2008. The aim was to bring together an international contingent of scholars for an interdisciplinary exploration of Manilius at an auspiciously significant time, close to the bimillennial celebration of the poem's composition. All of the contributors to the conference have revised their pieces for the current volume, with a further chapter subsequently commissioned. The international angle to the scholarship is particularly important for a study of Manilius. As Katharina Volk shows in her introductory chapter on the history of scholarship, Manilius has attracted significantly more attention from French, German, and particularly Italian scholars than it has from their Anglophone counterparts. Three leading exponents of this international Manilian surge—Josèphe-Henriette Abry, Wolfgang Hübner, and Enrico Flores respectively—are represented in the present volume. As none of the major works from these scholars has found its way into English, however, one important additional aim of the present volume (and the original conference) is to bring together the important cultural or national scholarly traditions that have so far existed largely in isolation.

The range of perspectives from which Manilius is approached in the present volume is testament to both the complexity of Manilius and the differing fruitful avenues for modern interdisciplinary inquiry. Matters of literary interest, especially generic affiliation and intertextuality, are complemented by approaches which assess the socio-political, philosophical, scientific, and astrological resonance of the poem. Moreover, as a salutary counterbalance to the relative neglect of our author in recent times, the popular reception of the poem, especially in Renaissance times, is also explored. The volume is organized under five subheadings—Intellectual and Scientific Backdrop, Integrity and Consistency, Metaphors, Didactic Digressions, and Reception. These divisions are, of course, somewhat artificial, as there are frequent internal dialogues between papers from different sections, and they should be treated as convenient means of reader orientation rather than definitive statements of content and critical approach.

The editors would like to thank the Columbia Classics Department for hosting the conference and especially Marvin Deckoff for his generous financial support and unflagging good cheer. We also gratefully acknowledge funding from the Stanwood Cockey Lodge Foundation. In addition, we are most grateful to Hilary O'Shea for her support of the volume, as well as to Jenny Wagstaffe and the staff at OUP for their assistance during the book's production. Special thanks go to our editorial assistant Sarah Kaczor for her help in preparing the typescript.

And finally, a note of real sadness. It was with great regret that news was received of the untimely death of Josèphe-Henriette Abry just a week or so after the conference in October 2008 (to which she had been too ill to travel). The editors would like to dedicate this volume to dear Joette, whose appreciation and enthusiasm for Manilius permeate this book and provide inspiration for future studies on the author.

SJG and KV

Leeds and New York
March 2010

Contents

List of figures	xiii
Abbreviations	xv
Contributors	xvii

1. Introduction: A century of Manilian scholarship   1
   Katharina Volk

I. INTELLECTUAL AND SCIENTIFIC BACKDROP

2. More sentiment than science: Roman stargazing
   before and after Manilius   13
   Elaine Fantham

3. Manilius' conflicted Stoicism   32
   Thomas Habinek

4. Myth and explanation in Manilius   45
   Daryn Lehoux

II. INTEGRITY AND CONSISTENCY

5. Watch this space (getting round 1.215–46)   59
   John Henderson

6. On two Stoic 'paradoxes' in Manilius   85
   Wolfgang-Rainer Mann

7. Manilian self-contradiction   104
   Katharina Volk

8. *Arduum ad astra*: The poetics and politics of horoscopic
   failure in Manilius' *Astronomica*   120
   Steven J. Green

III. METAPHORS

9. Tropes and figures: Manilian style as a reflection of
   astrological tradition   141
   Wolfgang Hübner

10. Sums in verse or a mathematical aesthetic?   165
    Duncan F. Kennedy

11. *Census* and *commercium*: Two economic metaphors
    in Manilius   188
    Patrick Glauthier

IV. DIDACTIC DIGRESSIONS

12. Digressions, intertextuality, and ideology in didactic
    poetry: The case of Manilius   205
    Monica R. Gale

13. Cosmos and imperium: Politicized digressions in
    Manilius' *Astronomica*   222
    Josèphe-Henriette Abry

14. A song from the universal chorus: The Perseus and
    Andromeda epyllion   235
    James Uden

V. RECEPTION

15. Augustus, Manilius, and Claudian   255
    Enrico Flores

16. Renaissance receptions of Manilius' anthropology   261
    Caroline Stark

17. Lorenzo Bonincontri's reception of Manilius' chapter
    on comets (*Astr.* 1.809–926)   278
    Stephan Heilen

Bibliography   311
Index Locorum   339
General Index   342

List of figures

4.1 Jan Baptist Weenix, Portrait of René Descartes (*c*.1648). 56

9.1 The mixed figure of Capricorn. Codex Leidensis Vossianus
lat. 79 (9th c.), fo. 50^{v}. 143

9.2 The comic characters of Menander according to *Astr.* 5.472–3. 146

9.3 The characters of the four planets according to *Astr.* 5.472–3. 146

9.4 Planetary geography according to Ptolemy, *Tetrabiblos* 2.3. 147

9.5 Quincunx of the planets. Codex Leidensis Vossianus lat. 79
(9th c.), fo. 80^{v}. 148

9.6 The idealized *enantiodromia* of the zodiacal Fishes.
Impression of a marble slab from Roman Egypt. 150

9.7 The real configuration of the two zodiacal Fishes. 151

9.8 The 36 *decani* distributed over the twelve zodiacal signs. 154

9.9 The system of signs that are 'regarding' or 'hearing' each other. 156

17.1 King Ferrante praying during the earthquake of 1456.
BNF Ms. Ital. 1711 (Giuniano Maio, *De maiestate*), fo. 19^{r}. 309

Abbreviations

References to classical texts typically follow the style of abbreviations of the
Oxford Classical Dictionary (3rd edn.).

A&R	*Atene e Roma*
AC	*L'Antiquité classique*
AClass	*Acta classica*
AFLN	*Annali della Facoltà di Lettere e Filosofia dell'Università di Napoli*
AJA	*American Journal of Archaeology*
AJP	*American Journal of Philology*
ANRW	W. Haase and H. Temporini (eds.), *Aufstieg und Niedergang der römischen Welt: Geschichte und Kultur Roms im Spiegel der neueren Forschung* (Berlin: De Gruyter, 1972–)
BIBR	*Bulletin de l'Institut Historique Belge de Rome*
CCAG	*Catalogus Codicum Astrologorum Graecorum*
CCC	*Civiltà classica e cristiana*
CCJ	*Cambridge Classical Journal*
CErc	*Cronache ercolanesi*
CJ	*Classical Journal*
CP	*Classical Philology*
CQ	*The Classical Quarterly*
CR	*The Classical Review*
EMC	*Échos du monde classique*
EphK	*Eygetemes Philologiai Közlöny*
GIF	*Giornale italiano di filologia*
G&R	*Greece and Rome*
GW	*Gesamtkatalog der Wiegendrucke* (1925–38, 1978–)
HSCP	*Harvard Studies in Classical Philology*
ICS	*Illinois Classical Studies*
JHI	*Journal of the History of Ideas*
JRS	*Journal of Roman Studies*
LICS	*Leeds International Classical Studies*
LS	A. A. Long and D. N. Sedley, *The Hellenistic Philosophers*, 2 vols. (Cambridge: Cambridge University Press, 1987)
MC	*Il mondo classico*
MD	*Materiali e discussioni per l'analisi dei testi classici*
Neuer Pauly	H. Cancik and H. Schneider (eds.), *Der Neue Pauly:*

	Enzyklopädie der Antike, 16 vols. (Stuttgart: Metzler, 1996–2003)
OCD	S. Hornblower and A. Spawforth (eds.), *The Oxford Classical Dictionary*, 3rd edn. (Oxford: Oxford University Press, 1996)
OLD	P. G. W. Glare (ed.), *Oxford Latin Dictionary* (Oxford: Oxford University Press, 1983)
OSAPh	*Oxford Studies in Ancient Philosophy*
PACA	*Proceedings of the African Classical Association*
Pauly-Wissowa	A. F. von Pauly, G. Wissowa, and W. Kroll (eds.), *Real-Encyclopädie der classischen Altertumswissenschaft*, 24 vols. (Stuttgart and Munich: Metzler/Druckenmüller, 1894–1982)
PBSR	*Papers of the British School at Rome*
PVS	*Papers of the Virgil Society*
RBPh	*Revue belge de philologie et d'histoire*
RCCM	*Rivista di cultura classica e medioevale*
REL	*Revue des études latines*
RFIC	*Rivista di filologia e di istruzione classica*
RhM	*Rheinisches Museum*
RRC	M. H. Crawford, *Roman Republican Coinage*, 2 vols. (Cambridge: Cambridge University Press, 1974)
SicGymn	*Siculorum gymnasium*
SIFC	*Studi italiani di filologia classica*
SVF	H. F. A. von Arnim, *Stoicorum Veterum Fragmenta*, 4 vols. (Leipzig: Teubner, 1903–24)
SyllClass	*Syllecta Classica*
TAPA	*Transactions and Proceedings of the American Philological Association*
TLL	*Thesaurus Linguae Latinae* (1900–)
WS	Wiener Studien

Contributors

Josèphe-Henriette Abry† taught for many years at the University of Lyon. One of the leading Manilius scholars of the twentieth and early twenty-first centuries, she is the author of numerous articles on the *Astronomica* and other topics in ancient astrology.

Elaine Fantham is Giger Professor of Latin emeritus of Princeton University. She has edited commentaries on Seneca, Ovid, and Lucan and has recently brought out an Oxford World Classics selection of eighty Letters of Seneca. In 2009 she published *Latin Poets and Italian Gods* on the cult and poetic treatment of country gods with University of Toronto Press.

Enrico Flores is Ordinary Professor of Latin Literature at Naples University and the author of many books and essays on Greek and archaic Latin literature. He has published critical editions of Manilius, Lucretius, and Ennius' *Annales* as well as *Elementi critici di critica del testo ed epistemologia* (Naples, 1998).

Monica R. Gale is Associate Professor of Classics at Trinity College, Dublin. She is the author of *Myth and Poetry in Lucretius* (Cambridge, 1994), *Virgil on the Nature of Things: The* Georgics, *Lucretius and the Didactic Tradition* (Cambridge, 2000), and other books and articles on late Republican and Augustan poetry.

Patrick Glauthier is a Ph.D. candidate in the Classics Department at Columbia University and works mainly on Latin literature of the late Republic and early Empire. He is currently writing a dissertation on Roman scientific literature of the first century AD.

Steven J. Green is Senior Lecturer in Classics at the University of Leeds. He is author of *Ovid* Fasti *I: A Commentary* (Leiden 2004), co-editor of *The Art of Love: Bimillennial Essays on Ovid's* Ars Amatoria *and* Remedia Amoris (Oxford, 2006), and has written several articles on the interaction between Roman literature and imperial politics and religion.

Thomas Habinek is Professor and Chair of Classics at the University of Southern California. He has published extensively on topics in

Latin literature, Roman cultural history, and classical rhetoric. His current research focuses on materialist models of mind, past and present.

Stephan Heilen is Professor of Classics at the University of Osnabrück, Germany. His research focuses on astrological texts from antiquity through the Renaissance, on Neo-Latin poetry, and on the history of classical scholarship. Among his publications are several critical editions, including of Lorenzo Bonincontri's didactic poem *De rebus naturalibus et divinis* (1999).

John Henderson is Professor of Classics at the University of Cambridge and a Fellow of King's College. He teaches like crazy, but has also written stellar books, mostly on Latin literature (e.g. *A Plautus Reader*, 2009), and fateful articles across the range of classical topics: an obvious Gemini.

Wolfgang Hübner, Professor of Classics at the Westfälische Wilhelms-Universität Münster and the author of several monographs, editions, commentaries, and articles on Greek, Latin (including medieval and Renaissance Latin), Italian, French, and German literature, specializes in the history of science, especially astrology.

Duncan F. Kennedy is Professor of Latin Literature and the Theory of Criticism at Bristol University and author of *The Arts of Love* (Cambridge, 1993), *Rethinking Reality: Lucretius and the Textualization of Nature* (Ann Arbor, 2002), and *Antiquity and the Meaning of Time* (forthcoming).

Daryn Lehoux is Associate Professor of Classics at Queen's University and author of *Astronomy, Weather and Calendars in the Ancient World* (Cambridge, 2007) and *What Did the Romans Know?* (Chicago, forthcoming), as well as many articles on ancient science.

Wolfgang-Rainer Mann is Professor of Philosophy at Columbia University. His research is focused primarily on ancient Greek philosophy, but he also works on German Idealism. He is the author of *The Discovery of Things: Aristotle's* Categories *and their Context* (Princeton, 2000).

Caroline Stark is a doctoral candidate in Classics and Renaissance Studies at Yale University. Her dissertation, *The Role of Knowledge in Ancient and Renaissance Conceptions of Man*, explores ancient stories of the birth and development of man and their reception among Italian humanists.

James Uden is a graduate student at Columbia University, where Katharina Volk taught him about Manilius. He is the author of articles on Catullus, late antique elegy, the Latin fable, and the *Carmina Priapea*.

Katharina Volk is Associate Professor of Classics at Columbia University and the author of *The Poetics of Latin Didactic: Lucretius, Vergil, Ovid, Manilius* (Oxford, 2002), *Manilius and his Intellectual Background* (Oxford, 2009), and *Ovid* (Malden, Mass., 2010), as well as numerous articles on Greek and Latin poetry and the history of ideas.

1

Introduction

A century of Manilian scholarship

Katharina Volk

Despite being a Classical Latin poet in the tradition of Lucretius and Virgil, Manilius has been neglected by modern scholarship, especially in the Anglophone world. True, over the centuries since the *Astronomica*'s rediscovery by Poggio Bracciolini in 1417, its difficult text has not failed to attract editors and has often been mined as a source for ancient astrology;[1] however, critical interest in the work's poetic qualities and larger philosophical and scientific ideas has arisen only in the last few decades and has been mostly restricted to Germany, France, and especially Italy. Our aim in this volume is to encourage readers to discover Manilius, and we have invited a group of international scholars—some of them veteran Manilians, others relative newcomers to the poet—to offer stimulating and diverse perspectives on the *Astronomica*, its background, content, purpose, poetics, and reception.[2] To put their contributions in context, this chapter provides an overview of scholarship on Manilius from the early twentieth century onward, tracing important lines of inquiry and discussing the most significant publications. It is intended as an introduction not only to this

---

[1] On the editorial history of Manilius, see Maranini 1994, with a list of all editions at pp. 350–64.

[2] With the exception of Enrico Flores, all contributors participated in the conference 'Forgotten Stars: Rediscovering Manilius' *Astronomica*', organized by the editors and held at Columbia University on 24–25 October 2008.

volume, but generally to Manilius, a fascinating Latin poet who presents, we believe, a promising and rewarding subject for further scholarly study.

EDITIONS, TEXT, COMPLETENESS

Modern scholarship on Manilius begins with the commented edition of A. E. Housman (1903–30).[3] Published in five volumes over a span of nearly thirty years, and followed by an *editio minor* in 1932, this imposing work was probably consciously intended by the author to make his reputation as *the* outstanding classical scholar of his time and succeeded in doing so—though not without adding more than a shade of notoriety.[4] The edition is characterized by the editor's superior command of the manuscripts; his outstanding astrological expertise; and his bold handling of the text, including numerous transpositions and a high number of emendations.[5] It is also famous for Housman's vitriolic attacks on other scholars, found both in the Latin commentary and in the various English introductions, especially the notorious one to book 1, '75 pages of sustained and all but actionable abuse of the editors of Manilius, the editors of other Latin authors, Latin scholars as a whole, mankind in general and indeed even God' (Goold 2000: 143). Many classicists who know little about Manilius are nevertheless familiar with Housman's most famous jabs: at, for example, the edition of Elias Stoeber (it 'saw the light in 1767 at Strasburg, a city still famous for its geese', Housman 1903–30: 1.xix); the *Aetna* of Siegfried Sudhaus ('I imagine that Mr Buecheler [Sudhaus's teacher], when he first perused Mr Sudhaus' edition of the Aetna, must have felt something like Sin when she gave birth to Death', 1.xliv); and the critical abilities of Robinson Ellis ('his readers were in perpetual contact with the intellect of an idiot child', 5.xxiii).

Housman's work eclipsed all contemporary editions, including those by Theodor Breiter (1907–8), H. W. Garrod (1911; book 2

---

[3] On Housman's Manilius, see Goold 2000 and Courtney 2009.

[4] For Housman's intentions, see Goold 2000: 137–42 and Courtney 2009: 29, both of whom point out that the critic deliberately turned to Manilius only after giving up on his ambition to produce a definitive edition of Propertius.

[5] Shackleton Bailey 1979: 161 counts 236 textual changes in the *editio minor*; Courtney 2009: 333 arrives at 339.

only), and Jakob van Wageningen (1915 and 1921), all three of which were savaged by Housman in the introduction to his fifth volume (1903–30: 5.xxiii–xxxii). His influence is palpable in the work of G. P. Goold, whose Teubner (1985; 2nd edn. 1998) and Loeb (1977; 2nd edn. 1992) are now the most widely used texts of the *Astronomica*. Goold largely follows Housman's progressive approach, adopts a significant number of his emendations, and (unlike Housman) even includes in his text some verses of his own, 'exempli gratia', to fill putative lacunae. A conservative reaction to Housman's influence is apparent in the two recent Italian editions with commentary, Liuzzi 1991–7 and Feraboli *et al.* 1996–2001. The latter, whose text and apparatus were prepared by Enrico Flores, now presents serious competition to Goold and prints a version of the *Astronomica* that is, for better or for worse, much closer to the manuscripts.

Significant work on the manuscript tradition of the *Astronomica* was done by Goold, who, among other things, plausibly suggested that a copy of the work existed at Bobbio in the tenth century and was able to reconstruct the appearance of the archetype (see Goold 1954 and the introduction to Goold 1998). Michael Reeve has crucially added to our knowledge of many of the Renaissance manuscripts (see esp. Reeve 1980*a*); his concise discussion in Reeve 1983 is the best introduction to the text and transmission of the poem. In a number of publications, Enrico Flores has suggested a somewhat different scenario for the textual tradition (see e.g. Flores 1993 and Feraboli *et al.* 1996–2001: 1.lxvii–lxxix); the resulting controversy between Reeve and Goold is partly documented in Maranini 1994: 319–24.

Related to the issues surrounding the manuscripts is the question whether the *Astronomica* is complete as we have it. It is striking that, contrary to his own announcements, Manilius never treats the planets; a lacuna between lines 709 and 710 of book 5 adds further uncertainty. While many readers, through the centuries, have concluded that the poet did not finish the work, others have argued that additional books once existed but were lost in the process of textual transmission. See on this topic Thielscher 1956, Gain 1970, and especially Costanza 1987, who provides an extensive *historia quaestionis*. On a somewhat different note, Goold 1983 proposes that the missing discussion of the planets was contained in the great lacuna.

DATE AND POLITICAL CONTEXT

The only securely datable event mentioned in the *Astronomica* is the Battle of Teutoburg Forest (AD 9; cf. *Astr.* 1.898–903), which functions as a *terminus post quem* for any attempt to pin down the time of the work's composition. In the first centuries after the poem's rediscovery, there was near-general consensus that Manilius wrote during the last years of Augustus' reign. It was only after this belief was called into question in 1815 by Karl Lachmann—who suggested that references to the emperor that had been taken as pointing to Augustus might be better understood as being about Tiberius (see Lachmann 1876: 42–4)—that a fierce controversy erupted, one that shows few signs of abating even today. There are three possible scenarios: Manilius wrote exclusively under Augustus; he wrote solely under Tiberius; or he began his composition under Augustus and continued beyond the emperor's death into his successor's reign. While the Tiberian hypothesis of Lachmann and his followers appears to have lost some ground (though see the recent defence by Neuburg 1993),[6] both the Augustan and the Augusto-Tiberian theories have their dedicated defenders. Owing, no doubt, to the fact that the hybrid scenario was championed by Housman and taken over by Goold, it has entered the scholarly mainstream and is now found in such reference works as the *OCD* (= Wilson 1996), the *Neuer Pauly* (= Hübner 1999),[7] Conte 1994: 429, and von Albrecht 1994: 769. However, especially in the wake of an important article by Enrico Flores (1960–1; see also Flores in this volume), the all-Augustan hypothesis has had strong support, particularly in Italy, where it is maintained, for example, in the editions of Liuzzi 1991–7 and Feraboli *et al.* 1996–2001.[8] I review the evidence for the date in Volk 2009: 137–61, concluding that it strongly points to composition under Augustus, with no indication that Tiberius was emperor at any time while Manilius was writing.

---

[6] Other 20th-cent. proponents of a Tiberian date include Bickel 1910, Pauer 1951, Gebhardt 1961, and Baldwin 1987.

[7] Already in the 'old' *Pauly-Wissowa*, Jakob van Wageningen (himself the author of a paper on Manilius' date, 1920) championed the Augusto-Tiberian view (1928: 1116–17).

[8] Other supporters of an Augustan date include Bechert 1900, Kraemer 1904, Prinz 1912, Griset 1931, Liuzzi 1979, and Brind'Amour 1983*a*: 62–71.

Since the exact historical context of Manilius (about whose life and personal circumstances we know absolutely nothing[9]) is thus hard to determine, teasing out the poet's political stance and/or relationship to the emperor(s) is likewise difficult. The most comprehensive treatment is now found in the dissertation of Valentina S. DeNardis (2003); see also Flores 1960–1 and 1982 and Neuburg 1993. In this volume, Josèphe-Henriette Abry shows how three important digressions in the *Astronomica* poetically evoke three major Augustan monuments (the Forum Augustum, the sundial of Augustus, and the map of Agrippa), creating an intricate connection between *cosmos* and *imperium*.

A vexed question concerns Manilius' decision to write a poem on astrology in what might be considered a political atmosphere hostile to this practice. An edict of Augustus from AD 11 forbade the consultation of diviners in private or about the topic of anyone's death, and under Tiberius (who was himself a fervent believer in astrology), the putative use of horoscopes could be used as evidence against those accused of plotting against the emperor.[10] Bajoni 2004 suggests that in this context, Manilius intended his *Astronomica* as the positive advertisement of an art unfairly maligned. However, some scholars believe that the poem shows evidence of self-censorship: Manilius decided to give up on his project, especially his treatment of the astrologically significant planets, once he realized that the political situation was not propitious (see most recently Herbert-Brown 2002: 126, but cf. Volk 2009: 171 n. 95). Steven Green in his contribution to this volume proposes that the poet kept his astrological teaching deliberately obscure so as not to divulge an art potentially dangerous to the emperor; his real audience would then be not his increasingly frustrated student of astrology, but the emperor himself, uniquely positioned to appreciate both Manilius' subject matter and his discretion.

---

[9] Attempts to construct a biography and social context for Manilius are fraught with peril. Herrmann 1962, Hamblenne 1984, and Scarcia in Feraboli *et al.* 1996–2001: 1.xix–xxiii speculate on connections between the poet and an astrological writer Manilius Antiochus of the 1st cent. BC, who is mentioned once by the elder Pliny (*HN* 35.199); see Goold 1961 on Manilius' purported circle of fellow-intellectuals.

[10] On astrology under Augustus and Tiberius, see F. H. Cramer 1954: 81–108, 236–40, and 248–51, Barton 1994*a*: 41–4, and Volk 2009: 132–7 and 160–1.

WORLD-VIEW, ASTROLOGY, PHILOSOPHY

As the earliest extant comprehensive treatment of astrology, the *Astronomica* is an important source for the history of science. That a Latin author would have dedicated a lengthy poem to the topic of celestial influence is indicative of the great fascination—partly fuelled by the reception of Aratus—that the stars held for the Romans of Manilius' period. In this volume, Elaine Fantham traces this Roman interest in the heavens from Plautus to Pliny, considering the views of individual authors on such topics as cosmic order, stellar immortality, and determinism, while Daryn Lehoux discusses Manilius' relationship to another important contemporary discourse, that of myth, raising important questions about the role of mythological thought within the history of science in general.

Treatments of Manilius' astrology include Franz Boll's discussion of the *paranatellonta* of book 5 in his famous *Sphaera* (1903: 378–88). More recently, Wolfgang Hübner has dedicated a number of publications to elucidating the various features of the poet's system, including the signs of the zodiac (1982; see also Schwarz 1972 more generally on the significance of the zodiac in the *Astronomica*) and the *dodecatropos* (1995a); his article in *Aufstieg und Niedergang der römischen Welt* (1984) remains the standard introduction to the astrological aspects of the poem. In his contribution to this volume, Hübner revisits some of the themes of his earlier work, demonstrating how Manilius artfully employs poetic figures to mirror astrological ones.

The *Astronomica* presents, and celebrates, a rationally ordered cosmos in which everything is related to everything else by the principle of *sympatheia* and in which fate unfolds according to an unbroken chain of cause and effect. Most scholars consider the poem's world-view (described in detail by Lühr 1969, Reeh 1973, and Volk 2009: 217–26) to be fundamentally Stoic; see especially Salemme 2000: 27–56, as well as Lapidge 1989: 1393–7 and Luck 1984 (differently MacGregor 2005). Thomas Habinek's chapter in this volume (cf. also Habinek 2007) explores the ways in which Manilius represents the corporeality of the Stoic universe, focusing on the world's palpable bodily continuum. While it used to be fashionable, especially in German scholarship, to view Posidonius as a major source of Manilius' Stoic thought (see esp. Müller 1901, as well as Blum 1934), the lack of reliable information about this influential thinker has given recent scholars cause for scepticism (see Salemme 2000: 10–21 and Volk 2009: 231–2).

In addition to finding Stoic features in the *Astronomica*, a number of critics have posited the influence of Hermetic thought, as suggested by Manilius' claim that astrology was brought to mankind by Mercury, that is, Hermes Trismegistos (1.30). While the extant *Corpus Hermeticum* postdates the *Astronomica*, earlier Hermetic writings, including on astrology, may well have left their mark on Manilius. Kerényi 1923, Vallauri 1954, Valvo 1956 and 1978, and Volk 2009: 234–9 discuss aspects of the poem's Hermetism, while Salemme 2000: 21–6 dismisses—too dogmatically—the possibility of Hermetic influence.

A recent focus of Manilian scholarship has been the question whether there are inherent contradictions in the poet's world-view. Building on earlier work (Volk 2001, 2002, and 2009; see also Neuburg 1993: 257–82), my own contribution to this volume examines systematically various types of inconsistency in the *Astronomica* and argues that fundamental Manilian self-contradictions arise from the poet's use of different conceptual languages at different points in his poem. This approach has its critics (see already Habinek 2005: 276 n. 55 and 2007: 235–6 + n. 28). In the present volume, John Henderson discusses Manilius' treatment of the sphericity of the earth in book 1, making the case that perceived mistakes and contradictions in the passage have been misunderstood by unsympathetic readers convinced of the poem's inferiority. In a different vein, Wolfgang-Rainer Mann tackles the seeming inconsistency—for which he finds Stoic parallels—between Manilius' claim that the universe reveals itself to all humans and his statement elsewhere that only a few will be able to gain knowledge of the cosmos.

GENRE, POETICS, INTERTEXTUALITY

Major discussions of the *Astronomica* as a didactic poem include Effe 1977: 106–26, Calcante 2002, and Volk 2002: 196–245 and 2009: 174–82; Neuburg 1993 specifically treats the role of the work's addressee(s). In keeping with the conventions of the didactic genre, Manilius (or, strictly speaking, his persona) throughout the text reflects intensively on his own status as poet and teacher and his relationship to the literary tradition, stressing in particular his originality and his elevated status as *vates mundi* (cf. 2.142). These statements of poetics, which are found especially in the proems to books 1, 2, and 3, have been the subject of much recent scholarly interest: see especially Dams 1970: 15–37, Schrijvers 1983, Wilson 1985, Baldini Moscadi 1986, Perutelli 2001, Volk 2002: 209–45 and 2009: 197–215, Landolfi 2003, and Abry 2006*b* (and cf. Schindler 2000: 216–75 on the *Astronomica*'s similes). Two contributions to this volume discuss a set of striking poetic metaphors that Manilius employs in speaking about the cosmos and the ways in which human beings, including the poet, might approach it: Duncan Kennedy examines the central concept of *ratio*, pointing out that the term implies the notion of '(ac)counting', while Patrick Glauthier discusses the poet's economic language, in particular his repeated reflection on the 'wealth' and 'commerce' of the universe.

Manilius is an intensely intertextual author, who engages creatively with a number of poetic predecessors (cf. Volk 2009: 182–97). As a poet of the starry sky, he is obviously writing in the tradition of Aratus (see esp. Romano 1979*a*: 27–36, Salemme 2000: 79–90, and Abry 2007), whose description of the constellations he imitates in book 1 but whose myths of catasterism he appears to criticize in 2.37–8. A major poetic model is Virgil (see esp. Di Giovine 1978: 398–402, Wilson 1985: 289–92, Scarcia 1993, and Hübner 2006*b*). Manilius mines his work for stunning phrases, which he re-employs in different contexts (beginning with the famous *conscia fati / sidera*, *Astr.* 1.1–2 = Verg. *Aen.* 4.519–20), while also occasionally 'correcting' the classical poet's position: for example, on the history of civilization, which Manilius presents in a more optimistic light (see Effe 1971).

Manilius' most important predecessor in the genre of Latin scientific poetry is Lucretius, and the *Astronomica* maintains a continuous dialogue with the *De rerum natura* (see esp. Rösch 1911, Lühr 1969, Di Giovine 1978, Flores 1996, Abry 1999*b*, and Gale 2005: 111–12). While the Augustan poet follows his Republican model's ambition to create a monumental 'Weltgedicht' that comprehensively explains the workings of nature (the five books of Manilius are the second-longest ancient didactic poem after Lucretius' six), he takes strong exception to his Epicurean world-view and polemicizes against it at a number of places in the *Astronomica* (most notably 1.483–93, where the poet ridicules the idea that the universe might be a random conglomerate of atoms). Manilius has thus been fairly described as a veritable 'anti-Lucretius'.

Two contributions to this volume focus on Manilian intertextuality. Monica Gale examines how Manilius creatively engages with his didactic predecessors, most notably Lucretius and Virgil, in a number of digressions. James Uden tackles the most extensive excursus of the poem, the story of Perseus and Andromeda in book 5, showing the ways in which Manilius has carefully adapted his sources in order to produce a version of the myth in keeping with the ideological thrust of his poem.[11]

RECEPTION

No ancient source mentions Manilius, but allusions in a number of authors prove that his poem continued to be read throughout antiquity and was known to, among others, Lucan, Petronius, Calpurnius Siculus, Tertullian, and—as Enrico Flores demonstrates in his contribution to this volume—Claudian.[12] There are significant parallels between the *Astronomica* and Germanicus' translation of Aratus; however, given that the two poets were contemporaries and that their works cannot be dated exactly, it remains unclear who influenced whom.[13] The ancient author most indebted to Manilius is the fourth-century astrological writer Firmicus Maternus, who in book 8 of his *Mathesis* closely follows the *Astronomica*'s discussion of the *paranatellonta*, without, however, giving his model any credit.[14]

Following his rediscovery, Manilius was widely read by scholars and poets of the Italian Renaissance (see Hübner 1980 and Maranini 1994). Two chapters in this volume treat the *Astronomica*'s reception in this

---

[11] On Manilius' intertextuality with Ovid, see further Di Giovine 1978: 402–6 and Flores 1995. For the large literature specifically on the Perseus and Andromeda episode, see Uden's paper.

[12] On the reception of Manilius, see generally Maranini 1994; on echoes in ancient authors, see van Wageningen 1928: 1130–1, as well as Schwemmler 1916 (Lucan), Eriksson 1956: 71–8 (Petronius), and Costanza 1984 (Calpurnius Siculus and Tertullian).

[13] On Manilius and Germanicus, see Wempe 1935, Fantham 1985, and Abry 1993*b*.

[14] On Manilius and Firmicus, see Boll 1903: 394–412, Skutsch 1910, Fontanella 1991, and Abry 1999*a*.

period. Stephan Heilen discusses how the humanist Lorenzo Bonincontri (*c.*1410–91) reacts to Manilius' treatment of comets, both in his 1484 commentary on the *Astronomica* and in his two didactic poems titled *De rebus naturalibus et divinis* (on which see further Heilen 1999). Caroline Stark traces the reception of Manilius' anthropology in both Bonincontri and the *Urania* of Giovanni Pontano (1429–1503), showing how the *Astronomica* served as an inspiration for Renaissance debates about the status of man and his place in the universe.

APPROACHING MANILIUS

Since Manilius is not currently much studied even by classicists, I have thought it useful to conclude this chapter with a few (necessarily subjective) tips for the reader who is approaching the *Astronomica* for the first time (for a more detailed commented bibliography, see Volk forthcoming). G. P. Goold's Loeb, with its lucid translation and extensive introduction, is the obvious place to start. Anybody embarking on a close reading of the Latin text would do well to have Goold's Teubner and Feraboli *et al.* 1996–2001 open at the same time, and to keep Housman 1903–30 in easy reach. The Italian edition also contains the best available commentary on Manilius, which is especially strong on the astrological background and literary parallels. An understanding of the basics of ancient astrology is necessary for any appreciation of the poem; Bouché-Leclercq 1899 remains the classic discussion, while Barton 1994*a* and Beck 2007 are more user-friendly.

The most comprehensive general introductions to Manilius are Salemme 2000 and now Volk 2009 (for a more concise treatment, see Effe 1977: 106–26). Lühr 1969 and Reeh 1973 provide detailed surveys of the *Astronomica*'s world-view, while Hübner 1984 discusses the poem's astrological system, Romano 1979*a* its structure, Landolfi 2003 its proems, and Volk 2002: 196–245 its didactic poetics. Maranini 1994 offers a wealth of information on the poem's reception. Particularly useful recent articles indicative of the revived interest in the poetic qualities of Manilius include Schrijvers 1983, Wilson 1985, Baldini Moscadi 1986, Neuburg 1993, and Abry 2006*b*. It is our hope that the present volume will likewise provide an attractive avenue to Manilius and will contribute to a readerly and scholarly rediscovery of the *Astronomica* two millennia after its composition.

Part I

Intellectual and Scientific Backdrop

2

More sentiment than science

Roman stargazing before and after Manilius

Elaine Fantham

Although I appreciate many non-technical aspects of Manilius' didactic poem, I cannot claim to understand his astrology enough to contribute to this expert gathering. Instead I think—or at least I hope—that I can make myself useful by providing some Roman background to his account of the stars.

I will delegate the prologue of my account to Arcturus, one of the very few star-personalities in Latin literature. Like the dog star of scorching August Arcturus was bad news meteorologically because of the association of his late October setting with sea storms.[1] But Plautus, or more likely his model Diphilus, brings on Arcturus to introduce the *Rudens*, his drama of moral restitution, offering an interpretation of the function of the stars which we shall not meet again—as Jupiter's morality squad, on duty like American drones over Waziristan or British security cameras in city centres to detect human criminality and ensure its punishment.[2]

> qui gentes omnes mariaque et terras movet
> eius sum civis civitate caelitum.
> ita sum ut videtis splendens stella candida

---

[1] Cf. Hor. *Carm.* 3.1.27–8: *nec saevus Arcturi cadentis / impetus* ('nor the savage onslaught of setting Arcturus').

[2] How did the prologue speaker present his star-identity? My guess is that he wore a star bound to his brow on a headband like the image of the deified Julius Caesar on Octavian's denarius of 36 BC (*RRC* 540).

signum quod semper tempore exoritur suo,
hic atque in caelo. nomen Arcturost mihi.   5
noctu sum in caelo clarus atque inter deos,
inter mortales ambulo interdius.
et alia signa de caelo ad terram accidunt;
quist imperator divom atque hominum Iuppiter;
is nos per gentes aliud alia disparat   10
qui facta hominum mores pietatem et fidem
noscamus, ut quemque adiuvet opulentia.
qui falsas lites falsas testimonias
petunt, quique in iure abiurant pecuniam
eorum referimus nomina exscripta ad Iovem. (Plaut. *Rud.* 1–15)

I am a citizen from the community of heaven-dwellers, [subjects] of him
who moves all races, earth, and seas. I am a glittering white star, as you
see, a sign which always rises at its due time, here and in the sky. My
name is Arcturus. By night I am brilliant in the sky and among the gods,
by day I walk among men. Other stars too come down from sky to
earth, who obey Jupiter, commander of gods and men. He distributes us
individually to individual tribes, to discover the deeds and character of
men, their piety and trustworthiness, and how each man's abundance
aids him. Those who seek false suits and testimony and renege on debt
in court: we report their names on record to Jupiter.

Arcturus will be the agent of divine providence in the comic action,
rewarding the virtuous old man and his virgin daughter, punishing
the wicked pimp, and giving a salutary lesson to the greedy slave. Like
the divine Lar of *Aulularia* he triggers the event which will start the
action moving to restore social justice. This share of divine power and
providential beneficence is about all Arcturus will have in common
with the fixed stars in the prose and didactic texts discussed in this
survey.[3]

Moral allegory is the link between Arcturus' role and the best
known of all Roman celestial episodes, Cicero's adaptation of the
myth of Er from the tenth book of Plato's *Republic*, which turns the
vision of a man returned from the dead into a dream of Rome's
ancestral heroes gathered in the realm beyond the Milky Way as a
reward for their lives of public service (*Rep.* 6.15). Scipio's translated

---

[3] See Fraenkel 1942, who cites Hes. *Op.* 249–56 (the 30,000 *daimones* who watch
over human misdeeds for Zeus) and Pl. *Epin.* 984c ('when the heavens become full of
living creatures, they interpret among themselves (*hermeneusthai*) and to the highest
gods all men and all things').

grandfather Africanus and father Aemilius Paullus have the task of instruction which Virgil will transfer to Anchises. Romans certainly gave cult to their ancestors as heroes (the Greek equivalent of *Lar familiaris* was *Heros*) and endorsed the deification of Romulus modelled on that of Hercules: posterity had already gone a long way towards deifying Africanus by Cicero's time. While Cicero himself wished rather than hoped to earn a place among them he would live to hear Octavian's announcement of the comet of July 44 BC as the *sidus Iulium*,[4] either as sign or embodiment of the murdered Caesar's apotheosis.

But just as the whole system of the (geocentric) spheres developed in *Republic* 10 was only a *mythos* for Plato, so Cicero's politicized image of heroes among or beyond the stars cannot be treated as more than an allegory. Scipio Aemilianus' dream surely influenced Seneca's consolation to Marcia in which her dead son Metillius has been raised to the heights of heaven and moves among the blessed souls:

> paulumque supra nos commoratus, dum expurgatur et inhaerentia vitia situmque omnem mortalis aevi excutit, *deinde ad excelsa sublatus inter felices currit animas.* excepit illum coetus sacer, Scipiones Catonesque, inter contemptores vitae et <mortis> beneficio parens tuus. ille nepotem suum adplicat sibi nova luce gaudentem et vicinorum siderum meatus docet, nec ex coniectura sed omnium ex vero peritus in arcana naturae libens ducit, utque ignotarum urbium monstrator hospiti gratus est, ita sciscitanti caelestium causas domesticus interpres et in profunda terrarum permittere aciem <iubet>. iuuat enim ex alto relicta despicere...puta itaque *ex illa arce caelesti* patrem tuum...dicere....(*Marc.* 25.1–2, 26.1)

> Lingering a little while above us until he is purified and shakes off all the clinging faults and dirt of mortal life, then raised to the highest he moves among the blessed souls. The sacred band has welcomed him, the Scipios and Catos, among those who despise life, and through the grace of death, your father. He attaches his grandson to him rejoicing in the new light, and teaches him the courses of the stars, his neighbours, and gladly introduces him not from guessing but being expert in everything from the truth, to the secrets of nature, and as a guide to unfamiliar cities is welcome to a stranger, so he is a family interpreter to the young man seeking to know the origins of the heavenly bodies, and orders him

---

[4] See the narrative of Cass. Dio 45.7.1–2, as well as the scholarly discussion of Ramsey and Licht 1997 for both a scientific analysis and a study of the political exploitation of the phenomenon. Dio quotes a formal statement by Caesar's heir that this comet was or conveyed the soul of his father on his way to heaven.

to direct his sight to the depths of the earth. For it thrills him to see from
on high what he has left behind.... Imagine then that your father is
speaking from that citadel of heaven-dwellers....

For himself, in the living death of exile on Corsica Seneca proposes
the exhilaration of contemplating the heavenly bodies:

undecumque ex aequo ad caelum erigitur acies, paribus intervallis
omnia divina ab omnibus humanis distant. proinde dum oculi mei ab
illo spectaculo cuius insatiabiles sunt non abducentur, dum mihi solem
lunamque intueri liceat, dum ceteris inhaerere sideribus, dum ortus
eorum occasusque et intervalla et causas investigare vel ocius meandi
vel tardius, <dum> spectare tot per noctem stellas micantis et alias
immobiles alias non in magnum spatium exeuntis ... dum cum his sim
et caelestibus qua homini fas est immiscear, dum animum ad cogna-
tarum rerum conspectum tendentem in sublimi semper habeam, quantum refert mea quid calcem? (*Helv.* 8. 5–6)

From whatever place on level ground your sight is raised to the sky, all
divine things are equally distant from all human affairs. Accordingly
while my eyes will not be distracted from that vision with which they
cannot be sated, while I am permitted to gaze on the sun and moon and
fix my gaze on the other constellations, while I may explore their risings
and settings and distances and the causes of their faster or slower
motion, and gaze on so many stars glittering through the night, some
motionless and others not moving out over a great distance ... while
I am with them and mingle with the heaven-dwellers as far as is lawful
for a man, while I constantly keep my soul aloft straining to see its
kindred beings, what do I care what ground I am treading?

His nephew Lucan, in many ways a rebel against the divine, goes
further, asking his readers to believe that the murdered Pompey's soul
ascended to the heavens to look down pityingly on mankind before
dividing itself in the separate inspiration of Cato and Brutus. Did any
Roman have faith in such a prospect?

qua niger astriferis conectitur axibus aether,
quodque patet terras inter lunaeque meatus,
semidei manes habitant, quos ignea virtus
innocuos vitae patientes aetheris imi
fecit et aeternos animam collegit in orbes.
      ...
            illic postquam se lumine vero
implevit, stellasque vagus miratus et astra

fixa polis, vidit quanta sub nocte iaceret
nostra dies, risitque sui ludibria trunci. (Luc. 9.5–9, 11–14)

> Where the black sky is linked to the star-bearing vaults, the half-divine
> spirits inhabit the space open between the earth and orbits of the moon,
> men whom their fiery virtue has made untouched as they endured the life
> of the lower heaven, and gathered their soul into the eternal cycles. There
> after Pompey filled himself with true light, marvelling at the constellations
> and stars fixed to the vaults, he saw under how deep a night lay our day,
> and laughed at the mockery of his own mangled corpse.

I come now to Roman beliefs about the nature of the stars, but before
reviewing Cicero's later, more scientifically oriented treatises, this
survey should pause briefly over the Epicurean school of thought,
which Cicero ignores or rejects. There is little on the stars in Lucretius,
largely because Epicurean thinking did not distinguish the stars from
any other compound formed from Democritus' atoms. As a poet
Lucretius clearly delighted in the stars, using the language of Homer
as translated by Ennius. They first appear early in book 1 when
Lucretius includes in his programme the question 'whence does the
aether feed the stars' (*unde aether sidera pascit*, 1.231)[5] but does not
answer it. Stars feature more frequently in books 5 and 6. Lucretius
calls the ether or heaven 'star-bearing' (*signifer*[6] *aether*, 5.689; *orbis*,
6.481) and imitates Ennius' variations on 'studded with stars' (*stellis
micantibus fixum*, 5.1025; *stellis fulgentibus apta* / . . . *caeli domus*,
6.357); the stars in turn are 'embedded in the vaults of the sky'
(*aetheris adfixa cavernis*, 4.389). In twenty lines of book 5 (609–30)
Lucretius offers alternative and conflicting explanations of the motion
of the stars:

> Is it 1 that the sphere of heaven turns? Or is 2 the sky fixed while the
> bright constellations move? Either 2a because rapid tides of air are
> enclosed . . . and roll the stars throughout the nightly regions of the
> sky, or 2b because an external current of air, flowing from some source

---

[5] Compare Verg. *Aen.* 1.608 (*polus dum sidera pascet*) and Cic. *Nat. D.* 2.43, where
the stars are nourished *marinis terrenisque umoribus longo intervallo extenuatis* ('on
sea and land moisture refined by the great distance'); cf. also 3.37: *ali autem solem
lunam reliqua astra aquis, alia dulcibus, alia marinis* ('now the sun and moon and
other stars are nourished by waters, some fresh and some salt').

[6] *Signifer*: cf. *Aratea* 317–18 (*Zodiacum hunc Graeci vocitant, nostrique Latini /
orbem signiferum perhibent nomine vero*) and *Nat. D.* 2.53. The word will act as a
substantive denoting the Zodiac in later authors, cf. *OLD* s.v. *signifer* 2B.

flows and turns the starry fires, they themselves may make their way, going where each star's pasture summons and invites and nourishes their fiery bodies throughout the whole sky?

Russell Geer, whose 1965 translation I have quoted in modified form, refers us to Epicurus' letter to Pythocles (92–3), where the same multiple explanations are left unresolved.[7]

Let us turn instead to the orderly account of Balbus the Stoic in *De natura deorum* 2.49–60. While Cicero's umpire Cotta in this three-book dialogue does not endorse the Stoic account in what is left of book 3, nor does he refute this part of Balbus' exposition. Balbus devotes 2.39–45 to establishing the divinity of stars, based on their substance (they are composed of the purest and most mobile part of the heavens), their heat, and their luminosity, which justify their being called animate and capable of thought and understanding, as Cleanthes argued relying on evidence of touch and sight. Indeed their motion can neither be coerced nor accidental, so it must be voluntary.

Continuing in 2.49, Balbus distinguishes the two kinds of star:

> cum duo sint genera siderum quorum alterum spatiis immutabilibus ab ortu ad occasum commeans nullum unquam cursus sui vestigium inflectat, alterum autem continuas conversiones duas iisdem spatiis cursibusque conficiat, ex utraque re et mundi volubilitas, quae nisi in globosa forma esse non potest, et stellarum rotundi ambitus cognoscuntur.

> There are two kinds of star, of which one moves in an unchanging course from rising to setting, never bending any trace of its course, but the other kind completes two constant revolutions in the same laps[8] and courses; from each fact we know the rotation of the universe, which is only possible for a spherical shape, and the round orbits of the stars.

After he has elaborated in 51–2 on the cycles of the five known planets, Cicero returns to the fixed stars in 54–5:

---

[7] Geer 1964: 39. Another explanation we can gladly eliminate from mainstream thinking at Rome is the theory of Hicetas of Syracuse, quoted from Theophrastus by Cic. *Luc.* 123, namely, 'that heaven, sun, moon, stars and everything in the upper regions (*supera denique omnia*) stands still and nothing in the universe moves except the earth. This moves and curves itself at the greatest speed around the axis, so that all these phenomena look as if the earth stood still while the heavens did the moving.'

[8] Latin *spatium* evokes the chariot race and the laps of a race-course, a metaphor latent in many of the following passages.

hanc igitur in stellis constantiam, hanc tantam tam variis cursibus in omni aeternitate convenientiam temporum non possum intellegere sine mente, ratione, consilio. quae cum in sideribus inesse videamus, non possumus ea ipsa non in deorum numero reponere. nec vero eae stellae quae inerrantes vocantur non significant eandem mentem atque prudentiam . . . nec habent aetherios cursus neque caelo inhaerentes, ut plerique dicunt physicae rationis ignari; non est enim aetheris ea natura ut vi sua stellas complexa contorqueat, nam tenuis et perlucens et aequabili calore suffusus aether non satis aptus ad stellas continendas videtur . . . habent igitur suam sphaeram stellae inerrantes ab aetheria coniunctione secretam et liberam. earum autem perennes cursus atque perpetui cum admirabili incredibilique constantia declarant in his vim et mentem esse divinam.

I cannot understand this consistency in the stars and this great congruity of times in such varied orbits throughout eternity without assuming a mind, reason, and design.[9] Now since we see this in the constellations, we cannot avoid counting them in the number of the gods. Nor indeed do the stars called fixed fail to indicate the same mind and purpose. They do not have cycles in the ether nor cling to the heaven, as most people ignorant of physics declare, for the nature of the ether is not such as to be able to enfold and direct the stars by its own force: it is thin and transparent and diffused with even heat, and is not fitted to hold the stars . . . so the fixed stars have their own disc separate and free from the heavenly connection. And their eternal and perpetual courses affirm with marvellous and incredible consistency that they have in them a divine force and mind.

The next step is taken at 60 when the beauty and purity of the stars makes them seem to have conspired to protect and preserve all things: the stars are part or active partners in the providential divinity that operates the *mundus*. Add to this Balbus' claim that the stars are nourished, not by the aether as in Lucretius, but by the waters of earth, a doctrine of Posidonius:[10]

---

[9] The stars are the prime argument, then, for what is now called Intelligent Design.

[10] Posidonius fr. 118A Kidd quotes Macrob. *Sat.* 1.23.2 for the sun (not specifically stars) for which the waters of the Ocean serve as food. For Posidonius' definition of the stars, cf. fr. 127 (Arius Didymus): 'Posidonius says that a star is a divine body composed of aether, radiant and fire-like, never stationary but forever moving in a circle. The term star (*astron*) used specifically is applied to the sun', etc.; fr.128 (Achilles Tatius, *Introduction to Aratus*): 'according to Diodorus a star is a divine body, a body in the heavens that shares the same substance as the place where it is, a

pulcherrima forma praediti purissimaque in regione caeli collocati ita feruntur moderanturque cursus, ut ad omnia conservanda atque tuenda consensisse videantur.

Endowed with the most fair and pure of forms and set in the sky they sweep along and control their courses and seem to have conspired to preserve and protect all things.

I have said nothing so far about Aratus' *Phaenomena*, which Cicero translated in part at least as a young man. It is not known whether he translated the whole poem, but substantial excerpts survive because he took good care to quote it extensively in book 1 of *De divinatione*. Compare the following passage (*Nat. D.* 2.104):

atque hoc loco me intuens 'utar' inquit 'carminibus Arateis, quae a te admodum adulescentulo conversa ita me delectant quia Latina sunt, ut multa ex iis memoria teneam. ergo ut oculis adsidue videmus, sine ulla mutatione ac varietate

> cetera labuntur celeri caelestia motu
> cum caeloque simul noctesque diesque feruntur'.

And at this point he gazed at me and said, 'I shall use the Aratus poems which were translated by you when quite a young man, and give me such pleasure because they are Latin, that I have memorized a large part of them. So as we see constantly with our own eyes, [the stars move onward] without any change or variation, "the other heavenly bodies glide with swift motion and are carried along with the heaven through night and day"'.

A transitional passage from the longer and independently preserved text of *Aratea* shows that after listing and describing the constellations, Aratus/Cicero passed over the planets, something Manilius will also do: it is thought by some scholars that the latter did so deliberately to obstruct readers eager to conduct horoscopes, though note the different argument in Volk 2009: 48–57 and 116–26.[11]

> haec sunt quae visens nocturno tempore signa
> aeternumque volens mundi pernoscere motum
> legitimo cernes caelum lustrantia cursu.
> nam quae per bis sex signorum labier orbem

body that is radiant and never stationary, but forever moves in a circle. The same definition was given by Posidonius the Stoic before him.'

[11] For a version of the deliberate-obstruction theory, see the contribution by Steven Green to this volume.

quinque solent stellae simili ratione notari
non possunt: quia quae faciunt vestigia cursu
non eodem semper spatio protrita feruntur.
sic malunt errare vagae per nubila caeli
atque suos vario motu metirier orbes.
(*Aratea* 223–31 = 451–9 Soubiran)

These are the signs which you will see at night and wanting to know the eternal motion of the universe you will discern traversing the skies in law-abiding course. For the five stars (planets) which are wont to glide through the cycle of twelve constellations cannot be marked in the same way, because the traces they make in their movement are not always trodden along the same course. Thus do they prefer to wander errantly through the clouds of heaven and measure out their cycles in varying motion.

To compensate for this omission, the Muse Urania's address to the consul Cicero in *De consulatu suo* 6–10 puts the planets in context:

et si stellarum motus cursusque vagantes
nosse velis, qua sint signorum in sede locatae,
quae verbo et falsis Graeorum vocibus errant
re vera certo lapsu spatioque feruntur,
omnia iam cernes divina mente notata.

And should you wish to know the motions and wandering orbits of the stars, and in what position of the zodiac they are placed, those which in language are called by false Greek names 'wanderers', but which truly are swept on with fixed glide and trajectory, you will see everything marked out by the divine mind.

Perhaps it is even possible to reconcile these texts with Cicero's Latin version of Plato's *Timaeus*, which shows how Cicero and Plato converge in affirming the divinity of the stars and their nature as living beings:[12]

ex quo genere ea sunt sidera quae infixa caelo non moventur loco, quae sunt animantia eaque divina ob eamque causam suis sedibus inhaerent et perpetuo manent. (Cic. *Tim.* 36)

---

[12] Note the cross-reference to Plato at *Nat. D.* 1.30: *idem et in Timaeo dicit et in Legibus et mundum deum esse et caelum et astra et terram et animos et eos quos maiorum institutis accepimus* ('Plato also says in the *Timaeus* and the *Laws* that the universe is a god and the sky and stars and earth and souls and those [humans] whom we have learned about from our ancestors' traditions').

> ... and of this kind are the stars fixed in the sky which do not move
> from their post, which are ensouled and divine and for this reason cling
> to their positions and stay there for ever.

Cicero goes further in *Timaeus* 43, adapting the theory of a deliberate
matching of an equal number of souls and stars:

> toto igitur omni constituto sideribus parem numerum distribuit ani-
> morum et singulos adiunxit ad singula atque ita quasi in currum
> universitatis imposuit commonstravitque leges fatales ac necessarias et
> ostendit primum ortum unum fore omnibus eumque moderatum atque
> constantem neque ab ullo imminutum, satis autem et quasi sparsis
> animis fore uti certis temporum intervallis oreretur animal, quod esset
> ad cultum deorum aptissimum ... atque ille qui recte atque honeste
> curriculum vivendi a natura datum confecerit, ad illud astrum quocum
> aptus fuerit revertetur. (Cic. *Tim.* 43 ~ Pl. *Tim.* 41–2)

> So when this entire whole had been set up he distributed an equal
> number of souls to the stars, and attached individual souls to individual
> stars, and seated them as if on the chariot of the universe and pointed
> out the necessary laws of fate and showed that there would be a first
> rising for all of them, and one moderated and consistent and not
> reduced by any factor, and that when these souls had been sowed and
> scattered it would come to pass that an animal would be born at fixed
> intervals of time most suited to the worship of the gods ... and the man
> who had rightly and honourably completed the course of life given to
> him by nature would return to the star to which he had been attached.

This is probably as near as Cicero comes to suggesting the personal
attachment or influence of stars over their human protégés. But his
own choice was to follow Panaetius in questioning the Stoic belief in
any kind of divination; in the thunderbolts and bird-signs of augury,
in the scrutiny of entrails by *haruspices*, in dreams and inspired
prophetic utterance, but above all in the astrological predictions of
the Chaldaei. To judge from his detailed attempt at refutation, he was
more concerned to dispute the validity of the 'science' of astrology
than alarmed by its practitioners. In this we will see a sharp contrast
with the following century and Augustus' later years.

Lucretius had already protested that the interpretations of astrologers were at variance with the genuine predictions of astronomers
(*astrologi*, 5.727–8). In *De divinatione*, when the dialogue's 'Cicero'
answers in the second book the credulous claims of 'Quintus' for the
validity of divination, he devotes an extended set of arguments based

on Panaetius to showing the absurdity of *Chaldaeorum monstra* ('the unnatural claims of the Chaldeans', 2.87). Here I have found Long's explanation of apparently shifting Stoic response most helpful. He suggests that Hellenistic interest in horoscope astrology should not be dated before the second century BC; hence no comments in Chrysippus and Carneades, 'the qualified approval of Diogenes of Babylon, the opposition of Panaetius (to what were essentially newfangled theories), and the wholesale support of Posidonius' (Long 1982: 170).

Cicero indicates in some detail the alleged role played by a child's birth sign in the zodiac, the influence of nearby planets, and the effects of friendly and hostile cognate signs, two friendly signs determined by their positions as vertices of an equilateral triangle inscribed in the zodiac circle, and three hostile signs as the other vertices of an inscribed square.

> vim quandam esse aiunt signifero in orbe qui Graece *zodiakos* dicitur talem ut orbis eius una quaeque pars alia alio modo moveat immutetque caelum, perinde ut quaeque stellae in his finitumisque partibus sint quoque tempore, eamque vim varie moveri ab iis sideribus quae vocentur errantia; cum autem in eam partem ipsam orbis venerint in qua sit ortus eius qui nascatur aut in eam quae coniunctum aliquid habeat aut consentiens, ea triangula illi aut quadrata nominant. (*Div.* 2.89)

> They say there is a force in the star-bearing circle which is called Zodiac in Greek such that every part of this circle moves and changes the sky each in a different way, according to which stars are in these and neighbouring regions at each time, and this force is activated in different ways by those stars which are called planets, and that when they have entered that part of the circle in which is the origin of the man born, or one which has some relationship of adjacency or agreement, they call them triangulated or quadrated.

It was ridiculous to assume that a man's life or behaviour could be determined and predicted from the astronomical circumstances of his birth, his *natalicia*. Cicero's arguments against the plausibility of such *natalicia praedicta* are mostly circumstantial, ranging from the twins with a single horoscope and different deaths (*Div.* 2.90) to the thousands of casualties who shared a common death at Cannae though born under as many different horoscopes (2.97).[13] Surely,

---

[13] Here again see Long 1982: 172–8: he discriminates between Cicero's logically stronger and circumstantially weaker criticisms in this passage.

Cicero adds, the accuracy of any prediction would be prejudiced by man's weak eyesight (91) and it would be even harder for the observer to calibrate the influence of remote stars than the variations caused by local weather conditions: *plus terrarum situs quam lunae tactus ad nascendum valere* (2.91, 94). In fact these objections would not affect any horoscope based not on observation at the moment of birth but on consultation by adults of established tables (*ephemera*) for the natal situation on a given day in a past year.

In another distinct line of argument Cicero quotes the caution of Diogenes of Babylon (2.90) that only a man's character and aptitudes could reasonably be predicted from birth, and—an ostensibly incompatible argument of the same order—that heredity and environment were a stronger influence on body and deportment than any heavenly body (*et formas et mores et plerosque status ac motus effingere a parentibus liberos*, 2.94).[14] Keeping in mind post-natal influences on the developing child, he argues that one can point to changes of mental or physical condition effected by moral or physical training or by medicine, while at the level of communities traditional ethnography attributed divergences of physique and character between men of different regions not to the stars overhead but to their location and climate—to 'airs, waters, places' (2.95).

Finally it may be possible to apply the same predictive techniques to animals and even cities like Rome (2.98–9): 'Tarutius Firmanus drew up the horoscope of Rome: so did even the birthday of the city fall under the force of the stars and moon?' Such an idea is seen as an absurdity that discredits the whole discipline.

In recapitulation, three basic tenets—both Stoic and more generally accepted—link Cicero's apprehension of the stars with Manilius, and separately with Seneca:[15]

1. Stars by their continual regular but complex movement compel us to believe in some supernatural guiding hand. As Manilius puts it (2.67–71 and 73):

---

[14] Astronomical data needed to be calculated *ratione atque animo* (2.92–3). Chaldaeans don't even allow for the nature of the heavens, which are seen differently from different places. For example, the dog-star rises after the solstice in our region, but before the solstice in the land of the Troglodytes (i.e. Ethiopia; see the comment of Timpanaro 1988: 384).

[15] I owe this formulation, and the corresponding Manilian references, to the doctoral dissertation of my friend Jonathan Tracy.

> quod nisi cognatis membris contexta maneret
> machina, et imposito pareret tota magistro
> ac tantum mundi regeret prudentia censum,
> non esset statio terris, non ambitus astris
> ...
> nec sua dispositos servarent sidera cursus.

Unless the whole frame stood fast composed of kindred limbs and obedient to an overlord, unless providence directed the vast resources of the skies, the earth would not possess its stability, the stars their orbits ... the constellations would not keep their wonted courses. (Translation of Manilius here and elsewhere from Goold 1992.)

2. The human soul derives from the stars and returns to them in contemplation (*Astr.* 2.115–16):

> quis caelum posset nisi caeli munere nosse
> et reperire deum nisi qui pars ipe deorum est?

Who could know heaven save by heaven's gift and discover god save one who himself shares in the divine?

3. The stars display their permanence, proceeding along their appointed paths from one millennium to the next (*Astr.* 1.185 and 476–7):

> cum facies eadem signis per saecla maneret
> ...
> certa sed in proprias oriuntur singula luces
> natalesque suos occasumque ordine servant.

... since for centuries the constellations have displayed the selfsame features ... and each constellation without fail rises to display its proper stars, regularly keeping to the same times of coming up and going down.

4. Cicero does not add, as Seneca does in *Helv.* 12.9.2, that the stars remain the same not only through time, but in their relative arrangement and distribution over space (*ubique aeque apparent, ubique aeque splendent*, 'they are visible with the same clarity everywhere and glitter with the same strength'). Not of course that Seneca believed the risings and settings were identical and simultaneous in Corsica and Rome—or Corduba—but he knew that the stars themselves were constant, no matter how we might see them. Clearly by this time astrology and astrologers had become far more dominant; we have only to think of the anecdotes about Tiberius on Rhodes and his trusted companion Thrasyllus.

However, apart from Manilius himself, there is little evidence for the transmission of ideas about the stars and their influence in the generations between Cicero and Seneca, and the Senecan evidence comes from his later works. While Seneca does adhere to Stoic convictions about the providential benevolence of the celestial bodies, he does so only on the largest scale. The long tribute to the benefits conferred by the stars in *Ben.* 4.23 is chiefly remarkable for insisting that the uncountable anonymous fixed stars contribute as much to human history and human fates as the more visible planets.

> ipse mundus, quotiens per noctem ignes suos fudit et tantum stellarum innumerabilium refulsit, quem non intentum in se tenet? quis sibi illa tunc cum miratur ea prodesse cogitat? adspice ista tanto superne coetu labentia, quemadmodum velocitatem suam sub specie stantis atque immoti operis abscondant. quantum ista nocte, quam tu in numerum ac discrimen dierum observas, agitur? quanta rerum turba sub hoc silentio evolvitur? quantam fatorum seriem certus limes educit? ista quae te non aliter quam in decorem sparsa consideras, singula in opere sunt. nec enim est quod existimes septem sola discurrere, cetera haerere; paucorum motus comprehendimus, innumerabiles vero longiusque a conspectu nostro seducti eunt redeuntque, et ex his, qui oculos nostros patiuntur plerique obscuro gradu pergunt et per occultum aguntur. (*Ben.* 4.23.4)

What man does the universe itself, whenever it pours out its fires through the night and so great a crowd of countless stars shines out, not hold fascinated by itself? What man when he is struck with wonder has in mind that they are conferring benefits? Look at those stars gliding by in such a lofty assembly, see how they conceal their swiftness in the appearance of a still and motionless piece of work. How much is achieved in that night which you watch to count the number and limits of the days? How great a host of things is developed beneath this silence? What a mighty sequence of fates this trusty orbit[16] brings forth? Those stars which you consider simply as scattered for general ornament are individual in their function. Nor do you have reason to believe that only the seven are rushing around while the rest are stock-still; we understand the motion of a few, but countless stars set apart more remote from our gaze come and go, and of those which come into our sight most proceed with an unseen progress and are carried through a hidden space.

---

[16] For *limes* = 'orbit, revolution', see Le Bœuffle 1987 s.v.

The other passages that give serious consideration to the stars come from *Natural Questions*[17] and the *Epistulae morales*, works composed after AD 62 in Seneca's last phase of retirement. Here too Seneca insists that the criteria of the Chaldaean astrologers are too narrow and ignore the power of stars that are, or just seem, motionless (*Q. Nat.* 2.32.6):

> quinque stellarum potestates Chaldaeorum observatio excepit. quid, tu tot illa milia siderum iudicas otiosa lucere? quid est porro aliud, quod errorem maximum incutiat peritis natalium, quam quod paucis nos sideribus adsignant cum omnia quae supra nos sunt, partem nostri sibi vindicent? ceterum et illa quae aut immota sunt aut propter velocitatem universo parem immotis similia, non extra ius dominiumque nostri sunt.

> The observation of the Chaldaeans has taken up the powers of the five planets. What then, do you think that so many thousand stars are shining to no effect? What else is it that inculcates the greatest ignorance in those expert in horoscopes, if not that they assign a few stars to us, although all of those above us claim for themselves a share in us? What is more, even those which are motionless or seem like motionless beings because their speed is the same as that of the universe, are not beyond holding rights and mastery over us.

He reiterates the same claim for stars and sun in *Q. Nat.* 6.16.2, the passage which ascribes the nourishment of sun and stars to the earth:

> totum hoc caelum quod igneus aether, mundi summa pars, claudit, omnes hae stellae, quarum iniri non potest numerus, omnis hic caelestium coetus et ut alia praeteream, hic tam prope a nobis agens cursum sol, omni terrarum ambitu non semel maior, alimentum ex terra trahunt et inter se partiuntur nec ullo alio scilicet quam halitu terrarum sustinentur: hoc illis alimentum, hic pastus est.

> This entire sky which the fiery ether, highest part of the universe, encloses, all these stars whose number cannot be reckoned, this whole assembly of heavenly bodies and, to pass over others, this sun that drives its course so close to us, greater by many times than the entire circumference of the earth, all draw their nourishment from the earth and share it among themselves and are sustained only by the exhalations of the lands: this is their sustenance, this their grazing.

---

[17] On Seneca's adoption of criteria for scientific argument in the *Natural Questions*, see now the opening pages of Williams 2008.

Seneca remains a sceptic to the end of his *Natural Questions*. Compare the ambiguous comment on the predictive power of comets at 7.28.1: *quomodo illa quae Chaldaei canunt, quid stella nascentibus triste laetumve constituat* ('like those prophecies which the Chaldeans utter, as to what sad or glad prospect their star sets up for them at birth').

One of the most interesting of his comments is a deliberate diversion in Letter 88.14–16 of Virgil's allusion to Aratus at *Georgics* 1.336–7. Virgil refers to the planets in order to introduce the notion of forecasting the weather:

> frigida Saturni sese quo stella receptet,
> quos ignis Cyllenius erret in orbes . . . .

. . . whither the chilly star of Saturn is withdrawing, or on what cycles the fire of Mercury is wandering.

However, Seneca distorts this as if it referred to astrological prophecy and denounces such attempts:

> hoc scire quid proderit? ut sollicitus sim cum Saturnus et Mars ex contrario stabunt aut cum Mercurius vespertinum faciet occasum vidente Saturno, potius quam hoc dicam: ubicumque sunt ista propitia esse, nec posse mutari? agit illa continuus ordo fatorum et inevitabilis cursus; per statas vices remeant et effectus rerum omnium aut movent aut notant. sed sive quid evenit faciunt, quid immutabilis rei notitia proficiet? sive significant, quid refert providere quod effugere non possis? scias ista, nescias: fient.

> What good will it do to know this? So that I may be harassed when Saturn and Mars stand opposite each other or when Mercury makes its evening setting as Saturn looks on, rather than say this: that wherever they are they are favourable, and cannot change? That continuing order of the fates and inescapable progress drives them; they return according to fixed sequences and either arouse or mark the results of all events. But if they cause what happens, how will knowledge of an unchangeable event avail you? Or if they indicate it, how is it relevant to foresee what you cannot escape? Whether you know these things or are unaware, they will happen anyway.

Two later letters, 93.9 and 94.56, add no further details to what is still a geocentric universe (*praeter terram nihil stare*). Seneca has only admiration for the perfect mechanism of the celestial system with its predictable seasons (*per quas annum vices revocet*) and the swift and unremitting speed of the heavenly bodies (*continua velocitate*

decurrere, 93.9; cf. 94.56, *tardos siderum incessus si compares toti,*
citatissimos autem si cogites quanta spatia numquam intermissa ve-
locitate circumeant):

> scimus a quibus principiis natura se attollat, quemadmodum ordinet
> mundum, per quas annum vices revocet, quemadmodum quae usquam
> erunt cluserit et se ipsam finem sui fecerit; scimus sidera impetu suo
> vadere, praeter terram nihil stare, cetera continua velocitate decurrere;
> scimus quemadmodum solem luna praetereat, quare tardior velociorem
> post se relinquat, quomodo lumen accipiat aut perdat, quae causa
> inducat noctem, quae reducat diem: illuc eundum est ubi ista propius
> aspicias. (*Ep.* 93.9)

> We know the beginnings from which nature raises herself up, how she
> arranges the universe, through what seasons she brings back the year,
> how she has foreclosed whatever will be anywhere and made herself her
> own purpose, we know the stars proceed by their own motion, that
> nothing is still except the earth but the rest races onwards in continuing
> speed; we know how the moon passes the sun and why the slower body
> leaves the swifter one behind her, how she receives or loses her light,
> what cause brings on the night, what restores the day: we must go to the
> place from which you can see these things more closely.

Letter 94.56 differs only in stressing the generosity of Nature in
enabling man to walk erect and contemplate the stars above, a
theme expressed earlier by Cicero:

> celsos et erectos ut deorum cognitionem caelum intuentes capere pos-
> sint, atque caelestium quorum spectaculum ad nullum aliud genus
> animantium pertinet. (*Nat. D.* 2.140)

> Nature made men tall and upright so that they might gaze on the sky
> and take note of the heavenly bodies, since the sight of them concerns
> no other kind of living creature.

In Seneca's version, Nature

> vultus nostros erexit ad caelum et quicquid magnificum mirumque
> fecerat videri a suspicientibus voluit: ortus occasusque et properantis
> mundi volubilem cursum, interdiu terram aperientem, nocte caelestia,
> tardos siderum incessus si compares toti, citatissimos autem si cogites
> quanta spatia numquam intermissa velocitate circumeant.

> ... raised our faces to the sky and wanted everything marvellous and
> magnificent that she had made to be seen by us when we looked
> upwards; if you compare the risings and settings [of the stars] and

rapid course of the hastening universe, revealing the earth by day, and the heavenly bodies by night, the pace of the stars, dragging if you were to compare them to the whole, but galloping if you should think what immense laps they travel with uninterrupted speed.

I am not claiming exceptional shrewdness or originality for Seneca; only a decade later there is an equally emphatic disclaimer in the elder Pliny, who refuses to assign stars to individual men in proportion to their brilliance, or believe that their rising or setting is associated with any man's birth or death. Indeed Pliny may perhaps go further than any Stoic in disconnecting the activities of the heavens from those of mortals. But both Pliny and Seneca, like the majority of their educated peers, made an exception to their scepticism of abnormal phenomena such as comets and shooting stars:

> sidera quae adfixa diximus mundo non ita ut existimat volgus singulis attributa nobis et clara divitibus, minora pauperibus, obscura defectis et pro sorte cuiusque lucentia adnumerata mortalibus, nec cum suo quaeque homine oriuntur nec aliquem exstingui decidua significant: non tanta caelo societas nobiscum est ut nostro fato mortalis sit ibi quoque siderum fulgor. (*HN* 2.28–9)

> The stars which we called fixed to the universe are not assigned to us individually as the common herd thinks, with bright stars for the rich and lesser stars for the poor, and dim ones for the failing, counted out for mortals and shining according to each man's destiny, nor do they rise each with their own man, nor when they fall do they mean that someone is perishing: the sky does not have so great a bond with us that the brilliance of the stars should be mortal even there because of our fate.

What mattered historically was as much what men were willing to believe as whatever the stars might bring to pass. Any interest in future deaths was clearly sinister: hence Augustus had forbidden the taking of horoscopes in AD 11. On the other hand Suetonius accepted the common belief that abnormal phenomena—comets (*stellae crinitae*), shooting stars, etc.—portended the demise or fall of an emperor.[18] Seneca in a rare moment of frankness might have said 'no such luck!' Pliny was less philosophically inclined, and writing under a decent

---

[18] See Plin. *HN* 2.89–93 on comets in general and Suet. *Claud.* 46 for the comet which was seen in the skies for a month around the time of Claudius' sudden death. Hurley 2001 *ad loc.* helpfully gives cross-references to the comet which panicked Nero (Suet. *Ner.* 36) and another false alarm under Vespasian (*Vesp.* 23).

emperor, but as fully aware of the political dangers of misdirected astrology as of its scientific perversity. A combination of scientific scepticism and political caution may perhaps be the best explanation for the reduction of theories about the stars to a less controversial, indeed more pedestrian, representation of our world within the (geocentric) celestial system. The allegorical apotheosis of Rome's inspired statesmen persisted as an ideal, but seems to have become increasingly divorced from any quasi-scientific account of the world of the stars around us.

3

Manilius' conflicted Stoicism

Thomas Habinek

Debate over identification of Manilius as a Stoic hinges as much on the meaning of Stoicism as it does on interpretation of the five books of the *Astronomica*. If, as a recent article proposes (MacGregor 2005), we consider Stoicism to consist of a fixed and finite checklist of principles, entailing no more and no less than what can be found among the fragments gathered by von Arnim, then we can be reasonably certain that Manilius was not a Stoic. Unfortunately, the same procedure would de-Stoicize any of a number of self-identified Stoic authors, so little is gained by such an exercise. Why impose an intellectual straitjacket on a system that allowed for flexible response to varied experience?

More reasonable is the approach of Katharina Volk (2002, 2009; cf. Mann in this volume), who argues that Stoicism had so thoroughly permeated the learned discourse of early imperial Romans that it becomes difficult to attribute a distinctively Stoic identity or aim to Manilius' astrological assemblage. Yet, even if true (and it would be pointless to deny the multiple philosophical and poetic influences upon Manilius), this position does not diminish the need to consider Manilius in relationship to earlier and contemporary Stoicism. The success of Stoic ideas didn't make them any less Stoic. Stoic physics, in particular, is so thoroughly and coherently distinctive from other physical systems (especially those taken for granted, it would seem, by most classicists) that engagement with it on the part of the modern reader provides an important corrective to understandable tendencies to dismiss aspects of Manilius' project as imprecise or incomprehensible or, in effect, to rewrite Manilius to make his poetry fit a world-view that was not his own. Reading Manilius' poetry from the perspective of Stoicism clarifies much of what might otherwise seem puzzling about his language and argument. At the same time, instances of Manilian deviation from a system that offers a potentially powerful grounding for his central claims concerning stellar influence enable us to identify the stakes of both Manilian poetry and Stoic physics.

In the present chapter, then, I continue the line of inquiry followed by earlier scholars, such as Goold 1977, Lapidge 1989, and Abry 2003, who have used Stoicism to explicate Manilius, but I carry their discussion a step further by considering, albeit briefly, how Manilius' choices among the options Stoicism offered him reveal both the foundations and the limits of his intellectual enterprise. In effect, I see Manilius' Stoicism, in particular his use of Stoic physical thought, as conflicted, perhaps even to the point of bad faith. The distinctive physics of the ancient Stoics, with its emphasis on continuity, corporeality, and dynamic transformation, permeates Manilius' poem, sustains his argumentation, and animates his language, but only to a point. When it might lead to a new understanding of his and his audience's immediate historical and political context, the Stoic perspective is suppressed or contravened—a practice that in part explains the tensions in the Manilian project more generally. Stoicism, especially Stoic physical thought, helps us to comprehend Manilius; and Manilius, precisely in his adaptation of and resistance to key aspects of Stoicism, provides insight into that philosophy's transformative potential in his era and beyond.

The Stoics understood the universe to be a single living, rational body (Sambursky 1959; White 1992, 2003). They were monists, in that they were committed to the proposition that nothing exists but matter, and they made valiant attempts to account for cognition, the gods, and language in terms of physical laws and observable patterns of causation. From the outset, Stoics insisted on the unity and interconnection of physics, ethics, and logic, likening them to the yolk, white, and shell of an egg, or to productive soil and trees, fruit, and a garden fence, or to the soul, flesh, and sinews of an animal (Diog. Laert. 7.39–41). As such, their teachings provide a stark alternative to the Aristotelian distinction between form and matter, acceptance of nonphysical realities, and differentiation between a changeless ethereal realm and mutable sublunar world that provide the foundation for leading strains of Arabic and European thought for centuries to come (Lang 1998). A renewed interest in Stoic physics partially explains new

developments in the early modern period, including Cartesian
mechanics, Galilean dynamism, and Kant's early work on time and
the cosmos. And Stoic physical thought has special relevance today,
in that it anticipates both in general and in a surprising number of
particulars strong forms of determinism being advanced by an impressive array of evolutionary biologists and neuroscientists, along with allies
and collaborators in the humanities and social sciences (for discussion,
see Habinek 2010). To take just one example, Michael Spivey's recent
book *The Continuity of Mind* (2007) argues that thought is best understood as a probabilistic trajectory uniting brain, body, and environment:
a claim that could be rewritten in the language of Zeno or Chrysippus
without significant loss of meaning. Contemporary accounts of neural
plasticity, cross-modal integration of percepts, feedback loops between
higher and lower order sensory processes, and continuity between
organism and environment were all in one sense or another anticipated
by proponents of Stoic physics in Graeco-Roman antiquity.

Manilius' engagement with Stoic physical teaching has been rightly
noted by earlier scholars. They point to his presentation of a Stoic
version of cosmogenesis in book 1, where, after admitting the possibility of disagreement over the *origo rerum* (1.145–6), he nonetheless
proceeds to assert such Stoic commonplaces as the pre-eminence of
fire among the elements, the formation of the earth's atmosphere
from water vapours, and the equipoise of the earth or *tellus* as a
sphere suspended at the centre of the universe (1.147–81). Also
widely recognized is Manilius' commitment to the Chrysippan account of *pneuma*, or life-breath, as a material substance permeating
the universe and uniting its diverse parts through its varying distribution (2.60–81). Indeed, Manilius as much as states explicitly (2.82–6)
that such a theory provides the philosophical basis for belief in
planetary influence. As Katja Vogt has recently noted (2008), in at
least one strain of Stoic theology, the gods are planets whose movements are constitutive of the movement that defines the universe as a
living organism. Finally, Michael Lapidge (1989) has pointed to Manilius' use of words and phrases that, even in non-doctrinal contexts,
indicate familiarity with Stoic teachings concerning *heimarmenē*, or the
chain of causation (*rerumque catenas*, 4.394), *sympatheia*, or the harmonious interaction of parts of the universe (*mutua foedera*, 1.252;
consensus, 2.63), and *ekpyrōsis*, the fiery conflagration that marks the
end of one cycle of cosmic transformation and the beginning of
another (2.67–72, 2.804–7; cf. 5.210).

We can corroborate these arguments—especially Lapidge's, concerning the pervasiveness of Stoic language—by considering not just cosmology, but also theories of perception, psychology, theology, and biology, all of which were connected to or encompassed in Stoic physical teaching.

Consider for example the opening verses of Manilius' poem:

> carmine divinas artes et conscia fati
> sidera diversos hominum variantia casus,
> caelestis rationis opus, deducere mundo
> aggredior.... (1.1–4)

> Divine arts and foresighted stars
> Diversifying the destinies of mortals,
> Work of heavenly reason,
> In song I set out to draw down from the heavens.

(Translations from Manilius are my own unless otherwise indicated.)

What is the referent of *opus*? Surely the divine arts and the constellations, but also the process whereby the constellations diversify the circumstances of mortals. The latter interpretation fits the active force of *opus* found elsewhere in classical Latin (*OLD* s.v. 3, 4, 5) and signals a Stoic world-view from the outset. Stoic reason is not a system that exists independent of the cosmos by which we evaluate it, but the name given to the ordering activity of the universe. Diversifying the fates of mortals just is the *opus* or operation of heavenly *ratio*. To turn divine reason into an independent 'means' by which the stars 'diversify the chequered fortunes of mankind' (Goold 1977: 5) is both a violation of the appositive grammatical function of the noun *opus* and a suppression of an immanentist account of universal order—an understandable move for a modern editor or translator schooled in the separation of observer from observed, but unlikely for a poet with even a slight commitment to the continuity physics advanced by the Stoics.

Just a few lines further into the poem Manilius describes his practice in language too easily misunderstood if we fail to follow through on the implications of Stoic 'cosmobiology' (in the terminology of Hahm 1977, Barnouw 2002). As Manilius puts it:

> impensius ipsa
> scire iuvat magni penitus praecordia mundi
> quaque regat generetque suis animalia signis
> cernere. (1.16–19)

It's a pleasure
To probe deeply the entrails of the universe,
To discern how it rules and generates animate beings with its signs.

The Latin phrase *praecordia mundi*, innards or entrails of the universe, as others have noted, presupposes a distinctly Stoic view of the universe as a living organism. But what of the expression *quaque regat generet suis animalia signis*? Goold translates 'how it [the sky] controls the birth of all living beings through its signs' (1977: 5). In so doing, he turns the verbs *rego* and *genero* into metaphors, when the latter at least can perfectly well be taken literally: the universe as an organism 'generates' other organisms. The Stoics speak of the *spermatikoi logoi*, or inseminating reason of the designing fire (*pyr tekhnikon*) that is Zeus/nature/fate/the universe (Diog. Laert. 7.148–50, Aetius 1.7.33, Stob. 1.213.15–21). Indeed, elsewhere in the *Astronomica*, especially book 5, Manilius has the gods fashion (*fingo*, 5.60, 5.106, 5.220, 5.344; *effingo*, 5.315), create (*creo*, 5.648), bestow upon (*tribuo*, 5.200), and give birth to (*ingenero*, 5.272; *nascor*, 5.349, 5.648; *do partus*, 5.634; *suboles*, 4.269) those under their influence.

A further type of stellar activity again makes clear how easy it is for even the most responsible of modern readers to misconstrue or misrepresent the underlying physics of the poem. In speaking of the Pleiades, Manilius writes

quibus aspirantibus almam
in lucem eduntur Bacchi Venerisque sequaces. (5.142–3)

Goold's translation of *quibus aspirantibus* as 'beneath their influence' (1977: 311) sells Manilius' materialism short. What the Pleiades do, like the stars of Orion's belt, which elsewhere are also subject of the verb *aspiro* (5.175), is, to translate literally, 'breathe upon', or transmit their *pneuma*, to those who enter life when they are visible, that is, when their rays are not physically blocked by the curving surface of the earth.

Attending to the material nature of interactions between celestial and terrestrial bodies also clarifies Manilius' discussion of the geographical divergence in stellar influence as developed at some length in book 4. The theory that different stars govern different territories of the earth allows Manilius to reject one traditional objection to astrology, namely that people born on the same day don't lead the same lives. But that doesn't mean that regional influence is an *ad hoc* response to real or potential criticism, for it fits a broader Stoic and physicalist account of the material development of human personalities and cultures. As Manilius puts it, 'as great the number of regions of the world, just so the number of worlds under the regions' (*quot partes orbis, totidem sub partibus orbes / ut certis discripta nitent regionibus astra*, 4.741–2). In other words, to understand stellar influence we must treat each region of the earth as a separate ecosystem characterized by distinctive features at both the celestial and the terrestrial level. As he goes on to say, 'the stars, as they have been allocated, pour through (*perfundunt*) the peoples beneath them with their own air (*aere suo*)' (4.742–3). Use of the prefix *per-* (through) in *perfundo* would seem to imply the permeability of the terrestrial bodies that are the objects of the stars' attention (a key point in Stoic physics, which denies the reality of physical boundaries); and *fundo* makes best sense if taken in reference to the fluid mixing, or *krāsis*, that Stoic physics identifies as constitutive of bodily composition and transformation (Diog. Laert. 7.151, Alex. *Mixt.* 216–18; Sambursky 1959, Long and Sedley 1987: 1.290–6). The consistent physics underlying Manilius' account of regional influence is sustained by his precise use of the term *aer*, which in Stoic as in pre-Socratic thought refers not to the element 'air', but to the atmosphere as produced by the combination of vapours from the earth and fiery heat from the heavens (Kingsley 1995). Manilius suggests not so much that different stars exercise influence in different locales as that different stars interact with the different natures of the locales with which they are linked at particular moments in time.

A physicalist reading of Manilius' discussion of cultural diversity has interesting implications for our understanding of the influential Posidonian ethnography on which it seems at least in part to depend (Hahm 1989). It is not precisely accurate to say that, on the Posidonian model, cultural differences are 'innate' in human beings depending on locale (*pace* Hahm 1989: 1347). Rather, the language, food, and climate people experience—not to mention the stars that govern their homeland—operate together to constitute a settled disposition that, from the vantage point of an outsider, looks like an innate character. Without a materialist framework, we cannot appreciate Manilius' inclusion among the relevant differences between cultures such items as the sounds of voices (*sonos . . . vocum*, 4.731), languages (*linguae*, 731), customs (*mores*, 732), and rituals (*ritus*, 732). For the Stoics each item listed is a body that interacts with and affects other bodies and thus, following Manilius' line of thought, needs to be factored into an account of the interaction of celestial with human bodies.

Of course, much of the contact between heaven and earth described in the *Astronomica* takes the form of perception, specifically visual observation of the heavens. In this area, too, Manilius' approach matches Stoic physical doctrine. For example, to persuade the audience of the mind's power, despite its small size, Manilius uses the analogy of the pupil of the eye: though tiny, it sees the entirety of the sky (*parvula sic totum pervisit pupula caelum*, 4.927). The expression records the movement of the eye across the whole of the visible cosmos; but Manilius seems also to have in mind the specifically Stoic notion of vision entailing both extro- and intromission: a movement outward, along a cone of sight, from the eye, matched by a movement inward from object to observer (Dumont 1989, with ancient sources; Morales 2004: 8–35). He describes the latter trajectory when he remarks that 'god does not begrudge (*invidet*) the earth the appearance of heaven, but reveals his face and body by ceaseless revolution, and impresses (*inculcat*) and imposes (*offert*) himself' (4.915–17). Impression, Greek *typōsis*, was one Stoic term for the effect of a sensory presentation, or *phantasia*, upon the mind of the observer (Diog. Laert. 7.49–50, Plut. *Mor.* 1084f–1085a). In applying it to God's appearance before and impression upon humanity, Manilius plays upon the verb *invideo*: to begrudge or envy, but also the negation (*in*) of seeing (*video*). God does not interrupt the process of exchange that constitutes normal vision, but in fact reveals and imposes all perspectives on his countenance.

The physics of perception grounds epistemology (and epistemology, as we shall see, makes the world go round). In recounting the history of astrology, Manilius situates its commencement after human beings had determined the causes of natural phenomena closer to home: why is snow softer than hail? Why do volcanoes blaze and solid earth quake? From there man set about to understand the world beyond the atmosphere and comprehend the totality of the sky in his mind (*intendit totumque animo comprendere caelum*, 1.108). The verb *comprendo* is common enough, but it is also Cicero's choice for presenting the Stoic theory of *katalēpsis*, or secure cognition based on assent (*synkatathesis*) to presentations (*phantasiai*) that themselves grasp or lay hold of reality (Ioppolo 1990). Manilius' use of *comprendo* here in the context of a discussion of causation and, three verses later, of the *facies* or visual appearance of the universe, is both well-informed and subtly polemical. In effect, he turns astrology, the status of which was controversial in at least some Stoic circles (Long 1982), into a quintessential instance of Stoic cognition. At the same time, Manilius acknowledges the causal force of the sage's secure cognition: for it is the human who grasps the true causes of the universe who also assigns shapes (*formas*) and names (*nomina*) to it (1.109).

This idea of the causal power of the sage (who after all, is a god in all things but time) seems to underlie one of Manilius' most striking claims (assuming it is in fact Manilius' and not Goold's, whose text and translation I follow here), namely that 'the mind of man has the power to leave its proper abode and penetrate to the innermost treasures of the sky; to construct the mighty universe from its component seeds' (*seminibusque suis tantam componere molem*, 4.878). To present the activity of the poet as the actual construction of the object he is describing is, as Katharina Volk reminds me, a familiar trope in didactic poetry. But Manilius' emphasis on seeds (*semina*) as the source of the universe thus constructed gives a decidedly Stoic spin to the tradition. A phrase that might be taken to mean 'write an account of the development of the universe starting with the seeds of its creation' also conveys an understanding that the properly disposed human mind does indeed contribute to construction of the universe. The sage's alignment of his controlling-faculty with comprehending sense-presentations intensifies the flow of divine fire, what the Stoics explicitly describe as *spermatikoi logoi*, between perceiver and perceived, thus leading, in the familiar phrase, to the *genesis* of *kosmos* (e.g. Aetius 1.7.33, Diog. Laert. 7.156). Indeed, the potential ambiguity in the referent of the word *suis*—seeds belonging to the human mind, or seeds of the universe—matches the Stoic understanding of the universe as continuous body. As Manilius goes on to claim, 'we perceive our parent, of whom we are part, and having been born from the stars, draw near to them' (4.883–5).

For all that our understanding of Manilius' poem is strengthened by attending to the Stoic physical outlook that directly or indirectly shapes his world-view, there are two important aspects of his presentation that appear to revise the arguments of his Stoic predecessors and near-contemporaries. One of these—the importance assigned to geometry—is best taken as evidence of the flexibility of Stoic physics over time. The other—explicit contradiction of the doctrine of *ekpyrōsis,* or periodic universal return to elemental fire—indicates the limit to which Manilius is willing to pursue the implications of his own physical outlook.

As any reader of Manilius quickly learns, the poem and the poet are deeply interested in geometry. The geometry of circles makes it possible to calculate the height of the heavens (1.545–49); the basic architecture of the cosmos is described in terms of parallel planes and ecliptics (1.561–630); trigons, quadrates, and hexagons are crucial for understanding the relationship between various celestial objects (2.270–96, 2.358–84); the circle of observation is divided on the basis of cardinal points (2.788–840); and so forth. Yet, as Jean-Paul Dumont has noted, geometrical analysis and reasoning sit uncomfortably with the Stoic physical approach to matter (1978; cf. White 2003). In contrast to the geometry of Euclid and Eudoxus, Stoic (or at least Chrysippan) geometry operates under the assumption that a geometric figure can produce nothing but another geometric figure. As an incorporeal, it cannot affect bodies. This is what allows Chrysippus to maintain, for example, in his famous rejoinder to Democritus, that the surfaces generated when a cone is bisected by a plane parallel to its base are 'neither equal nor unequal', although the segments are unequal: circular surfaces, as geometric concepts, are incorporeal and thus not subject to measurement, whereas the real, material entities generated by the bisection of a real, material cone, being bodies, can be measured (Plut. *Mor.* 1079d; Dumont 1978).

This insistence on the incorporeality of geometric figures would seem to pose a problem for any Stoic astrologer. How can circles, degrees, trigons, etc., which are incorporeal abstractions, have any effect on the living, breathing bodies of human beings? In a sense, the question is the physical equivalent of the epistemological problem that also challenges the Stoic astrologer: it is clear enough how heavenly bodies can, through the transmission of *pneuma,* affect terrestrial bodies. But how can constellations, or *signa,* which are, by Manilius' admission, forms and names imposed by the human mind on physical reality, have a similar effect? The problem resembles the one Sextus Empiricus discusses when he criticizes as incoherent the Stoic teaching that *lekta,* or sayables, that is abstract notions articulated in material utterances, can alter the mind through a process equivalent to a child's imitation of his trainer's bodily movements (Sext. Emp. *Adv. Math.* 8.409; Habinek 2010). If the trainer doesn't touch the student, how can his instruction be said to consist of the effect of one body on another?

Rather than throwing up our hands and lamenting either the limitations of Stoic materialism or, more likely, the intellectual weakness of Manilius, we might want to use Manilius' engagement with geometry and semiotics as grounds for advancing our understanding of both Stoicism and Manilius. Stoicism is a flexible and evolving system of thought designed to protect core insights inherited from the pre-Socratics concerning the internal consistency of the physical universe and the desirability of human life in harmony with it. As such, more than other ancient (or for that matter, modern) philosophical schools of thought, Stoicism was deeply respectful of scientific discoveries as they became known. Julia Annas has shown how the Chrysippan concept of *pneuma*, which revises Zeno's singular emphasis on fire, responds to Alexandrian physicians' discoveries concerning the circulatory and nervous systems of the human body (1992: 22–6; cf. A. Jones 2003). Galen, too, remains open to new experimental discoveries while maintaining a broadly Stoic outlook on physical reality. Systematic astrology, as we know, is a relatively late arrival in the Hellenistic world (A. Jones 2003; Lawrence 2008) yet it takes hold in part because of its claim to be based on centuries of careful empirical observation. As Manilius puts it, 'experience fashioned this skill' (*artem experientia fecit*, 1.61). Whether he accepts its teachings or not, a Stoic can't afford not to take the claims of astrology seriously.

Manilius, it seems reasonable to infer, presents astrology from the perspective of Stoic physics and in so doing joins his predecessor Posidonius in expanding Stoic physics as well. As Dumont puts it, the Stoic use of geometry is contemplative not generative, 'geometric speculation consisting not in the production of entities, but in the perception of realities that are already present' ('la spéculation géométrique ne consistant pas à produire des entités, mais à percevoir des réalités déjà présentes', 1978: 123). Manilius' geometrical and semiotic account of the operations of the heavens is just such a mode of perceiving and describing realities that, in his view, are already present. He makes no explicit, doctrinal claims for the corporeality of geometric figures or constellations. Rather he tries to show that the knowledge generated by astrological science and observation is an effective means of aligning human experience with the order of the universe and thus serves the ultimate end of all variants of Stoic thought. Through *oikeiōsis*, or finding one's place in the physical universe, a process articulated and defended by means of dialectical engagement with geometric and other forms of reasoning, Manilius and his reader have one more opportunity to experience *sympatheia*, or a life in harmony with nature. When understood this way, the *Astronomica*, rather than teaching astrology fortified with philosophy (Abry's phrase, 2003: 250), recognizes in astrology an extension and validation of Stoic physical thought, with its distinctive insistence on the materiality, singularity, and continuity of the universal body.

Yet the overall picture is not quite so simple as that. For at the end of his poem, at least as we have it now, Manilius explicitly refers to another tenet of Stoic physics—namely the dynamic growth, decline, and reconstitution of the physical universe, characterized by the experience of *ekpyrōsis*, or periodic transformation into elemental fire—only to reject it as contrary-to-fact. In celebrating the magnificence of the heavenly firmament he remarks on both the extraordinary number of stellar fires and their careful, hierarchical ordering, which, he tells us, resembles that of great cities whose inhabitants are assigned to separate classes (*utque per ingentis populus discribitur urbes*, 5.734). Lest we fail to see which great city in particular is meant, Manilius employs the familiar language of the Roman political system: *patres, ordo equester, populus, vulgus, res publica* (5.735–8). For Manilius the beauty of the heavenly system, like the Roman, is that despite the numerical superiority of the people (*populus*, 5.742) over the elite (*procerum*, 5.740), the power of the inert mob (*vulgus iners*, 5.737) is insufficient to ignite the cosmic catastrophe that the final lines of the poem proceed to evoke:

> cui si pro numero vires natura dedisset,
> ipse suas aether flammas sufferre nequiret,
> totus et accenso mundus flagraret Olympo. (5.743–5)

> If nature had given them strength to match their numbers
> The heavens would be unable to endure their own fires
> And the whole universe would be ignited by the blazing sky.

The emphatic placement of this aborted *ekpyrōsis* can hardly be accidental. Fire imagery pervades the poem, indeed Manilius himself is virtually 'on fire' (e.g. *duplici circumdatus aestu*, 1.21). At one point he goes so far as to describe destruction by fire as the *supremum fatum* ('ultimate fate', 5.210) of the earth, of which the earth itself is apparently aware.

Perhaps more to the point, the juxtaposition of political order and the doctrine of transformation into fire appears elsewhere among the Stoic sources, although to an entirely different end. A key passage consists of an apparently verbatim citation of Aristocles in Eusebius' *Praeparatio evangelica*. In the translation of Long and Sedley (1987: 1.276), Aristocles reports that, according to Stoic doctrine:

> At certain fated times the world is subject to conflagration, and then is reconstituted afresh. But the primary fire is as it were a sperm which possesses the principles (*logoi*) of all things and the causes of past, present, and future events. The nexus and succession of these is fate, knowledge, truth, and an inevitable and inescapable law of what exists. In this way everything in the world is excellently organized as in a perfectly ordered society.

Coming from Manilius, we may well find this connection of cosmic conflagration with a perfectly ordered society unexpected, even inexplicable. What does periodic destruction have to do with social order? The Stoic answer becomes apparent from the broader context of Eusebius' treatise, where the underlying problem to which the doctrine of *ekpyrosis* speaks is that of continuity and change over time. Can a material universe persist eternally even as it undergoes change? For the Christian Eusebius, Porphyry's argument that fire cannot be eternal is sufficient to undermine the Stoic position (Eus. *Praep. Ev.* 15.16). But in the course of rejecting Stoic materialism, Eusebius preserves crucial evidence for the ways in which a Stoic might have used the doctrine of periodic conflagration. The citation just following the one from Aristocles reprises Arius Didymus' observation that for the Stoics the universe is eternal, but its arrangement subject to periodic change (Eus. *Praep. Ev.* 15.15). The parallel between a universe subject to periodic transformation and a well-ordered society is to be found in the persistence of substantive identity despite radical transformation. In other words, it can be used to draw exactly the opposite political inference from the one promoted by Manilius. Transformation, of which being consumed by fire is but an exceptionally intense version, is in the natural order of things. The prospect of dissolution and recomposition is reassuring rather than threatening.

Indeed, Seneca the Younger, writing at most a generation after Manilius, has the deceased Cremutius Cordus speak favourably of the very dissolution Manilius represents as being held at bay. In

Cremutius' speech, which concludes the *Consolation to Marcia*, the doctrine of conflagration becomes a reminder of all human beings' shared fate (*commune fatum, Marc.* 26.6). When the time comes, 'the present visible order will go up in flames. And we, too, fortunate souls . . . will return to our original elements' (26.6–7). An even more pointed lesson informs the *Consolation to Polybius*, where Seneca insists that contemplation of universal destruction is 'the greatest consolation' (*maximum solacium*) available to those who are sorrowing. Nature has made universal that which is most disastrous, so that 'equality becomes consolation for the cruelty of fate' (*ut crudelitatem fati consolaretur aequalitas, Pol.* 1).

As I have argued elsewhere, Manilian astrology suits the needs of an elite Roman population disconnected from the ritualized bodily practices that had shaped its subjectivity in generations past (Habinek 2007). Technical enough to be the purview of up-to-date experts, bodily enough to constitute a new way of being, astrology compensates for the rationalization of earlier familial and religious practices that characterized Rome's cultural revolution of the late first century BC and early first century AD. Stoicism could and did serve much the same purpose, with its intense commitment to reason and its equally intense commitment to the materiality of experience. But Stoicism's intellectual rigour ultimately undermined its ideological usefulness. Although it readily incorporated new scientific discoveries and responded creatively to changing historical experiences, its commitment to key principles concerning the materiality and unity of the entire cosmos made it an unlikely candidate for ideology's task of masking underlying contradictions in the social order. Individual Stoics were certainly capable of tolerating, even defending, what to us are deeply unjust social and political arrangements (Shaw 1985). But the system of thought the Stoics developed was (and is) more likely to disturb and expose the awkward compromises of conventional belief and action than to argue them away. And so it is with Manilius, the disorderliness of whose defence of Rome becomes apparent when we take his conflicted Stoicism seriously.[1]

[1] I am happy to thank Katharina Volk and Steven Green for their invitation to participate in the conference on Manilius held in New York in fall 2008 and for comments on an earlier version of this paper. The present study is part of a larger set of projects aimed at re-evaluating the place of Stoic physics in European intellectual and cultural history.

4

Myth and explanation in Manilius

Daryn Lehoux

EXPLANATIONS

I want to ask what turns out to be a disciplinary question. Some disciplines, from literature to history of religion, sociology, even psychotherapy, all have ready-to-hand categories within or against which *myth* is understood.[1] Scholars working in those traditions have some well worked-out ideas about what kind of thing myth is, where it has actions and responses in the world, and how we can understand its roles in various contexts ranging from ritual to ethics, to theology, politics, and psychology.

In the history of the sciences (as in the history of philosophy), though, the situation is quite different. On the one hand, the histories of the medieval, early modern, and modern sciences almost never have to deal with myth at all; religion, allegory, metaphor, perhaps, but not myth *per se*. Historians of *ancient* science, on the other hand, have a different kind of non-encounter with myth. We have, it seems, bracketed out myth quite deliberately. Myth is invoked, when it is confronted at all, as the very paradigm of NOT-science. It falls on the far side of the so-called *demarcation problem*. In the history of the sciences the demarcation problem is the difficult question of how (or whether) we can define science. To put it most crudely, it is reducible to this question: what is it that the history of science is the history *of*? Partial answer: not myth. When one looks around, though, one can find occasional mentions of myth by modern scholars, but

---

[1] Csapo 2005 offers a good overview.

almost always parsing it as some category of explanation that science supplanted: science posited natural causes in place of attributing causation in the universe to *super*natural entities (pick up almost any book on the Presocratics for example). That very move from supernatural to natural causation is, we are told, exactly what defines the birth of science, and perhaps of philosophy also.

Let me show this with some more or less randomly selected quotations from recent and respectable works:

> In Hesiod, to explain the world is to show how it arose from the interactions of supernatural persons. By contrast, in Anaximander the explanantia are natural events or things.[2]

> Hesiod's genealogical model was quickly superseded by a variety of others. Among these, the mechanical model is of particular importance to our story.[3]

> At some point a new and more critical attitude came about. People began to reject myths and explanations in terms of the gods as arbitrary and fanciful. Instead they began to use theories for which they could gather evidence and debate the merits.[4]

> The many different explanations by the philosophers of lightning had in common the principal feature that they did *not* attribute it to Zeus, as non-philosophical Greeks thought. . . . Rainbows, rain, comets, lightning: not only do they share in having *some* kind of natural explanation and in not having a divine explanation, but they are brought into natural philosophy *because* they are not divine. . . . The subject has not only its boundaries fixed but its subject matter determined by the absence of the actions of the gods in things that frightened people.[5]

> It is clear that preliterate people, no less than those of us who live in a modern scientific culture, have a need for explanatory principles capable of bringing order, unity, and especially meaning to the apparently random and chaotic flow of events. But we should not expect the explanatory principles accepted by preliterate people to resemble ours: lacking any conception of 'laws of nature' or deterministic causal mechanisms, their ideas of causation extended well beyond the sort of mechanical or physical action acknowledged by modern science.[6]

---

[2] Graham 2006: 10 uses this contrast specifically to define what Anaximander does as 'scientific'.
[3] Sedley 2007: 4.   [4] Gregory 2001: 2.
[5] French 1994: 17, emphasis his.   [6] Lindberg 1992: 7.

In comparison with Hesiod's account much has changed. Instead of Hesiod's whole range of independent cosmic factors, we now find a more *reductive approach*: various stages of the cosmogony [of Anaximander] . . . are explained by reference to only two factors (the hot and the cold) . . . Furthermore the basic explanatory factors are no longer more or less anthropomorphic gods. Instead, the genesis of the cosmos is explained in terms of recognizable elements of nature—in other words, the approach is *naturalistic*.[7]

One aspect that all these accounts share is an emphasis on the role of *explanation*. Both myth and philosophy are supposed to be providing explanations for why things are the way they are. For Geoffrey Lloyd, who takes a more nuanced approach, myth does not quite explain, but in a sense cocoons a number of difficult-to-rationalize phenomena: death, disease, madness, dreams. At the same time as he wants to argue in favour of this function for myth, he has also made the great advance of reminding us that the very category of myth was invented by a class of individuals who were trying for polemical and professional reasons to distinguish their discourse from myth.[8] These were the self-styled advocates of something they decided to call *logos*. This distancing of their own inquiry from that of the mythographers had considerable force, at least if the frequency of its deployment in antiquity is anything to go by. Moreover, the basic idea behind it is very compelling, and for all that Lloyd and others can trace it to an original polemical purpose, it still finds independent air to this day. Indeed, it is its continuing compellingness that lent Paul Veyne his shock value when he posed the question *Did the Greeks Believe in their Myths?* back in 1983.

But that categorization of myth, as dedicated to (and perhaps even only to) primitive peoples' explaining the incomprehensible universe by inventing invisible causes for all the apparent arbitrariness, that categorization would not last two minutes in an undergraduate course on myth in any department that would offer one. But there we have it in histories of the sciences. Rather than asking what is wrong with the conception, I want to look at why it is compelling, how the actors' category makes sense within a particular discourse, and then to re-ask the question of what we can do with it. Manilius, as

---

[7] Algra 1999: 48. One wonders what part of nature the *apeiron* is, however.
[8] Lloyd 1979. See also Detienne 1981; for a recent update of this theme, see Morgan 2000.

it turns out, is a perfect case study. Just as each discipline became interested in myth for different reasons, so also interpretations of myth get accepted or rejected within any one discourse community for a complex of reasons peculiar to that community. At the same time, discourses can operate on many different levels, and Manilius as poet/scientist/Stoic/theologian has a rich and complex use of mythology that belies the old myth-to-science story only with difficulty.

That Manilius is siding with *explanation* as one of the primary registers in which myth operates, he leaves us in no doubt. When he tells his creation story for how people discovered the laws of the stars, we see a good deal of divine intervention (god himself bringing them to god: 1.50) but nothing that a Stoic would not reduce to physical causation ultimately—no baldly supernatural or superstitious stories, at least not yet. Here is the history of astrology as Manilius tells it: before people acquired the knowledge of the heavens they lived in ignorance (1.66), surprised at the rising sun each day. Then came the arts, including language, and people began to invent fables to account for the causes of things. He does not say this last point directly, but instead tells us that, after much toil, reason (*ratio*) rose to heaven and captured darkest nature in the causes of things. Now people knew why thunder happens, why volcanoes explode, why earthquakes and wind and rain happen (1.98–9)—a veritable what's what of the purported explananda of myth, a fact Manilius does not fail to note by pointing out how knowledge of these causes 'snatched (*eripuit*) the very lightning from Jove' (1.104), instead attributing lightning's sound to the winds, its fire to the clouds themselves. We could not ask for a more deliberate characterization of the transition from mythical to naturalistic explanation. He reinforces the point when he says in the proem to book 2 that the world is nothing but fables for poets, and he adds that this means that the waters have become very muddied and he must start anew, 'travelling in his own car' (2.59).

But if the lightning, the movements of the sun and moon, the structure and order of the Cosmos are thus being attributed to natural entities, why does Manilius have such frequent recourse to myth? If it were a simple case of his paying homage to poetic tropes in the course of an otherwise physical set of explanations, that would be one thing.[9]

---

[9] On myth in didactic poetry generally, see Gale 1994; Taub 2008.

But that is not quite (or not just) what Manilius does. What we see instead is much more interesting. As Manilius moves through his catalogue of well-travelled poetic subjects, where we see myths aplenty, he suddenly breaks his catalogue off for a brief and isolated critical aside that explicitly condemns the shallowness and presumptuousness of one type of fable, catasterism myths, which is suprising, in that these would seem to be the very type most appropriate for him to be paying generic tribute to. He says:

> quorum carminibus nihil est nisi fabula caelum
> terraque composuit mundum quae pendet ab illo. (2.37–8)[10]

> In their songs heaven is nothing but fable, and the earth creates the Cosmos from which it hangs.

When at last he comes to the close of his list, it is noteable that he does not repeat this criticism. Instead he simply promises not to use other poets' worn words and to tread his own path assiduously. One may be tempted to read his list of traditional poetic topics (many of them mythical) together with his claim that the waters are now muddied and the streams no longer refreshing, as a broad if implicit criticism of mythology, but that would be to read more into his words than is actually there. He is clearly eager to establish the novelty of his project and so he needs to turn away from what he calls the trampled paths of other poets, but given the highly poetic language in which he summarizes their works, he is simultaneously showing us that he *could*, if he wanted to, play their game too. That he chooses not to do so should not be seen as a condemnation of what the greats among his forebears have achieved (indeed he lauds Homer and Hesiod explicitly) so much as a confident assertion of his own originality and his courage in taking on such an apparently unpromising subject for versification. Having said that, though, we need to look back at the little two-line break in the catalogue where Manilius really does appear to criticize the catasterism poets: 'heaven is nothing but fable, and the earth creates the Cosmos from which it hangs'. It is hard not to read this as a dismissal of the genre. But the reason is an interesting one: catasterism poets are not condemned because mythology as a whole is an unfit subject, but instead because these poets invert the priority of heaven and earth, by decorating the heavens based on insignificant 'accidents' (*ex variis casibus*) that

---

[10] On the issues raised by these lines, see Volk 2001 and 2009: 12–13 and 190–2.

happen to befall people and animals down here.[11] The particular
point of the criticism means that mythology as a whole has not
been ruled out of court, even if Manilius owes more of a debt here
to the catasterism tradition than he explicitly acknowledges.[12]

If we now turn to instances where Manilius uses mythology himself, we find a parallelism that is surprising—and perhaps a little bit
worrying—to the historian of science. A favourite technique for
Manilius is to set up parallel strings of explanations, some physical,
some mythological, as though they were equally likely *causes* for
certain phenomena. The most obvious way of understanding what
he is doing in these passages is to read him allegorically (a common
Stoic hermeneutic) but, as I hope to show, this has a possibly worrying side-effect in that it may unintentionally revitalize the myth-
to-science narrative.

ALLEGORIES

We know that allegoresis was a central method in Stoic theology, and
we find it littering the corpus from Chrysippus forward. It is perhaps
symptomatic of mainstream history of philosophy that neither the
word 'allegory' nor 'myth' make their way into the index to the
massive and authoritative *Cambridge History of Hellenistic Philosophy*.
But when one reads, for example, Balbus' defence of Stoic theology in
Cicero's *De natura deorum*, which includes a crescendo of allegory on
traditional mythology, one cannot help but be struck by both the power
of the method and what must be its familiarity to Cicero's readers.
Manilius, though, is grasping the stick at the other end.

The usual Stoic method is to take a myth or a story from Homer or
Hesiod and to then read it through a Stoic lens, showing how it
captures some truth or other about the Cosmos. At its extremes,
this led to the accusation by opposing schools that the Stoics made
even Homer into one of their own, *avant la lettre*. Thus Velleius in the
De natura deorum complains that Chrysippus saw all the poets as
Stoics (*Stoici fuisse videantur*, 1.41). At its more moderate end, we get
the softer and, I think, more interesting claim that *physica ratio non*

---

[11] *Astr.* 2.35. See Salemme 2000: 76–9, 86–90, for a discussion of this passage.
[12] See Salemme 2000: ch. 4.

inelegans inclusa est in impias fabulas ('there is a not inelegant physical logic behind common myths', 2.64). But this method of reading the old anew is not what Manilius is up to. Rather than a reader of poets, Manilius is a poet himself, and he is not reading myths for us, but inviting us to read them for ourselves. He is a Stoic consciously *writing* allegory rather than offering it to us on a plate.

Manilius' use of myth as allegory, then, is not quite the same as, say, Palaephatus trying to find the historical truth behind popular myths (Medea did not rejuvenate old men by boiling them in a cauldron, she was the inventor of hair dye!), nor is it exactly Balbus' point that people have always had certain kinds of knowledge about the gods, which we find in the hidden truths behind their myths. That is to say it is not the winnowing off of superfluity and a rather brutal correction of historical meaning (let us call this the sieve of Palaephatus), nor is it Balbus' somewhat more careful insight, which says that there is good theological truth behind common myths. Where normal Stoic allegorical practice wants to translate myths for us to make sure we get things right, Manilius is instead opening a book for us to read on our own.

CAUSES

But there is more in Manilius. Sometimes, to be sure, the myths are readily transparent poeticisms, as when he talks of the sun's chariot as a pretty way of describing the transit of that star. More complex are cases where the structures and the formulae of his mythologizing repeat themselves in the poem. Again and again, it is hard not to notice, he introduces mythological narratives in the middle of his explanations of physical causes in the Cosmos, and he does so with an innocuous-looking—but telling—'either/or' construction. Rarely this is just a very literal description of the ranges of opinion available to people, as in book 1, when he tells us how people eventually clawed their way up from ignorance and formulated and debated various causal accounts of phenomena: perhaps (*sive*) the universe is without end; or else (*sive*) Chaos separated matter out; perhaps (*sive*) all is little atoms; maybe (*sive*) it's all fire; or maybe (*aut*) there is not just one primary element, but four of them (1.122 ff.). Compare also his list of causes for the Milky Way at 1.684 ff. where he has an identical expository structure: PHYS₁, PHYS₂, MYTH₁, PHYS₃ . . . .

But then something entirely different is going on in other cases. At 2.485 ff. Manilius describes some of the secondary geometrical relationships between the signs, which are called 'hearing' and 'seeing', 'loving' and 'rebuffing' each other, relationships that allow for reinforcements of astrological events in their seen or heard signs, positive or negative according to the natures of the signs in relation to the events. As his list progresses, he comes to Taurus, which, he says, rebuffs the love of Aries (*insidiantia*), hears Pisces (*audientia*), and looks upon (*videntia*) Virgo with, says Manilius, longing. He now cannot help himself and adds that thus (*sic*) the bull was the dress in which Jove carried Europa on his back. The fact that Taurus longs for Virgo here is unusual, as they merely look at each other, and looking is otherwise an unloaded relationship throughout this section: Aries looks at Libra, Gemini looks at Leo, Scorpio looks at Pisces, Sagittarius at Aquarius, and vice versa. Looking is not longing for any of them. Their *loves and longings* by contrast run in a near perpendicular direction according to that unique and confusing Manilian schema of *amantia* and *insidiantia*. Only for Taurus looking at Virgo (and not, I note, the other way around) are his eyes the vehicles of longing. Manilius is here adding a nuance to Taurus' relationship with Virgo that has no parallel in the other signs, and he is doing it through a mythological allegory. Indeed, the particular nuance makes perfect sense, insofar as for people born under the sign of Taurus love itself must exist in an act of seeing: *semper amare parum est: cupient et amare videri* (5.156). This flags a double aspect for the intimate relationship between love and vision for Taurus: love happens through seeing, and (related to this) love is only real *if seen*.

Jupiter's disguises, it seems, pose a special fascination for Manilius. In book 1 when he introduces the constellation Cygnus, Manilius recounts the story of Jupiter's seduction of Leda and his placing of the constellation in the stars as reward. As with the loves of Taurus, Manilius comes back to Jupiter in Cygnus in book 5 when he uses the incygniation of Jupiter to *explain* why bird fanciers are so frequently born under this sign, having a special way of talking to birds or of teaching them even to talk.

A favourite framing device of Manilius emerges here: a myth first brought up in book 1, as part of Manilius' description of the geography of the constellations, is taken up again in book 5, where Manilius is outlining the astrological powers, the causal force, of each constellation. Orpheus and the Lyre (1.325, 5.324), Heniochus/Bellerophon the charioteer (1.361, 5.97), Jupiter drinking the milk of the Kids to nourish him for his bid for power (1.365, 5.128), Jupiter and the Altar in the battle with the Giants (1.420, 5.339), Aquila and Jupiter's thunderbolts (1.345, 5.486), Perseus and Andromeda (1.356, 5.538). It is worth noting that he uses all but two or three of the mythological stories in 1 and 5 as such literary bookends, and that we find these myths paired in books 1 and 5 but nowhere in between.[13]

In each of these cases the myth serves in book 5 to *explain* particular characteristics of those born under the sign. Where Aries, the ram, is self-explanatorily mild and the Bears so obviously powerful and strong over animals, it is more difficult to explain why those born at the rising of, say, Andromeda should be heartless executioners in the absence of the myth. Once we know the myth, though, we can understand the causal force: who else could have chained a helpless and blameless maid to a rock, Manilius asks, but such a heartless executioner?[14] Indeed, it is telling that, for one constellation, Manilius laments in both book 1 and again in 5 that there is no story behind it. Engonasin's characteristics are very hard to reconcile (desertion and bullying, courage and clumsiness), for which there is no mythical explanation on offer. Not only does Manilius thus explicitly lament the lack of an explanatory myth for Engonasin, but he does so twice, in books 1 and 5 respectively (1.314, 5.645).

In a sense, then, these myths are functioning as metonyms for the powers of the various constellations.

---

[13] In general: the repetition in book 5 of themes from the beginning of the poem seems to me to be strong evidence that the poem as we have it is complete (lacunae excepted). For this strategy in Ovid's *Fasti*, see Newlands 1995: 124–45. Compare also Goold 1977: xiv.

[14] It may be argued here that it makes little sense for Andromeda to preside over the births of executioners, the very people who would have been responsible for chaining her to her rock—would it not make more sense for her to be the patron star of the unjustly persecuted or some such thing? I agree that Manilius is making a stretch here, but I think the association of Andromeda with executioners is close enough for metonymic purposes, and in any case, Manilius is faced with trying to explain an accepted body of doctrine rather than having the power to simply make up astrological influences at will. He is, in this sense, saving certain phenomena rather than creating them. For the dynamics of the Andromeda epyllion in its context, see Uden in this volume. For an astrologically based argument for consistency between story and qualities given to natives under Andromeda, see Hübner in this volume.

ALLEGORESIS

If, on the other hand, we take the standard Stoic reading of myth to heart, we here run into a difficulty. On the Stoic model, myths cloak some true propositions, which can be uncovered through careful and proper reading. The idea here is that there are true statements about the natural world (or in other contexts, about history) embedded in the quaint stories of myth. Theology, closely related to physics in Stoicism, is a favourite subject for this hermeneutic method. Nevertheless, the basic output of Stoic allegoresis is a set of propositions, and as a set of propositions, it can be checked for agreement with the actual natural world. Myths, on this model, *can be true or false*, and that means that the complex readings of myth that we find in many modern disciplines become difficult to maintain if it is true that myths are just a kind of explanation. We may, if we are not careful here, find ourselves railroaded back into a myth-to-science narrative.

One way out may be to argue that Stoic hermeneutics is a later reaction to the mythic traditions and cannot tell us anything about the *origins* of myth or of science. This may work to keep the myth-to-science narrative from gaining uncritical traction in the very early (Greek) period, but it will not work for a reading of Manilius, where the myths are being retold with just such explanatory purposes in mind. This is first-century Roman scientific mythopoesis, not just a new-fangled reaction to myths of old.

But—and this is the main point—for Manilius to say that Cygnus was put in the sky by Jupiter is not just figurative or allegorical. The universe is, as Manilius himself emphasizes again and again, a providentially created Cosmos. Jupiter, god, *ratio* (however Manilius happens to be calling it in any particular passage) created the Cosmos, and created it wisely. The pretty pictures in the sky are there for a reason, and their effects fall out of their characters as a fundamental concomitant of the order and interdependency of the entire Cosmos (indeed, this may well be what Manilius means when he says that he must sing the Cosmos *sua totus sub imagine*, 'after its own likeness'). When Manilius claims that anyone born under the constellation of Delphinus will be swift upon the sea, this is not just quaint word-association or easy mnemonics.[15] It is

---

[15] Contrast Beck 2007.

instead a manifestation of the underlying *order* in the Cosmos, an order that is both divinely created and divinely maintained.

The constellations have shapes, and the constellations have powers. Their powers are related to their shapes because the universe is rational and ordered at every level. The powers and the pictures combine into what we might profitably treat as the *natural history* of each constellation. They have actions and abilities in the world, they have environments (geometrical), and they have characteristic interrelationships with us and each other. The mythical stories told by Manilius are part and parcel of that natural history. They encapsulate and explain the power of certain constellations.

CONCLUSION

André Laks joins many Continental thinkers, and a growing number of Anglo-American ones, in rejecting a simplistic 'from myth to reason' formulation.[16] Helpfully for our purposes, though, he still wants to try and settle what the transition is, partly on the grounds that our philosophical sources seem to have seen their own tradition as having somehow grown out of myth traditions. I think he is gesturing in the right direction with his point that the difference 'induit une redistribution des positions discursives' (Laks 2006: 59). Reason does not supplant myth. Reason has always been there and myth will continue to fare under the supposed hegemony of reason. But the 'inquiry concerning nature', as Lloyd has called it, asks different questions and is satisfied with very different answers than mythopoetic traditions. Its points of contact with the world, the entities it is talking about, its criteria for what can or should be said about them, are different. So too the cultural, political, and moral implications of its inquiry and its framing of the world differ. In that sense then, the difference between science and myth does not just lead to (*induire*) a redistribution of discursive positions, but rather *consists in* such a redistribution. There is a famous and puzzling portrait of that arch-rationalist René Descartes, painted by Jan Baptist Weenix in

---

[16] Laks 2006. See also Lloyd 1979; Detienne 1981; Veyne 1983; von Staden 1992; Brisson 1996; Buxton 1999; Morgan 2000; von Hendy 2002; Bonadeo 2004; Taub 2008.

Figure 4.1 Jan Baptist Weenix, Portrait of René Descartes (*c*.1648). Centraal Museum, Utrecht. Reproduced by permission.

1648 or so and now in the Centraal Museum, Utrecht (see Figure 4.1), which shows Descartes holding open a large book on which we can read the inscription *mundus est fabula*. Frankly, I have no idea how to make sense of this phrase with respect to Descartes' philosophy,[17] but it would be an appropriate summary for the reading I am arguing for Manilius, where the rational and divine order of the universe implies the *meaningful* arrangement of its particulars.

---

[17] I do not follow e.g. Nancy 1978.

Part II

Integrity and Consistency

5

Watch this space (getting round 1.215–46)

John Henderson

> alii...
> melius caeli... meatus
> describent radio et surgentia sidera dicent.
> (Verg. *Aen.* 6.847–50)

Now that the essays in Part I have set about setting Manilius' power-book in its early imperial cultural-intellectual frame,[1] my chapter revvs up on what goes around comes around: the attractions/resistances of *textual* volumetrics. I would claim that the Roman poet Manilius who figures in today's scholarship knows all the poetological topoi and knows them well, but I am not so sure that he yet owns his world, is granted the cosmotext he writes. By comparison with the recognition of systematic imprinting of Epicurean 'atomology' within Lucretian cosmopoetics,[2] the fit, the degree of fit, between doctrine and exposition in, and as, *Astronomica* has yet to straddle the whole 'di*verse*' epic.[3] I am not so much thinking of graphematic conceits, all

---

[1] See now Volk 2009: *Manilius* is indisputably booked into the Anglophone Latin Literature stakes (in my day we knew 'serious study... has been for the most part left to Germany and Italy', Wilson 1985: 283; cf. Volk 2002: 196–7). *Forgotten Stars* must've been in my stars—but I am really grateful to Katharina.

[2] Inaugurated by Friedlaender 1941, developed in Snyder 1980; cf. Volk 2002: 239.

[3] This after the Loeb translation (Goold 1977), with 'di*versify*' for *uariantia* at 1.2: *uerto* will prove to have been one of the most compactly overdetermined puncepts in the poem all along: compare Hübner in this volume (cf. 1.15, 67, 94; at 5, *uertice*: at 4.555 = 'pole'; *diuersos*, 2, 86, 248, cf. 252–4). I touch on the core role played by some variant varieties of 'variousness' and/as '(co-)variance' in generating *Astronomica* in what follows (*uarius* at 1.61, 70, 112, 237, 252).

the way through to acrostics or outré frills such as whether the opening salvo of 1.1–10 qualifies as a 'kosmos' (a perfect 1+2+3+4 figure, instead of the classic 7-line epic proem?), or the like exotic-esoteric quodlibeta; nor of the hermeneutic form of attention where you would stop, or let, your reading *wonder*, at <u>Helicona</u> *mouere | cantibus et uiridi nutantis uertice siluas*, 1.4–5, whether this traditional (*post*-Hesiodic) diction of 'mountain and winds getting up' already adds up, and spins fine, to mounting a 'wind-up' (i.e. does the spheroid uni*verse*, that astro-nomic joint, *already* start rocking, going round and round—'helically'?).[4] Rather, the common project as I see it now, orbits around the pervasive work of textual figuration as adumbrated, and magisterially keyed, by Hübner in this volume.[5] Are we ready, how ready, to embrace a thoroughgoing idiolectal (re-) troping of the poem's entire apparatus of spatial-temporal, causal-associative, 'literal'-descriptive vocabulary in line with the postulates of the dynamical system of his Roman astrostoicism?[6] When we can credit the crafting of every meme as directly 'influenced' by the persuasive project in a customized world-design, then we can unreservedly claim Manilius' epic ecosystem well and truly revalued. That's what makes a work go round.

Periods spiral down and jitterbug up the page, before any version of 'first-time' reader *can* be ready for the overdetermined ride.[7] But any second-guessing encounter, any *reading*, will be anticipating thematic prequels by way of entrée, as signalled by the elaborated trappings of proemial business, there for actual second-time reading to realize. As we find our feet, the writing can't launch us straight into the groove we're looking for, as we 'calculate' (*deducere*)[8] the designs it must have on us as, and before, we begin. Massaged as we are primed, we'll expect to realize retrospectively how theory-laden and persuasively tooled it

---

[4] But *mouere* (41, 51, 64, 76, 93, 102, cf. *motus*, 57), naturally, belongs with *uerto* as 'motor' for Man's kinesic poetics: compare Hübner in this volume.

[5] Cf. Hübner 1984: 214–27, etc.

[6] I resist Habinek's resistance (2007: 234; but see now Habinek in this volume) to sympathetic Stoicizing (as e.g. Volk 2002: 198, 240; 2009: 30–1, etc.) in favour of Pythagorean 'mutual mimesis between heaven and earth': humanity as 'cosmic replica' in the Anaxagoras tradition is more my Man (cf. Naddaf 2005: 149–50, after Cynthia Farrar).

[7] Cf. Schrijvers 1983: 143, 'une grande densité sémantique'. The etymology of 'ready' is obscure, but, as I read in Wiktionary s.v. 'read', is 'the development from "advise, interpret" to "interpret letters", unique to English'?

[8] See Kennedy in this volume on *deducere*, 1.3.

must already, unseizably, have been. Otherwise author forfeits authority and mission aborted. So, on he leads and we must follow, *per carmina* to *per ipsum* | *aera*,[9] from 1.12–13, *pandere . . . uacat tantum* (as we assimilate *ad tanta canenda*, 1.10),[10] to break on through to 14, the joys of *spatiantem uiuere caelo*: 'opening up, peacefully, all that *space*—to sing all this *stuff*', *as well as*: 'there's only free *time* under a *pax Augusta*'. This first sample programming encapsulates-pilots any trip we take with Manilius. At any rate, I shall be working my way round and back to this short step into a giant leap. One light year for *Man*power.

Still, to date, *Astronomica* is stuck in the penumbra of an editorial approach which was *not* locked onto the poetics of this cosmograph, and played blind to *his* rhetoric. To sum up what I mean in one all-round uni-verse, take the rounding-up flourish at 1.235, *ex quo colligitur terrarum forma rotunda.*| Even without visible brackets round this invitingly excisable flourish of a self-contained 'recap', it's easier to wish them away than expunge the trace from the memory. Even after Joette Abry has come to the rescue through appeal to Manilian metarhetoric, in her brilliant 2005 article,[11] working on and through the 'form' *of argumentation* tightly organized into this tautly 'rounded' shape for its meme, to vindicate the ouroborous circularity of reasoning which kneads 'glomeration' (in 214) into full-blown 'rotundity' (as in Cic. *Nat. D.* 2.117), still, as yet, daggers star-and-scar this one-liner of an epiphonema. Don't they? And this sort of incubus stays around, to hobble the poem's reclamation from scorn—yes, third-rate billing can lurk not least behind apologist denial![12] Does *Astronomica* really fall, before the first astrological fence, at the starting-gate—as imprinted on scholarship, so on us? Does Icaro-Man crash at the first corner?

---

[9] Cf. Volk 2002: 196, 225–6, with esp. 2.141–4, *per iter . . . per carmina . . . per orbem.* |, Volk 2001: 87, 91; 2009: 15. Qua astrophysicist Man's aim is to prescind bisection/dissection between 1.13–15 and 16–19: as if 'astronomy' *could* be non-coincident with 'astrology'!

[10] Schrijvers 1983: 144 n. 5.

[11] Abry 2005: 'La sphéricité de la terre: un poète aux prises avec la démonstration (Manilius, *Astronomiques* I, 173–235)'. I was so looking forward to meeting Prof. Abry, but the stars decreed *autrement*. The Unforgotten Star.

[12] Thus Wilson 1985: 295, with 'Manilius' view of his own role and powers may involve a certain arrogance not altogether justified by the results', buying 'A self-aware poet, self-conscious and sophisticated in his literary-programmatic allusions, emerges'.

In the course of driving home his first confident flashpast of mundane basic co-ordinates for his universe to come, Man speeds along through an organized rundown on standard current astrothinking at Rome,[13] as satirized by a crowing Lucretius; as paraded by Cicero, intersetting starburst *scintillae* from his own trek through heavenly verse in the *Aratea*;[14] and as synthesized with lead boots on by a Pliny Maior revving up for his catalogued and shelved cosmos.[15] As yet, our poet is catching us up for the ride, so he daren't dawdle here, in his preliminary sketching; and yet, his first cluster of 'errors' are supposed to hit us full-tilt, all in a row between 1.215 and 246. And, what's more, these are bound to set the mould/are standardly presented as symptomatic-paradigmatic.[16] I shall represent the case that this is

---

[13] Cf. Volk 2009: 10, 22–8, 'The two-sphere universe', at 30–1.

[14] See Fantham in this volume for Cicero on geocentrism and on sphericality.

[15] He fires one of his most amazing volleys at the moon (2.52): 'But the last of the stars beats the lot for being a marvel! Earth's closest neighbour, nature's invention to cure darkness: the Moon. She has so many different shapes, she's racked astronomers, peeved to know least about the star that's nearest. Forever either waxing or waning; sometimes her disc curves into horns, sometimes it halves, at other times it arcs out into the full ball; sometimes she's spotted and then suddenly becomes extra-bright; appears enormous with full disc, then in a trice is nowhere; at times lasting through the night, at others risen late, and aiding the light of the sun for part of the day, or waning and yet being visible as eclipsed—hides at the end of the month and yet is not supposed to be in trouble then (*quae mensis exitu latet, tum laborare non creditur*)— now down low or high up, and that not on a single cycle, but instead at one time raised up to the sky, at other times almost touching the mountains; now lifted up north, now flattened down south.'

[16] Esp. Goold 1977: xix–xx, 'Canopos is invisible north of *Rhodes*' (i.e. accepting Housman's conjecture *Heliacas* at 1.217). 'Lunar eclipses afford another proof of the Earth's sphericity... Herein the poet may have *misunderstood* his source, for the relevance of lunar eclipses to this enquiry consists not in what he says at all.... Unfortunately he has fallen into the *error* of confusing the western with the southern hemisphere....' Volk 2009: 11 opens up with the '*blatantly erroneous claim* about lunar eclipses at 1.221–35', as trailer to '2.3. The World according to Manilius (*Astronomica* 1)' (29–48, at 33; cf. ead. 2002: 208–9): 'Unfortunately, at this point the poet has *garbled* his argument, possibly because he *misunderstood* his sources or maybe *out of sheer ignorance*... It would seem that the poet is *mixing up* the observability of an eclipse with the fact that the Moon does revolve around the earth from east to west.... As a matter of fact.... It is perhaps because of the fantastic associations of this imagined people on the other side of the globe that Manilius does not mind that he is *committing an egregious error* in claiming that it is night "down there" when it is day up north. It is quite inconceivable that a poet writing an astrological poem (and one who just a few lines earlier discusses the westward course of the Moon) would not have known that the Sun moves from east to west and not from north to south, and I therefore suggest that this is one of the instances where Manilius, as it were, switches from one discourse to another in a way that *appears self-*

hang-over prejudice, which doesn't survive rereading, and no call for special accommodation; and call in the other texts to provide a control. I guess this will oblige me to treat the example as paradigmatic, too.[17]

*

Here is the suite of arguments, preceded by the immediate build-up for them,[18] from which they perpend:

> quodni librato penderet pondere tellus,
> non ageret cursus mundi subeuntibus astris
> Phoebus ad occasum et numquam remearet ad ortus,   175
> lunaue submersos regeret per inania cursus,
> nec matutinis fulgeret Lucifer horis,
> Hesperos emenso dederat qui lumen Olympo.
> nunc quia non imo tellus deiecta profundo,
> sed medio suspensa manet, sunt peruia cuncta,   180
> qua cadat et subeat caelum rursusque resurgat.
> nam neque fortuitos ortus surgentibus astris
> nec totiens possum nascentem credere mundum
> solisue assiduos partus et fata diurna,
> cum facies eadem signis per saecula constet,   185
> idem Phoebus eat caeli de partibus isdem,
> lunaque per totidem luces mutetur et orbes,
> et natura uias seruet, quas fecerat ipsa,
> nec tirocinio peccet circumque feratur
> aeterna cum luce dies, qui tempora monstrat   190
> nunc his nunc illis eadem regionibus orbis,
> semper et ulterior uadentibus ortus ad ortum,
> occasumue obitus, caelum et cum sole perennet.

contradictory' (cf. 47, 'another self-contradiction, which might be explained with the poet's momentary adoption of a popular, non-scientific point of view (as in his treatment of the antipodes)'; and the peroration at Volk 2009: 263, where the antipodeans in darkness when it is day in the northern hemisphere spell 'incoherence' out of 'eclecticism'): whence both this essay and the one by Volk in this volume, proposing 'cheating' through 'self-contradiction': 'This contention [1.242–5] is not only blatantly false, but also contradicts Manilius' cosmology in the rest of the poem. . . . He has his cake and is eating it too . . . ' (p. 110).

[17] It's too long to translate, but we still play off the *Loeb* hymnsheet, Goold 1977.

[18] *Ipsa mihi primum naturae forma canenda est*, 120, is the major incision for the topic closed at 254, before *nunc tibi flammas referam*, 255 (Neuburg 1993: 269; Volk 2002: 236–7).

nec uero natura tibi admiranda uideri
pendentis terrae debet. cum pendeat ipse   195
mundus et in nullo ponat uestigia fundo,
quod patet ex ipso motu cursuque uolantis,
cum suspensus eat Phoebus currusque reflectat
huc illuc agiles et seruet in aethere metas,
cum luna et stellae uolitent per inania mundi,   200
terra quoque aerias leges imitata pependit.
est igitur tellus mediam sortita cauernam
aeris e toto pariter sublata profundo
nec patulas distenta plagas, sed condita in orbem
undique surgentem pariter pariterque cadentem.   205
haec est naturae facies; sic mundus et ipse
in conuexa uolans teretes facit esse figuras
stellarum; solisque orbem lunaeque rotundum
aspicimus, tumido quaerentis corpore lumen,
quod globus obliquos totus non accipit ignes.   210
haec aeterna manet diuisque simillima forma,
cui neque principium est usquam, nec finis in ipsa,
sed similis toto ore manet perque omnia par est.
sic tellus glomerata manet mundique figura.
idcirco terris non omnibus omnia signa   215
conspicimus. nusquam inuenies fulgere Canopum,
donec Niliacas per pontum ueneris oras;
sed quaerent Helicen, quibus ille superuenit ignis,
quod laterum tractus habitant, medioque tumore
eripiunt terrae caelum uisusque coercent.   220
te testem dat, luna, sui glomeraminis orbis,
quae cum mersa nigris per noctem deficis umbris,
non omnis pariter confundis sidere dempto,
sed prius Eoae quaerunt tua lumina gentes,
post, medio subiecta polo quaecumque coluntur,   225
ultima ad Hesperios infectis uolueris alis
seraque in extremis quatiuntur gentibus aera.
quodsi plana foret tellus, semel orta per omnem
deficeret pariter toti miserabilis orbi.
sed quia per teretem deducta est terra tumorem,   230
his modo, post illis apparet Delia terris
exoriens simul atque cadens; quia fertur in orbem
uentris et accliuis pariter decliuia iungit
atque alios superat gyros aliosque relinquit.
ex quo colligitur terrarum forma rotunda.   235
hanc circum uariae gentes hominum atque ferarum

aeriaeque colunt uolucres. pars eius ad Arctos
eminet, Austrinis pars est habitabilis oris
sub pedibusque iacet nostris supraque uidetur
ipsa sibi fallente solo decliuia longa   240
et pariter surgente uia pariterque cadente.
hanc ubi ad occasus nostros sol aspicit ortus,
illic orta dies sopitas excitat urbes
et cum luce refert operum uadimonia terris;
nos in nocte sumus somnosque in membra uocamus.   245
pontus utrosque suis distinguit et alligat undis.
hoc opus immensi constructum corpore mundi
membraque naturae diuersa condita forma
aeris atque ignis terrae pelagique iacentis
uis animae diuina regit, sacroque meatu   250
conspirat deus et tacita ratione gubernat
mutuaque in cunctas dispensat foedera partes,
altera ut alterius uires faciatque feratque,
summaque per uarias maneat cognata figuras.   254

In re-verse order, the triple indictment reads:

1: 236–46 betrays elementary 'duh' confusion of antipody with
antichthony (see n. 16 above). But does it? Re-read with Abry, the
charge dispels, as the paragraph neatly halves between *hanc* (236)
circum ..., which pictures the round shape of the earth in terms of
place, north-south, longitudinally, over against the matching *hanc*
(242), east-west, latitudinally. In my opinion there is no difficulty in
vindicating this *cartographic* instance of writing 'sphéricité' into
volumetric bisection—at least in *these* terms this last point is today
generally agreed.

One pay-off that accrues from this construal is the elegant *écriture* of
246, *pontus utrosque suis distinguit et alligat undis*, a punctual flourish
to match its predecessor, 235, and surely a metarhetorical gem of
self-description for this global paragraph's own rhetorical wave/s
of antithesis aka (= *et*) parataxis. The line internally constitutes itself
through a combination of reciprocally defining, hence constituting,
'(com)bina(to)ry' operations, of distinction and association. And the
distributive '1 through 2' (*et*)/'2-in-1' (*utros-que*) completes a classic
reflection on/with self-reflexivity (*suis* ... *undis*). This has to rate as one
of Many classy closural fillips: making waves, before celebrating the
work that's gone into writing up the work of self-composition by

cosmic matter (*hoc opus . . . mundi*, 247),[19] out of elemental infinity
into the organic formation of every 'limb' of existents (*membra, partes,*
248, 252 ~ *membra*, 244, *pars . . . pars*, 237–8). This is brought about by
the 'pneumatic' sympathy of the imperial coordinating 'governance'
of divine *ratio* operative through celestial 'travel to-and-fro' (*animae,*
conspirat; gubernat, dispensat; meatu, 250–2): here is fully comprehen-
sive/comprehensible synthesis between impassive mathematical analysis (*pars* means 'fraction', 'degree', et sim., in *Astronomica; constructum,*
condita) and impassioned animist zen (*membra; conspirat, cognata*),
unpacking the polarized unity of/in *mundi* +/= *natura* (247–54). Out of
divine division plus part-icular distribution (*diuersa, dispensat*) cometh
forth a calculus that turns immeasurability into a sum (*immensi . . .*
summa) that totals up the whole by arithmetical procedures that *are*
cosmogony (248–54): four founding quantities-entities are 'formatively/
formally' identified/differentiated (four quarters occupying one 'verse'
to make our (hexa)metric universe, from two pairs of forces/principia,
with rhyme merged by elision between the hot light and by implication
'soaring' hemistich of *aeris-atqu-ignis* vs/plus the heavier hemistich of
non-harmonizing but never-so-weakly linked, opposing team of *terrae*
pelagi-que, which has borne down, along, through, to reach the end of
the line inertia of solid ground, grounded earth |, 249–50);[20] then they
can be transformed/factored into a stable/grounded, 100 per cent and
no-remainder (*cunctas . . . maneat*), formation 'through' the applica-
tion/invocation of the physical/numbered ecosystem/set of log. tables,
into the di-versified polyeidic plethora of configurations—shapes and
species, geometrical genera and/or/= biophysical beings promised for
creation/poem at the outset (*diuersa . . . per uarias . . . figuras*, 248–54).[21]
    The operative 'workings' are pinpointed and starred as the articu-
lation of mutual-reciprocal correlations that interlink components
into the dynamic packets that they comprise, together, as the
moving parts that power the whole cosmic engine that energizes
them/everything: *uis* → *uires* (then round again to → *uis*), via
mutua/cunctas → *alter/alterius* (250–3). In this algebra/world, active
'factor/ingredient' and passive 'result/product' are two turns of the
same cycle, where, in another guided/tooled verse-unit that takes us

---

[19] Ringing back to 1.3, *opus* (on which see esp. Kennedy in this volume).
[20] See 3.52, 4.889 for variants on 'all four elements in one verse', with Hübner
1984: 152.
[21] For the ever thematic *maneo*, cf. 145, 168, 180, 207, 211, 214.

down to the logic of reasoning itself, the foundational binary of active and passive is stripped down to its essential valency/ability to convey meaning (*uires faciat-que ferat-que*, 253): you can't have one without the other, but they cannot be the same, rather they cause one *alter* to exchange places with another *alter*, in any given and every imaginable case of 'alteration', so that sameness persists through shift in function/inflection, and generative 'alterity' survives interchange of referent without eliminating traction in terminology (as in the paradigm of grammatical termination, from nominative through genitive, *alterius*). Above, or rather through, it all runs the Manilian purrposiveness of that *per* . . ., running the dactyl/spondee alter(n)ation show, showing how the pulsar mind-machine runs and the quasar slide-rule beats. The poet almost contrives to verbalize the pre-/post-linguistic status of this programming of the cosmos as if committed to pre-linguistic thinking, calculation without symbols, information without words: *tacita ratione* (251); but his logocentric conspiracy (says it) owes its life to the breath that animates this cosmos, and the 'movement' that constitutes the paragraph (*meatu, regit, gubernat, in* . . . *per*) requires you to go width it, 'breathe' to make its breadth, read aloud along these epic lines at length.[22]

But I have surged ahead; I should settle back down again, to follow the argument round (*hanc circum* . . .). Inhabitants-cum-devotees of 'the lands" (plural = Earth's singular) orotundity themselves animate/embody the diversified cosmic economy: *terrarum forma rotunda.* | *hanc circum uariae . . . colunt* . . . (236–7). Man-kind have all sorts of earthbound territory for habitat, severally; species of fauna have their own separate ranges (on land or sea); between their countless types, the 'airy-vary' bird nations travel the skyways skywide (*uariae-aeriae*), migrating planet-wide, *sans frontières*, travelling through space like the minimi-heavenly 'hurtling' bodies they *are* (*uolucres*, 237: *uolo*[1] is a leitmotif of *Astronomica*).[23] A, or one, fraction, or half/50 per cent—'of it' (*pars eius*), namely, of the 'round form of lands which are/is Earth' (*hanc*), extends 'up' north, reaching for the northern pole-star; a, or the, other *pars* (*eius*, i.e. *huius*) is down south with its own

---

[22] 1.24 at once faced off *uerba* ↔ *figuris* (cf. 214, *forma*, 109, 120, 211, 235, 248; Volk 2002: 240–1). As the opening bulge of preliminary materials draws itself to a halt here, a rhetorical ring returns us to the starting-line, lacing *opus, diuersa, diuina, ratione, uarias*, 247–54 tight to *diuinas, diuersos, uariantia, rationis opus*, 1–3.

[23] So Hübner in this volume: cf. already 207, *uolans*, 197, 200, *uolitent*, 149, *uolucer* (of *ignis*), Landolfi 1999.

horizons (237–8 ~ 238–9). Just as these *partes* share designation through their 'polarity' as north-south opposites, so they interlock as each other's doubles because they share the same self-centred perspective that we have already smuggled in to our own survey: our bit is bound to 'be', to seem to be, to appear, phenomenalistically, to be pre-eminent, as if 'up' to heaven our way (| *eminet*, a self-enacting salience through enjambment, 238), whereas 'there' tolerates a population—'supports' life (*habitabilis*, 238). The *variatio* slips into the prejudice we're being trapped in/about to throw into the mix, concentrating on what we of the northern hemisphere unthinkingly refer to as 'underfoot', as (if) the bringdown (Epicurean) way of seeing is surreptitiously infiltrating Man's grasp on volumetric reality along with flattening and deadening the feet of his verse, as it obliterates the force of every *sub* in the poem (see below).[24] In this looking-glass world, the line puts what's down there before, so 'above', what seems/ looks like the right way up from 'their' point of view down under. What they see is what is visible, it is evident-apparent and so 'is' the experience-truth of the world they are given to inhabit, their worldview. So they are no more wrong than we are; but what we say, all the same, is that when they regard themselves as 'on top', they must seem to tread and trample us underfoot, because the solid ground tricks them by imperceptibly masking its 'down-ward slope' over ever-extending distances, just the way that a volumetric body must to any observer stationed at any point anywhere on the surface (*fallente solo*, 240). We can't say or think all this without binding *ourselves* in as well, as if we know no better, to this very partial and so partisan sightedness of living down at ground level: no, it's not going to be a breeze for Man

---

[24] The 'Lucretian' line-opener | *sub pedibus*... (239) in fact opens Virgil's starry-eyed paragraph on 'the zones' (G.1.231–56, *idcirco*..., at 243) just before he concocts *his* astonishingly 'literary' (sc. 'unscientific') version of (?) the antipodes as an *impossible* hell: but this *is* distanced (from Eratosthenes, and Virgil, and Lucretius) by the marker *ut perhibent*, 247; and when Seneca lams into zomboid nightbirds (*Ep.* 122.1–3), we should *not* note (e.g. Volk in this volume) that he gets *all* bases covered, by quoting this unnatural version of *natura*, as the poet's (*ut ait Vergilius*), *as a simile*, and *as first half of a mirror-image* of his own, in which Cato stars as the antipodes to Virgil: *talis horum contraria omnibus non regio sed uita*: the upside-downies are matched by their opposite numbers *here* amongst us (*sunt quidam in eadem urbe antipodes*): so the graphically rasping prophet put/s it, anyway (*ut M. Cato ait*), *nec orientem umquam solem uiderunt nec occidentem*. Seneca is not signed up to the inside-out fantasy quoted by Virgil, but on his way to painting *his own picture* of perversion (15): *infamiam: hanc petunt omnes isti qui, ut ita dicam, retro uiuunt!*

to teach *us* to reconceive every *de-* (and *e(x)*) in the book/world without implicating *himself* in the ordinary implications of mundane language. Even when we know no trick of the light is involved and things could not be otherwise, this 'delusion', or 'illusion', or *trompe l'œil*, is no trick, yet the 'trick' is still both being played on people and on orotund earth itself, in it together (*sibi*). Man does not *need* to spell out that the same goes, arsy-versy, for *their* other. Instead he winds himself up for a consummate self-contained ouroborous rounding off.

Taking both sources of prejudicial parochialism out of the reckoning, the *de-* and *cliu-* in the foxy longueur of *decliuia* (240), he shrinks/abstracts the graph to map every single simple *uia* anywhere in the universe, not just down on earth, but everywhere, no matter how short on syllables (241). There can be no 'movement', uphill and down dale, between Norway and South Georgia, that does not *simultaneously* 'rise and—set', any more than there can be a hexameter that does not enact the eternal round of 'masking' then 'declining' its construction, even when it is arranged to defeat its linear trajectory by axial circling round the most inconspicuous of words passing on its understated 'way' at the weak caesura (*uia*):[25] *par-iter* and *par-iter* reiterate the equivalence between polarized 'opening' and 'cadence', here chiming with/written in the core language of astropoetics, *surgente/cadente* | (241).[26] For as this 'period' falls away, the 'trick' that treated us to *fallente solo* before the line-break displaces it with *surgente uia*, before/while mashing this into its antithesis, *cadente*, as every stationary substantival co-ordinate on earth is transmuted into the terrain for motion, to be conceptualized as a trek in correlation with and reciprocally plotted against every instance of travel through/around celestial space. Or would you like to swing on a star?

To reprise, *hanc* (242) refers to neither *uia*, nor either *pars*, but to *eius*, that is, *hanc*, sc. *terrarum rotunda forma* | (235).[27] This second half of the paragraph, 242–6, parallels whereabouts with whenarounds. 'Where-so-when' (*ubi*) the sunlight drives on to where counts as west 'for us, into the sunset' (*nostros ad occasus*), 'over there-at-that-point in time' (*illic*) it's sun-up, and that awakens myriads of people: 'back

---

[25] For *uia* cf. 32, 180, 188, 197 . . . .

[26] This was set up by the *perverse adynaton* at 175, *ab occasu . . . ad ortus* |, and the reassuring reality at 181, *cadat . . . rursus resurgat* | and 205, *undique surgentem . . . cadentem.* |

[27] The incubus here: '**236** *hanc*, <u>terram</u> (230), <u>non Deliam</u> (231)'.

round again' are fetched that twosome, the daily round of the working day (*refert*, 242–4). Their daylight coincides with our dark of night: try to think of it this (satirical) way, it's the same the whole world over, none of us want to get up, but we make each other clock in as if each morn we're to attend court, whereas we actively try and 'summons' sleep to show up for each dock on our bodies' corridor (*in membra . . . uocamus*: an ingenious inside-out phrase for the *comédie humaine*, 245). Whether we see this or not, 'night-and-day' is a dimension for living lives, and it runs us like 'sea-and-land', in that the solar round does to time what ocean does to space. *Except* that whereas the continents pretty well stay put, solar-powered temporality achieves permanence by constantly shifting what *counts* as east or west at/from any point in steady cyclic revolution, with no GMT or international dateline to say 'when-where is when' by reference and in relation to anything, bar sunshine. That is, Man relativizes 'the eastern' and 'western hemispheres', ~~defined~~ in terms of the moving orbit of the sun, the very principle that makes *sol* = *dies* = *lux* (242–4), as *orta* changes places with *occasus* (242–3), and 'we' circle *nostros . . . nos . . . . -que* around 'them there', *illic . . . et*, (sc. out westward, ho, 242, 245 ~ 243–4) with just half a day's grace between the furthest apart conurbations there can be on Earth (*urbes* | *. . . terris* |, 243–4). We're all in the same boat; must be; and (we won't like this) it's beyond our say-so!

**

2: 221–35 is not so straightforward a 'case'. It is acknowledged as serious, catastrophic, error even by Abry: who has Man messing up on the lunar *eclipse*, which does *not* steadily travel through time and space east through west.[28] This, however, takes its rise from reading 222 as ushering in, precisely, lunar eclipse, gone haywire;[29] and then glares when we find 230–4 modulating towards the banal truth of ordinary night time heading west on its daily basis. Only allow Man a writerly modicum of send-up satire, at the expense of benighted flat-

---

[28] Summed up by Goold 1977: n. *ad* 242 (where the translation supplies 'When the Sun reaches our occident and looks upon this lower world'), 'the poet has confused the western with the southern hemisphere': see Volk 2009: 11, 32, and n. 16 above.

[29] Goold 1977 *over*translates 222, 'when at night your star is plunged into utter darkness *and suffers eclipse*'.

earthers, and the whole description is all along about that special but regular nightfall across the earth, *per noctem*, when each 'moonth' the earth calls as evidence of its own curvature, its convex 'globousness' (*glomeramen*), the blanking out of moonlight, as the dark/new moon, 'throws unenlightened humans into confusion', as it sinks in black shade (221–3).

For *this* routine not-so-weird occurrence of a 'when' *does* arrive in a westerly traverse across the earth, complete with the moon 'rolling' along and around (226, *uolueris*), the way stars do, on its way out west where (sc. for our look-out) it's 'too late' for the peoples on the edge to bang their dustbin lids if they're wanting to save *our* black-out! (227) There *are* no ultimates, no edges, naturally, because the earth is, we're attesting, a globe, and that's why this light doesn't go out 'at the same moment' across the earth's crust. It *should* be *our* earthbound problem if we still think of Rome as centring a disc of inhabitable continent athwart what would have to be a particular cut of flattened hemisphere. But *Astronomica* sees it as *funny* to think that a duly 'rolling' heavenly body wears *simultaneously* 'by now dusky-dyed' *and/=* 'still non-existent-to be made wings' (*in-fectis uolueris alis*) each time it cycles round on the wane, or that any throwback anywhere on earth could still think the moon is fading fast, a gonna every month, let alone—*everywhere* (229, *toti . . . orbi*). A static earth *would* find the lunar phases coming their way as if 'later in the day' from East to West, and for any *other* 'star' to stop shining *would* amount to chaos—but only a world full of unreconstructedly loony flat-earthers would let each new moon phase them out as if we were back to treating a celestial orbit like primitive peoples coming out in sympathy to revive a dead-again divinity with heavy percussion. Just because we—we Romans—still have to use the word *deficio* (222, 229) as if we thought the moon 'fades out, *and dies*', it doesn't mean we should treat the menstrual syzygy as if it were the scarily erratic full-moonty eclipse, which is synchronously *non*-dependent on observer location, and very likely does make informed people still want to find a hilltop and make one helluva racket.[30]

The *forma rotunda* | of 235, which undifferentiates *alios* from *alios* and so leaves the apparently contrasted *superat* and *relinquit*

---

[30] Cf. Ov. *Met.* 4.331–3, *hic color . . . est . . . sub candore rubenti* | *cum frustra resonant aera auxiliaria lunae*. Naturally, *defectus* spans the range between 'waning' and 'eclipse'.

superimposed, as they encircle the encirclement of *gyros* (234), also capped the preceding version, where the pivot *pariter* conjoins the two sides of the same phenomenon, *accliuis/decliuia* (233), into mutually constitutive equivalents that collapse in the theoretician's model, where their diametrical opposition can never reduce but must always cruise through, and past, the viewpoint on the ground: round and round. In turn, *this* succeeded the version that has the virgin goddess of childbirth preside over the swelling, 'bulging', surface of the earth which is the paradoxical product of earth's 'reduction/slightening' (*deducta*, 230), which 'smoothes' and rounds it off/out/up as the etymological-geometric sum *terra per teretem* = *apparet Delia* (from Greek *phainetai* + *dēlos*, 230 ↔ 231). Here, q.e.d., the moon turns out to equate with its appearance, from our point of view, since it shares barrenness of luminosity with earth as against the sun (which generates its own perceptibility with 'real', reifying, light: 208–10). The roundness of the earth is locked into symmetry with the roundness of the heavenly bodies compounded by the roundness of their orbits, and the whole system is obscured from anyone on earth by the very configuration that brings light, and dark, to and across our enlightened/benighted viewpoint. For the way the moon looks/shows herself to us is simultaneously/dividedly the successive rounds of mutual exchange of places between *his* and *illis* through time, *modo/post*, as each *terra* in line is blessed with moonshine upon all the *terris*, precisely because the same body is at once both *exoriens*-and-*cadens*, the more strikingly because both incompatibles obtain in respect of the same entity in both dimensions of space and of time, and contrive to find graphic representation in the successive yet virtually distributive phrasing with *simul* and *atque* converging towards fusion in a *simulatque* (232). This is all straight physics, not 'magic' (*nec uero admiranda tibi* . . . , 194).[31]

No moonwalk, no silver shoon. Rather, the correlation between the two contributing bodies, the always already static figuration of the terrestrial condition and the continually self-replicating dynamism of lunar lapping further rings round their interlocking between *quia* (230) and *quia* (232), which between them unpack the plain flatness of the first, unreal-counterfactual, formulation of the logic of Ms Flat-Earth Geometry, which *would* spell just one-for-all, same-and-equal,

---

[31] 'Where *tibi* indicates for the first time the presence of an addressee' (Volk 2002: 199).

synchronous and geographically indifferent, 'birth-and/as-death' for
her ladyship (*orta/deficeres*), so far as all of the (other) globe would
be concerned: *tellus = orbi; semel...per omnem → pariter toti*
(228–9).[32] Which brisk elimination of a pathetic misprision of how
properly informed cosmic sympathy operates, rather than our whole
species joining for a planet-wide fest of death-bed trauma every time
the moon's round is done, yields through the appearance of *its per,
pariter, orbem*, to the twin-channelled, bipolar, stereophonic causal
ex-plan-ation (*quia-quia, atque-et/atque—que*, 230–3), through to
the conclusive conclusion to the 'syllogism' (*colligitur*, 235), which
summarizes, in a word, as the form of the form *forma rotunda.* ||
(235). Perfect, beautiful, and no way about to be rubbished, these
words set out to fix on the relativistic conversion-processes that make
up the make-up of our cosmos. When the rotary firmament rubs its
way round the globe and rubs surface *away* to make it round (*tero*,
Latin, as on a lathe, Greek *tornos*), that is only and exactly the other
way round of saying/seeing that it's this same subtractive process that
actually stuffs and swells and rounds out and provides the convex
surface for rotating abrasion, sticking the 'tumid bun' in oven Earth to
accrete ever more solidity to compensate for wear and tear through
eternal elemental displacement, and *make* mater Terra firma (*tumorem*, 230).[33] As the poem already explained (1.149–72) and
I shall insist (down) below, '*de*-duction' is the other side of this
bulging 'addition'. In Man's world, everything's a journey to the
centre (of/,) the earth, and that's the same as the sky's the limit.

∗ ∗ ∗

3: Now back round to 215–20;[34] for a truly worldwide/antipodean
phenomenon of stardom:

> When you look deep into the pockets of the universe
> You never know what you'll find

---

[32] *Pariter* keeps these preliminaries on a subliminal even keel: 124, 203, 205–5, 223,
229, 233, 241.

[33] Cf. *tumore* |, 219, *tumido*, 209; *teretis...figuras*, 207, with *facies...facit*, 206–7).
This polished poem swells shaping of smooth-talking into bodily form *passim*.

[34] Volk 2009: 32; see n. 16 above. On 'Gli scandalosi antipodi di Marziano Capella',
see Sclievenin 2009: 89–103.

> *Because stars don't shine in singular places*
> Open up your mind's eye
> And light up familiar faces
>
> (Minogue 2007, 'Stars'[35])

Pace Man, science informs us that the star Canopus is visible well
north of the Nile delta. For Abry, rounding on and starring the
favourite Manilian metarhetorical operator **idcirco** for us (215),[36]
our cringeworthy fudger deserves only a ticking-off—this is an 'approximatif' lapse (253). But *as* 'approximatif', I don't see it *is* a lapse:
arriving over the sea to any *oras* | is going to be about shifting
'horizons'; 'edges' to the Nile effluence do blur out to sea; and in
any case *the* place to see the *-opos* of Kan-opos 'dazzle' is precisely
when you get to Egypt at the place on earth called Kanopos—the only
town to watch its uniquely homonymous star from (217; 216).[37] Yes,
this is the spot where you'll look for Ursa Maior (218), only to find
you can't have everything, and though the reason Graeco-Romans
call it 'Helike', 'The Winding Star', is because it's always orbiting
gently in (our) view, it *couldn't* spell that to an Egyptian, for whom
Kah Nub served as a southerly 'pole star' equivalent (second brightest
star in the nocturnal canopy, after Sirius).[38] This time round, the
point makes a 'where' (*nusquam*, 215), to pair off with the moon's
'when' (*ubi*, 222)—and ring with the 'where-and-when' of those other
versions of us, on the other sides (from the Eurocentric-bound view
the backsides and hindquarters), and its daily round.

* * * *

In threefold, the arguments here all address the relativization of celestial
activity *vis-à-vis* observer point on the ground, following through the
rhythmic 'uncoiling' of the instant cosmogony rapped out so far: with *per
pontum* (217), Man gets under way to our destination *pontus*, 246, and
our 'opening paragraph' manages to co-implicate all four elements under

---

[35] Trumped by Man, and, as Shirin Borthwick came far north to tell me, the
University of Sydney <u>mutato</u>: *sidere mens eadem mutato*.
[36] Cf. 168 (and 235, *circum*).
[37] See Brind'Amour 1989 for defence of the paradosis *Niliacas*.
[38] For Helice, cf. 'Helicon', 1.4, above (already mocked in *Acheronta mouere* |, 93).

its horizon (*pontum, ignis, terrae caelum*, 217–20), as compressed in
the coda (249). But naturally, qua 'rider', the cruise to the Nile is heavily
para-sitic on the language and ideas of the theorizing it follows (up on).
Sun, Moon, and Earth were just conjoined, as suspended in space,
together with the universe itself (194–203). And the same *mise en
abyme* held for shape, same as for position, when we encountered them
as rings in a ring, so many circling circles—firmament, orbits, and axis:
globe, orb, sphere (204–14, in turn itself flowing from 173–93).[39] Thus we
already pretended alarm at the unreal nightmare that if the earth didn't
hang fire and stay put, the Sun and Moon would lose track (173–8 ~
228–9; 175 ~ 241–2; 176–7, esp. *summersos* ~ 222, esp. *mersa*)—and
dawn and dusk wouldn't live up to their names, light-bearing *Lucifer* at
matins and Greek Hesperos, 'Evening' (177–8, *nec...fulgeret* ~ 216,
nusquam...fulgere). As it is, however, the Sun is on course (174 ~ 198,
currus) and the Moon, too, is doing her thing (176 ~ 200, *per inania*): the
permanent, radiate/radiant configuration of the cosmos brings around
what comes around, each day every day (*circum...feratur*, 189), with
different locations taking turns to receive the same 'times' (*nunc his nunc
illis*, 191 ~ *his modo post illis*, 231), and forever sunrise is 'further away' if
you head for sunrise, and sundown if you're off into the sunset. To
complete our set of congruent-concentric sets, the universe plays ball,
too, and between them they come up with 'solar year on year—to eternity'
(*caelum et cum sole per-ennet. |*, 193 ~ *aeterna cum luce dies*, 190).

As Man says/sees, universal roundness rounds the stars, but our
eyes *see* the Sun is round and so is Sister Moon, though in her case it's
the fact that she's forever 'looking for more light' to bulge out into a
'full disc' with (*orbem...rotundum* ↔ *globus...totus*, 208–10), but
her sphere never gets it face-on all over, that amounts to us seeing she
is round (208–09,...*quaerentis...lumen*): which traces through to
the 'rider' when us—we sailors—can't spot the—*their*—pole star here,
while Egyptian southerners 'look for' the Great Bear which lights our
sky (*fulgere...quaerent*, 216–18); and then we move on to Mankind
which is *not* alarmed by the waning non-appearance of the moon,
and does *not* 'look for her light', freaked out as the heavens turn and
observers in turn across the lands can't spot her 'wings' as 'dusky'
turns imperceptibly into 'non-existent' and the new moon awaits
sighting (*quaerunt tua lumina*, 224; *infectis...alis*, 225).

---

[39] On the *mise en abyme* structure: esp. Lefebure 1991.

Now in the course of rounding up circular arguments about the roundels of our universe, we ran into a very clear reminder of Moon's unique, natural, contribution to the astrophysical zoo, *per totidem luces mutetur et orbes* (187),[40] that is, exactly, the perpetual motion of *the* moonthly pattern: the *un*alarming periodicity of waxing-and-waning, 'same number of days, same number of phases' of the 'disc', on the lunar 'orbit'. Man's Latin has luxuriated in starburst equivocations on the core term *orbis* from the start,[41] and it would not be out of synch to give a run, with the Loeb, to the notion that in shuttling from *orbi* (229) → *in orbem* (232), we lurch between (solid intern) 'sphere' and (stellar) 'disc', and interface earth's *orb* with the moon's *orbit*, as if both were 'bumps': *hence* 'it is carried in a bellying orbit'. Filling out the pathway around the earth into a diagrammatic 'belly bulge' would stand as joined-up volumetric writing/reckoning, testing to the limit credence in creation as a monistic process within the material continuum, ruling out void and positing instead homogeneity between ever inter-converting form-and/as-substance. But the context here is the idiosyncratic but normal, astro-nomic, behaviour of the moon, as clear as moonlight to all of us waiting in longitudinal line: Man names the observer-dependent and so apparently staggered 'rising-and/=-setting' of each night's routine (232); next, he explains, we all can see the moon is the moon, because it plainly behaves the way it does: the *first* item is the pregnant ph(r)ase: *fertur in orbem | uentris* (232–3). 'Moon works her passage round the curvature of the Earth.' To be sure, this means travelling round in orbit (too). The *second* characteristic, *accliuis pariter decliuia iungit* (233), tacks on Moon's relativized/time-lapsed 'downward-and/= upward' trajectory through the sky. In *third* place and out, *alios superat gyros aliosque relinquit* (234) widens the time-lapse lens to 'the circuits it completes, one after another, met and mastered as-and/=-after they are left in its wake'. Just as every lap round a track replicates but trumps/overrides the last one, each 'identical-and-differentiated' loop 'mounts up/sheds', on a monthly basis, adding to/subtracting from the tally for the annual version of the perennial race. In the process, as he 'joins up' t/his chain of commonplace lunar observations, the poet 'overcomes' all obstacles and 'leaves' the moon, before coming down to earth and 'collecting' thoughts on the globe,

---

[40] For *muto* as prime cosmogonic cue, Hübner in this volume.
[41] 1.8, 23, 32, 76, 101, 131, 165, 191, 204, 208, 232 . . . .

by sliding at the 'juncture/hinge' of *iungit | atqu'* (233–4), to 'go over the top' and 'leave' on a positive, upbeat, note. Man on the Moon conjugates the cosmos round moon going round her round trip round earth while rounding out, and then in, her own roundness—

* * * *

* * *

* *

*

To come round 'full circle', we should certainly class all this heated astrophysics as freshed-up 'commonsense' *captatio* for enterprising readers on Starship Man, confidently displayed by the poet going through his most polished paces. *Astronomica* is always already teetering, of course, over the brink and into the madness of the astrology invasion. 'Come on in, the sky's lovely: no, we won't have to pretend to have all the answers here' (*semper erit pugna ingeniis*..., 145)—but *Astronomica*, for all its first base station within the realms of sanity, is launching into the blue beyond. Just at the point where others—[42]

Cicero[43] saved *his* credentials with a curse on would-be measurers of universal immensity—as will Pliny; and Cicero pulled back

[42] Cue 'Abbruch', rhetoric of.

[43] For what follows, cf. esp. Cic. *Nat. D.* 2.84, 'And there being four classes of physical body, the make-up of the cosmos consists in shuffling them. You see water originates from earth and air from water and ether from air, then in reverse by exchange (*retrorsum uicissim*) air from ether, then water, and last at the bottom earth from water. As these physical entities which make up all things travel up down thither hither (*sursus deorsus ultro citro commeantibus*) the linkage of all the sectors is maintained'; 115–18, 'These aren't just marvels but there's nothing more important than the fact that the cosmos is so stable and hangs together so well, for permanence, that nothing can even be thought up that gets it better. You see all its sectors pitch on the central spot from all quarters and apply equal thrust (*undique medium locum capessentes nituntur aequaliter*). Bodies with components joined together with each other last best, when they hook up with an (ahem) sort of chain around them, and this is the handiwork of the Nature that floods through the whole cosmos, producing everything with intelligence, with reason: she exerts centripetal force (*ad medium*), she brings together what is off at the margins. 116, Consequently, if the cosmos is spheroid, and if that's why all its parts, which match up from all quarters, hold together through their very own doing and between themselves (*aequabiles ipsae* per se *atque inter se continentur*), the same must inevitably hold for the Earth, so that as all its parts seek the centre (in a sphere, that's the lowest part) (*omnibus eius partibus in medium uergentibus* (*id autem medium infimum in sphaera est*)), there is

precisely from 'seeing too much into [what he calls] astronomy',
and descends swiftly to raptures on Life on Earth.

For his part,[44] Pliny will draw the line at, round, the *uulgus* for
swallowing the notion that stars are assigned to individual humans

no breach of continuity by which all this great pressure of gravity and heaviness
(*ponderum*) could be shaken. In the same way, too, although it is above the earth, the
sea is nevertheless, as it heads for the earth's centre (*medium*), matched together from all
quarters into a sphere, and never overflows or overspills (*undique aequabiliter neque
redundat umquam neque effunditur*). 117, Air, now, which abuts the sea, while it is
indeed carried upwards by its sublime lightness, but still diffuses itself in all directions
(*tamen in omnes partes se ipse fundit*); it therefore both abuts and links with the sea, and
also is carried by its own nature to the sky, whose combination of lack of density with
heat temper it, thereby providing animate creatures with healthful, life-supporting
breath. Embracing it is the highest part of the sky, which is called after "ether", and
which, while it keeps its own blazing heat thin/fine and unclogged by any admixture, is at
the same time in contact with the outermost edge of the air. The stars revolve in the ether
(*astra uoluuntur*), and they are made spherical so they hold together by their own gravity
(*nisu suo*), while they maintain their movements through their actual shape and form:
you see, they are round, and forms of that kind, as I reckon I said earlier, are least able to
be harmed. 118, The stars are fiery by nature; they therefore feed on steam from the
earth, sea, and the rest of the waters, the steam which gets roused by the sun from soil it
has warmed, and from water; then the stars plus the whole ether, once fed and renewed
by these, pour the same back and draw them again from the same source (*effundunt
eadem et rursum trahunt indidem*), so that pretty well nothing is lost, or just the very
little which the fire of the stars and the flame of the ether consume.'

[44] For what follows, cf. esp. Pliny *HN* 2.1–2, 'The cosmos, or whatever other name it is that
we've been pleased to call this sky, surrounded by the vault of which (*circumflexu*) all things
live, is—dead right—believed to be a deity: eternal, unbounded, neither created nor heading
any time for destruction. To investigate what is beyond it is no concern of man, nor can the
human mind take it in. 2, It is sacred, eternal, and bounded, totally in the totality—no, in fact, it
is *itself* the Totality, infinite, yet like what is finite; certain of all things, yet like what is uncertain,
externally/internally embracing all things in itself; one and the same the work of nature and
itself nature itself (*totus in toto, immo uero ipse totum, infinitus ac finito similis, omnium rerum
certus et similis incerto, extra intra cuncta conplexus in se, idemque rerum naturae opus et
rerum ipsa natura*)'; 5, 'That its form is a perfect globe shape is the lesson we learn especially
from human unanimity in calling it a "ball", as also from proofs in Physics: not only does a
figure of this kind lean everywhere into itself, to sustain and be sustained by itself, enclosing
and holding itself together, requiring no bindings, insensitive to either end or beginning in any
of its parts (*omnibus sui partibus uergit in sese ac sibi ipsa toleranda est seque includit et continet
nullarum egens compagium nec finem aut initium ullis sui partibus sentiens*); not only is it best
fitted for that motion, which, as will soon become clear, has it continually turning round; but,
as well, by our own eyes' confirmation it is perceived to be in every part convex and central
(*conuexu mediusque quacumque cernatur*)'; 10–11, 'On the elements: I don't see any doubts
about they're being four: zenith goes to fire, next all those winking stars lighting them up;
second place to breath—what Greeks and us Romans both call "air", same word, alive and
here, at once permeating right through all kinds of matter and linked in with the Totality (*per
cuncta rerum meabilem totoque consertum*); suspended by the power of air together with the
fourth element, water, balancing at the centre of space (*medio spatii*) is Earth. 11, So from the
mutual embrace of difference results a hook-up, and light things are restrained from flitting

(*HN* 2.28); and he'll wind up setting *litterae* versus *uulgus* on the sticking-points of the antipodeans (2.161) and on the curvature of the seas (2.163).

Yes, seeing stars is a mindfield—Cicero the diviner, he takes the one ~~small~~ step, to *ekpurosis* and *renouatio mundi* in his stride (*Nat. D.* 2.118): as little help to the thriller from Manilia as Big Bang squabbling over the Origins of the Universe—which he already praeteritioned at 1.147, before we started wondering if the *origo* should have *influenced* the Astrophysical Cosmos. No, *Astronomica*, for *its* part, will only face the implosive abyss—the delete button—for its own meltdown closedown. There, *dis*astrous oblivion came imag(in)ed in the nightmare guise of communist revolution from the intergalactic proletariat, where only the ruse of an unreal conditional saves world(s') order from glimpsed burn-out: 'Had physics powered the stellar

out/away by heavy, and vice versa heavy items are suspended so they don't crash down while light ones head up into the sublime. So by matched impetus in opposite directions each lot stays stabilized (*pari in diuersa nisu in suo quaeque consistere*), tied in by the restless circling (*circuitu*) of the very cosmos, which forever orbits back round on itself with the Earth at the bottom and at centrepoint in the Totality, the same Earth is suspended, so stabilized, by the cosmic axis, balancing what keeps it suspended (*semper in se recurrente imam atque mediam in toto esse terram, eandemque uniuerso cardine stare pendentem, librantem per quae pendeat*), and so alone motionless as the cosmos revolves round it (*uolubili uniuersitate*), and the same Earth is webbed into everything and all things downthrust on Earth (*eandem ex omnibus necti eidemque omnia inniti*)'; 56, 'Every year on set days at fixed hours occur eclipses of both constellations down beneath the Earth and yet, even though they occur up above on high, they are not observed everywhere—on some occasions because of cloud, but more often when the Earth's sphere gets in the way of the concavity of the cosmos (*saepius globo terrae obstante conuexitatibus mundi*)'; 160, 'It is the prime figure, the agreed verdict on it. For sure we call it the Earth's "ball" and concede it is enclosed by twisters (*uerticibus*). You see its shape is not a perfect ball, across such soaring mountain heights, such dead flat plains, but instead its embrace if all its parts are caught by lines of circumference will create the shape of a perfect ball, as the physics of matter compels—but not for the same reasons as we adduced in the case of the sky. You see with and in the sky, a concaveness leans in toward itself and from all quarters weighs on its axis, viz. Earth. Earth, as it is hammered together solid, expands upwards like something bloating, and heaves pushing out beyond its arc (*non isdem causis, quas attulimus in caelo. namque in illo caua in se conuexitas uergit et cardini suo, hoc est terrae, undique incumbit. haec ut solida ac conferta adsurgit intumescenti similis extraque protenditur. mundus in centrum uergit, at terra exit a centro*). The cosmos leans in toward the centrepoint, whereas the Earth moves out from its centre, as the constant revolving motion (*uolubilitate*) of the cosmos around Earth compels its immense sphere into ball shape'; 162, 'But what does that matter now another marvel arises, that Earth is in suspension and doesn't fall down, along with us, as though the force of breath, especially breath enclosed by the cosmos, is in doubt, or could fall, combatted by the physical world which denies it anywhere to fall. You see just as there is no settled place for fire except in fire, for water except in water, for breath except in breath, so there's no place for Earth, since all else repels it, except in itself (*sic terrae, arcentibus cunctis, nisi in se locus non est*)'.

masses in proportion with their numbers, the Sky Reactor (*aether*, Greek 'Furnace') would lack capacity to sustain its own blaze, and the whole of the universe (*totus . . . mundus*) would go up in flames when Heaven catches alight. ||' (5.743–5).[45] Between the come-on first proem and this endgame scenario intervene all the lessons in the peril of astronautica, the long conditioning by cautions to proceed no further, past this mission's Symplegades.[46] But here, finally, fate—the fate of astrology—hangs by an ultimate thread, when . . . the text snaps shut with *total* discontinuity between aeons. Cosmogonic theorizing means cosmophthoric horrors *somewhere* down the track; and that's a black hole in the head when it comes to being determined to read your starsign stars.

* * *

* *

*

Which brings us back/round to Lucretius.[47] Lucretian sarcasm neatly marks out the starwarzone—his attacks on standard 'current thinking' on the processual universe:

---

[45] For this as the end (?) for Man: Volk 2009: 109–11 (with 263 on 1.735–49 (Phaethon) and 5.209–12 (Sirius) as hints of 'cosmic disruption'); Volk in this volume.

[46] See Green in this volume.

[47] Lucr. 1.1052–60, 'In this matter about matter, Memmius, run a mile from believing their mantras/claims: "All things gravitate inward to the centre (*in medium . . . niti*), and the reason the physical cosmos stands firm with no external stimuli, and highest and lowest (*summa atque ima*) cannot be disaggregated in any direction, is that all things always gravitate inward to the centre (*in medium . . . nixa*)"—if you believe that anything can "stabilize upon itself" (*ipsum si quicquam posse in se sistere credis*)—and "The heavy bodies which are under Earth (*pondera . . . sub terris*) all gravitate upwards and come to rest stationed backwards upon the earth (*sursum | nitier in terraque retro requiescere posta*), like the images of things we see through water"'; cf. 956–1091, esp. 956–7, 'Let's look through, see (*peruideamus*) if it's a stable whole, bounded, finite, and founded/from the bottom up (*funditus*), or opens out to infinity (*immensum pateat*), to a vast depth (*profundum*)'; 984–94, 'Besides, if all the space of the whole totality were stabilized by enclosure within fixed (*certis*) edges/ shores/horizons, so finitely bounded, then the glut of matter would flow together by solid weight (*ponderibus solidis*) from everywhere to the bottom of the world (*ad imum*), and nothing could happen under the sky cover, nor could there *be* a sky at all, nor sunlight, not considering that there all matter would lie piled in a heap (*cumulata*) by sinking/settling down (*subsidendo*) during infinite time. But as it is, you bet, no rest is allowed for any elemental bodies, because there is no fundamental bottom (*funditus imum*) where they could (ahem) flow together, where they could take up their settled positions'; 1083–91, 'Besides, since they fake it that "not all bodies gravitate inward to

(Q1) How can *imum* mean *medium*? (1.1052–60; as e.g. in Cic. *Nat. D.* 2.116, Plin. *HN* 2.5)

(Q2) How can anything *in se sistere*? (1.1057;[48] as e.g. in Plin. *HN* 2.11, 162)

Turning these round:

(A2) We know it follows sure as night follows day that *everything* must *in se sistere* in so far as that follows, definitionally, from selfhood.

And:

(A1) We know that in a volumetric world everything must be going 'in(to)' when it goes 'down', and everything else must be going 'out of' when it goes 'up'. That is how weight works, in 3D, in 'space'. And so too displacement/levitation.

Less abruptly—(A1), first, this time around:

(A1) In the quasi-religious world of cosmographic anti-logic, the paradox of cult appears in linguistic form as the cult of paradox: as e.g. in Pliny's formulae for the 'set of sets including itself as one of its sets, a set' (*HN* 2.2). In phrasal form, Cicero *Nat. D.* 2.84, *sorsus deorsus ultro citro*; Pliny *HN* 2.1, *extra intra omnia*; cf. Man 1.142, *discordia concors*.[49] Now the *self-flexivity* of the holistic organic unitary cosmos which is the sine qua non for all totalizing systems of grand theory issues in a myriad variants on internal division/linkage of self to itself: a roll-call of ne'er-to-be-forgot star turns from Man, who is an obsessive/genius at them, must feature 1.40, *seque ipsa reclusit*, 50, *inque deum deus ipse tulit patuitque ministris*;[50] 2.38, *terraque composuit caelum quae pendet ab illo*,[51] 107–8, *in unum | descendit deus atque habitat seque ipse requirit*;[52] 115–16, *quis caelum posset nisi caeli munere nosse,| et*

centre (*in medium niti*), no, only those of earth and water (marine liquid, big rollers from the mountain slopes, and whatever's encased in"—ahem—"earthen body"), to the contrary, they set out how "The thin air and hot fire together get diffused from the centre (*a medio*) and the reason that the whole of the ether all around (*circum*) quavers with bright stars, and the sun's flame is fuelled through the sky's blue, is that heat, running for it from the centre (*a medio*), all hooks up there'". Cf. Sedley 1998: 41 for the original inclusion and placement of the Epicurean 'Critique of the centrifocal universe theory' in *Peri Physeōs*.

[48] See n. 47.

[49] Offsetting the options *concordia discors* (Hor. *Epist.* 1.12.19) and *discors concordia* (Ov. *Met.* 1.433).

[50] Volk 2009: 223.

[51] Ead. 2002: 222, 2009: 265. See Volk, Hübner, and Stark in this volume, as well as esp. Uden: 'Hanging, then, with its implications of reliance on something above us and outside of our control, may well be the poem's dominant metaphor' (p. 252).

[52] Volk 2002: 205; 2009: 222.

reperire deum nisi qui pars ipse deorum est?,[53] 124–5, *caeloque ueniret* |
quod uocat in caelum, 129, *uelut in semet captum deducere in orbem?*;[54]
4.392, *transire tuum pectus mundoque potiri*,[55] 884–5, *mundo nos-*
trumque parentem | *pars sua perspicimus genitique accedimus astris*
and 893–4, *noscere mundum* | *si possunt homines, quibus est et mundus*
in ipsis,[56] 910, *cognatumque sequens corpus se quaerit in astris*.[57]

And, most re-orientationally read-ying:

(A2) When the topic is spatial conformation, the paradoxes are bound to
run every which way, with the prepositional directionality that
saturates language in whatever *discourse*: so, going into extra-terres-
trial *Astronomica*, how far is *SVB*—including *surgo, subeo, sublimis,*
suspendo, sublatus—going to turnaround, under the sky where
'down', *DE*, signifies 'into', and as such is locked into conveyor-belt
reciprocity with 'up', *E*, meaning 'away' and 'out'? As in Lucr.
1.1084, 1086, etc; in Plin. *HN* 2.160; and all round Man, especially
1.149–70:[58]

> ignis in aetherias uolucer se sustulit oras   149
> summaque complexus stellantis culmina caeli   150
> flammarum uallo naturae moenia fecit.
> proximus in tenuis descendit spiritus auras
> aeraque extendit medium per inania mundi;
> ignem flatus alit uicinis subditus astris.
> tertia sors undas strauit fluctusque natantis   155
> aequora perfudit toto nascentia ponto,
> ut liquor exhalet tenuis atque euomat auras
> aeraque ex ipso ducentem semina pascat.
> ultima subsedit glomerato pondere tellus,
> conuenitque uagis permixtus limus harenis   160

---

[53] Ead. 2002: 216–17; 2009: 206; Volk and Stark in this volume.

[54] See Habinek 2007: 236, vindicating pluralvalency for *in semet* ('onto itself/the
person of the dragger'; cf. Glauthier in this volume): *aliter* Volk 2001: 92–5; 2002: 221
esp. n. 46. The play between in *caelum, in semet . . . in orbem* (127, 129) is *starred* by
the etymological figure in *quis neget esse nefas*, 128.

[55] Volk 2009: 257 and in this volume.

[56] Ead. 2001: 90, 112; 2002: 205; 2009: 221–2, 258; Habinek and Kennedy in this
volume.

[57] 'The poet invokes the utmost resources of language to reproduce the reciprocity
of the universe' (MacGregor 2004: 151); Volk 2009: 220, 224.

[58] Start from 1.32, *sublimis aperire uias imumque sub orbem*, and run on into:
203–5, *aeris e toto pariter sublata profundo* | *nec patulas distenta plagas, sed condita in*
orbem | *undique surgentem pariter pariterque cadentem*, 213, *perque omnia par est*,
232, *exoriens simul atque cadens*, 234, *alios superat gyros aliosque relinquit . . .* Read*y*.

paulatim <u>ad summum</u> tenui fugiente liquore;
quoque magis puras umor secessit <u>in</u> auras,
et siccata magis struxerunt aequora terram,
adiacuitque cauis fluidum conuallibus aequor,
<u>e</u>mersere fretis montes, orbisque <u>per</u> undas   165
<u>ex</u>siliit uasto clausus tamen undique ponto.
<u>im</u>aque <u>de cunctis mediam tenet undique sedem</u>,   167
idcircoque manet stabilis, quia totus <u>ab</u> illa
tantundem <u>refugit mundus fecitque cadendo</u>
<u>undique ne caderet (medium totius et imum est</u>).   170

* *
*

In the circumscriptances, the problem of dis/continuity in (or, as we should rethink this, *as*) imagery,[59] slippage between analogy and ontology in cosmography, starting from the ringing ring-structure of *circumdatus . . . circumstrepit* around the duplicity of *carminis et rerum* (1.21–3)[60] and lately dubbed the 'Have one's cake and eat it too' principle is,[61] you might say, literally *PER SE* the precipitate, in this context, of the commonsense spheroid principle that a centripetal *mundus* depends on the centrifugal geocentre that depends on *it*. That is, whatever 'part' of the 'parent' whole we look at will produce and deliver *Volkish* 'ascent' running/run through *Hübnerian* patterns of 'descent' (or is it the other way round, the other round way?).[62]

See especially Cic. *Nat. D.* 2.84 and *passim*; and Pliny, especially *HN* 2.160: up and down, up is down, neither are up or down—they are *PER*, two-way traffic in 4D, the rhythm of life, *animated* Physics (see e.g. Man 1.32, <u>*sublimis aperire uias imumque sub orbem*</u>, 97, <u>*caelum ascendit ratio cepitque profundam*</u>, 113, <u>*hoc mihi surgit opus*</u> ↔ 118–19, *quoniam <u>caelo descendit carmen ab alto,</u>* | *et uenit in*

---

[59] See Anderson 1960 on 'Discontinuity in Lucretian symbolism': telling/showing how flux meets imagery to make a world of (what I shall dub) 'theorhetoric' sense (with the 'reservations' articulated in Gale 1994, esp. 3 n. 8, 204 n. 164).

[60] Volk 2002: 235–6.

[61] Ibid. 202, 222–3, 242, 244 n. 92, 245; ead. 2009: 13, 170, esp. 258, 263, and in this volume; for criticism, see the contribution by Mann.

[62] See Volk 2002: 232–4 ~ Hübner 1984: 245. But Man's way up *is* the way down, that is how the displacement *per* the cosmos that makes up the seething cosmos works (see esp. 1.241, above).

terras, 149, *ignis* in *aetherias uolucer <u>se sustulit</u> oras* ↔ 152, *proximus <u>in</u> tenuis <u>descendit</u> spiritus auras*, 159, *<u>subsedit</u>* ↔ 161, *<u>ad summum</u>*, 181, *<u>qua cadat et subeat caelum rursusque resurgat</u>*, 205, *<u>surgentem pariter pariterque cadentem</u>*, 239, 241 (under/over), *<u>sub pedibusque iacet nostris supraque uidetur</u>* and *<u>et pariter surgente uia pariterque cadente</u>*, 4.887, *<u>in caelumque redire animas caeloque uenire</u>*).

This contrariwise traffic flow was, to Epicurean consternation, so embedded in 'current Roman thinking' that the point of each formulation is to cultivate the irreconcilable rift in 'logic' that 'scientific' belief revolves round when it appropriates, moves to expropriate, our language for its discourse: as when Plin. *HN* 2.10 puts it across that 'vital' air is, beautifully, at once *per cuncta rerum meabilem totoque consertum*. Or, to return to Man 1.14 for test case, as premised: if the earth is 'in' the *mundus*, then its surface is 'in' the *caelum*, and any earthly walk is a walk in the celestial park, and if you take Manilius at his word, it's the walk of life:

> iuuat spatiantem uiuere caelo.[63]

*

If you're read-y: the difficulty was never with standard geocentric volumetrics, but with reluctance to believe it's owed to Man to allow astrophysics, astronomy, and astrology to belong to the same holistic ecosphere of existence.

---

[63] See Volk 2001: 86–92; 2002: 225–6; 2009: 15–16, 212.

6

On two Stoic 'paradoxes' in Manilius

Wolfgang-Rainer Mann

PRELIMINARIES

In order to account for a number of tensions, paradoxes, or even outright contradictions in the *Astronomica*, Katharina Volk suggests that Manilius

> is . . . operating according to a kind of have-one's-cake-and-eat-it-too principle. Put differently, the poet behaves not like a philosopher, who wishes to present a coherent explanation of the universe, but like a student of rhetoric, who is happy to draw arguments from different backgrounds, with an eye not to internal coherence, but to the maximal effect at each individual moment. He finds a number of discourses ready for him to use . . . , and he wants to use them *all*, exploit the potential of *every* single one of them, without regard to the contradictions that might arise from such a procedure.[1]

Relying on a principle that has him—and that therefore also has us—be so easy-going ought, however, to be resisted, or at least, be resisted as long as possible. For embracing it amounts to giving up on the project of trying to address these tensions directly. Instead, we first lower our expectations. Then, with those lowered expectations in place, Manilius' failure (if that is what it is) to meet higher ones proves wholly irrelevant.

I should like to suggest that two features of Manilius' position which Volk identifies as problematic (that is, as problematic *absent* her 'have-your-cake-and-eat-it-too' principle) can be rendered

---

[1] Volk 2002: 196–245, here at 208 (emphases added). See also her contribution to the present volume.

unobjectionable by recalling the specifically Stoic context, and to some extent, even the broader context of ancient philosophy, in which they originally figure. To adopt a more conciliatory tone: Volk clearly recognizes this as a possible way out; what I should like to do here is offer the outlines of a strategy for pursuing it a bit further than she does. Now, before actually mentioning the tensions or paradoxes I have in mind, two caveats. Nothing in what I shall say is meant to take a stand on the issue of whether there might not be other reasons, deriving from other elements in the poem than those I shall be discussing, for none the less ascribing such a principle to Manilius; and so nothing is meant to rule out that we might not, at the end of the day, need to turn to *some* version of the easy-going principle after all. Secondly, the form of my proposal will be that there are good philosophical grounds—at any rate, good grounds within more or less standard Stoicism—for finding the paradoxes much less paradoxical than they initially appear; perhaps better: for finding them 'paradoxical' in a way that is predictable and wholly consistent with other parts of Stoic doctrine. This deliberately narrow focus brings with it the obvious defect of neglecting the *Astronomica*'s poetic project; and such neglect is (arguably) especially troubling in the case of Manilius, who already with the first word (*carmine*) of his work signals his acute self-consciousness as a poet and makes clear that he will be using poetic language self-referentially to speak about the enterprise of poetry itself. If it is inconceivable that the *Astronomica* could have been written except against a certain philosophical background, it is still far more inconceivable that it would have taken the shape it did take without Manilius' metapoetic and poetological concerns, both of specifically situating his own efforts within what amounts to virtually the whole tradition of ancient poetry from Homer on, as he understands it (see 2.1–56 and 3.1–30)—a tradition he sees as having, for all intents and purposes, exhausted itself[2]—and of announcing his aim to treat subjects that he takes to be (close to) inherently intractable, and to be particularly intractable *in verse*

---

[2] Commenting on *Astr.* 2.49–52, Volk writes: 'The scene described is a Callimachean's nightmare (trodden paths, dirty rivers, crowds), and given the generalizing diction of the passage . . . , one might well think that a poet who arrives at this stage of the game has no chance of producing anything original' (Volk 2002: 213). As she notes, this of course allows Manilius to go on to make all the more ambitious claims about his own achievement of having, as it were, escaped from the hideous world of that nightmare.

(3.31–42). In short: the evidently important question of how the poetic enterprise and the Stoic background—the *carmen* and the *res* (cf. 1.20–4)—are to be viewed in relation to each other is one about which I shall have nothing to say. I trust, though, that what follows is not incompatible with what such fuller and richer accounts of the project of the *Astronomica* would provide.[3]

So, on to the two sources of difficulty. (i) Manilius is committed to the thought that every person, simply in virtue of being a human being equipped with reason, is in a position to understand, and so to benefit from, his teaching (see 4.916–35, esp. 916–23). From this perspective, his approach looks egalitarian, and his teaching, universal. Yet at certain moments he adopts a far more elitist or exclusionary tone, saying that he is addressing only a chosen few, who in these passages seem much more like some sort of privileged acolytes than like rational inquirers (e.g. 1.48–65). (ii) Given the nature of the universe (it is a fully rational and wholly divine being), the universe itself wants us—and this means, wants each of us—to understand it and its principles (cf. 2.105–36). Moreover, given the correspondence between, as it is sometimes put, microcosm and macrocosm, each person is in a position, simply in virtue of having a mind, having reason, (to come) to understand the universe and its workings. More specifically, each person is by nature suited for, among other things, learning about the celestial bodies and learning 'how to read them': the stars and planets, their motions, and indeed the whole of nature thus are *open* or *transparent* to reason. Yet Manilius also, at times, makes it sound as if the universe (so to speak) wishes to *conceal* itself, and that it thus becomes necessary for someone—namely, for Manilius himself, in his role as visionary poet[4]—to *reveal* its truths, truths which would otherwise remain inaccessible to us, even if we were inclined towards inquiry and learning (cf. 2.137–49).

---

[3] Besides being important in its own right, the question of the relation between the *carmen* and the *res* bears directly on the issue of how best to understand Manilius *vis-à-vis* Lucretius. Is it because of doctrinal, *philosophical* differences between them that Manilius sets out to write the *Astronomica*; or is it rather a desire to outshine Lucretius *poetically* that he chooses his subject matter—which, arguably, is at once both more technically difficult (in its details, namely, the actual astrology) than Epicurean philosophy and more sublime or grand in its overall outlook (i.e. in the 'loftier', Stoic metaphysical picture underlying and underwriting the astrological programme)?

[4] Cf. the use of *vates* at 1.23, 2.142, 3.41, and 4.121.

To put all this more succinctly. Why should something that could, in principle, be understood by anyone, and that would be of value for everyone, be communicated only to the few? And why would a universe that wants us to know its workings seek to conceal them in such a way that a special intermediary is needed to disclose them?

To make progress here, I suggest, we need to recall three parts of Stoic doctrine: (1) the Stoics' account of the structure of the universe; (2) their account of the place of human beings within the universe; (3) their account of wisdom, and of the special role of the wise within the universe.

But before turning to (1)–(3), one final cautionary note. On the one hand, it is obvious that Manilius is *not* himself a philosopher; thus it would be quite misguided to assume that he is as thoroughly grounded in, or as conversant with, the relevant technical details of Stoicism, as a fully trained philosopher could be expected to be. On the other hand, as P. A. Brunt (among many others) has maintained, the core notions of Stoicism were broadly disseminated among educated Romans during the early years of the Empire, and later.[5] Now

---

[5] 'The wide circulation of Stoic ideas among Romans of the upper class from the time of Panaetius in the second century B.C. to the reign of Marcus Aurelius (A.D. 161–80) is a familiar fact. Few Romans of note can indeed be marked down as committed Stoics, and even those like Seneca who avowedly belonged to the school borrowed ideas from other philosophies. Still, even if eclecticism was the mode, the Stoic element was dominant. Stoicism permeated the writings of authors like Virgil and Horace who professed no formal allegiance to the sect, and became part of the culture that men absorbed in their early education. One might think that it exercised an influence comparable in some degree with that which Christianity has often had on men ignorant or careless of the nicer points of systematic theology.' These are the opening sentences of Brunt 1975. As Brunt notes, the point is a thoroughly familiar one. I cite him because he goes on to show, in considerable detail, how both champions and critics of the Empire (and of the office of the emperor) were able to draw on Stoicism for their arguments, *pro* and *contra*, but were able to do so without contradicting themselves (or each other). The actual Roman Empire, and many actual emperors, are of course easily criticized from within Stoicism; in fact, an 'orthodox' Stoic would presumably want to say that the Empire is not really an empire, and the emperors, not really emperors. But asserting this is wholly compatible with advocating, on strictly Stoic grounds, the claim that empire is the optimal form of political organization, and that someone who really was an emperor would be best suited to ruling such a genuine empire. And such a true emperor would in turn need to be a *sophos*, a wise person as the Stoics conceive him. As we shall see, the *de facto* elitism and epistemological pessimism evinced by Manilius on the one hand, and his commitment, on the other hand, to cognitive egalitarianism and epistemological optimism can be seen as standing in a wholly analogous relation to each other, as do, on Brunt's account, the Stoic criticisms and defences of the Empire and its institutions.

even if Manilius is not a philosopher, he presumably is a Stoic
(i.e. draws on Stoic materials) in a way that goes beyond the pervasive,
diffuse kind of Stoicism which Brunt identifies and which would have
been widely shared by, and thoroughly familiar to, large parts of
Manilius' intended or imagined audience. He rather uses Stoicism,
I suggest, in a manner analogous (say) to how many people nowadays, in their thinking, rely on central psychoanalytic notions—like
'repression', 'projection', 'object', and so on—often in fairly sophisticated ways, without though themselves being trained psychoanalysts,
or more to the point, even without themselves having studied pro-
fessionally any works by Freud, Melanie Klein, D. W. Winnicott, or
other major theoreticians. In setting out relevant parts of the Stoics'
view, I shall, however, at times advert to texts which present more
detailed claims, and more specific formulations of them, than what
I think we can confidently attribute to Manilius; my aim in doing this
is a limited one: to get clearer about the *contours* of the philosophical
picture needed to defuse the threat of paradox mentioned at the
outset, not to address the no doubt interesting historical question
of whether Manilius is closer to the 'orthodoxy' of the Old Stoa
(i.e. Zeno and Chrysippus), or is instead following certain innovations
deriving from, for example, Panaetius or Posidonius.

1

The world is divine and rational. Two accounts of Zeno's teaching
illustrate this familiar Stoic claim. Sextus Empiricus reports Zeno as
saying:

> The rational (*to logikon*) is superior to the non-rational (*to mē logikon*).
> But nothing is superior to the world (*kosmos*). Therefore, the world is
> rational. And similarly with 'intelligent' (*noeron*) and 'having a share in
> being animate' (*empsuchias metechon*). For the intelligent (*to noeron*)
> is superior to the non-intelligent (*to mē noeron*), and the animate
> (*to empsuchon*) to the non-animate (*to mē empsuchon*). But nothing is
> superior to the world. Therefore the world is intelligent and animate.
> (Sext. Emp. *Math.* 9.104, tr. LS 54 F (1), with changes.[6])

---

[6] LS = Long and Sedley 1987. Vol. 1 contains their translations and brief philosophical commentary; vol. 2, the Greek or Latin originals together with textual notes.

Cicero relates something quite similar:

> Zeno also argued as follows: 'Nothing lacking sensation can have a sentient part. But the world (*mundus*) has sentient parts. Therefore the world does not lack sensation.' He then proceeds to a stricter (*angustius*) argument: 'Nothing without a share of mind (*animus*) and reason (*ratio*) can give birth to something animate (*animans*) and rational (*compos rationis*). But the world gives birth to beings that are animate and rational. Therefore the world is animate and rational.' (Cic. *Nat. D.* 2.22, tr. LS 54 G, with changes.)

Moreover, the world as a whole possesses sensation, mind, reason, and intelligence to the *highest degree*; in fact, it is *perfect*:

> ... there is not anything besides the world (*mundus*) which has nothing missing (*cui nihil absit*), and which is equipped from every point of view, perfect, and complete in all its measures and parts. As Chrysippus cleverly puts it ... with the exception of the world everything else was made for the sake of other things: for example, the crops and the fruits which the earth brings forth were made for the sake of animals, and the animals which it brings forth were made for the sake of men.... Man himself comes to be in order to contemplate and imitate the world (*ad mundum contemplandum et imitandum*),[7] being by no means perfect (*nullo modo perfectus*), but a tiny constituent of that which is perfect (*sed est quaedam particula perfecti*). But the world—since it embraces everything, and since there is nothing that is not included in it—is perfect in every respect (*perfectus undique est*).
>
> How, then, can it lack what is best? But nothing is better than intellect and reason (*mens et ratio*). Therefore, the world cannot lack these.... [Chrysippus] argued that that which is the best thing in the whole world should be found in something which is perfect (*perfectus*) and complete (*absolutus*). But nothing is more perfect (*perfectius*) than the world, and

---

Long and Sedley assign numbers to the different sections (with the division into sections based on the topics to which the fragments or testimonia are devoted); within each section, each individual fragment or testimonium is identified by a capital letter. Thus LS 54 F serves to identify this passage from Sextus Empiricus as text F in section 54. In what follows, all further references to passages collected by them will be given as LS + number + letter. In some instances, I also provide a number in parentheses after the letter (e.g. here: 54 F (1)); this is to indicate a specific subsection, again as numbered by LS, within the given passage.

[7] This is an established topos in the philosophical tradition. Aristotle (*Eth. Eud.* 1.5.1216a10–14) reports that Anaxagoras answered someone who asked, 'For the sake of what should one choose to be born rather than not?', by saying: 'For the sake of viewing/contemplating (*theōrēsai*) the heavens and the whole order of the cosmos'.

nothing better (*melius*) than virtue (*virtus*). Therefore, virtue is intrinsic to the world. Indeed, human nature (*hominis natura*) is not perfect, yet [none the less] virtue is achieved in man (*in homine*)—then how much more easily [sc. can virtue be realized] in the world! Therefore, there *is* virtue in the world. Therefore, the world is wise (*sapiens*), and hence is god (*deus*).[8] (Cic. *Nat. D.* 2.37-9, tr. LS 54 H, with changes.)

And if we proceed in the other direction, we learn that god is the world:

They [sc. the Stoics] say that god is an animal which is immortal, rational, and intelligent,[9] perfect in happiness, not admitting of any evil, provident towards the world (*kosmos*) and the things in the world, but not anthropomorphic. He is the artificer of the whole (*dēmiourgos tōn holōn*) and, as it were, the father of all, both generally and, in particular, that part of him which pervades all things, which is called by many titles (*prosēgoriai*), according to its powers (*kata tas dunameis*). They call him *Dia* because all things are through (sc. *dia*) him; *Zēn* insofar as he is responsible for, or pervades, life (*zēn*); *Athēna* because his commanding faculty (*hēgemonikon*) extends to the aether; *Hēra* because it extends into the atmosphere (*aer*); *Hēphaistos* because it extends into the craftsmanlike (*technikon*) fire; *Poseidon* because it stretches to the sea; *Demeter* since it reaches the earth. Similarly men have given god his other titles (*prosēgoriai*), fastening as best they can on some one or another of his proper attributes. (Diog. Laert. 7.147, tr. LS 54 A and Hicks 1925, with changes.)

2

Moreover, human beings, in virtue of possessing reason, have a *special place* within this divine and rational cosmos. Philodemus reports Chrysippus as saying that 'the world is a single entity of the

---

[8] Compare also Philodemus' report of a detail from Chrysippus' *On Nature*, book 5: 'he [Chrysippus] puts forward arguments about the thesis that the universe (*kosmos*) is an animal and rational (*logikon*) and exercises understanding (*phronoun*) and is a god' (*P. Herc.* 1428, cols. VII.30–VIII.4, tr. Obbink, with changes); see Obbink 1999: 185. For the Greek text, see (besides Obbink 1999) Henrichs 1974; the text of the papyrus, with facing German translation, is printed on pp. 12–26; the quoted remark occurs on p. 18 (not on p. 20, as Obbink reports).

[9] Read: *zōon athanaton, logikon ē noeron, teleion en eudaimonia(i)*, with David Sedley, in place of the *textus receptus*: *zōon athanaton, logikon, teleion ē noeron en eudaimonia(i)*. See Long and Sedley 1987: 2.321, *ap. crit. ad* 54 A, line 1.

wise (*kosmos heis tōn phronimōn*), its citizenship being held jointly (*sumpoleiteumenos*) by gods and human beings' (*P. Herc.* 1428, col. VII.22–6, tr. Obbink 1999).[10] (The plural gods mentioned here obviously cannot be *the* god identified with the world as a whole. They must rather be both the different 'aspects' of that god, mentioned by Diogenes Laertius, and, as we shall shortly see, the various divine celestial bodies.)

Arius Didymus provides a less compressed formulation of essentially the same point:

> The world is said to be an organization (*sustēma*) of heaven and atmosphere and earth and sea and the natures within them. The world is also called the dwelling-place (*oikētērion*) of gods and men, and the structure (*sustēma*) <consisting of gods and men> and the things created for their sake. For just as there are two meanings of *polis*—first as dwelling-place (*oikētērion*) and secondly as the structure of its inhabitants along with its citizens (*to ek tōn oikountōn sun tois politais sustēma*)—so the world is like a *polis* consisting of gods and men, with the gods serving as rulers and men as their subjects. They are members of a community (*koinonia*) because of their participation in reason (*dia to logou metechein*), which is, by nature, law (*phusei nomos*). . . . In consequence of which it must be believed that the god who administers the whole exercises providence for men, being beneficent, kind, well-disposed towards men, just, and possessing all the virtues. (Arius Didymus *apud* Euseb. *Praep. evang.* 15.15.3–5, tr. LS 67 L (part) and Vogt 2008: 91 and nn. 51–2, with changes; the supplement is von Arnim's (cf. *SVF* 2.528), whom LS follow.)

(NB: Here, too, we must assume that the gods (plural) who share the world with human beings are not, or are not simply, *the* god 'who administers the whole'.)

In fact, the *Astronomica* closes with the magnificent (and obviously related) image of the universe as a cosmic *res publica* created by Nature, a cosmic *urbs* established in the heavens (5.734–45, here at 738–9). (It is presumably because Manilius wants, for his grand finale,

---

[10] See Obbink 1999: 185. (Obbink also offers an alternative translation of the first phrase: 'the world is a single entity for the wise', ibid.; cf. his comments at 184–6.) For the Greek text, cf. again also Henrichs 1974, who translates, 'der Kosmos sei einer der Weisen und gehöre zum Staat der Götter und Menschen' (18). Obbink rejects Henrich's translation and argues persuasively in favour of the stronger reading of *heis* (viz. *hena*) (ibid.; cf. his nn. 13–14). For further discussion of this passage, see Vogt 2008: 97–8.

to fix our gaze upon the majesty of the stars and the empyrean realm that human beings are here passed over in silence. But passages like 2.105–36 make clear that we humans, too, have a special kinship with the cosmos and the gods, and thus must also be a part of that *res publica*, even if this is not stated explicitly at 5.734 ff.: *quis caelum posset nisi caeli munere nosse, / et reperire deum, nisi qui pars ipse deorum est?* ('Who could know heaven save by heaven's gift / and discover God save one who shares himself in the divine?', 2.115–16, tr. Goold 1977).

Now, in order to get a sense of the special place that human beings occupy, we need to recall that, for the Stoics, the world as a whole is a complicated system consisting of many parts, more importantly, consisting of many *kinds of parts*, each of which has its own role to play in the functioning of the whole. And these kinds form a sort of hierarchy:[11]

   (i) At, so to speak, the bottom are 'lifeless things, stones and logs, and our bones, which resemble stones' (LS 47 P (2)). These things are held together by what the Stoics call *hexis* (standardly translated as 'tenor' in these contexts), where *hexis* is 'a kind of tensile movement (*kinēsis tonikē*) which moves simultaneously inwards and outwards—the outward movement producing quantities and qualities, and the inward one, unity/unification and substance (*henōsis kai ousia*)' (LS 47 J).[12]

   (ii) Next come plants and plant-like things; these possess *phusis*, described as *hexis* that is already moved (*ēdē kinoumenē*) (LS 47 P). (Let us leave aside the delicate question of how this motion differs from the basic tensile movements characteristic of the *hexeis* as such.)

---

[11] On this hierarchy, see also the lengthy extract from the beginning of Hierocles' *Ēthikē stoicheōsis* (preserved in *P. Herc.* 1020), which LS give as 53 B.

[12] The suggestion seems to be that the *kinēsis tonikē* makes each individual object both be individual and have the features it has. Thus the absence of *kinēsis tonikē* would leave things being some sort of homogeneous, undifferentiated mass. I cannot here go into the subtle and difficult question of what, for the Stoics, accounts for the difference between determinate, differentiated *stuffs* (like air or water, which differ from each other by being different *kinds* of stuff), and determinate, particular *objects* (which can differ from one another even if they belong to the *same* kind; e.g. Socrates and Plato are both human beings, but each is a distinct individual).

   (iii) Then there are animals, which have *phusis* together with impressions (*phantasiai*) and impulses (*hormai*), and thus are said to have soul (*psuchē*) (cf. LS 53 B (4)).

   (iv) Still higher are rational animals, which have reason (*logos*) in addition to souls. (Or perhaps more accurately: which have rational souls.)

Many of the details of this *scala naturae* are obscure.[13] All that matters for us now is recalling that God—or Nature—has so designed all of the non-rational things that they will behave in ways that fit in with the plan for the whole simply on the basis of both how they are constituted (this tenor of theirs, if you will) and their interactions with other things. If two moving billiard balls collide, their properties (due to their tenor) and the motions that had been imparted to them account for how they will continue moving, after the collision. If a plant, as it grows, turns towards the sun, its *phusis* accounts for the heliotropism. Animal behaviour is obviously more complex. But equipped with certain impulses, for example, to seek out food and to avoid danger, and equipped with the capacity to receive impressions (for example, of food, or of danger), an animal will behave as it does in response to the impressions it receives from its environment.[14] And in behaving as they do, all of these things— from rocks and billiard balls to the non-rational animals—make

---

[13] The details of the Stoic theory of *hexis* are difficult, with levels (i) and (ii) posing the greatest challenges to interpreters; but in whatever way, precisely, those distinctions are to be understood, it is clear that the Stoics see an important difference between (iii) and (iv), and that *rationality* is the hallmark of (adult) human beings which serves to distinguish them from non-rational animals (and from non-rational human infants and small children). To get a sense of what the Stoics are aiming at with this series of levels, it may help to recall an analogous hierarchy Aristotle presents: mere aggregates (e.g. heaps and puddles); things which are one 'by continuity' (e.g. a dictionary with entries in alphabetic order); artefacts; living organisms; and the forms (*eidē*) of living organisms. According to Aristotle, as one moves 'up' in the hierarchy, the items at each successive level are characterized by a higher degree of unity (and are also better candidates for counting as *ousiai*, as substances). The details of Aristotle's schema and that of the Stoics are obviously different; but they share the thought that different sorts of items are characterized by greater or lesser internal unity, and that these degrees of unity can be drawn on for a hierarchical classification of things.

[14] C. Brittain provides a useful account of Stoic discussions of the impressions of non-rational animals; see Brittain 2002, esp. 256–74. As he notes (273 n. 57), a proper understanding of these impressions is also relevant to understanding *human* cognition, since we, according to the Stoics, start out as mere animals and only come to be rational animals in the course of our development (see also below, with n. 21).

their contribution to the overall functioning of the whole. While each of them lacks reason, since the plan for the whole is a rational one, there is a straightforward, albeit indirect, sense in which they can be said to be behaving rationally, namely, by behaving in conformity with that plan; and thus each of them can also rightly be seen as sustaining the rational workings of the whole.

At this point it is important to recognize that they just are the parts of the whole they are, and they just do make the contributions they make, without (as it were) being in a position to make better or worse contributions. But things are different when it comes to rational animals. Of course, by being in the world as parts of it, we necessarily contribute to the functioning of the world. Yet by having reason, we are in a position to contribute to the functioning of the world in a distinctive way—by us *ourselves* exercising *our* reason. What does this mean?

One thing it means is that our behaviour depends on something else besides only on our having the various impressions and impulses we have.[15] According to the Stoics, we also need *assent* (= *sunkatathesis*). Why? I may, for example, have the impression that there is champagne in the refrigerator. (Let us call impressions of this kind representational impressions; this is my term, not the Stoics'.[16]) For me actually to have the *belief*—or, if I were wise, the *knowledge*[17]—that this is so,

---

[15] I am extremely grateful to Katja Vogt for several thoughtful comments about, and suggestions for improving, an earlier version of the formulations of the points in this and the following paragraph (and in the notes accompanying these two paragraphs).

[16] I call them 'representational' impressions in order to highlight the following. (i) Any such impression purports to describe, or represent, a state of affairs. (ii) Each such impression either is itself propositionally structured, or is associated with the particular propositional content—in Stoic terminology, a *lekton*—that corresponds to the impression. (Reed 2002 provides a subtle and illuminating argument for preferring the second of these alternatives.) Accordingly, in the example given, my impression (or: its content) is not of the champagne, or of the refrigerator, or even of the champagne and the refrigerator, it rather is: *that the champagne is in the refrigerator.* Indeed, the Stoics are prepared to say that the impressions of rational beings are *rational* impressions (Diog. Laert. 7.51 *ad fin.* = LS 39 A (6); cf. Sext. Emp. *Math.* 8.70 = LS 33 C). But saying this is simply a way of stating the point that these impressions—perhaps better: the *lekta* corresponding to them—*are* propositionally structured; it is *not* a way of making the further claim that they are rational in the stronger sense of being fully reasonable, or of being impressions one is rationally justified in having. On *lekta*, see Barnes 1993 and Frede 1994.

[17] Here we need to remember that the Stoics *reject* the single most familiar philosophical account of knowledge, one whose distinguished history reaches back

I need to assent to that representational impression.[18] I may also have the impression that I ought to drink the champagne. (The Stoics call impressions of this sort 'hormetic impressions' (Stob. 2.86.17 = LS 53 Q (1)).) But for me to have the impulse, the *hormē*, to drink the champagne, I need to assent to the impression. Simply in virtue of interacting with my environment, I shall, unavoidably, end up having all sorts of impressions, many generated directly by sensation, others generated by operations of my mind on those basic, sensation-based impressions. A central component of the project of Stoic epistemology is to articulate the standards we can (and must) rely on so as never to assent either to any representational impressions that would yield mere belief, or to any hormetic impressions that would lead to impulses to pursue what one ought not to pursue. The details of this project are difficult and controversial. But what is perfectly clear is that by creating such a special role for assent in the formation of cognitive states and motivations, the Stoics make each of us *responsible* for

at least to Plato's *Theaetetus*: knowledge *is* true belief plus something else (e.g. a *logos* of a certain kind). The Stoics, by contrast, insist on a sharp, binary opposition between knowledge and belief, i.e. the presence of knowledge entails the absence of belief, and the presence of belief entails the absence of knowledge—a point secured by C. Meinwald, in her incisive Meinwald 2005, via a review and analysis of the relevant evidence. Most salient for us right now is the following consequence of this tenet: in the case of all those who are not wise, the grasp or cognition (*katalēpsis*) of things provided by *even the epistemically most privileged impressions*, the so-called cognitive impressions (*phantasiai katalēptikai*), amounts only to belief; in the case of a sage, by contrast, such grasp amounts to knowledge. But in some situations—e.g. clearly seeing the champagne in the refrigerator, in good light, while fully awake, sober, and so on— there will be no difference whatsoever *in the impressions* (they are fully accurate and in no way deficient) of the non-wise and the wise perceivers to account for the different epistemic statuses of the assents (namely, belief vs. knowledge); there is instead a difference *in the condition of the minds* of the two perceivers (namely, lack of wisdom vs. wisdom), and it is this difference that makes for mere belief in the one case, and actual knowledge in the other. On the distinction between knowledge and belief, and wisdom and lack of wisdom, see Arthur 1983, esp. 75–8, and, in particular, again Meinwald 2005. On the *phantasia katalēptikē*, see Frede 1983; he somewhat modifies his views in Frede 1999*b*, see esp. 300–11. Reed 2002 offers a useful account of the debates (both ancient and modern) about the *phantasia katalēptikē* in the light of contemporary discussions in epistemology. See also section 3 below, for a bit more on wisdom.

[18] Reed 2002 argues that the 'considered view' of the Stoics is that, when we assent to something, we strictly speaking assent not to the impressions themselves, but rather to the propositions associated with those impressions (168 and n. 40). Fortunately, this complication does not matter for present purposes. Thus throughout my discussion I use the simpler language of 'assenting to impressions', etc.

the cognitive states and motivations we have.[19] Thus, for example, given the way the world is (including, the way human visual perception works), a stick partially inserted in water just will *look* bent or broken. But in order for me actually to hold that it really *is* bent or broken requires my assenting to that impression. If I do so assent, I acquire and express a false belief ('the stick is bent or broken'); and *I* shall be the one who is responsible for having this false belief, *not* the world.

Now the Stoics hold that Nature has so constructed us that we *could*, by never assenting to impressions that we ought not to assent to, come to have only *katalēpseis* (grasps or cognitions of things; see n. 17) which can result in, or ultimately amount to, knowledge (see section 3 below, esp. n. 25), but that, in actual fact, most of us hold many, many *false* beliefs. And these stand in the way of our leading happy and truly rational lives.[20] (While I cannot go into the matter here, the Stoics' developmental account of how human beings make the transition from non-rational animals to adults possessing reason helps explain how it is that most of us so easily come to have many false beliefs.[21]) Of course, the world as a whole is so rational and so

[19] I use 'motivations' here as an umbrella term, to cover both the *impulses* (or *choices*) of the wise, i.e. the outcomes of assenting to the *right* kinds of impulsive impressions in the *right* kind of way, and the *desires* of the non-wise, i.e. the outcomes of either assenting to the right kinds of impulsive impressions in *wrong* sorts of ways, or assenting to the *wrong* kinds of impulsive impressions, ones which represent things that, in fact, ought *not* to be pursued, as to be pursued. 'Cognitive states' is likewise used as an umbrella term, to cover both the knowledge of the wise and the beliefs of the non-wise.

[20] The same thing, *mutatis mutandis*, is true with respect to hormetic impressions: Nature has so constructed us that we *could* only have impulses to pursue what we ought to pursue (by never assenting to a hormetic impression that would lead us to pursue what we ought not to pursue); but as a matter of fact, most of us have many, many desires for various things we ought not to pursue. And such desires, of course, very much also stand in the way of our leading happy and truly rational lives.

[21] Since we start out as mere animals, Nature has equipped us with impressions (i.e. the capacity to receive impressions) and impulses in much the way it has so equipped all animals; in particular, we are equipped with a first, or primary, impulse (*prōtē hormē*) towards self-preservation (*to tērein heauto*) (Diog. Laert. 7.85 = LS 57 A; see also the whole of Sen. *Ep.* 121; cf. again Brittain 2002: 256–74). This impulse leads animals (to seek) to preserve themselves qua animals, i.e. qua living things. (On the notion of primary impulses, see Brunschwig 1986.) Such an impulse will, say, impel a small child to shrink back from intense, searing heat or extreme cold. As a part of our transformation into rational beings (= the result of a natural process which, the Stoics hold, culminates at either around age 7 or age 14), two things occur. First, that original impulse is replaced by an impulsive impression (which, recall, only becomes

provident that it has a place even for those rational animals that are failing to make the best or fullest use of their rationality. Thus every human being, no matter how foolish, is playing his or her part in that whole.

3

Here we come to the special role for *wisdom*. It would hardly be the mark of a perfect intelligence to have made a place only for such rational beings as are *not* making the best use of their rationality. The entire point of having reason, one is inclined to think, is to use it well. And this clearly is the Stoic view. Thus while any human being, simply by possessing reason, has his or her part to play in the cosmos, the *wise* have a special role to play: it is they who can, in words of Cicero's we have already seen, truly *contemplate and imitate the world* (see *Nat. D.* 2.37, quoted above). And it is they who, together with the

---

motivating of action if assented to). And secondly, since we now are rational beings rather than mere animals, we ought to be concerned, if we are being fully rational, not about preserving ourselves as mere animals, but about something else: in the first instance (or so it is sometimes argued) about preserving ourselves as rational beings; but this, if properly understood in the light of Stoic theory, really rather amounts to an attachment to reason and, according to Michael Frede, to the good. (See Frede 1999a, esp. 90–4, where he remarks: '[The] Stoic view presupposes that the original impulse to go for certain things and to avoid their opposites, though appropriate in the pre-rational stage, is no longer reasonable once we have become rational, but is replaced by an attachment to the good. And it is only as a consequence of this new attachment that we will, when appropriate, have a derivative concern with what we were impelled towards in the pre-rational stage. But, as, for instance, the Stoic doctrine of suicide shows, there will be situations where it is not appropriate to act to maintain one's life' (92).) Brittain 2001 offers grounds for questioning the claim that the ends of action are always chosen *sub specie boni*; see 247–53, esp. 252. Yet quite independently of how, exactly, this issue is to be resolved, it is clear that that attachment will only come about in a person if s/he assents to various relevant impressions, and if s/he refrains from assenting to various merely natural-*seeming* impressions—e.g. in certain circumstances, the impulsive impression that one ought to act so as to preserve one's life—impressions which may seem *natural*, precisely because the impulses from which they derive once *were* natural, namely, during the pre-rational stage of the person's life (i.e. infancy and early childhood). The Stoics hold that almost all of us develop improperly, by *failing* to assent to the kinds of impressions it would (actually) be natural to assent to (and also by all too hastily and rashly *assenting* to those impressions it would (actually) be natural to refrain from assenting to), and that we thus find ourselves in fact attached to things that it would not be rational to be attached to, if we were being fully and genuinely rational.

gods, have perfect (or perfected) reason and so help constitute what the Stoics call the cosmic *polis*. As Katja Vogt has recently argued, although each of us is an inhabitant of the cosmos—where else, after all, could any of us live?—only the wise and the gods have the higher status of being its citizens (for an attractive account of what this comes to, see Vogt 2008).

What, then, is wisdom for the Stoics? This is another large and difficult topic which cannot be adequately treated here; thus a few remarks will need to suffice. The sage (*sophos*) is characterized by possessing *epistēmē* (knowledge or understanding). There are several dimensions to this. First of all, *epistēmē* may refer either to a bit of knowledge or to a branch of knowledge. More importantly, it may refer to the tenor for receiving impressions (in the wise person's soul), a tenor which is unchangeable by argument (*ametaptōtos hupo logou*).[22] Most importantly, *epistēmē* is a whole system of cognitions (*katalēpseis*) which are secure and unchangeable by argument.[23] How are we to understand this?

Here it may be useful to recall Socrates' encounters with various supposed experts (as depicted, for example, in any number of Plato's Socratic dialogues). These experts present themselves as possessors of knowledge in their respective areas of expertise. But Socrates, via his questioning, is able to induce them to grant things that are incompatible with the claims they maintain they know (or to deny things which follow from such claims). Thus Socrates is also able to induce them—at least if they are being honest with him and with themselves—to concede, at the end of their question-and-answer exchanges, that they are now in a state of *aporia* with respect to their initial claims (asserted on the basis of their supposed knowledge) and the various points they had granted (or denied) in the course of their encounter with him. In other words, at the end of their exchanges

---

[22] For a helpful analysis of what this comes to, see Arthur 1983: 74–5.

[23] Stobaeus provides the crucial report: '[The Stoics say] (1) Scientific knowledge (*epistēmē*) is a cognition (*katalēpsis*) which is secure (*asphalēs*) and unchangeable by argument (*ametaptōtos hupo logou*). (2) It is secondly a system (*sustēma*) of such *epistēmai*, like the rational cognition of particulars which exists in the virtuous man. (3) It is thirdly a system of expert *epistēmai*, which has intrinsic stability (*to bebaion*), just as the virtues do. (4) Fourthly, it is a tenor (*hexis*) for the reception of impressions which is unchangeable by argument, and consisting, they say, in tension and power (*tonos kai dunamis*)' (Stob. 2.73.16–74.3 = *SVF* 3.112 (part); tr. LS 41 H, with changes.)

with Socrates, they find themselves unable to choose which of the various incompatible statements to reject, and which to retain. The conclusion to be drawn from this outcome, as Socrates sees it, is that these 'experts' are not really experts, because they (in effect) lack firm and unchangeable knowledge of a sort which, had they possessed it, would have allowed them to survive the Socratic *elenchus* unscathed.

Now, given the way Socratic questioning works, it is very natural to assume or posit two things, the first of which itself comes in two parts. No individual bit of knowledge can be firm and unchangeable *on its own*, or rather, any bit of knowledge will be firm and unchangeable to the extent that it is *embedded* within a (much) larger system of firm and unchangeable knowledge; in addition, each bit of knowledge will *derive* its stability from that whole.[24] Thus, at the most basic level, possessing knowledge needs to be understood as possessing a *body of knowledge*, comprising *systematically interrelated truths*, where that systematicity is what confers stability onto the whole body of knowledge.

Secondly, the *minds* of those who do possess such knowledge will also be said to be firm and unchangeable, because their grasp of any individual piece of knowledge involves grasping the much larger system of knowledge, the place of that piece within in the entire system, and the systematicity of the whole body of knowledge—and grasping all of this in such a way that even so clever and resourceful a questioner as Socrates will not be able to induce them to grant anything conflicting with that given bit of knowledge, and so will also *not* be able to 'loosen' the grasp they have of it and of the larger body or system to which that piece of knowledge belongs.[25] (See *Resp.* 7.531d–534e for Plato's elaboration of these two Socratic assumptions in the context of the metaphysical and epistemological programme of

---

[24] A further, absolutely central assumption Socrates, Plato, and the Stoics are prepared to make is that there can only be a *single* consistent system, and that that consistent system will in fact be *true*: thus not only is inconsistency a sign that something (in the inconsistent set of claims) is false, but consistency actually is a hallmark of truth.

[25] A difficult question I cannot address here: how do the *katalēpseis* become, or lead to, *epistēmē*? Is it that if a person has sufficiently many of them, then their interconnectedness and systematicity will also, so to speak, almost automatically, impress themselves on him or her in such a way as to create in the mind the stability characteristic of *epistēmē*, or must the person rather do something more active, e.g. him- or herself reflect on the various *katalēpseis* in the right sorts of ways so as to *discover* their interconnectedness and systematicity, with that discovery then creating, or amounting to, the requisite stability?

the *Republic*.) The Stoics take over both parts of this Socratic-Platonic picture.[26]

These are obviously extraordinarily strong requirements on knowledge and wisdom.[27] Indeed, given the sharp, in fact, the *physiological*, differences between the wise and all those who fall short of wisdom, it might be appropriate to add a fifth level to the *scala naturae* we saw earlier:

(v) Still higher are the wise, who not merely possess reason, but have perfected it.

Furthermore, we may wonder if these requirements are so strong as to entail that a wise person must in fact be omniscient. Yet even if one does not go as far as maintaining this—and I think it would be a mistake to hold that a Stoic sage is omniscient[28]—the wise person will be able, on the basis of possessing such knowledge, to do something only slightly less impressive than knowing everything: she or he will 'live in agreement with nature' (which is happiness, i.e. the *telos* of life, according to one of Zeno's definitions; Diog. Laert. 7.87 = LS 63 C). That is, a true sage will be able to harmonize his or her own reason with Nature's reason. And we can see, at least roughly, why this should make for 'a smooth flow of life'—which is one of the other definitions Zeno gives of happiness (LS 63 A, cf. 63 C (4)).

Now here we can perhaps also recognize a special role (in relation to human beings) for the divine celestial bodies. As far as virtue or excellence is concerned, there is no difference between a wise person and a god (see e.g. LS 61 J or Epictetus, *Diss.* 1.12.26). But gods and humans are still different kinds of beings.[29] First, gods are immortal and we are not. Secondly and perhaps more importantly, the gods just

---

[26] Again, see Frede 1983 and 1999*b*, as well as Meinwald 2005.

[27] Indeed, these requirements are so very strong that one can readily see why various *Sceptical* opponents of the Stoics seek to argue that a sage ought in fact—i.e. ought given the stringent conditions the Stoics insist on—to suspend judgement. Frede 1983 provides a useful *entrée* to this issue. See Allen 1994, for discussion of various refinements introduced by both Sceptics and Stoics in the course of their centuries-long debate, and Reed 2002, for discussion also of several of the key underlying epistemological questions.

[28] On the question of whether or not the Stoic sage is omniscient, see Kerferd 1978, Frede 1999*b*, and Vogt 2008: 118–30.

[29] On Stoic theology, see Frede 2005 and Vogt 2008: 113–60; the place of Stoic theology within the broader context of Hellenistic philosophical theology is treated in Mansfeld 1999.

are fully rational while we, at best, can *come to be* so.[30] Thirdly, their rationality and the 'smooth flow' of their lives are on display:

> The orderliness (*ordo*) and regularity (*constantia*) of the heavenly bodies is the clearest indication of their powers of sense perception (*sensus*) and intelligence (*intelligentia*)—since there is after all nothing which could move in an orderly and regulated way without a rational plan (*sine consilio*), which contains nothing haphazard or random or accidental. But the orderliness and perpetual regularity (*in omni aeternitate constantia*) of the heavenly bodies neither points to nature[31]—for they are full of rationality (*plena rationis*)—nor to chance (*fortuna*), who is a dear friend (*amica*) of change and despises constancy (*constantia*). It follows, therefore, that they are moved through themselves (*sua sponte*), out of their own perceptions and divinity. (*Nat. D.* 2.43, tr. Inwood and Gerson 1997: 149, with changes.)

The motions of the heavenly bodies can serve as an image of what a perfectly reasonable, wholly well-ordered life looks like. Moreover, these motions harmonize so completely with the overall movement of the cosmos that they actually form integral parts of that very movement and order. Nevertheless, each heavenly body very much remains a distinct individual, because each one engages in its *own* motions. I thus find attractive the suggestion offered by Vogt that the celestial bodies can be a *model* for what human lives that were fully rational would look like: they are governed each by their own reason, producing reasonable actions, but they do so in a way that not only is consonant with, but clearly is part of, the rational workings of the whole.[32] A thorough understanding of the heavens and their motions might, therefore, well deserve pride of place within the knowledge—i.e. the *system* of knowledge—that is the sage's wisdom.

How does any of this help with our initial questions about Manilius? The answers, it seems to me, are relatively straightforward, at least in outline. The universe does want us to be happy, and it does want us to know about its workings (indeed, our happiness will in part consist in our understanding the rational order of the universe). That rational order and those workings, however, are enormously

---

[30] See Vogt 2008: 116 and n. 9.

[31] See Vogt 2008: 144 n. 73, who points out that 'nature' (*natura*) cannot here be being used in the standard Stoic sense, since Nature, according to the Stoics, is something fully ordered and is, indeed, pervaded by reason.

[32] See Vogt 2008, esp. 144–8.

complex. Moreover, the causes of things are, for the most part, non-evident (*adēla*); that is, *coming* to know them will require the use of reason; and only a mind in good condition will actually be able to come to *know* them (as opposed to assenting to a whole host of impressions, many of which will yield false beliefs). Thus, looked at in one way, the universe is wholly open to reason; but given the overall complexity of the system in all its details, given the non-evidence of causes, and given the actual condition of the minds of most of us, it can very readily seem *as if* the universe were concealing itself, and hence *as if* a guide or instructor were needed. Similarly, it is part of the Stoic conception of things that truths are there to be known and understood by minds, that is to say, there are no truths which are, in principle, or by their very nature, inaccessible to reason and thus simply unknowable. (On this fundamental point, as in so much else, the Stoics again show themselves to be inheritors of the Socratic-Platonic tradition.) But insisting that all truths are there to be known is wholly compatible with the thought that it might require a great deal of intellectual effort so as to be able to grasp certain truths. Manilius' suggestion that only a select few will really be able to benefit from his teaching, it strikes me, is wholly in line with this thought. In any event, the seemingly odd mixture of, if you will, elitism and anti-elitism that appears to characterize his stance towards those who would come to know the truth about the stars seems perfectly at home in Stoicism. It corresponds to a conception of reason as being, on the one hand, an intrinsic capacity present in any rational being as such, and as being, on the other hand, a hard-won and, very likely, a surpassingly rare achievement.

7

Manilian self-contradiction

Katharina Volk

Manilius is not an author famous for his consistency. For centuries, critics have pointed to the poet's incoherence, self-contradictions, and downright mistakes, sometimes in a purely disparaging fashion, but occasionally with the purpose of throwing light on the underlying ideological tensions of Manilius' work.[1] There have also been attempts to absolve the poet of the charge of inconsistency and to explain perceived self-contradictions as having been misunderstood and not in fact being contradictory at all.[2] In this chapter, I build on my earlier work on the topic and attempt to formulate a general approach to the problem of Manilian self-contradiction. In doing so, I am guided by the belief that there is indeed inconsistency in the *Astronomica*, but that this very lack of conceptual coherence yields important insights into Manilius' world-view and modus operandi.

Inconsistency has for some time now been a fashionable topic in Latin studies, a trend examined, and exemplified, in a recent article

---

[1] E.g. Joseph Scaliger at numerous points in his commentaries on Manilius maintains that the poet has no idea what he is talking about (see Grafton 1983–93: 1.201 + 328 n. 100 for discussion and references). Following in part the important observations of Neuburg 1993: 257–82, I discuss, and attempt to interpret, self-contradictions in the *Astronomica* in Volk 2001; 2002: 204–9, 220–4; 2009: 12–13, 33, 47, 111–15, 169–70, 251–8, 263–5.

[2] Criticism specifically of my own scholarship on the topic is found in Habinek 2005: 276 n. 55 and 2007: 235–6 + n. 28; see also the contributions of John Henderson and Wolfgang-Rainer Mann in this volume. For a different, astrological, approach to explaining many perceived mistakes and inconsistencies in *Astronomica* 5 in particular, see the work of Wolfgang Hübner, esp. Hübner 1984: 174–213 and 2010.

and monograph by James J. O'Hara.[3] Since these two publications provide both useful summaries of previous work and handy formulations of the author's own approach, they serve as a convenient starting point for the present investigation. Tellingly, the title of the article is 'Trying Not to Cheat': in O'Hara's opinion, scholars all too often attempt to explain away inconsistencies by 'cheating', that is, by ascribing them to external factors such as the author's incompetence, textual problems, or the unfinished state of the text. Instead of resorting to such easy ways out, O'Hara believes that self-contradictions should be 'thematized', that is, considered meaningful and interpreted as far as possible.[4]

However, even those who share the desire not to gloss over inconsistency may come to the conclusion that, in some cases, what O'Hara calls cheating is ultimately the most honest solution. Consider, for example, what is perhaps the most egregious self-contradiction in the *Astronomica*. In his discussion of methods of calculating the ascending degree of the zodiac (3.203–509), Manilius first introduces what he calls the *vulgata ratio*, that is, the assignation of a rising time of two hours to every sign on the zodiac (218–46). However, as the poet himself is quick to point out, this is little more than a rule of thumb since, owing to the obliquity of the zodiac, the rising times of individual signs actually differ and there are further divergences owing to different latitudes and different times of year. After a detailed and sophisticated discussion of the issues involved (247–482), Manilius finally presents yet another method, one that involves assigning fifteen degrees of the zodiac to each passing hour (483–509). Unfortunately, this is nothing but the *vulgata ratio* in disguise: if fifteen degrees rise each hour, every sign, occupying thirty degrees, will take two hours.

How to react to this blatant self-contradiction? A. E. Housman thinks that Manilius has shown himself to be incompetent:

> Alas, alas! This alternative method of yours, my poor Marcus, is none other than the vulgar method which in 218–24 you said you knew, and which in 225–46 you exposed as false. The wolf, to whom in his proper

---

[3] See O'Hara 2005 and 2007. Note that for the sake of convenience, I am using 'inconsistency' and 'self-contradiction' more or less interchangeably in this chapter.

[4] See O'Hara 2007: 10, with reference to Scodel 1999, the source of O'Hara's term 'thematize'.

shape you denied admittance, has come back disguised as your mother the goose, and her gosling has opened the door to him. (1903–30: 3.xxi)

By contrast, Pierre Brind'Amour, to whom we owe the most detailed discussion of the passage, believes that the lines must have been interpolated since the poet simply would not have contradicted himself in such a way; he maintains that 'the care with which this whole question of the Ascendant is treated rules out any mistake due to carelessness or inattention' (1983*b*: 148). Finally, Josèphe-Henriette Abry suggests that the passage shows signs of hasty composition (1993*a*: 210: 'une composition rapide ou fragmentaire du poème'), implying, I assume, that Manilius might have eliminated the inconsistency had he but had the opportunity to revise his text. In the parlance of O'Hara, all three scholars are 'cheating', albeit in different ways. It seems to me, however, that all three comments are perfectly valid reactions to the problem—they are, of course, also quite revealing of each individual critic's temperament—and that some self-contradictions simply cannot be interpreted.

If we now turn to those inconsistencies that can, perhaps, be made meaningful, it is again instructive to look at O'Hara's discussion. His standard working hypothesis—and this approach is by no means particular to O'Hara, but widespread in contemporary Latin literary studies in general—is that if there is an inconsistency, it has most likely been deliberately set up by the author in order to make a point. More often than not, the supposed point is that there are two ways of looking at the issue in question; the author wants to show us the two sides of the same coin. The deliberate ambiguity of the text is thus meant to mirror the inherent ambiguity of the world, the human condition, or whatever else is at stake. It is obvious from O'Hara's discussion that much of his and other scholars' interest in the apparently self-contradictory nature of many Latin texts has its origin in Virgilian scholarship, where the two or more 'voices' and the resultant ambiguity of Virgil's *Aeneid* and other poems have been the object of study for decades. Whether dealing with Virgil or other authors, scholars who propose readings of this kind typically reckon with conscious authorial agency.[5]

---

[5] O'Hara allows for the unintentional generation of self-contradiction in certain cases, but it is clear that his preferred scenario is that of the author who consciously produces inconsistency.

As has been pointed out by Charles Martindale, among others, this approach, with its tell-tale use of the term 'ambiguity', has developed out of New Criticism, and it is probably at this point the default critical modus operandi in the interpretation of inconsistency in Latin poetry.[6] Martindale himself discusses two additional ways of conceiving of self-contradiction, each informed by a different theoretical framework: instead of assuming intentional ambiguity, we can take a deconstructionist stance and argue that language itself is inherently inconsistent and always implies its own contradiction; alternatively, we can, in the manner of reception studies, move the focus from the author to the reader and see inconsistency as generated over time by a plurality of different readers and interpretive communities. In my opinion, any of the approaches discussed so far (authorial ambiguity; the indeterminacy of language; and the history of reading) can throw light on perceived self-contradictions, as can the explanations denounced as 'cheating' by O'Hara; of course, different texts and different instances of inconsistency may call for different explanations. To Manilius' self-contradictions, though, I propose yet another approach.

I submit that, at least in a large number of cases, inconsistency or self-contradiction in the *Astronomica* is the unintentional (if often very revealing) by-product of Manilius' use of certain traditional conceptual 'languages'—what one might also call 'discourses', 'metaphors', 'ideas', 'memes', or simply 'ways of thinking and speaking' about the world.[7] My suggested approach is similar to one that has been employed, in various permutations and for some decades now, in the study of Lucretius. Scholars such as P. H. Schrijvers, Monica

---

[6] Martindale 1993 is an important critical study of approaches to inconsistency in Latin poetry. The influence of New Criticism especially on discussions of Virgilian ambiguity has often been noted; see e.g. Connolly 2001 on the *Eclogues*.

[7] This jumble of terms, all with their own advantages and disadvantages, is meant to indicate my lack of commitment to any particular jargon. While 'idea' highlights the conceptual content of a particular notion, 'language', 'discourse', and 'metaphor' refer primarily to its expression in language ('metaphor', of course, denotes a very specific type of linguistic encoding, one whose use in scientific texts has been much discussed (see e.g. Black 1962: 25–47 and 219–43; Hesse 1966; Leatherdale 1974); note that some but not all of my examples in what follows involve metaphors or other instances of figurative language). 'Meme' (a term invented by Dawkins 1976: 203–15 and made palatable to the humanities by Dennett 1990, among others) has the advantage of collapsing the form-content divide but is not (yet) widely employed by classicists (though see G. Campbell 2002, 2003). I use 'ways of thinking and speaking' in Volk 2009—a clumsy circumlocution, but it fits my purpose quite well.

R. Gale, Duncan F. Kennedy, and Gordon Campbell have shown that
Lucretius is consciously employing for his own rhetorical purposes
certain established ways of thinking and speaking, even though their
implications in fact contradict the poet's own Epicurean message.[8]
For example, Lucretius uses such attractive tropes as the metaphor of
Mother Earth; the image of the universe as a text; and the idea of the
early history of mankind as a Golden Age. However, in his world,
there is no divine agency in nature; the physical world is a random
conglomerate of atoms; and there was no original blessed state.[9]
There is strong reason to believe that Lucretius is doing this on
purpose and that he is, in the words of Kennedy, 'playing a dangerous
rhetorical game for high stakes' (2002: 93). He attempts to avail
himself of the attractiveness of the discourses he is using (this is the
honey on the cup in the famous simile), but of course risks being
misconstrued—and, as a matter of fact, has been, as the various
versions of the anti-Lucrèce-chez-Lucrèce theory show.[10]

   On this reading, Lucretius is consciously waging a kind of linguistic
guerrilla warfare, using his philosophical enemies' language as ca-
mouflage. Manilius (to return to the topic at hand) is doing nothing
of the kind: he is neither all that self-conscious in his choice of
language nor in the situation of having to write against the philosophical grain, as Lucretius does.[11] Nevertheless, I suggest that his self-
contradictions result from his use of traditional conceptual language
in a similar way to tensions that we see at work in the *De rerum*

---

   [8] See Schrijvers 1978; Gale 1994; Kennedy 2000, 2002; G. Campbell 2002, 2003;
compare now Garani 2007; more sceptical Schiesaro 1990: 72–87.
   [9] For 'Mother Earth', see Lucr. 1.250–64; 2.598–660, 991–8; 5.772–836 with
Schrijvers 1978: 90–4; Gale 1994: 26–32; and Garani 2007: 81–93; for the universe
as a text, see the poet's repeated analogy between the atoms of the physical world and
the letters of the alphabet, esp. those used in his own poem (1.196–8, 823–7, 907–14;
2.688–99, 1013–22), with Schrijvers 1978: 84–7; for the 'Golden Age', see esp. Lucr.
5.925–1104 with Gale 1994: 156–82 and G. Campbell 2002, 2003.
   [10] Cf. Schrijvers 1978: 87: 'la fécondité de la métaphore entraîne des risques pour
l'auteur d'origine en ce sens que des implications qu'il n'a ni envisagées ni voulues sont
déduites et exploitées par des lecteurs vivant dans les traditions culturelles différentes de
celles qui prédominaient du temps de l'autheur lui-même'. On versions of and reactions
to the anti-Lucrèce-chez-Lucrèce theory (the phrase goes back to the 19th-cent. French
scholar H. J. G. Patin), see Gale 2007*a*.
   [11] The first point is, of course, debatable; see my discussion below in the text. As for
the second, Lucretius' Epicurean physics is not only counter-intuitive, but also at
variance with mainstream ancient ideas about the natural world (cf. Bakhouche 1996:
309–12); by contrast, Manilius' cosmology is by and large conventional (cf. Volk 2009:
14–57).

natura. Neither in the case of Manilius nor with Lucretius is the conflict simply one of 'poetic' versus 'philosophical' discourse.[12] Obviously, certain ways of thinking and speaking are more associated with poetic, others with philosophical genres; still, as I hope will become clear in what follows, the contradictions do not necessarily evolve along a supposed fault line between philosophy and poetry, two discourses that at any rate were not necessarily as clearly distinguished in the time of Manilius as they are today.

For the sake of convenience, I have identified three types of Manilian self-contradiction, though there is clearly a strong continuity among them and they constitute but different points on the same spectrum. The first is what I have in earlier publications called the have-one's-cake-and-eat-it-too principle.[13] What I mean by this is that Manilius, at different points in his poem, is participating in different discourses, employing a number of traditional ways of thinking and speaking about the world, either without noticing or without caring that this leads to self-contradictions. For example, in his argument for the sphericity of the earth, Manilius discusses the antipodes, mentioning in passing that the sun rises in the southern hemisphere once it has set in the north:[14]

> hanc ubi ad occasus nostros sol aspicit actus,
> illic orta dies sopitas excitat urbes
> et cum luce refert operum vadimonia terris;
> nos in nocte sumus somnosque in membra vocamus. (1.242–5)

---

[12] To contrast Lucretius' poetry with his philosophy has been readerly practice for centuries (see e.g. Volk 2002: 71–3, 94–118; Gale 2007*a*); arguably, such an approach is suggested by the poet's own distinction between philosophical content and poetic form in the honeyed-cup simile (Lucr. 1.936–50 ~ 4.11–25). In the case of Manilius, tensions between his poetic medium and his scientific-philosophical subject matter have been noted by many scholars; see now esp. Abry 2006*b*, who suggests that the poet 'wins out' in the end, as apparent from Manilius' decision in book 5 to treat the (poetic) paranatellonta rather than the (scientific) planets.

[13] See Volk 2002: 208 and index s.v. 'Manilius, "Have-one's-cake-and-eat-it-too" principle' and 2009: 13, 170, 258, 263; cf. also Volk 2001: 113–14. If I had known that I would continue to work on this topic, I would have coined a less unwieldy term. For an independent use of the phrase 'have one's cake . . .' to describe a similar phenomenon (inconsistency in Aratus), see Pendergraft 1990: 104 (thanks to Steven Green for the reference).

[14] Cf. Volk 2009: 33. For a different interpretation of this passage, see Henderson in this volume.

Once the sun looks on this part of the world, having reached our sunset, day begins there and awakens the slumbering cities and brings back to these lands their appointed labours together with the light; we instead dwell in night and summon sleep to our bodies.

This contention is not only blatantly false, but also contradicts Manilius' cosmology in the rest of the poem, where the heavenly bodies circle the earth from east to west and not from north to south. However, the idea that the antipodes live in an upside-down world where everything is the opposite of what we find in our half of the earth was a well-established topos, and the claim that it is day in the south when it is night in the north is found in other sources as well.[15] In treating the southern hemisphere, Manilius for a moment appears to dip into this largely non-scientific discourse about the antipodes, while elsewhere he hews to an astronomy-based, less fantastic view of the universe. He has his cake and is eating it too, happily using two different ways of thinking and speaking about the world in the same work.

The same procedure may explain a number of additional self-contradictions within the *Astronomica*.[16] A central inconsistency, first pointed out by Matt Neuburg and discussed also by Wolfgang-Rainer Mann in this volume, concerns Manilius' pedagogical stance.[17] For most of the poem, the poet keeps reassuring his student that he will succeed in gaining cosmological and astrological knowledge since the universe is eager to reveal itself to all mankind (see esp. 2.105–25 (partly quoted below) and 4.866–935). By contrast, in a central passage in the proem to book 2 (2.136–49), Manilius suddenly maintains that only the happy few are granted this kind of insight and that he himself is not singing 'for the crowd' (*turbae*, 2.137). Here, too, the poet seems to be availing himself of two traditional, if contradictory, ways of thinking and speaking, utilizing both the topos of cosmic self-revelation with its resultant pedagogical optimism and the elitist idea of the initiation of a select group of chosen *mystae*.[18]

---

[15] See esp. Verg. *G.* 1.249–51 and Sen. *Ep.* 122.1–3. Generally on ancient views of the antipodes as an upside-down world, see Moretti 1994*a*: 31–48 and 1994*b*: 246–55, as well as Hiatt 2008: 14–37.

[16] For examples in addition to the one discussed immediately below in the text, see my earlier publications mentioned in n. 13.

[17] See Neuburg 1993: 276–82 and cf. Volk 2002: 207–9. On Manilius as a teacher and his relationship to his student, see also Green in this volume.

[18] Mann in this volume explains this perceived contradiction with reference to Stoic doctrine: according to the Stoics, the universe is in principle intelligible to all

Many cases of the have-one's-cake-and-eat-it-too principle in the *Astronomica* admit at the same time of a more traditional ('cheating') explanation of inconsistency, that is, the assumption that Manilius is drawing on different, contradictory sources. It is inherently likely that an author who gives voice to a variety of divergent and sometimes inconsistent ideas has derived these from a number of texts and contexts. On occasion, it is possible to reconstruct where a particular image or concept comes from, though often—especially with commonplace ideas—the search for an exact source may well turn out to be futile.[19]

If we accept that a number of Manilius' self-contradictions arise from his indiscriminate employment of diverse traditional, but not always compatible, ideas, this raises the question of whether the poet is simply not conscious of the inconsistencies his procedure creates (a lack of sensitivity or attentiveness that one might consider a weakness or failure) or whether he is fully aware of contradicting himself but unbothered by it. If the latter, this might be an idiosyncrasy of Manilius (who may have been more concerned with orchestrating effects at individual points in his text than with creating a coherent whole) or it might be indicative of the writing and reading habits of a culture whose ideas of coherence and unity were different from ours. I do not have a ready answer to this quandary, but although I am willing to allow for a certain carelessness or cavalier attitude on the part of Manilius specifically, I am inclined to believe that the poet's contemporaries, attuned to the highly rhetorical nature of much of oral and written Roman discourse, were much more tolerant of inconsistency, which they may not necessarily have experienced as such. I cannot develop this argument further here but suspect that some form of the have-one's-cake-and-eat-it-too principle may not only be operative at many places in Manilius' text but also be able

---

humans qua rational beings; however, only very few (the 'wise') will in fact attain this kind of knowledge. This point is very well taken, but it seems to me that Manilius in 2.136–49 is doing more than just stating the fact that not everybody will manage to arrive at wisdom. He appears to be rejoicing in the exclusivity of the small group to whom the heavens 'have not begrudged knowledge of their sacred motions and of themselves' (143–4), taking an elitist pride in the fact that his song is not for the masses.

[19] Since the *Astronomica* is the earliest comprehensive ancient treatment of astrology that has come down to us, the question of its source(s) has been surrounded by uncertainty.

to explain supposed self-contradictions in other ancient authors as well.

My second type of Manilian inconsistency has to do with what we might call flipsides. Self-contradiction can arise not only from the use of different conceptual languages at different points in the poem, but from the creative exploration of one and the same idea or set of images, which may carry the potential for ambiguity in itself.[20] Take, for example, what has been called Manilius' anthropology, a topic I already briefly touched on above in the context of the poet's pedagogy.[21] Throughout the *Astronomica*, Manilius stresses that human beings, intimately related to the cosmos, are called upon to investigate the heavens. The divine universe positively encourages them and willingly reveals itself to their scrutiny. Thanks to this benevolent invitation, man is able to 'rise to heaven' and ultimately achieve union with the divine. This kind of cosmic spirituality is widespread in Hellenistic and Roman texts (cf. Volk 2009: 226–51) and fits perfectly with Manilius' world-view, which is why he employs its language and concomitant imagery so extensively in his poem. There is, however, a flipside. If at the invitation of the divinity man can heroically rise to the heavens and gain knowledge of the universe, perhaps he can do the same even without divine sanction.

Let us consider a set of passages, taken from all over the *Astronomica*, that have a bearing on this issue. The first, from the proem to book 2, describes knowledge of the sky straightforwardly as a gift from the gods and an invitation from heaven itself to 'enter heaven':[22]

> quis caelum posset nisi caeli munere nosse,
> et reperire deum, nisi qui pars ipse deorum est?
> quisve hanc convexi molem sine fine patentis
> signorumque choros ac mundi flammea tecta,
> aeternum et stellis adversus sidera bellum
> ac terras caeloque fretum subiectaque utrisque
> cernere et angusto sub pectore claudere posset,
> ni sanctos animis oculos natura dedisset
> cognatamque sibi mentem vertisset ad ipsam

---

[20] This is the point where my argument comes closest to the deconstructionist approach mentioned above.

[21] Compare also Stark in this volume.

[22] On the striking final image of man's *commercia* with the heavens (2.125), see Glauthier in this volume.

et tantum dictasset opus, caeloque veniret
quod vocat in caelum sacra ad commercia rerum? (2.115–25).

Who would be able to understand the cosmos unless through the gift
of the cosmos or to find god unless he had a place among the gods
himself? Or who could see and encompass in his narrow mind
the mass of the infinitely vaulted sphere, the dances of the stars, the
flaming roofs of the universe, and the eternal war of planets against
constellations, and the land and sea beneath the sky and what is
beneath both, unless nature had given sacred eyes to the soul and turned
the kindred mind toward herself and dictated such a great work, and
unless there came from heaven something to call us into heaven for a
sacred exchange of things?

The next passage, from Manilius' first of two responses to the dis-
couraged student in book 4, presents a neutral statement of man's
desire to rise to the upper cosmic reaches and find god:

> quod quaeris, deus est: conaris scandere caelum
> fataque fatali genitus cognoscere lege
> et transire tuum pectus mundoque potiri. (4.390–2)

What you are looking for is god: you are attempting to scale heaven and,
born by the law of fate, to know the fates and to transcend your mind
and gain possession of the universe.

However, in the next two passages, we see the flipside of man's trans-
cendental urge, where the visit to heaven becomes an invasion and
attack on the gods reminiscent of the gigantomachy. In his celebration
of human ability in the finale of book 4, Manilius stresses the boldness
of man, the 'tamer' and 'capturer' of the natural world, as he casts his
eyes on the heavens and enquires after Jupiter:

> secessit in urbes,
> edomuit terram ad fruges, animalia cepit
> imposuitque viam ponto, stetit unus in arcem
> erectus capitis victorque ad sidera mittit
> sidereos oculos propiusque aspectat Olympum
> inquiritque Iovem. (4.903–8)

He [man] moved into cities, tamed the earth for (bearing) fruit, caught
animals, and imposed a pathway on the sea; he alone stood with his
head lifted up and, victorious, raises his starlike eyes to the stars and
looks closer at Olympus and asks for Jupiter.

Even more strikingly, human reason in the proem to book 1 is presented as literally rising to heaven and snatching his weapons from the king of the gods:

> nec prius imposuit rebus finemque modumque
> quam caelum ascendit ratio cepitque profundam
> naturam rerum causis viditque quod usquam est
>
> . . .
>
> eripuitque Iovi fulmen viresque tonandi. (1.96–8 + 104).

No earlier did reason impose an end or limit to its endeavours until it scaled heaven and grasped the deepest nature of things according to its causes and perceived whatever there is . . . and snatched from Jupiter his lightning bolt and power of thunder.

It seems that Manilius simply cannot resist the dark flipside of his own imagery, and as a result, cosmological activity in the *Astronomica* appears strangely violent in a number of instances.[23] One could argue, of course, that the poet is undercutting himself on purpose and, like the Virgil of much recent scholarship, is pointing his readers to the inherent ambiguity of the endeavour of astrological research, which can be viewed as an act of both piety and impiety at the same time. To me, it seems that Manilius is in fact strongly promoting his pious approach to cosmology and that his occasional notes of impiety are an unintentional side-effect of his use of language that is too multifaceted for its implications to be contained. Claims of intentionality or the lack thereof can hardly ever be proved or disproved. However, unlike Lucretius, who reflects, for example, on the circumstances when it is appropriate to use an expression like 'Mother Earth' (see 2.644–60 and 5.795–6, with Gale 1994: 31 and Garani 2007: 32–3), Manilius does not display any awareness of the pitfalls of his imagery.

My third and last type of Manilian self-contradiction concerns what is probably the central inconsistency in the *Astronomica*, one likewise caused by the poet's use of, and entanglement in, traditional ways of thinking and speaking about the world (cf. Volk 2009: 111–15, 263–5). In his poem, Manilius upholds a system of 'strong' and 'hard' astrology, which means not only that the stars hold the key

---

[23] Cf. Volk 2001 (specifically on the image of the gigantomachy); 2002: 220–4; 2009: 251–8.

to our exact fate down to the last detail, but also that they in fact cause this fate and all the events that take place on earth:[24]

> hic igitur deus et ratio, quae cuncta gubernat,
> ducit ab aetheriis terrena animalia signis,
> quae, quamquam longo, cogit, summota recessu,
> sentiri tamen, ut vitas ac fata ministrent
> gentibus ac proprios per singula corpora mores. (2.82–6)

Hence this god and reason, which governs all, derives earthly beings from the constellations in the sky and forces their power to be felt, even though they are removed at a far distance, so that they provide lives and fates to the peoples and to everybody his own character.

This stellar influence works along the lines of similarity: whatever happens in the sky is replicated on earth. This is apparent, for example, from the following passage, which concerns the relationships the signs of the zodiac have with one another:

> per tot signorum species contraria surgunt
> corpora totque modis totiens inimica creantur.
> idcirco nihil ex semet natura creavit
> foedere amicitiae maius nec rarius umquam.
> . . .
> scilicet, in multis quoniam discordia signis
> corpora nascuntur, pax est sublata per orbem,
> et fidei rarum foedus paucisque tributum,
> utque sibi caelum sic tellus dissidet ipsa
> atque hominum gentes inimica sorte feruntur. (2.579–82 + 603–7)

Through so many configurations of signs, hostile bodies arise and are so often and in so many ways made one another's enemies. Therefore nature never created anything out of herself greater and rarer than the bond of friendship.... Surely, since under many signs bodies of a discordant disposition are born, peace is removed from the world, and the bond of faith is rare and granted to few, and the earth, just as the sky, is at variance with itself, and the races of men are carried along by hostile fate.

---

[24] For 'strong' astrology (the entirety of a person's fate can be read in the stars), see Hankinson 1988: 133–5; 1998: 287–93; for 'hard' astrology (the stars not only signify but actually cause fate), see Long 1982: 170 n. 19. Cf. Volk 2009: 59–67, specifically on Manilius.

Sad to say, most relationships of the signs are hostile, which explains
why on earth, too, enmity is much more common than friendship.
It is specifically *because* of the hostility in the sky that aggression is
rampant on earth: *utque sibi caelum sic tellus dissidet ipsa* (2.606).
Throughout the poem, Manilius insists on this mirroring effect between heaven and earth; it is probably fair to say that analogy between
the above and the below is his main mode of explanation.[25]

This kind of cosmic similarity, however, also leads to major self-
contradictions. The following passage concerns the astrological influences of the sign Leo, which, not surprisingly, brings forth leonine
people. The equivalent is true for all the signs, which—according to
the principle of causality just mentioned—engender human beings in
their own image:

> quis dubitet, vasti quae sit natura Leonis
> quasque suo dictet signo nascentibus artes?
> ille novas semper pugnas, nova bella ferarum
> apparat, et spolio vivit pecorumque rapinis;
> hos habet hoc studium, postes ornare superbos
> pellibus et captas domibus praefigere praedas
> et pacare metu silvas et vivere rapto.
> sunt quorum similis animos nec moenia frenent,
> sed pecudum membris media grassentur in urbe
> et laceros artus suspendant fronte tabernae
> luxuriaeque parent caedem mortesque lucrentur.
> ingenium ad subitas iras facilisque recessus
> aequale et puro sententia pectore simplex. (4.176–88)

Who is in doubt as to the nature of the huge Lion and what pursuits he
decrees by his sign to those being born? He always prepares new battles,
new wars against animals, and lives off booty and his prey of flocks.
They are eager to decorate their high doorposts with animal skins and
to nail caught spoils to their houses and to bring peace to the woods
through fear and to live off what they catch. There are also those whose
similar inclinations the city walls do not keep out, but they walk around
with body parts of animals in the middle of the city, hang bloody limbs
from their storefront, prepare slaughter for the sake of luxury, and make
money by killing. They are given equally to sudden anger and easy
withdrawal and have a simple mind in their pure heart.

---

[25] On resemblance as a central principle in Manilius' cosmos, see e.g. Hübner 1982:
517; 1988: 26–9; Abry 1993*a*: 201–10; generally on thinking in correspondences as
typical of astrology, see von Stuckrad 2003: 17.

The natives of Leo are bloodthirsty hunters or butchers (180–6), prone to anger but blessed with a simple heart (187–8), and they have these character traits because such is the 'nature' (*natura*, 4.176) of Leo himself. But why would we think of Leo as aggressive in the first place? The reason, of course, is that he is a lion and, as Manilius hints elsewhere (2.32), specifically the Nemean Lion defeated by Hercules and subsequently raised to the sky. To think of the constellations as stellified human beings, animals, or objects was of course commonplace, and stories of catasterisms abound in the works of the authors of Latin *Aratea* and especially Manilius' contemporaries Germanicus and Ovid—as well as in the *Astronomica* itself. However, the concept of catasterism undermines the unidirectional chain of causality that is at the heart of Manilius' astrology: if Leo is a lion similar to those we know, then heaven is like earth, and not the other way around. The poet is in fact aware of this problem, as is apparent from his attack, in the proem to book 2, on writers who treat the *aetia* of the constellations and present the heavens as being made up of earthly creatures:

> astrorum quidam varias dixere figuras,
> signaque diffuso passim labentia caelo
> in proprium cuiusque genus causasque tulere.
>
> . . .
>
> quorum carminibus nihil est nisi fabula caelum
> terraque composuit mundum quae pendet ab illo. (2.25–7 + 37–8)

> Some have treated the various patterns of the stars and have connected to their proper origins and causes the constellations that glide everywhere through the wide sky. . . . In their songs, heaven is but a story, and earth has made up heaven, though the one [earth] really depends on the other [heaven].

Despite this verdict, though, Manilius himself throughout the *Astronomica* is practically doing the same thing.[26]

The problem is that once one operates with a principle of similarity, it becomes extremely difficult to control what is the original and what the copy. For Manilius' doctrine, it is necessary that the heavens

---

[26] On the problems this passage raises, see Effe 1977: 123–5; Romano 1979a: 51–3, 62–4; Feraboli *et al.* 1996–2001 *ad* 2.25–38; Salemme 2000: 75–104; Volk 2001: 95–6; 2002: 221–2; 2009: 111–12, 190–2. For an elegant solution, see Uden in this volume.

are always primary, and terrestrial and human affairs secondary;
however, his language very often contradicts his beliefs. A case in
point is the famous simile at the end of book 5, where the different
magnitudes of stars are compared to the different orders in a human
city that looks not a little like Rome:

> utque per ingentis populus discribitur urbes,
> principiumque patres retinent et proximum equester
> ordo locum, populumque equiti populoque subire
> vulgus iners videas et iam sine nomine turbam,
> sic etiam magno quaedam res publica mundo est,
> quam natura facit, quae caelo condidit urbem.
> sunt stellae procerum similes, sunt proxima primis
> sidera, suntque gradus atque omnia iusta priorum:
> maximus est populus summo qui culmine fertur;
> cui si pro numero vires natura dedisset,
> ipse suas aether flammas sufferre nequiret,
> totus et accenso mundus flagraret Olympo. (5.734–45)

And just as the populace is divided up in great cities, and the patricians
hold the most prominent position, and the equestrian order the next
place, and you see how after the equestrians follow the people, and after
the people, the ineffectual crowd and nameless masses—thus there is a
commonwealth also in the great heaven, which nature brings about,
creating a city in the sky. There are stars similar to nobles, constellations
close to these leaders, and there are orders and all leaders' privileges.
Greatest is the common people carried along on the firmament: if to
them nature had given strength in proportion to their number, heaven
itself would not be able to bear its flames, and the whole universe would
burn, with Olympus having caught fire.

Strikingly, the poet makes it sound as though the celestial *res publica*
were but a copy of that on earth: nature founded a city in the sky
(739), and the stars resemble human citizens, not the other way
around.

The inherent ambiguity of resemblance is, in a way, another
example of my category of flipsides: if one thing can be said to be
like the other, then the second can easily also be described as being
like the first. It is just that this flipside has particularly important
implications since it points to a tension at the heart of Manilius'
world-view, and not just his. Ultimately, we are dealing here with
the problem of anthropocentrism in science, the question of whether
human beings always construct reality in the image of what they

already know, that is, ultimately themselves.[27] Manilius, as we have
seen in the passage about the poets of catasterisms, is a fierce anti-
constructionist, but his habit of thinking and speaking about intra-
cosmic relations in terms of similarity makes him fall prey to the
language of constructionism and anthropocentrism again and again.
He himself nicely explains the guiding principle of his cosmological
'invention' in the passage about the infamous Southern Bears
(1.451–5), where he gives the following reason for why we expect
the Antarctic circumpolar constellations to mimic the Arctic ones
and why we therefore posit the existence of a Great and a Little Bear
at the celestial south pole as well:

> mens fugientia visus
> hunc orbem caeli vertentis sidera cursu
> tam signo simili fultum quam vertice fingit. (1.453–5)

The mind imagines that this (southern) sphere of heaven, which turns
about stars that escape our vision, rests on similar signs just as it rests on
a similar pole.

Extrapolating from the known to the unknown is the natural modus
operandi of the human mind, a tendency that continuously undermines the stability and unidirectionality of the posited top-down
organization of Manilius' universe.

To sum up: while every instance of perceived self-contradiction in
the *Astronomica* needs to be considered individually, I have suggested
an interpretive approach that I believe explains—without explaining
away—a large number of them. On my reading, Manilius, unlike
perhaps Virgil, is not deliberately employing self-contradiction to
make points about the inherent ambiguity of his topic and he is
also not, like Lucretius, endangering his coherence through the daring
use of hostile language. Rather, his inconsistencies more often than
not arise from his use of the language of his *own* world-view, which
carries its self-contradictions in itself.

---

[27] On anthropocentrism in science, see Guthrie 1993: 152–76, with many references. Cf. Kennedy 2002 on viewing the scientific enterprise as either 'discovery' (the
scientist finds and describes a pre-existing reality) or 'invention' (the scientist's work
consists in constructing reality).

8

Arduum ad astra

The poetics and politics of horoscopic failure in Manilius' Astronomica

Steven J. Green

If Manilius' *Astronomica* has suffered an unfavourable modern reception, especially from the Anglophone world, it is largely due to the complexity of its astrological instruction.[1] As it is a self-consciously didactic poem, following a long tradition of Greek and Roman poetry which purports to teach a specific skill, philosophy, or way of life to a less-specialized, 'student' audience, the reader is led to expect a lesson which is accessible to the average learner.[2] But this is not the case with Manilius. Those readers who approach the text with a certain eagerness for the topic but without detailed astrological knowledge and, as such, slip into the role of the 'model' student constructed in the text, have often found Manilius' teachings very tough to chew. Those who

---

[1] The socio-political reading of Manilius and his near contemporaries which I advance in this chapter is currently being developed in greater detail as part of a book-length study, provisionally entitled *Discourses of Discretion in Roman Astrology: Manilius and his Augustan Contemporaries*.

[2] Literature that we readily label 'didactic' was often grouped by metre with epic in antiquity. The first tangible evidence of didactic as a specific genre of literature comes from late antiquity (Diomedes the grammarian, 4th–5th cents. AD), and it is a matter of scholarly debate as to whether poets of the late Republic and early Empire were consciously operating within such a generic category; see Volk 2002: 26–34. At any rate, all modern commentators regard the intratextual exchange between teacher and student, such as we find in Manilius, as a defining feature of such literature; see esp. Toohey 1996: 1–5, Volk 2002: 34–43.

approach the text with knowledge of astrology have (also) found it strewn with astrological errors.

Scholarship on the poem has often felt the need to explicate Manilius, to explain what he actually *means*, what he *meant to say*, where he is *in error*, or more drastically, where his text is *spurious* or where verses have become *displaced* or *lost*.[3] Underlying this approach to the text is a desire to preserve the integrity of the ancient lesson and render the poem a useful guide to the workings of ancient astrology. Such noble scholarly intentions, however, run the risk of obscuring important tensions in Manilius' didactic strategy. Some more recent scholarship has helped to redress the balance, and there is now general awareness of two significant ways in which Manilius' astrological lesson effectively collapses by the end of the extant work. First, and most notably, Manilius does not offer any substantial detail about the planets, the very entities on which horoscopes depend, despite several promises of a fuller discussion later in the work.[4] Secondly, and at a more conceptual level, one must acknowledge inherent tensions between didacticism and the rigid deterministic form of astrology advocated by Manilius. Not only is it far from clear that astrology is even teachable exclusively within a mortal sphere but, even if it is, there is a jarring contrast between the ineluctable determinism of the workings of heaven and Manilius' role as a teacher, capable of influencing students and, thus, becoming instrumental in changing the course of those future events.[5]

---

[3] Goold's 1977 Loeb edition, with introductions, copious notes, and illustrations, is monumental in its aim to explain Manilius to a lay reader. For the various scholarly attempts to account for Manilius' inconsistencies, see now Volk in this volume.

[4] The importance of the planets in determining destiny is regularly drawn to our attention (e.g. 1.15, 51–2, 670–1, 2.643–4), and on two occasions Manilius begins to speak about the planets, before ultimately deferring the discussion to a later stage (2.738–54, 961–7; cf. also, more generally, 3.586–9). To suggest that this discussion has been lost somewhere in the lacunae of book 5 is wishful thinking. Such 'forward glances' are, I suspect, part of a rhetorical strategy to keep us reading to the end of the work before we realize that we have been cheated. Failure to deal with the planets is, to some extent, a matter of generic inheritance: the father figure of astronomical poetry, Aratus, refuses to include discussion of the planets as they do not adhere to the determinability of his Stoic design for the universe (*Phaen.* 450–3). But Manilius' refusal does, I argue below, have an important additional socio-political dimension to it. For the riddle of the missing planets, see also Volk 2009: 48–57, 116–26.

[5] Manilius himself flits between astrology as knowledge acquired (i.e. capable of being taught) and knowledge inspired or revealed by celestial forces (i.e. outside the control of any mortal teacher); see *Astr.* 1.1–117 with Stark's discussion in this

These conclusions come to light once one has reached the end of the (extant) work: and one may well be inclined to read until the end before passing any judgement on the lesson's effectiveness, given that Manilius' professed teaching strategy is to scatter related pieces of information and advice across his entire poem.[6] In the first part of this chapter, I wish to further this line of inquiry by suggesting that there is a sense of *progressive* difficulty built into the text for the 'model' student: on my reading, a sense of student despondency is reached some way before the end of the work, pivotally in book 4.

Let us take, then, a brief journey through the first four books of the poem, focused through the experience of the student addressee and my own candid experiences as reader, as I choose to identify with this student. As my own knowledge of the workings of ancient astrology is very limited, in comparison to some of the other contributors to this volume, it should become clear that my personal experience and that of the model student are actually quite comparable.[7]

READING A FAILING LESSON

Manilius starts, in book 1, by mapping out the *sphaera*, detailing the positions of and interrelations between the constellations in the sky. This book is a gentle opener as it is easy enough for both a literate Roman and a modern reader to comprehend and digest: it amounts to a descriptive, static representation of the heavens; one can sometimes verify what is said by resorting to autopsy, a tactic encouraged by the poet himself; a learned reader can draw on his familiarity of the subject from previous literature, especially Aratus.[8] The information in book 1, then, is easy to comprehend, and makes the student (myself

---

volume. For useful discussions of the tension between teaching and determinism in the poem, see Neuburg 1993: 257–82, esp. 276–80; Volk 2002: 202–9.

[6] More precisely, on two occasions, Manilius uses the analogy of children learning to read and write (2.755–64) and (more effectively) the building of a city (2.772–83) to justify his decision to discuss facts, data, or 'building blocks' before teaching us how to use the information or make appropriate connections.

[7] As I am referring to myself, I refer throughout to the student as masculine.

[8] For Manilius' appeals to student autopsy, cf. 1.209 (*aspicimus*), 216 (*conspicimus*), 260 (*possis caelo numerare sereno*), 552 (*quodcumque supra te suspicis ipse*); for the intertextuality between Manilius' first book and Aratus, see esp. Abry 2007.

included) feel that Manilius' most optimistic exhortation may be realizable: that we all, simply by virtue of being human, can uncover the secrets of the heavens (2.105–8). Then again, the student has not learnt anything strictly *astrological* from book 1: all Manilius has done so far is to map out the cosmic backdrop for a study of astrology, and we have not yet been introduced to the variables and calculations necessary in order to cast our own horoscope.

It is to this more specific purpose that Manilius turns in books 2 and 3. Book 2 details the signs of the zodiac and their complex relationship with each other. In order to grasp what Manilius means, the current reader needed to seek the advice and illustrations of Goold's Loeb edition. Book 3 represents the dense heart of the work—the calculation of the degree of the ascendant—and is unanimously recognized as the most technical and difficult book, not helped by some internal inconsistencies.[9] The current reader understood very little from Manilius' own words, and again had to resort to Goold's edition.

In view of this, book 4 offers some genuine light relief, as it sets forth—in very easy-going, non-technical language with common-sense sentiment—the influences that the signs of the zodiac have on those humans born under them: for example, those born under the Ram work with wool, those born under the Lion delight in plunder (4.124–291). For the first time, the student (myself included) has been able to grasp something truly *astrological*!

My feeling of relief here would, I think, have been shared by the model ancient student, if one considers a passage from Petronius' *Satyricon*, in which the ludicrous dinner host Trimalchio attempts to impress his guests by serving a course which represents, in the fashion of a rebus, the twelve signs of the zodiac (Petron. 35–6). In a typically theatrical scene, Trimalchio uses the occasion to show off his sophistication by explaining the influences that the signs exert on those born under them (Petron. 39–40). Trimalchio's explanations chime with existing astrological texts (including Manilius), albeit with some embellishment, and the host is even capable of taking on the authoritative air of the astrologer.[10] The implication of this is clear: even

---

[9] On the famous problem of Manilius' self-contradiction in discussing the degree of the ascendant, see Volk in this volume.

[10] As in astrological treatises, Trimalchio commences his discourse with Aries; he uses a technical term, *genesis*, to refer to the natal star (Petron. 39.8). Moreover,

Trimalchio, who is typically seen as unsophisticated and ignorant when it comes to topics such as literature and history, has been able to learn these basic elements of astrology to bluff his way in front of his captive audience.

So any Roman fool, Petronius informs us, can understand some of the basic links between the nature of the constellation and the influence it exerts on those born under it. Coming back to Manilius, the student finds some comfort in his own ability to comprehend some basic elements of astrology set out at the start of book 4 . . . but this comforting feeling is only momentary, as the teacher abruptly applies a layer of difficulty by informing the student about the decans, which affect the influence exerted by the individual signs (4.294–386). Manilius sums up the implication of this new information for the student (4.380–6):

> nec tantum lanas Aries nec Taurus aratra
> nec Gemini Musas nec merces Cancer amabit,
> nec Leo venator veniet nec Virgo magistra,
> mensuris aut Libra potens aut Scorpios armis
> Centaurusque feris, igni Capricornus et undis
> ipse suis Iuvenis geminique per aequora Pisces;
> mixta sed in pluris sociantur sidera vires.

Not only will Aries take pleasure in wool, nor Taurus in the plough, nor the Twins in the Muses, nor the Crab in trade, nor only will the Lion come forth as a huntsman, nor the Maiden as a teacher, nor will the Balance have power only over the measures, nor the Scorpion over arms and the Centaur over wild beasts, Capricorn over fire and the Youth himself over his own waters or the two Fishes over the sea: but the stars are mixed up and become associated into more powers.

What Manilius means here, of course, is that his previous discussion of the (basic) influences of the constellations (4.124–291) needs to be complemented with the (more complex) discussion of the decans (4.294–379). It is hard to imagine, however, a less sensitive way in which Manilius could have conveyed this to the struggling student: with its polysyndetic structure, its relentless repetition of negative connectives (*nec, aut*), and its insistence on mentioning all

---

Petronius subtly casts Trimalchio in the role of Stoic creator of the world by referring to him as 'creator of matter' (*materiae structor*, Petron. 35) and making him allude to the classic Stoic conceit that nothing is created 'without reason' (*nihil sine ratione*, Petron. 39.14). See further Smith 1975: 89–92; Connors 1998: 112–14.

the constellations, 4.380–6 reads like a deliberate and systematic undoing of all the knowledge the student thought he had grasped so far.[11]

It seems entirely fitting, then, that this should be the point at which the voice of the didactic student is directly evoked, in a distinctly epic cry of despair (4.387–9):[12]

> 'multum' inquis 'tenuemque iubes me ferre laborem,
> *rursus* et in magna mergis caligine mentem,
> cernere cum facili lucem ratione viderer.'

'Extensive and subtle is the toil you bid me undergo', you say. '*Once again*, indeed, you are plunging my mind into great darkness, just when I was beginning to appear to see the light with some easy principle.'

This is a noteworthy event. Didactic poets usually construct their students as passive recipients of information. In some cases, we may be aware of more active participation from the student, in that the teacher appears to respond to (unquoted) questions posed by the student.[13] Whether we are meant to interpret these student questions as having been posed in advance or during the course of the teacher's instruction, the important thing to note is that the student's actual voice remains undocumented in the text: the teacher is the master of ceremonies in his own didactic text, and he is not interrupted once he has started to speak.[14] Only on two occasions prior to Manilius is this didactic protocol compromised by having the words of the intervening student directly quoted. Both examples occur in Lucretius, book 1 (803–8, 897–900), where they follow the same general pattern. Let us take the latter Lucretian exchange as representative (Lucr. 1.897–903):

---

[11] For Manilius' predominant strategy of 'retuning' didactic advice, making the student aware that what he has so far grasped is only part of the story (often using the transitional phrase *non/nec satis est*), cf. e.g. *Astr.* 1.458, 2.270, 297–302, 331, 570, 643, 722; for this didactic strategy elsewhere, see Green 2004: 52–3 on Ov. *Fast.* 1.49–52.

[12] With *Astr.* 4.387, cf. the structure of Aeneas' opening words to Dido at Verg. *Aen.* 2.3 *infandum, regina, iubes renovare dolorem.*

[13] For the frequent pose of the didactic teacher responding to student questions, typically introduced by *quaeris*, cf. e.g. Lucr. 5.1091, Verg. *G.* 2.288, Ov. *Med.* 79, *Ars* 1.49, 1.375, 3.750, *Rem.* 487, 803.

[14] This is a defining feature of the didactic genre according to Diomedes, as it is poetry 'in which the poet himself speaks without interruption from others' (*in quo poeta ipse loquitur sine ullius personae interlocutione*, Diom. *Gramm. Lat.* 1.482.21 Keil).

'at saepe in magnis fit montibus' inquis 'ut altis
arboribus vicina cacumina summa terantur
inter se validis facere id cogentibus austris,
donec flammai fulserunt flore coorto.'
scilicet et non est lignis tamen insitus ignis,
verum semina sunt ardoris multa, terendo
quae cum confluxere, creant incendia silvis.

'But often it happens on big mountains', you say, 'that the top branches
of the high trees, being close together, are rubbed one against another
when the strong South wind compels them to do so, until they burn
bright when the flower of flame breaks out.' Assuredly, and yet fire is
not implanted in the wood, but there are many seeds of heat which,
when they stream together by rubbing, create fires in the woods.

Manilius shares with Lucretius the use of *inquis* (cf. also Lucr. 1.803), but
this only serves to underline the difference between the student/teacher
exchanges in Lucretius and Manilius. In both examples in Lucretius, the
exchange takes place in a spirit of intellectual curiosity and debate. First,
the student makes a valid point based on autopsy—an observation about
plants (Lucr. 1.803–8) and trees (1.897–900)—which is used to draw an
inference: respectively, that plant life contains the four elements and that
wood contains flame. In both cases, the teacher immediately responds
cordially by respecting the truth of the observation (with the encouraging
scilicet, Lucr. 1.809, 901) before informing the student that the inference
drawn is incorrect (Lucr. 1.809–13, 901–3). The relationship between
student and teacher here in Lucretius, then, is one of mutual intellectual
respect and progressive learning.

This is a very different scenario from the exchange in Manilius. The
desperate complaint of confusion from the floundering student at *Astr.*
4.387–9 should not be taken in any localized sense to refer to a momentary loss of clarity:[15] it is, rather, a reflection on the entire experience of
the student since the beginning of the poem/lesson. On my reading, this
is the first time that the student has been able to grasp something truly
astrological in the work and, especially as it comes after the intricacies
of book 3, it is all the more distressing when that long-awaited sense of
surety is suddenly taken away: the student could see for but a brief time
before he was plunged, once again (*rursus*, i.e. as in books 2–3) into
darkness. Manilius has truly articulated the feelings of the would-be
student—I felt exactly the same. . . .

---

[15] It is taken in this way by Neuburg 1993: 273; cf. Volk 2002: 206.

Manilius' response to this student outburst is predictably Stoic and lacks the more personalized encouragement of Lucretius: you are seeking god; not everyone will get there; it's up to you; be thankful that you have been given the chance to inquire; only if you give up earthly passions do you stand a chance of achieving it (4.390–407). After this dubious 'encouragement', Manilius continues relentlessly by applying an additional layer of difficulty (4.409–10): taking on board all this information is *still* not enough (*nec satis est*, 4.409). In the course of book 4, Manilius has moved from discussion of the signs (30°, 4.122–293), to the decans (10°, 4.294–386), to individual degrees (4.408–501), to changes within a degree (4.502–84). At each stage, the student does not see the complication coming, but is rather fooled into thinking that he knows the full picture, before successive layers of difficulty are applied. This will lead to a further outburst from the student towards the end of book 4 (4.866–72):

> sed quid tam tenui prodest ratione nitentem
> scrutari mundum, si mens sua cuique repugnat
> spemque timor tollit prohibetque a limine caeli?
> 'conditur en' inquit 'vasto natura recessu
> mortalisque fugit visus et pectora nostra
> nec prodesse potest quod fatis cuncta reguntur,
> cum fatum nulla possit ratione videri.'

But what is the use in probing into the shining firmament with such fine reasoning, if anyone's own mind fights against it and if fear banishes hope and bars access to the threshold of heaven? 'Look!', he says, 'nature is buried in a vast cavern and flees our mortal gaze and heart; nor can it be of use that all things are governed by the fates, since fate cannot be seen by any reasoning.'

This outburst from the student is a lot more serious than the former. First, it is longer, as the student feels it necessary to cause greater interruption to the teacher to express his frustration: and note here that Manilius may have constructed this as a 'real' interruption, in that the words are uttered by the student (*inquit*, 4.869) rather than being mouthed by the teacher (*inquis*, 4.387).[16] The sentiment is also more serious, as it raises fundamental questions about the capacity of

---

[16] The text of 4.869 is problematic: *inquit* is Richard Bentley's conjecture, following on from *en*, the conjecture of Friedrich Jacob; both critics are trying to make better sense of the MSS *enim quid* or *enim quod*.

any mortal to comprehend the essence of an art which lies beyond his heart and mind—note the all-encompassing *cuique* (4.866) and *mortalis ... nostra* (4.870). This strikes at the heart of the tension (mentioned earlier) between (earthly) didacticism and the (extraterrestrial) nature of astrology, and constitutes a direct challenge to Manilius' earlier pledge that anyone is capable of comprehending astrology simply by virtue of being human (2.105–8):

> quis dubitet post haec hominem coniungere caelo,
> <cui, cupiens terras ad sidera surgere, munus>
> eximium natura dedit linguamque capaxque
> ingenium volucremque animum, quem denique in unum
> descendit deus atque habitat seque ipse requirit?

> Who after this can doubt that heaven is joined with man, <to whom, in his desire for earth to rise to the stars>, nature gave outstanding <gifts>—speech, keen intellect, and a winged mind—and into whom alone a god ultimately descends and resides, the god himself seeking himself?

Who can doubt that heaven is not joined with man, asks Manilius? Well, the student can, and does so directly two books later....

To summarize this part, reading Manilius' poem is not a didactic transaction from which the student only feels short-changed once he has finished reading the extant text. Rather, the intratextual relationship between teacher and student unfolds as a progressive drama, reaching in book 4 the level of confrontation between teacher and student when the latter feels a real sense of despondency. With the student disillusioned by the end of the penultimate book of the poem, one is entitled to ask just how many students are still listening to their teacher in book 5, and what part the deterioration of the student–teacher relationship plays in the abrupt ending to the (unfinished) lesson in this final book.

MOTIVES FOR STELLAR DECONSTRUCTION

Overall then, I am in agreement with scholars such as Neuburg and Volk when they suggest that there are unnegotiable complexities to Manilius' astrological lesson in *Astronomica*. And yet, the same scholars have not considered the possibility that Manilius may have *deliberately* set up his astrological lesson to fail.[17] Neuburg 1993: 280–1 maintains that there is a positive learning outcome for the student: the teacher is seeking to inculcate an almost 'religious' feeling of awe and wonder in his students, bidding them to worship the absolute power of the stars rather than question their apparent inconsistencies. Volk 2002: 208 prefers to see the didactic teacher as a speaker of shifting rhetorical poses rather than an advocate of consistent philosophy, a tutor who intends to draw arguments from different sources with little interest for internal coherence. Whilst these theories are interesting, I feel it an equally valid approach to assess the merits of the teacher from the 'feedback' from the student, and it is quite clear from the 'outbursts' at 4.387–9 and 4.866–72 that the student has not succumbed to any acquiescent and reverent worship of the stars, nor does he acknowledge or take delight in a polyphonic speaker: on the contrary, the student feels that this was supposed to be a lesson, and that it is seriously failing.

For anyone who feels uncomfortable with the notion that a poet's central aim might be to construct a lesson which is designed to deconstruct, I hope to offer some reassurance by considering two interconnected factors which I feel are important in comprehending Manilius' strategies more fully: namely, the political place of astrology in the early Empire, and the development of the playful genre of didactic.

Astrology, politics, and the early Empire[18]

As a branch of divination, there are several reasons why astrology might, at first glance, appear to be at odds with Roman state religion. Astrology was an art directed towards the benefit of the *individual* rather than the good of the *state* (like, for example, augury); it was a distinctly foreign practice (Mesopotamian/Egyptian) and had entered

[17] Herbert-Brown 2002: 126 comes closest when she floats the idea, in passing, that the absence of planets might be intentional: 'Was omission of the planets Manilius' way of foiling any accusation of providing procedures which could incite subversion?' Whilst I agree with Herbert-Brown, I am arguing for a much more deep-rooted strategy of deception on Manilius' part.

[18] For fuller discussions of the role of astrology in the politics of 1st cent. BC and AD, see Barton 1994*b*, 1994*c*: 33–62, and esp. the monumental work of F. H. Cramer 1954, esp. 58–104.

Rome at a discernibly late period (early third century); as it lay outside the official priestly college system, with its own set of experts, it might be felt to represent a dangerous sect which was difficult for the Roman authorities to monitor; and conceptually, its inherent determinism clashes with a Roman religion which believes fundamentally in the ability to alter the future course of events through proper and timely worship of the gods.[19]

These are all fair charges against astrology. And yet, it is a practice which takes hold quickly in elite circles in Rome from the late Republic onwards, as the rise of the political individual appears to have brought with it a corresponding desire for a more individualized form of divination. Roman leaders as far back as Octavius (87–86 BC) and Sulla (80s BC) attract anecdotes about influence from astrologers (Plut. *Mar.* 42, *Sull.* 37); horoscopes were apparently cast for Pompey, Caesar, and Crassus (Cic. *Div.* 2.99); and Nigidius Figulus, praetor in 58 BC, emerges as the first high-profile Roman astrological practitioner (cf. e.g. Luc. 1.639–72).

The chance occurrence of a comet that appeared during Caesar's funeral games in late July 44 BC seems to have marked a turning point in the credibility of astrology among the Romans and, consequently, in the authority of astrology among the different forms of divination. Astrology provided the most popular interpretation of the comet, in that it represented the catasterism of Caesar, the so-called *Iulium sidus* (Suet. *Iul.* 88, Cass. Dio 45.7.1). It is from this pivotal point—the first time that astrology had been used in the service of dynastic/imperial ambitions—that astrology appears to have become widely acknowledged as a science. From now on, criticism of the practice was largely reserved not for the art itself but for certain untrustworthy *practitioners* of the art: with so many apparent astrologers at Rome—from imperial courtiers to the street seers that loitered around the Circus—one had to be on one's guard in order to differentiate the learned and authoritative from the con man.[20]

Octavian/Augustus consolidates the political use of astrology and establishes a pattern for future Emperors. Octavian publicizes his

[19] See in general, Beard *et al.* 1998: 1.211–44, esp. 231–3.

[20] Vehement criticism of astrology such as we find most famously in Cicero's *De divinatione* (2.87–99), which is traditionally dated just before the Julian comet (45–44 BC), does not extend into the imperial period, which focuses on practitioners and assumes the veracity of the art; see my discussion below.

birth-sign on coins throughout the Empire from 28 BC: Capricorn is later taken up by successive Emperors eager to legitimize their rule and advertise their membership of the imperial house.[21] Stories emerge to strengthen the connection between the Emperor and the movement of the heavens. On the day of his birth, for example, Nigidius Figulus is reputed to have predicted that Octavian would be ruler of the world (Suet. *Aug.* 94.5, Cass. Dio 45.1.3–5).

A further landmark in the consolidation of astrology's power in imperial circles occurs from AD 2 onwards, when Tiberius returns to Rome from exile with his learned associate, Thrasyllus, an astrologer who quickly attains official status in the imperial court.[22] It may be no coincidence, then, that the early years AD see some of the most fervent astrological action. In AD 11, Augustus produces an edict proscribing astrological consultations about death or without witnesses, a clear attempt to keep this political tool within the hands of the imperial family and outlaw private astrological investigation into the fate of the aged Emperor (Cass. Dio 56.25.5).[23] The atmosphere of imperial nervousness at unauthorized astrological practising only intensifies under Tiberius, whom our sources depict as an unsettled Emperor housing a clandestine group of astrologers with the express purpose of marking out those destined for greatness, so that they could be destroyed (Cass. Dio 57.19.3–4, Juv. 10.94). The famous trial of Libo Drusus, who consulted astrologers for his own political future, duly follows in AD 16 (Tac. *Ann.* 2.27–32). This year also sees the (third) high-profile expulsion of astrologers from Rome.[24]

In the early Empire, then, profound imperial respect for astrology and its political power is matched by an acute awareness of the danger of this art in the wrong hands, a complex later articulated by Tacitus when he says that astrology 'will always be prohibited and always retained' (*et vetabitur semper et retinebitur, Hist.* 1.22). Authors of

---

[21] All the more strange given that Octavian was actually born in September, under the sign Libra; for the debate, see Barton 1995.

[22] See esp. F. H. Cramer 1954: 92–108.

[23] Augustus' nervousness towards unauthorized prophetic utterances was felt over twenty years earlier, in 12 BC, when, in the midst of problems of imperial succession, he had all prophetic writings collected up and scrutinized; many of them were destroyed (Suet. *Aug.* 31).

[24] Octavian had also banished astrologers from Rome in 33 BC, at a time when the propaganda war with Marc Antony was at its height. This followed an earlier edict against astrologers made by the praetor Cn. Cornelius Hispalus in 139 BC.

this period readily pick up on this complex. I do not intend to offer here a wide-ranging analysis of the presence and role of astrological material in early imperial literature.[25] Instead, I will focus on three authors who, through different means, share a common strategy of refusing to disclose the secrets of astrology whilst at the same time drawing attention to its prominent contemporary status.

Let us turn first to possibly the most prominent appearance of the art in Augustan literature, the figure of Horos in Propertius 4.1. Horos, a Babylonian astrologer, appears suddenly in Propertius 4.1 (71–150) in an apparent bid to advise the poet to abandon his poetic intention, outlined earlier in the same poem (1–70), to create a Roman aetiological work. The complex (and unresolved) issues of Horos' exact purpose in the poem and his contribution to the literary programme of Propertius' fourth book do not concern us here. Instead, I wish to focus briefly on the representation of Horos as astrologer, one who apparently operates at Rome and in Propertius' own (Augustan) age. Despite some views to the contrary, it is now generally regarded that Horos cuts an amusing and unreliable figure in Propertius' poem. His immediate obsession with establishing his credentials as an astrologer suggests a lack of confidence, and only makes us more suspicious of his authority.[26] Our initial suspicions are confirmed when Horos attempts to bolster his reputation as an astrologer by recalling previous examples of his successful predictions, some of which have nothing to do with the art: one does not need astrology to 'predict' death in warfare (89–90) nor to advise a woman in labour to pray to Juno Lucina (99–102)![27] Even when Horos offers an accurate account of Propertius' upbringing (121–34), he fails to present any astrological evidence on which he might have based this information: on the contrary, it would appear that Horos has gleaned at least some of this information from the less impressive

---

[25] See F. H. Cramer 1954: 83–98; Barton 1994c: 47–54; and my own monograph in preparation (n. 1). Cramer tends to argue that the literature of the early imperial period mixes acceptance of astrology as a science with scepticism. I do not see criticism of the art *per se* during this period—outside 'mock' debating halls (Sen. *Suas.* 4.3)—but rather a complex of admiration and proper restraint.

[26] For Horos' obsession with credentials, especially his predilection for *certus* and *fides*, cf. Prop. 4.1.75–6, 79–80, 91–2, 98. Stahl 1985: 270 is perhaps right to suggest that Horos evokes the image of 'a cheap seer in the streets of Rome', though I would argue that this only serves to ridicule the practitioner: it does not, as Stahl suggests, ridicule the art of astrology *per se*.

[27] See further Hutchinson 2006 *ad loc.*

means of 'eavesdropping' on what Propertius was saying in the earlier part of 4.1.[28]

Horos is, then, a fraud, a figure of fun, a con man who, despite appealing to credibility, manages to offer no tangible evidence of his ability to predict things from reading the stars. Laughing at the phoney practitioner, however, does not in any way entail an attack on astrology itself: Propertius offers no views either way about the science itself, and has certainly not revealed any of its secrets. This is one way of safely handling astrology in the Augustan age.

A reluctance to reveal credible information about the astrologer's craft manifests itself in a different form in Vitruvius and Ovid. Vitruvius, writing in the early Augustan age,[29] professes (1.1.3) that his subject, architecture, requires competence in a range of disciplines, including mathematics, music, philosophy, medicine, and astronomy. A working knowledge of astronomy, specifically the movement of the sun and moon, is required in the accurate construction of clocks and sundials (1.1.10). In book 9, Vitruvius duly embarks on a description of the heavenly movement of the moon and sun (9.2, 3), and shows additional enthusiasm for his stellar material by including a description of the northern and southern constellations (9.4, 5). When he comes to the topic of natal astrology (9.6), he praises its noble practitioners as men of great wisdom (*sollertia . . . acuminibusque . . . magnis*, 9.6.2) to whose special skills we must yield (*Chaldaeorum ratiocinationibus est concendum*, 9.6.2). Natal astrology is outside Vitruvius' thematic scope as teacher of architecture—it has nothing to do with the calculations required for making clocks or dials—and yet he has drawn attention to the practice only to concede it to specialists: a perfect means of toeing an appropriate imperial line between respect for an important, en vogue art and awareness of the need not to unlock secrets.

It is not surprising perhaps that Vitruvius, an avid supporter of Octavian/Augustus,[30] should tread so carefully in this area. Much more startling, however, is the fact that the mischievous Ovid also

---

[28] E.g. Horos' information about Propertius' birthplace (121–4) might well have been drawn from his eavesdropping on Propertius' words at 63–4.

[29] Scholars tend to locate Vitruvius in the 20s BC before 22 BC; see Howe and Rowland 1999: 3–5.

[30] For the evidence for Vitruvius' apparently close (working) relationship with Julius Caesar and Octavian/Augustus, see Howe and Rowland 1999: 5–7.

appears to have actively thought against dealing with such a topic. In a fascinating piece on Ovid's *Fasti*, Herbert-Brown 2002 draws our attention to the absence of astrology from the poem. In particular, she analyses Ovid's eulogy to stargazers early in the poem (1.295–310) and draws specific attention to a contextual inconsistency. Having sung the praises of stargazers, Ovid purports to deal with the *vaga signa* (1.314), the 'wandering constellations', a clear reference to the planets, the bodies on which the art of astrology depends. This is quite understandable from a thematic point of view, as one can well imagine the sort of creative (and subversive) potential such a topic would have offered a poet like Ovid. It is all the more surprising, then, that the extant work does not comment on any planets. Rather than trying to explain the discrepancy by changing the meaning of *vaga signa*, Herbert-Brown interprets it as the clearest sign of an *excision* of astrological material from a revised edition of the poem following the Augustan edict of AD 11.[31] Whether or not we are prepared to hang such a bold interpretation on a few words of text, Ovid's astrological reticence certainly fits the wider context of contemporary political nervousness surrounding the art and would (if true) be fascinating evidence of Ovid's recognition of the need to react to fast-changing official imperial postures towards astrology, especially if he is still holding out a hope for a return from exile.

Augustan writers then, whilst not abandoning all treatment of astrology, are sensitive to the lines that should not be crossed. At the time when Manilius is composing his *Astronomica*, traditionally *c.*AD 9–16,[32] the imperial nervousness surrounding astrology is, as we have seen, at its most fervent. And yet Manilius does not shy away from purporting to teach astrology to the lay reader who, simply by virtue of being human, is in the position to understand the principles of horoscopic astrology. Just in case we allow ourselves to think that Manilius is being politically absent-minded here, producing a poem as if divorced from its socio-political climate, this impression is

[31] For the unfinished state of the poem, and the question of revision of the text (from exile), see Green 2004: 15–25.

[32] For the continuing debate about the dating of the poem, see the introductory chapter by Volk in this volume. I am certainly not restricting myself to a dating of the poem after the edict of AD 11 (though this seems likely): the spirit of the law would surely have been felt many years beforehand; for Augustus' nervousness at unofficial prophetic utterances, see also n. 23 above.

quickly dispelled by the address to a *Caesar* (*Astr.* 1.7), probably Augustus.[33] It is important to recognize that there need not have been any address to the Emperor in this work—it is not required of the genre, the Emperor is never addressed again, and he appears not to have been the inspiration for the work nor an individual that requires instruction.[34] Manilius does attempt to create a flattering causal nexus between his subject matter and the Emperor—by suggesting that the peace brought by the *princeps*, as well as his divine status, make heaven more ready to disclose its astrological secrets (*Astr.* 1.7-13)—but it remains a very bold move to include an imperial dedicatee for this work in light of the socio-political climate: who in their right mind would advertise to an Emperor that he was intending to divulge all astrological secrets to the general Roman reader? The answer to that question is, I suggest, one who is in fact complicit with the Emperor, someone who has no real intention of doing what he purports to do, and intends instead to ensure that astrology remains an obscure, overly specialized, and ultimately inaccessible craft.

What I am suggesting, at a poetic level, is that Manilius constructs two different addressees in the work: an imperial dedicatee and a generalized reader, both of whose interests he purports to serve. These addressees are quite different from each other: the generalized reader constructed by the text, with whom the Roman reader might want to identify himself, is eager to learn about astrology; the Emperor, by contrast, has no need to learn this lesson (as he has others to construct positive astrological discourse around him) and has no desire for others to learn it. Manilius, I argue, ultimately serves the interests of his less visible addressee, the Emperor.

---

[33] For the ambiguities surrounding the identity of the Caesar(s) at Man. 1.7 and 4.935, see esp. Neuburg 1993: 244–57; Volk 2002: 200–1. For my purposes, it is the imperial (and hence intensely political) nature of the addressee that is important, rather than his specific identity. Even without a direct reference to an emperor, the very process of reading a self-purported 'manual' on astrology at this time may be interpreted as a subversive political act, as one colludes with the 'teacher' to learn something prohibited; for the politics of early imperial didactic in general, see Sharrock 1994, esp. 103–8.

[34] Even Lucretius maintains the pretence that he is instructing his political addressee, Memmius: addressed first at Lucr. 1.21–8, he is 'instructed' at regular intervals (e.g. Lucr. 1.1052, 2.142, 2.182, 5.1282).

Didactic: developing the poetics of obscurity

In attempting such a bold project—purporting to teach a frontline student but actually serving the interests of a less obvious reader—Manilius turned fittingly to the poetic medium and the didactic genre, which by his day had become malleable enough to accommodate such a complex agenda.[35] In Roman times, the didactic genre was far more complex than is suggested by its surface façade of providing instruction to student(s) in a poetic form. It was a playful medium in which the author could: create disjuncture between message (content) and medium (form and style); speak with various differing voices, providing 'polyphony' if not open contradiction; speak to the interests of differing audiences.[36]

All three elements of play are in evidence in Manilius. The disjuncture between instruction and medium is most obviously felt in book 3, where complex mathematical calculations are unhelpfully confined to hexameter and obscured behind poetic periphrasis.[37] Moreover, as I have suggested above, Manilius' didactic voice is by no means uniform, in that outward exhortations to the student's ability to grasp the material are matched with more subtle but sustained attempts to undermine the student's current knowledge. But it is the third element of play—the speaking to different audiences—which interests me most, as Manilius appears to develop a strategy that he may have picked up from his immediate predecessor, Ovid, in his erotodidactic works.

In general terms, one can readily detect an influence from Ovid's *Ars Amatoria* and *Remedia Amoris*, since (on my reading) both authors set out to teach the unteachable: how to fall in love, how to manage a relationship, how to rid oneself of love, and how to cast a horoscope are all 'arts' which are, for one reason or another, resistant to static instruction. But *Ars* 3 in particular may have provided

---

[35] That didactic *verse* is not a potentially serious medium for instruction (compared to didactic *prose*) is a popular modern misconception. On the contrary, poetry in the ancient world was thought to command authority as an instructional medium; see Hutchinson 2009: 197–8.

[36] For various useful formulations of the dynamics of didactic literature, see Effe 1977: 26–39; Heath 1985: 253–5; Toohey 1996; Volk 2002: 44–68.

[37] Manilius specifically draws attention to the challenge of fitting technical instruction into (hexameter) verse—*Astr.* 1.20–4, 3.31–42, 4.431–42—sentiments which reveal a desire for literary notoriety even if it is at the expense of useful instruction.

inspiration for Manilius.[38] After two books instructing men on how to find, approach, and keep hold of a woman, Ovid turns his attention in *Ars* 3 ostensibly to the amatory instruction of women. Recent scholarship, however, has persuasively argued that women are not really offered independent instruction from Ovid in *Ars* 3: rather, they are being groomed to look attractive and take on a passive role so that they become 'sophisticated accomplices' in the male game of love as expounded in *Ars* 1 and 2. Male-oriented instruction in *Ars* 3 implies the presence of a male audience for the book, and scholars have detected that *Ars* 3 actually has two groups of addressees, the more obvious female audience and a more covert set of men whom Ovid appears to address in transitional passages: and it is this less obvious, 'eavesdropping' set of addressees whose interests the instruction of *Ars* 3 ultimately serves.

In summary, Manilius is an author steeped in the traditions and dynamics of the didactic genre. It is tempting to read his poem as a culmination of the various playful generic features that have been developing in the past decades of Roman didactic poetry: like Virgil's *Georgics*, Manilius does something other than teach; like Ovid's *Remedia Amoris*, Manilius teaches a lesson that ultimately fails; and like Ovid's *Ars Amatoria* 3, he takes on and develops the technique of serving the interests of an audience in the background.

CONCLUSION

Astrology was, by the early years AD, a most fashionable subject and the most authoritative form of divination around. Manilius' poem, along with the stellar literature of Ovid and Germanicus, are certainly part of this new trend. Other contributions to this volume have drawn attention to the positive political resonance of Manilius' poem, such as the poet's promotion of Augustan architecture, the boundlessness of Rome's empire and knowledge, and the flattering comparison between the workings of the Emperor and the divine.[39] My chapter has continued this line of inquiry by drawing attention to something potentially anti-imperial which Manilius makes a specific point of *not*

---

[38] For what follows on *Ars* 3, see more fully Green 2006: 11–14.
[39] See, respectively, Abry, Kennedy, and Gale in this volume.

doing. I would argue that the poem operates as a subtle form of imperial propaganda which attempts to negotiate a path through the political problems that surround the issue of astrology. In the light of the popular interest in the practice and the corresponding insecurity on the part of the imperial household, it was both appropriate and tactful for Manilius to deal with astrology but present it as an obscure, highly technical, and hence essentially specialized practice. Astrological knowledge is hot property...if you can get it. Though the poem is ostensibly addressed to the lay reader, it actually serves an imperial purpose by ensuring that the lesson gradually overwhelms its readers. Only the divine Emperor is left standing.

Part III

Metaphors

9

Tropes and figures

Manilian style as a reflection of astrological tradition

Wolfgang Hübner

Manilius lived in the late Augustan/early Tiberian period, at around the same time as Ovid, with whom he may be justly compared in terms of style and poetic versatility. Joseph Justus Scaliger appreciated Manilius' style with the following words: 'Ovidio suavitate par, maiestate superior'.[1] This judgment is appropriate not only for the philosophical passages, but also for the more distinctly astrological material.

Poetry and astrology are both essentially metaphorical. The entire starry firmament can be comprehended as a sum of metaphors, since the human mind transposes the real world that surrounds it up into the sky, and this initial transfer from earth up to heaven is then followed by a reversal from heaven down to earth, when the figures and movements of the constellations are related back to human life by prognostication.[2] Manilius expresses this mutual relation between mortals and the

---

[1] Scaliger 1655: 18: 'poeta ingeniosissimus, nitidissimus scriptor, qui obscuras res tam luculento sermone, materiam morosissimam tam iucundo charactere exornare potuerit, Ovidio suavitate par, maiestate superior' ('a very ingenious poet, a very elegant writer, who was able to decorate obscure arguments with such clear language, the very morose material by such a pleasant quality, equal to Ovid in sweetness, in majesty superior'). See also Garrod 1911: lxxiv: 'he has in addition a grace and charm, a fluency and limpidity of style which brings him near to Ovid'.

[2] Topitsch 1972: 24 and 115 'Projektion und Reflexion'; see also Denningmann 2005: 3–7.

universe in an elegant verse (2.38):[3] *terraque composuit caelum quae pendet ab illo* ('the earth fashioned the sky on which it depends'). Note the timelessness of the present tense (*pendet*) in comparison with the historical act of inventing the celestial constellations (*composuit*).[4]

As such, poetry and its subject matter in the *Astronomica*—or, as Manilius terms it, the *carmen* and the *res* (1.20–4)—are more closely related to each other than in other didactic poems, not only those classified by Effe 1977 as 'sachbezogen' ('straightforwardly instructional') but even Virgil's *Georgics*. It is indeed a fundamentally incomplete approach to deal with Manilius, as so often happens, without paying attention to his investment in the astrological tradition. Over the years, stylistic particularities have encouraged me on several occasions to investigate the astrological sense hidden behind them. I shall here select only a few examples, arranging them either according to stylistic tropes and figures or to astrological data. Often, different stylistic phenomena are combined, reminding us that there is no clear dividing line between tropes and figures, or indeed between individual specific phenomena.[5]

FIGURES

The concept of *figura* touches upon both stylistic and astrological phenomena.[6] All constellations are 'figures', sometimes merely geometrical ones like the Triangulum, the rhombus of the Dolphin, or the square of

---

[3] I generally follow the edn. and translation of Goold: *Astr.* 2.38: *caelum* trad., *mundum* Housman 1903–30, 1932; Liuzzi 1983; Goold 1977, 1985; Fels 1990; Feraboli *et al.* 1996–2001. Cf. Volk 2001: 95 n. 16; 2002: 222. For *caelum*, see Lühr 1969: 28 n. 3; Liuzzi 1991–7: 2.125; Hübner 2002: 68 n. 73. On *caelum* and *mundus* in Manilius, see Liuzzi 1986: 43. *Caelum* here is a synecdoche meaning 'the stars of heaven', see below.

[4] Compare Volk in this volume who, continuing to read *mundum*, believes that Manilius here actually endorses the philosophical view that it is the earth which depends on heaven.

[5] I omit from the discussion the accumulation of effects in the contrasting stories of the two constellations rising with the Crab, the huge hero Orion and his little dog Procyon (*Astr.* 5.174–96, 197–205), which create a higher and lower stylistic level, respectively; see Hübner 2010: 2.99–114.

[6] Manilius says that the universe could hardly be described even in prose: *vixque soluta suis immittit verba figuris* ('scarce allowing even words of prose to be fitted to their proper phrasing', 1.24). This line has generated significant philological discussion. Bentley 1739, van Wageningen 1915, and Liuzzi 1991–7: 1.115 are most

Figure 9.1. The mixed figure of Capricorn. Codex Leidensis Vossianus lat. 79 (9th cent.), fo. 50ᵛ. University Library, Leiden University. Reproduced by permission.

Pegasus.[7] Moreover, the constellations form triangular, quartile, or sextile aspects within the zodiac when viewed from the central earth.

One of the strangest zodiacal signs is represented by Capricorn, the goat whose anterior part ends in a fish-tail (see Figure 9.1). Manilius

---

convincing in taking this to refer to the shapes of the constellations; see Waszink 1956: 589–90, who shows that only Manilius uses this word for the stars (*TLL* 6.729.40–4). Ambiguity, suggested by Volk 2002: 240–1, is less probable. Some material on stylistic figures has been collected by A. Cramer 1882: ch. 4, 'De Manilii figuris et tropis'. Fine observations can be found in Salemme 1983: 107–46 (= 2000: 105–43), ch. 5, 'Il realismo espressivo'.

[7] Hipparchus (*apud* Eratosth. *Cat.* 23 extr.) sees a triangular shape in the Pleiades. On the Triangulum, see Hübner 2006*a*.

emphasizes its 'figure'—*regione tuae, Capricorne, figurae* (5.390)[8]—in order to indicate conformity between this sign and its first extrazodiacal companion (*paranatellon*), Ophiuchus (Serpentarius), which is likewise composed of two elements: a human figure carrying a snake. So *figura* may reveal the extreme associative and speculative relationship between the zodiacal signs and their extrazodiacal companions.[9]

Already the simple figure of enumeration can have an astrological meaning. Ptolemy uses the stylistic term ποικιλία ('variation') in order to proceed to an extreme individualization provoked by the five planets or the variegated series of the twelve zodiacal signs.[10] Manilius often enumerates *mille artes* ('thousand activities') or *innumerae artes* ('unnumbered activities'), but in the context of the zodiacal Fishes, this abundant enumeration corresponds to the extremely prolific nature of fish that astrology transferred to the complete fourth triangle composed of beings far away from human nature (Crab–Scorpio–Fishes).[11]

----

[8] In general, the Greek word for the double or mixed signs, δίσημον, 'of two bodies', is translated by *bicorporeus* only later; in the classical period it is dismembered into two separate words, cf. *Astr.* 2.660 *duplici . . . figura*; see Hübner 1982: 74–7, no. 1.311, and 104–10, no. 2.21.

[9] More conventional is the circular composition Manilius employs in describing the round figure of the Crown (Corona). The poet frames the related passage with *Coronae*, a word which concludes the verse at the beginning and, in a punch line, at the very end of the passage: *Astr.* 5.253 *Ariadnaeae . . . Coronae* and 5.269 *floresque Coronae*.

[10] Ptol. *Tetr.* 4.4.9 πρὸς τὸ ποικίλον τῶν πράξεων ('towards the variation of the activities'), cf. 2.9.19; 3.14.2; 4.9.2. Vett. Val. 1.3.45 πᾶσαι δὲ ἐν τῷ Τοξότῃ [sc. μοίραι] ποικίλαι περὶ πάντα τὰ πράγματα ('all degrees within the Archer are manifold concerning all the activities'). More prolix Firm. *Math.* 3.6.26 (Venus culminating above): *sicut enim in imaginibus artifex pictor liniamenta membrorum ex varia mixturarum diversitate persignat et temperatis coloribus certam corporis formam imitatione facit similitudinis corporalis, sic et stellarum coniuncta radiatio societatis consensu pariter temperata vim quandam vicissim ex coniunctis sibi potestatibus mutuatur et substantia sibi ex diverso ignium colore collata fata hominum ad picturae modum aequata societatis moderatione depingit* ('For as a painter designs in his pictures the lines of the members by a different variety of mixture, and creates, by imitation and the mixture of colours, a certain form of the body, in the same manner the combined radiation of the stars, tempered equally by consensus of participation, modifies a certain effect from the powers that are connected with it, and the substance that is joined from the different colours of the starry fires paints, like in picture, the destiny of men, by the tempered mixture of partnership').

[11] *Astr.* 4.277 *innumerae veniunt artes* ('there rise innumerable activities'). In the zodiacal geography, 4.805 *innumeris vix complectenda figuris* ('that can scarcely be comprehended by (verbal) figures'). For the fertility of the Fishes, cf. *Astr.* 2.237 *partu*

Dealing with the constellation of the Arrow (Sagitta) that rises together with the Balance, Manilius gives three examples of skilful archers,[12] following the strange *Sphaera barbarica* invented by Teucer of Babylon (probably Babylon in Egypt).[13] According to Manilius, Sagitta rises with the eighth degree of Libra, which was at that period commonly accepted as the autumnal point, where Hipparchus had detected the precession of the annual points.[14] The prediction of archers is related to the 'stochastic' art, and the name of the first archer, Teucer, may have inspired Teucer of Babylon to his pseudonym.[15] The enumeration of three mythical examples alludes to the name of two uncanonical constellations that rise with the Balance (perhaps only two variants of the same constellation):[16] first 'The three Heros, also named Archers' (Τρεῖς Ἥρωες οἱ καὶ Βαλλισταί), second the Trident (Greek Τρίαινα), at which Manilius had already hinted (*cuspide vel triplici securum figere piscem*, 'or piercing with three-pronged spear the fish that deemed itself so safe', 5.297[17]). So the number of examples—three—is of high astrological importance. They seem, by the way, to correspond to the three stars in Sagitta's shaft listed by Ptolemy in his *Almagest*.[18]

From simple enumeration, we move to word order. When dealing with the constellation of Cepheus, under whom are apparently born budding playwrights, Manilius refers to the comedies of Menander and, in particular, his comic characters (5.472–3):

> ardentis iuvenes raptasque in amore puellas
> elusosque senes agilisque per omnia servos.

> Burning youths and abducted maidens in love,
> deceived old men, and slaves quick-witted in all matters.

---

complentes aequora Pisces ('the Fishes, filling the sea with their offspring'); 4.582 Venus instilled her fire into the Fishes (see Hübner 1982: 156–64, no. 3.321).

[12] *Astr.* 5.298–310: Teucer (the brother of Ajax from Salamis), Philoctetes, and Alcon (an ancient precursor of Wilhelm Tell).

[13] Boll 1903; Gundel 1949; Hübner 1975, 1995*b*: 1.92–3.

[14] Neugebauer 1975: 1.286–7 and 2.594–8; see also Hübner 2007.

[15] Hübner 1993: 22–3.

[16] Teucer, ed. Hübner 1995*b*: 1.118–9 (1.7.6) and 1.125 (1.12.10), with commentary.

[17] Differently Firm. *Math.* 8.12.1 *tridente vel cuspide* ('with a trident or a spear'). Skutsch 1910: 632 blames an erroneous translation, but Firmicus depends on the common source (see Hübner 1975: 401–3).

[18] Ptol. *Alm.* 7.5 p. 72–3.14 Heiberg τῶν ἐν τῷ καλάμῳ τριῶν ('of the three (stars) situated in the shaft').

We will notice here a chiasmic arrangement from active to passive (*ardentis ... raptas*) and back from passive to active (*elusos ... agiles*): the young men desire the girls, the old men are tricked by the slaves. As I have shown elsewhere,[19] the four characters as described here could be equally reminiscent of four of the five real planets that are visually arranged in a quincunx figure in ancient diagrams (see Figure 9.2). This order is far from arbitrary, as Manilius alludes first, with the use of *ardentis*, to the two hot planets surrounding the central sun, namely, the well-known couple of Mars and Venus (the erotic overtones of these two planet deities are also captured in *iuvenes ... puellas*); then, with the contrast between *senes* and *agilis*, Manilius alludes to the two planets furthest away from the sun, the old and slow Saturn and the young and quick Mercury (see Figure 9.3).[20] Given that in the Chaldaean system Venus ranks between the sun and Mercury, in the series of the five real planets (not counting the two luminaries, sun and moon), Saturn and Mercury represent the extreme positions of the scale: the slowest and the quickest. In both pairs the exterior planet precedes the interior one.

Figure 9.2. The comic characters of Menander according to *Astr.* 5.472–3. Diagram Wolfgang Hübner.

	exterior planet	interior planet
near the sun	MARS	VENUS
far from the sun	SATURN	MERCURY

Figure 9.3. The characters of the four planets according to *Astr.* 5.472–3. Diagram Wolfgang Hübner.

---

[19] Hübner 1984: 215.
[20] For another articulation of this antithesis, cf. Verg. *G.* 1.336–7 (quoted also by Sen. *Ep.* 88.14): *frigida Saturni sese quo stella receptet, quos ignis caelo Cyllenius erret in orbis* ('where retires the frigid planet of Saturn, in what circles errs the fire of Mercury in the sky').

	North Jupiter		
West Mars	Mercury	Saturn **East**	
	Venus **South**		

Figure 9.4. Planetary geography according to Ptolemy, *Tetrabiblos* 2.3. Diagram Wolfgang Hübner.

In his *Almagest*, in an explanation of his theory of planetary epicycles, Ptolemy arranges the five planets in a similar way, first one single planet and then two pairs: Mercury (book 9), Venus and Mars (book 10), Jupiter and Saturn (book 11). His planetary geography could be reduced to Figure 9.4.[21]

But in Manilius one planet is missing, namely the 'jovial' Jupiter, the reasonable deity in his best age, exempt from all comic features. He would occupy the middle in a quincunx-figure, comparable to what we see (in another planetary distribution with Saturn in the middle) in the Carolingian Codex Leidensis Vossianus (Figure 9.5).

This kind of two-dimensional figure was well known in antiquity, and it could be read in four directions: from left to right, right to left, top downwards, or bottom upwards.[22] A parallel is offered by Servius during his discussion of how the souls sink down from heaven to earth. The souls assume in each planetary sphere a different vice, and—though writing in prose—Servius adopts a similar chiastic formula (Serv. *ad Aen.* 6.714):[23]

> cum descendunt animae, trahunt secum
> torporem *Saturni, Martis* iracundiam,
> libidinem *Veneris, Mercurii* lucri cupiditatem,
> *Iovis* regni desiderium.

[21] Ptol. *Tetr.* 2.3; see Hübner 1998: 99.
[22] I have collected some examples in Hübner 1989: 58–62.
[23] See also Hübner 1997: 45–81, esp. 51.

Figure 9.5. Quincunx of the planets. Codex Leidensis Vossianus lat. 79 (9th cent.), fo. 80ᵛ. University Library, Leiden University. Reproduced by permission.

> When the spirits descend, they drag with them
> the sloth of *Saturn*, the anger of *Mars*,
> the sexual appetite of *Venus,* the desire for profit associated with
>   *Mercury*,
> and a longing for kingdom associated with *Jupiter*.

Here again Jupiter is excluded from the two chiasmic arrangements. We have to read the Manilian quartet (Figure 9.3) on the left bottom upwards and on the right top downwards to get the Servian order. So the stylistic chiasmus that we witness in both Manilius and Servius might well correspond to the astrological and mnemotechnic classification of the planets.

By another stylistic phenomenon, comparison, Homer opens within the heroic world a kind of window onto real life.[24] Didactic poets developed this epic form for their own purpose, as demonstrated in Claudia Schindler's excellent thesis (2000). Manilius also employs it for the interpenetration of macrocosm and microcosm. Having already treated the melothesia (the correspondence of the zodiacal signs and the members of the human body) in book 2,[25] he repeats it before exposing the zodiacal geography in book 4 in the parenthetic form of an epic comparison.[26] In this traditional epic technique, he found a tool to embrace the world-wide ubiquity of the twelvefold structure.

There are two verses written about the messengers born under the winged Pegasus, which rise together with the equally winged Fishes (5.640–1):[27]

> nam quis ab extremo citius revolaverit orbe
> nuntius extremumve levis penetraverit orbem?

Who more swiftly could fly back from the ends of the earth
as a messenger or with light foot to the earth's end make the way?

By describing the movement back from far away, and then—by return of post—a repeat of the outward journey, Manilius adopts the point of view of somebody who first receives and then delivers a message. The repetition of the hyperbolic expression[28] *ab extremo . . . orbe* and *extremum . . . orbem* corresponds to the reciprocal position of the two zodiacal Fishes, called *enantiodromia* (crossing position) by Jung and visible in idealized form in Figure 9.6.[29] This depiction is a fanciful interpretation of the real configuration of the Fishes, which may be seen in Figure 9.7.

---

[24] Schadewaldt 1952.

[25] *Astr.* 2.453–65, following the *tutelae* of the twelve gods.

[26] *Astr.* 4.704–9, one of the numerous zodiacal hexasticha that contain a pair of signs in each line. For the repeated melothesia, see Hübner 1984: 237–42.

[27] For the winged Fishes, cf. Rhetorius, *CCAG* 7.4 (216.13): 'in the winged signs, I mean in the first degrees of the Fishes because of (simultaneously rising) Pegasus'; see Hübner 1982: 125–6, no. 2.313.2.

[28] See Flores 1966: 99. On hyperbole in Manilius, see A. Cramer 1882: 51; Müller 1903: 82 n. 20; Breiter 1907–8: 119 *ad Astr.* 4.262; Bühler 1959: 475–6 *ad Astr.* 5.222 and 494 *ad Astr.* 1.926; Salemme 1983: 130 (= 2000: 128), who follows Breiter. On hyperbole in general, Hunziker 1896 is still illuminating.

[29] See Jung 1978: 81–103, esp. 103; see also 96 ('Gegensatzvereinigung').

Figure 9.6. The idealized *enantiodromia* of the zodiacal Fishes. Impression of a marble slab from Roman Egypt. From Boll 1903, Table VI, reproduced by permission.

Apart from the repetition there is an important difference between the two verbs. The verb *revolaverit* alludes to the winged nature of the northern fish, named 'Swallow-Fish' by the Babylonians,[30] whereas *penetraverit* (not rendered verbatim by Goold) corresponds to the aquatic nature of the diving southern fish. The contrast between the two verbal metaphors corresponds to the fundamental struggle

[30] See Bouché-Leclercq 1899: 148 + n. 2; Boll 1903: 196–7; Boll and Gundel 1924–37: 46–54, 979.

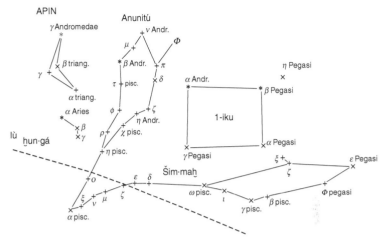

Figure 9.7. The real configuration of the two zodiacal Fishes. Diagram B. van der Waerden. From *Journal of Near Eastern Studies* 8 (1949), p. 15, reproduced by permission.

between *water*, the element of winter and the Whale, and *air*, the element of springtime and of both Pegasus and Perseus, who defeated the Whale in a contest only recently described in the Andromeda epyllion (5.538–618).[31]

While the repetition of *orbe/orbem* occurs in two subsequent verses, the repetition of *extremus* recurs at a ten-verse interval at the end of the zodiacal year. The two last true companions of the Fishes are contrasted on both sides of the ecliptic. First there is Engonasin, today referred to as Hercules (5.647): *dextra per extremos attollit lumina Pisces* ('brings forth its stars on the right simultaneously with the last portion of the Fishes'). Then there is Cetus, the Whale (5.656–7):[32] *laeva sub extremis consurgunt sidera Ceti / Piscibus* ('On the left, together with the last portion of the Fishes rise

---

[31] Here and in later examples in this chapter I maintain that the action of the Andromeda epyllion has an astrological meaning, and that there is a strong connection between the epyllion and its outer, Piscean context; see Hübner 1984: 197–201. For a different argument for the integrity of the Andromeda epyllion in the poem, see Uden in this volume.

[32] This parallelism is all the more significant since, in other cases, the poet uses different expressions, as for the signs of the first triangle: *Astr.* 5.128 (Capella with Aries 30°) *ultima . . . pars*; 5.234 (Crater with Leo 30°) *ultima pars*; 5.365 (Cygnus with Sagittarius 30°) *ter decima sub parte*.

the stars of the Whale'). Once more the poet alludes to the fundamental struggle between the two elements representing the seasons and between North and South—which provides another argument for identifying Engonasin-Hercules with Perseus, the subduer of Cetus (otherwise omitted as *paranatellon* in this book).[33] So the antagonism between Perseus and Cetus corresponds to the opposition between the two zodiacal Fishes, one of whom is winged while the other is merely an aquatic being.

You may have strong reservations about all these combinations. But there is a parallel to be found in modern Manilian research. Calcante 2002: 132 tries to replace a discarded and rebutted kind of 'Quellenforschung' with a new semiotic approach. Dealing with the epyllion of Andromeda and the effect of her constellation that engenders cruel hangmen (5.619–30), he compares the hangman with Perseus, the saviour of Andromeda, calling him an 'anti-Perseo' and vice versa Perseus an 'anti-carnefice'—without paying attention to the fact that Andromeda is a *paranatellon* of the two Fishes that swim in opposite directions, bound together by a band (Figure 9.6) as Andromeda is chained to the rock.[34] Without being aware of this, the ahistorical semiotic research works in the same manner as astrologers do.

The enantiodromia leads to verbal antithesis. In the astrological tradition, the weak stars of the zodiac are said to cause blindness by overstraining the eyes of the observer:[35] first of all the Cloud (Νεφέλιον, *Nubecula*) situated within the Crab. Manilius expresses blindness in a bold zeugmatic antithesis of two opposite verbs (4.534):[36] 'everyone lives and buries himself' (*se quisque et vivit et effert*).[37] The Crab is the first sign of the already mentioned last triangle that is composed of beings far from human nature. Under the third sign of this triangle, the Fishes, death will no longer be 'half', but definitive, as it has been

---

[33] See Hübner 1982: 623–34; 1984: 193–203.

[34] See Hübner 1984: 197–212; 2007: 98 and 102.

[35] See Hübner 1982: 193–6, no. 3.423.3.

[36] For the astrological explanation Manilius employs a nominal polyptoton; cf. 4.531–2 *qua velut exustus Phoebeis ignibus ignis / deficit et multa fuscat caligine sidus* ('where his own fire fails, as though burnt out by the Sun's, and darkens the signs with impenetrable fog').

[37] Other examples: 1.253 *faciatque feratque* ('furnish and receive'); 1.537 *veniuntque caduntque* ('coming into view and setting'); 1.862 *sequiturque fugitque* ('pursues and shuns'); 2.88 *redditque rapitque* ('gives and takes away'). As an effect of the tropic Ram, 5.49 *pelagus Xerxes facietque tegetque* ('Xerxes will open up a new sea and cover over the old'). See Christiansen 1908: 203–5.

described in cruel detail under the last *paranatellon*: the Whale (*Cetus*) is itself cruelly killed in the battle with Perseus.[38]

A good example of verbal antithesis reflects a stellar configuration near the North Pole. The septentrional Dragon both separates and embraces the two Bears: 1.306 *dividit et cingit*.[39] In this formula, the two opposite verbs correspond to the well-known dialectic ambiguity of the copula 'and': first we have to distinguish two objects before bringing them together again.[40] As for Ophiuchus and his snake, the two verbs are not paralleled, but syntactically combined: 'he displays the snake that embraces him' (1.331–2):[41]

> serpentem magnis Ophiuchus nomine gyris
> dividit et torto cingentem corpore corpus.

> The so-called Ophiuchus holds apart the serpent
> which with its mighty spirals and twisted body encircles his own.

Here, instead of the verbal antithesis, the interpenetration of the two bodies is expressed by the noun polyptoton *corpore corpus*.

This figure becomes all the more forceful when the verb remains the same, and such interpenetration induces the poet to eliminate the distinction between active and passive. In the distribution of the thirty-six *decani* (thirds of zodiacal signs, each of ten degrees)[42] over the twelve zodia, the two opposite signs of the solstices, Cancer and Capricorn, concede their first *decanus* to each other (Figure 9.8).

When Manilius comes to deal with Capricorn, he expresses the mutual interpenetration by eliminating the distinction as follows (4.351):[43] *munus reddit Cancro recipitque receptus* ('he (Capricorn) discharges his obligation to the Crab: welcomed himself to the Crab's domain, he welcomes the Crab to his').

---

[38] 5.558–681. See in greater detail Hübner 1984: 169–74.

[39] Cf. 1.452 [sc. *Arctos*] *distingui medias claudique Dracone* ('that (the Bears) are separated and encircled by the Dragon'). More generally, 4.364–5 [sc. *ratio*] *caelum / dividit et . . . sociat . . . orbem* ('it divides the heavens and associates the universe').

[40] It is well known that in general the former aspect is expressed by the Latin *et* and *atque*, and the second by the generalizing *-que*, as in *quisque, quicumque, ubique*, etc.

[41] In describing the two colures that cross the tropic point and the two poles, Manilius uses the same figure: 1.603 *quos recipit ductos a vertice vertex* ('which are drawn from one pole and received by the other').

[42] *Astr.* 4.312–62; cf. Bouché-Leclercq 1899: 217–19; Gundel 1936: 246–7.

[43] More conventional is 3.16 *victam quia vicerat urbem* ('conquered because of its conquest'); with an erotic touch, cf. 5.571–2 *victorque Medusae / victus in Andromeda est* ('the vanquisher of Medusa was vanquished at the sight of Andromeda').

zodiacal sign	first *decanus*	second *decanus*	third *decanus*
Aries	Aries	Taurus	Gemini
Taurus	Cancer	Leo	Virgo
Gemini	Libra	Scorpius	Sagittarius
Cancer	**Capricornus**	Aquarius	Pisces
Leo	Aries	Taurus	Gemini
Virgo	Cancer	Leo	Virgo
Libra	Libra	Scorpius	Sagittarius
Scorpius	Capricornus	Aquarius	Pisces
Sagittarius	Aries	Taurus	Gemini
Capricornus	**Cancer**	Leo	Virgo
Aquarius	Libra	Scorpius	Sagittarius
Pisces	Capricornus	Aquarius	Pisces

Figure 9.8. The 36 *decani* distributed over the twelve zodiacal signs. Diagram Wolfgang Hübner.

Once again, the same figure appears near the North Pole, in the description of the constant circular movement of the two Bears: 1.304 *sequiturque sequentem* ('and she follows her pursuer').[44] It should be added that the deponent form *sequitur* initiates the reciprocity, because the idea of active pursuit is expressed by a passive form. So already in the act of pursuing, she is also the object of pursuit.

As for polyptoton involving nouns, the following examples show a stronger astrological background. Like all 'tropic' (moveable) signs, the Crab favours trading: 4.169 *orbisque orbi bona vendere* ('selling the goods of the earth to the earth').[45] Here the polyptoton

---

[44] This is a Virgilian formula; cf. Verg. *Aen.* 11.695 (Camilla and her pursuer, compared by van Wageningen 1921: 59). Cf. the Bears at Arat. *Phaen.* 30.

[45] See Hübner 1982: 549–50 on *Astr.* 4.166 *quaestus artemque lucrorum* ('acquisition and the art of earning'). Cf. 3.86 *venit orbis in orbem* (mostly misunderstood): 'the circle comes back to itself (i.e. to its beginning)'. On this, see Valvo 1956: 116; she compares Asclep. 40 p. 351 *cum omnia se semper et praecedere videantur et sequi* ('when all seems always to precede itself and to follow'), which recalls the already mentioned verbal polyptoton on the two Bears at 1.304, *sequiturque sequentem*. Note

is facilitated by another typically Manilian stylistic figure, synecdoche, that is, the use either of a specific element to denote the entire
object, or—as Manilius prefers—of the general term to denote the
specific item (*totum pro parte*). The first form *orbis* strictly means
the habitable world, whereas the dative *orbi* refers via synecdoche
only to the inhabitants of the world.[46] Typical Manilian synec-
doches of this kind have often been misunderstood or changed by
inept conjecture.

Near the opposite winter solstice appears a corresponding combination of polyptoton and synecdoche under Capricorn and Cepheus,
signs that create together, among other natives, comedians or comic
writers who, like Menander, 'show real life to life':[47] 5.476 *vitae
ostendit vitam*. Elsewhere I have demonstrated in more detail that
this formula goes back to one literary and two astrological roots.[48]
Literary tradition compares New Comedy to a mirror that reflects real
life. The stereotype of comic characters mentioned above resembles
the typology of astrological determinism. In this special case two
astrological data can be added, first the system of zodiacal signs that
regard (or hear) each other (see Figure 9.9).[49] In the middle of Cancer
and Capricorn the parallels of regarding converge into one point,
with the result that Capricorn regards itself, creating the mirror of
comedy. The second astrological root is a strange constellation of
Teucer's *Sphaera barbarica* that, in the circle of the so-called *dode-
caoros*, corresponds to Capricorn: the Ape (*Πίθηκος*), the mimetic
animal *par excellence*.

the astrological interest in the repetition of 'merchandise' by a distance of 180° in *Astr.*
4.167 *merce* (Cancer) and 4.252 *mercem* (Capricorn).

[46] Cf. 3.591 [sc. *mundus*] *redit in terras* ('the sky comes back to earth [i.e. into the
field of vision for terrestrial inhabitants]'); compare the dative at 5.104 = 5.129 *terris*.

[47] See Salemme 1983: 114–15 n. 11 (= 2000: 112–13 n. 10), who classifies this under
'Influenza della retorica', hinting at Lanson 1887: ch. 4 'Quam rhetorice Manilius rem
astrologicam tractaverit'.

[48] For greater detail, see Hübner 1984: 187–91.

[49] See Hübner 1982: 64–72, no. 1.221. The acoustic complement under Lyra with
Libra 26° depicts a solitary singer who sings only for himself: 5.336 *solus et ipse suas
semper cantabit ad aures* ('and, left to himself, he will ever sing to his own ears').
Manilius uses a reflexive construction, in the opposite equinox, for the Ram—2.485
consilium ipse suum est Aries ('the Ram is his own counsel')—and once more for
Capricorn: 2.507–8 *Capricornus in ipsum / convertit visus* ('Capricorn turns his gaze
upon himself'), hinting at the autarchic Augustus.

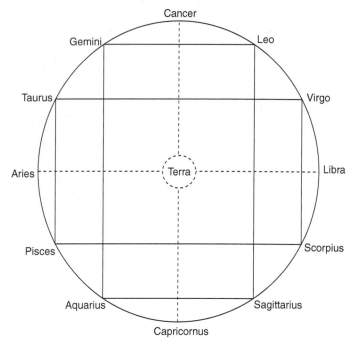

Figure 9.9. The system of signs that are 'regarding' (horizontal lines) or 'hearing' each other (perpendicular lines). Diagram Wolfgang Hübner.

TROPES

In stylistic terms, τρόπος means 'version',[50] a slight distortion of the sense; in astronomy τροπή signifies the turning point of the sun within the two zodiacal signs that are furthest removed from the celestial equator, Cancer and Capricorn. Astrology designates as tropic signs also the two equinoctial signs, Aries and Libra. So the four signs of the so-called first square are all 'tropic', signs of change.[51] Manilius translates the term τροπικός by *mutare*[52] or

---

[50] Calcante 2002: 126 (on *Astr.* 5.121 *rerumque tumultus*) speaks about 'il tropo tropico della sedizione come tempesta' without hinting at the fact that the Hyades are rising together with the tropic Ram; see Hübner 1982: 536.

[51] Bouché-Leclercq 1899: 170–1; Hübner 1982: 74–80, no. 1.311.

[52] Cf. *Astr.* 2.191 *mutantque in tempora signum* ('they change the sign to suit the change of season').

vertere.[53] For the related prognostications he uses the former in different metaphors: the sailor born under Argo with Aries 4°, that is, near the vernal equinox, 'inverts sea for land' (*mutabit pelago terras*, 5.42). The merchant born under the Southern Fish and the tropic Capricorn 'purchases at a fixed wage another's labour and exchanges it' (*emit externos pretio mutatque labores*, 5.407). Victories are also turning points. When the Romans defeated an enemy they believed that they owed their success to *Jupiter Versor* or *Mars Versor* and dressed a τρόπαιον. But Manilius goes further: the constellation of Argo causes both a victory and a defeat in sea-battles, as a former victory (Salamis) is balanced by a subsequent defeat (Syracuse): *versa Syracusis Salamis non merget Athenas* ('(without this constellation) Salamis, reversed by Syracuse, will not immerse Athens', 5.50). The metaphor *versa* here is facilitated by the metonymy, since *Syracusis* stands for the defeat and *Salamis* for the victory.[54]

Metonymy

Synecdoche—in both directions—expresses the interpenetration of macrocosm and microcosm. It often concerns the expanded regions of the universe, earth, ocean, and heaven, and these regions are associated with three of the four astrological elements, the homonymic earth, water, and air (fire is excluded). Since Parmenides, the heaven is designated either by the mountain Olympus or by its northern πόλος[55] and the horizon by Ὠκέανος, conceived as a large river surrounding the earth.

At the beginning of the Andromeda epyllion, Manilius says that the parents 'exposed their daughter to the wild sea': 5.543 *vesano dedere ponto*. A similar idea is expressed a little later when the poet speaks of Perseus (5.575): *destinat in thalamos per bellum vadere ponti* ('he resolves to enter into marriage through war against the sea').[56] Critics

---

[53] Cf. *Astr.* 3.621–2 *quae tropica appellant, quod in illis quattuor anni / tempora vertuntur signis* ('which they call tropic signs, since in them turn the four seasons of the year'). Cf. also 3.666 *tempora vertunt* ('they change the seasons').

[54] Examples of metonymy and synecdoche were collected by A. Cramer 1882: 52–3. Synecdoche, in which the particular aspect stands in for the whole, is a linguistic form of magic analogy: Cassirer 1922: 42–3 = 48–9; 1925: 66 and 83.

[55] *Astr.* 1.225; esp. the northern part of the heaven: 5.131 and 693. If one is aware of this, one may avoid unnecessary conjectures like 2.38 *terra . . . composuit caelum.*

[56] Voss 1972: 416 is right in translating 'durch einen Kampf mit dem Meer'.

have pointed out that it was not the sea, but the Whale (*Cetus*) to whom Andromeda was offered.[57] But this is to overlook the astrological background. The synecdoche in *ponto* reveals the fundamental meaning of Perseus' struggle from the air above to the sea below, as I suggested a little earlier. The sea represents water, winter, and the South. In the same manner, the Ram, situated at the vernal equinox, which carried Phrixus and his sister Nephele across the Aegean and the Black Sea, like another Perseus, is named *ponti victor* ('conqueror of the sea', 5.21).[58] At the end of the passage about Argo, a third *ponti victor* is related to us: none other than Octavian, in the battle of Actium.[59]

Metonymy is combined with polyptoton when the fish-tailed Capricorn engenders, together with the Dolphin, swimmers of different kinds, and finally also divers 'looking for the treasures of the sea within the sea': 5.431 *in ponto ... quaerere pontum*. This expression reinforces the connection with the wet and cold element. In his corresponding chapter, Firmicus Maternus introduces the planet Saturn, which passes as humid because it moves the furthest from the sun.[60] It is more likely that Manilius replaced the planet by the stylistic metonymy than that Firmicus replaced the stylistic figure by the planet. Moreover, the Southern Fish, rising together with the beginning of Capricorn when the sun reaches the deepest point of its course, creates divers that bring up pearls from the depths of the sea. With a moralizing touch, Manilius says: *oneratur terra profundo* ('the land is burdened by the treasures of the depth', 5.405). The metonymy *profundo* enhances the contrast between earth and water, the two elements rivalling for the deepest position in the universe,[61]

---

[57] See e.g. Paschoud 1982: 138 n. 54: 'ce n'est évidemment pas la mer, qu'il va combattre, mais le monstre venu de la mer, qui n'est que le lieu du combat'. A similar metonymy misled Housman to a conjecture, accepted by some later scholars. At *Astr.* 5.660—*pontum vinclis armare furentem* ('to equip the wild sea with chains (= nets))'—he changes *furentem* to *furentes*, thereby shifting the fury from the animals of the sea to the fishermen. The parallels given before justify the transmitted text.

[58] According to Teucr. 1.1.4, Perseus rises exactly with the vernal point Aries 8°–10°; see Hübner 1995*b*: 1.108–9.

[59] *Astr.* 5.52–3, and since the parallels of hearing converge in one point (Fig. 9.9), another reflexive idea follows: 5.55 *coit ipsa sibi tellus* ('the earth comes together with itself'—either in commerce, or in the battle of Actium).

[60] Firm. *Math.* 8.15.2 *cum Saturni testimonio urinator erit* ('under the witness of Saturn he will be a diver').

[61] For this rivalry, see Hübner 1984: 150–8.

and recalls the two elements that comprise Capricorn itself: earth (in the form of the goat) and water (in the form of the fish).

The 'burdening of earth' also agrees with the astrological hierarchy whereby water was regarded as heavier than earth. This metaphor finds its complement at the very end of the Andromeda epyllion, that is, near the vernal point in quartile aspect to the winter solstice. The story does not end with the catasterism of Andromeda, but with the defeated Whale, whose weight 'lightens' the sea (5.617–18):[62]

> concidit ipsa
> Gorgone non levius monstrum pelagusque levavit.

> A monster no less terrible than the Gorgo herself
> perished and relieved the sea.

In a further sense, Andromeda is 'lightened' from a cruel death, and in this sense we find the corresponding metaphor at the opposite position under the Arrow, which rises with Libra 8°, the autumnal point. Alcon, the third of the three archers mentioned above, saves his son by striking a snake that had slithered across the sleeping boy. Once more, impending death is averted. As Manilius says, *et pariter iuvenem somnoque ac morte levavit* ('and he (Alcon) lightened the young man likewise from sleep and death', 5.309).[63] The two metaphors *pelagus . . . levavit* and *morte levavit* functionally form an opposition at the two decisive equinoctial points of the year.

Metaphor

As I pointed out at the beginning, metaphor is a fundamental operator of astrology. In modern literary theory we observe an inflation of this term that tends to embrace all kinds of symbolism, by metaphor of metaphor, but in this case we are really allowed to use the notion of *translatio*. The human mind has invented in the firmament all kinds of beings: human, animals, and soulless objects—flying, swimming, walking, running, standing, sitting, or extended. The ancients were aware

---

[62] The translation of Goold, 'relieved the sea of a curse', is misleading; cf. 5.581 *onus monstri* ('the weight of the monster').

[63] This linguistic parallel enhances the observation made by Feraboli *et al.* 1996–2001: 2.530 *ad Astr.* 5.538–639: 'due eroi del mito, Perseo e Alcone, salvano una creatura inerme prossima ad essere uccisa da un mostro'. Compare the zeugma at 4.534 (*se quisque et vivit et aufert*).

that the so-called 'fixed' constellations move during the daily rotation. The heavenly population therefore offers poetry manifold possibilities for metaphors, and Manilius does not fail to exploit this potential.[64] Here are just a few examples. Since the air and the sky are often equated, all constellations seem to 'fly'.[65] But when speaking about the six opposite pairs of zodia, Manilius uses the frequentative verb *volitare* ('keep flying') only for the winged signs Virgo and Pisces (2.414–15):[66]

> Pisces et Virginis artus
> adversi volitant, sed amant communia iura.

> The Fishes and the limbs of the Virgin
> keep flying in opposition but cherish the bonds they share.

The opposite position suggests some difference between the two constellations, but there is also conformity, alluded to already in the former part of the sentence: the noun *artus* evokes parts of their bodies, their wings, as does the verb *volitant*. Not only is the Virgin winged, in conformity with Aratus' goddess Dike (Justice),[67] but the two Fishes are likewise counted among the winged zodiacal signs because of the 'Swallow-Fish' (for which see the discussion above).

A special case is the rising of the Southern Fish, of which Manilius says, *alienis finibus ibit* ('it will walk in an unusual region', 5.395).[68] While Aratus and his translator Germanicus often use, respectively, the verbs ἰέναι and *ire* and composita for the movement of the constellations,[69] Manilius generally avoids them. In this case the metaphor emphasizes the constellation's relationship to Capricorn. The Fish 'walks' on heaven, as if it were on land, and this corresponds once again to the hybrid figure of the 'goat-fish', whom he accompanies. Heaven appears to be like land, just as the rising ship *Argo* is

---

[64] Many examples have been collected by A. Cramer 1882: 53–5.

[65] *Astr.* 1.200 *cum luna et stellae volitent per inania mundi* ('when the Moon and the stars wing their way through empty regions of the sky'); 1.806 *terram caelumque inter volitantia pendent* ('(the planets) in their swift orbit are poised between heaven and earth'); 2.18 *omnia . . . immenso volitantia lumina mundo* ('all the luminaries that fly through the vast heavens'). Of winged beings, cf. Cygnus (5.366 *evolat*), Pegasus (5.633 *caelo . . . volabit*).

[66] See Hübner 1984: 223 with n. 279.

[67] Cf. the end of her catasterism at Arat. *Phaen.* 134 ἔπταθ' ὑπορανίη ('she flew up to heaven').

[68] In the preceding line we read *se patrio producens aequore* ('heaving itself from its native waters'): it demands effort to rise from the extreme depths.

[69] See Santini 1981: 179–80.

'drawn from the sea to heaven' (*in caelum subducta mari*, 1.413; the verb *subducere* is the term for drawing ships on land).[70] Furthermore, *Argo* moves backwards, just as ships were drawn on land.[71]

The Southern Fish, situated below Capricorn at the winter solstice, has a rival on the northern hemisphere: the Dolphin, jumping from the water upwards to the air or sky. It procreates among other things *petauristae* (acrobatic jumpers) 'landing on the ground softly as in water' (*ut liquidis ponuntur in undis*, 5.443). Here, the two elements water and earth are connected by comparison instead of metaphor.

I omit special cases of metaphor such as hyperbole[72] in order to proceed to another typical Manilian procedure, 'interiorization', by which I mean the poet's transferral of real activities to internal movements of the mind. With the winter solstice under Capricorn, two extrazodiacal constellations rise: the Southern Fish (below) and the Lyre (in the North). Unlike Firmicus,[73] Manilius calls the Lyre *Fides*, a move which allows him to make clever use of a double-meaning, as *fides* is both a musical instrument and an instrument of torture.[74] Metaphor allows Manilius to express two different but corresponding prognostications. The divers born under the Southern Fish bring up to the surface their hidden riches (5.398–400):[75]

---

[70] For more detail, see Hübner 1984: 260 n. 414.

[71] Only half of *Argo* is represented, namely its stern; see Boll 1903: 141 and 437; Boll and Gundel 1924–37: 1005.44–1006.5.

[72] In the battle between Perseus and Cetus, Manilius first mentions the flying Perseus—5.577 *concitat aërios cursus* ('he quickly cuts a path through the air')—but in the culmination of the struggle specific mention is made of the upper region: Perseus always withdraws up to the spacious ether (5.599 *laxum . . . per aethera ludit*, 'moves through the yielding air'). It is true that the poets confuse the two words: see Kießling and Heinze 1898 *ad* Hor. *Carm.* 1.28.5 *aërias* (*aetherias* Meineke); Pfeiffer 1932: 201; Lunelli 1969: 30; Zwierlein 1987: 283. But the context always has to be considered. In this case, Manilius emphasizes the ethereal nature of the advantageous upper region that favours Perseus' position.

[73] Firm. *Math.* 8.15.3 *in X. parte Capricorni oritur Lyra* ('in the tenth degree of Capricorn rises the Lyre').

[74] This ambiguity presupposes the Latin language and cannot be drawn from the Greek source; cf. 5.416 *caeruleus* 'coloured like the sky' for the Dolphin that inhabits sea and air.

[75] There is a similar prognostication for the Dolphin that vies with the Southern Fish for the position under the winter-solstice (Firm. *Math.* 8.15.2 gives Capricornus 8°, the exact turning point): 5.434–5 *exportantque maris praedas . . . / . . . atque imas avidi scrutantur harenas* ('they bring forth the spoils of the sea . . . and eagerly search the sandy bottom'). The terrestrial counterpart can be found in the first zodiologion (= set of prognostications for each of the twelve zodiacal signs) under Capricorn: 4.246 *scrutari caeca metalla* ('to pry for hidden metals'), and under Cassiope with the following

> pendentem et caeco captabit in aequore piscem
> cumque suis domibus concha valloque latentis
> protrahet immersus.

He will capture fish as they swim poised in the hidden depths,
and, immersed himself, will bring them forth together with the homes
of protective shell wherein they lurk.

The torturers, however, born under *Fides*, bring to the surface hidden
knowledge (5.411–13):[76]

> quaesitor scelerum veniet vindexque reorum,
> qui commissa suis rimabitur argumentis
> in lucemque trahet tacita latitantia fraude.

There shall be born a man to investigate wrongdoing and punish the
    guilty,
he will get to the bottom of crimes by sifting the evidence for them
and will bring to light all that lies hidden under the silence of deceit.

By employing such a metaphor, the activities of the diver and the
investigative judge are brought into close contact, as is appropriate for
the two constellations on both sides of the zodiac that accompany the
deepest point of the solar course.

Elsewhere Manilius expresses an interior and an exterior action
with the same verb *pendēre*: Andromeda hangs on the rock, but 'in
her mind she is even more in suspense', when she witnesses Perseus'
struggle against the monster: 5.607 *animoque magis quam corpore
pendet.*[77] The poet gives here a double interpretation of the two Fishes

---

Aquarius: 5.525–6 [sc. *Cassiope*] *imperat et glaebas inter deprendere gazam / invitamque
novo tandem producere caelo* ('she bids them (the natives) detect the treasure in lumps of
ore and finally, for all its reluctance, expose it to a sky it has never seen').

[76] Cf. the end of the passage: 5.415 *alto qui iurgia pectore tollat* ('the man who
removes dissensions from the depths of the heart'). Inappropriately, Shackleton Bailey
1956: 168 glosses 'with profound intelligence'; *alto . . . pectore* must be separative, cf.
the quoted text under the Southern Fish, 5.399–400 *latentis / protrahet.*

[77] Housman criticizes the translation by Pingré 1786—'son esprit agité est moins
libre que son corps'—but the French scholar is defended by Paschoud 1982: 140 n. 55.
Another example of this: when Pisces and Andromeda and their common chains are
rising, a 'gaoler' is born (5.621 *carceris . . . custos*); the naked Andromeda 'is a guardian
of her own appearance' (*ipsa suae custos est illa figurae*, 5.555). Nearer to the original
sense comes the net of fishermen (under the Whale equally rising with Pisces): 5.662
[sc. *phocas*] *carceribus claudent raris* ('they will confine them in spacious prisons').

tied by the band (see Figures 9.6 and 9.7), benefitting from the polysemy (expansion of meaning) of *pendēre*.

Polysemy relates to the interrelation of cosmic *sympatheia*, which brings together what had previously been mentally distinguished. The verb *pendēre*, most highly appreciated by the poet, can signify not only the acts of flying and swimming (of fish, men, or ships),[78] but also the earth, which is suspended in the middle of the universe (1.201):[79] *terra quoque aerias leges imitata pependit* ('the Earth, too, in obedience to celestial laws, has hung suspended'). The ancients were always aware of the frail balance of cosmic energy. It is only during the last years of our own time that mankind has become aware of this anew.

As for birds and fish we find two corresponding expressions. The Arrow rising with Libra 8° (at the autumnal point) creates bird-catchers that snare their prey down from the air (5.296):[80] *pendentemque suo volucrem deprendere caelo* ('hitting a bird in the wing of the sky that is its home'). The Southern Fish however, rising with the beginning of Capricorn at the winter solstice, creates fishermen that catch their prey upwards from the depth of water (5.398): *pendentem et caeco captabit in aequore piscem* ('he will capture fish as they swim poised in the hidden depths').[81]

This phraseology, which emphasizes vertical movement, corresponds to the movement downwards and upwards, according to the quartile aspect of two critical points of the sun's course, the autumnal equinox and the winter solstice: in Libra, the sun crosses the equator down to the inferior hemisphere, while in Capricorn it begins a new ascent from the depths upwards towards the North.

We have seen that Andromeda, exposed to the monster, dangles in chains from the rock (5.552, 565, 569, 607), in parallel to the band of the zodiacal Fishes (Figures 9.6 and 9.7). But Perseus her saviour, is likewise 'hanging, suspended from the air' (*caelo pendens*, 5.593). Both lovers are thus shown in the act of *pendēre*. As *paranatellon* of the Fishes, Perseus was replaced by a strange constellation named Engonasin ('the kneeling man'), and those born under this sign will

---

[78] See Hübner 1984: 225–7.

[79] Cf. also 3.49–50 *orbem . . . / undique pendentem in medium* ('the terrestrial globe . . . / everywhere poised in the centre').

[80] At this point already, the fisherman follows: 5.297 *cuspide vel triplici securum figere piscem* ('or piercing with three-pronged spear the fish that deemed itself so safe'). For similar examples, see *TLL* 10.1.1035.23–65.

[81] As for birds, cf. 4.898 *in aere pendent* ('they hang in the air').

be rope-dancers, which equally appear to be 'suspended' in the air.[82] Manilius uses another elegant pun here. The rope-dancer, 'suspended on the rope [drawn from the band of the Fishes as well] will bind his spectators to himself': 5.655 *pendens populum suspendet ab ipso*.[83] With this verbal polyptoton, Manilius once more transfers physical hanging to an internal suspense. The interdependence between artist and spectators, another effect of the two zodiacal Fishes, may also be an image of the interrelation between the didactic poet and his audience. Scaliger had the brilliant idea to compare this passage to a text from book 1, where the *galaxis*, the only of the eleven heavenly 'circles' which is visible, stupefies its observers, 'causing mortals to incline their heads backwards to it' (*resupina facit mortalibus ora*, 1.715). [84] This may also be compared to what Manilius says elsewhere: 4.121 *pendentem . . . ad sidera vatem* ('the poet being in suspense towards the stars').[85] The divine universe, too, is acting as an artist that fascinates its observers. So finally, polysemy and verbal polyptoton correspond to astrological determinism, to the fundamental interdependence that connects human beings with the universe.[86]

---

[82] See Hübner 1984: 193–6. Here we find another exaggeration—5.654 *caeli meditatus iter* ('he attempts an upward route to heaven')—as if he were a constellation like the preceding Pegasus: 5.633 *caeloque volabit* (see n. 65 above).

[83] *Pendens* is my conjecture (Hübner 1984: 194–5); for greater detail, see Hübner 1990: 264–6. We find a similar expression in August. *En. Ps.* 39.9 *didicit enim homo magno studio in fune ambulare, et pendens te suspendit* ('for the man learnt eagerly to walk on a rope and, hanging, put you in a state of suspense').

[84] See Scaliger 1655: 421: 'si vera est haec lectio, nihil elegantius potuit dici' ('if this reading is correct, nothing could be said with more elegance').

[85] *Pendentem . . . ad sidera vatem* (*versum* del. Bentley, Housman, Goold), defended by Lühr 1969: 136–7; Flores 1993: 19 (but Manilius would have deleted the verse later); Liuzzi 1991–7: 4.96 *ad loc.*; Hübner 2002: 62 n. 49; Volk 2001: 88 n. 4. Cf. also 1.68 [sc. *vita hominum priscorum*] *stupefacta novo pendebat lumine mundi* ('(the life of ancient mankind) was in suspense at the strange new light from heaven'). The idea has been christianized by August. *Mag.* 2 *ut homines . . . suspendantur in deum* ('in order that mankind . . . be in suspense towards god').

[86] On the significance of *pendēre* for Manilius, see also Uden in this volume.

10

Sums in verse or a mathematical aesthetic?

Duncan F. Kennedy

Scholars of Latin poetry have a penchant for bewailing the loss of works of literature they would love to read. Surely, you would think, they would kill for a poem in five books from the Augustan period on one of the obsessions of the age, written by, in the words of A. E. Housman, 'the one Latin poet who excels even Ovid in verbal point and smartness'.[1] Yet, in the Anglophone world at least, the *Astronomica* of Manilius languishes largely unread, and generally unloved by the few who have bothered to read him. As Katharina Volk has justly remarked: 'The only thing that most classicists know about Manilius is that his poem on astrology was edited by A. E. Housman. Tellingly', she says, 'it is not Housman who is remembered for Manilius, but vice versa'.[2] His edition of Manilius was designed to be his monument as a textual critic, to set him beside two of the critics he most admired, Joseph Scaliger from the sixteenth century and Richard Bentley from the eighteenth, who had both produced editions of Manilius, and who come in for the sort of lavish praise that Housman is reluctant to give to the poet himself. Housman for the most part eschewed aesthetic judgements on the texts he edited. Apart from that passing comparison of Manilius with Ovid (one that he may have expressed in deference to Scaliger's elegant judgement that Manilius was Ovid's equal in sweetness, his superior in grandeur, 'Ovidio suavitate par, maiestate superior'[3]), he is most famous for an oft-cited quip about 'that eminent aptitude for doing

---

[1] Housman 1903–30: 1.xxi.
[2] Volk 2002: 196.   [3] Scaliger 1600: 21.

sums in verse which is the brightest facet of his genius'.[4] Manilius himself had anticipated an aesthetic resistance on the part of his readers to the unavoidable preponderance of numbers in the exposition of his chosen subject (4.431–5), a passage we shall return to in due course. There is a strain of contempt in 'sums in verse' that is at odds with Scaliger's injunction to 'observe the fecundity of the poet's imagination in finding the means to express these rebarbative numbers' ('nota fecunditatem ingenii poetae in istis morosis numeris concipiendis') with—again—the suggestion that even Ovid could hardly have handled it better ('nescio an Ovidio melius cessisset');[5] and with Bentley's judgement that the many ways in which the poet adapted his style of expression in dealing with the same theme is worthy of admiration ('admiratione dignum est; quot modis in eadem re narranda variaverit faciem loquendi'),[6] both of which Housman himself cites with apparent approval in his note to 4.444–97. It is not that Housman himself was immune to the rhetorical pleasure to be had in numbers. He spent thirty years painstakingly editing the text of Manilius, producing at intervals between 1903 and 1930 an austere volume on each of the five books. Housman remarks at the start of the final volume:

> All were produced at my own expense and offered to the public at much less than cost price; but this unscrupulous artifice did not overcome the natural disrelish of mankind for the combination of a tedious author with an odious editor. Of each volume there were printed 400 copies: only the first is yet sold out, and that took 23 years; and the reason why it took no longer is that it found purchasers among the unlearned, who had heard that it contained a scurrilous preface and hoped to extract from it a low enjoyment.[7]

Housman is a master of this satirical mode, the all-consuming loathing of self and the world, and rejoices in the persona of the *scurra* he adopts, but any potential pleasure this 'tedious author' may have afforded his readers becomes swallowed up by its 'odious editor', only to be excreted as 'low enjoyment'. Housman's authority has prejudiced potential readers of the *Astronomica*, and successfully cowed 'the unlearned': Manilius has attracted but a fraction of the

---

[4] Housman 1903–30: 2.xiii.   [5] Scaliger 1600: 303.
[6] Bentley 1739 *ad* 4.434.   [7] Housman 1903–30: 5.v

kind of literary critical attention that has been paid to other Augustan poetry.

But if Manilius is a 'forgotten star', it would be unjust to lay all responsibility for this at Housman's door. For many twenty-first-century readers, the subject of the *Astronomica* presents an immediate disincentive to an appreciation of the poem. The text will always present ample opportunity for research into the technicalities of astrology, and from that perspective Manilius will not be entirely 'forgotten', but if the *Astronomica* is ever to lay claim to being of more than historical and antiquarian interest, if Manilius is ever to be accorded the status of 'star' once more, the question of his exploded discourse cannot be sidestepped. We cannot simply wish the intervening centuries away and transport ourselves back even to the lifetime of Scaliger, when astrology could still command widespread intellectual credibility and give its leading practitioners access to the palaces of princes, as Anthony Grafton has so brilliantly depicted in his study of the world and works of Giralomo Cardano.[8] Our present moment of reception is one fashioned by intellectual change that Manilius could not have foreseen, but by which we live. Is there anything of his poem that still speaks, and speaks memorably, to our concerns? The analogy of Lucretius suggests that the attempt is at least worth making. Epicurean physics has long been rejected as a viable description of the physical world, but its demise has not carried the *De rerum natura* down with it. Though the Epicurean atom bears little resemblance to the primary particles invoked in the discussions of physicists nowadays, Lucretius' poem retains the capacity not simply to provoke continuing intellectual reflection on the issues it raises, but to thrill, in a way that the writings of his master Epicurus never could, with its vision of the prospect of final explanation that the concept of the atom opens out.[9] What Lucretius said of Epicurus—'who surpassed the human race in his genius and, like the sun rising in the heavens blotted out all the stars' (*qui genus humanum ingenio superavit et omnis / restinxit stellas exortus ut aerius sol*, Lucr. 3.1043–4)— might more appropriately be applied to Lucretius himself. The star of Manilius never shone out as brightly as that of Lucretius, to be sure,[10] but has it just collapsed into a black hole from which no light whatsoever can emerge?

---

[8] Grafton 1999.   [9] See Kennedy 2002, 2006.
[10] For a survey of responses, see Fletcher 1973.

Such a task needs to pay attention to the narratives of intellectual history it generates. One type of narrative sees Science as a unified project directed towards the goal of the discovery of incontrovertible truth, and retrospectively it is not difficult to pick out ideas or discoveries that became incorporated in this enterprise. But within such an emplotment of progress, there is a tendency to see rejected ideas as eliminated by reason, and consigned to the categories of myth, superstition, or magic. Another type suggests there are rather multiple discourses, which see themselves as engaged with notions of truth, but which are provisional and may be succeeded by other forms of description in the future. If one positions oneself within such a narrative, there is no single form of science, and what counts as *a* 'science' depends on where and whence you are looking. Neither form of narrative offers a definitive account. The study of the stars is an excellent test-case. Working out how the planets and stars move across the sky demands a set of technical skills that is vital for modern cosmology and for the practical task of getting a man-made satellite to ride gravitational slingshots so as to track and land on a comet. Earlier observers were no less determined to devise techniques to pin down those movements, but with the aim of relating those movements to events on the earth on the assumption that there was some connection. It is easy to be cynical, in the case of a discourse seen within a positivist narrative of knowledge to be definitively superseded and consigned to the realm of non-science, to see astrologers as accommodating their interpretations to the circumstances, or the assumed desires, of their clients. Tamsyn Barton has suggested that the increasing prominence given to astrology is associated in general with the rise of a monarchical system when so much revolved around the fortunes of a specific individual, and in particular, with the use Augustus himself made of it.[11] But such a socio-political analysis marginalizes the epistemic pretensions of astrology, the investment its practitioners made in the interpretations they put forward, and the disputes amongst them (let alone the lay members of the public) about the validity of their modes of interpretation. In a less positivist spirit, Andrew Wallace-Hadrill has written of the transition from the traditional Roman modes of prediction, such as augury, to astrology: 'a form of knowledge predicated on the application of rational

[11] Barton 1994*a*: 38–41.

principles to a highly complex body of material by professionals displaces the traditional forms of knowledge embedded in the ruling class'.[12] The desire for predictive knowledge, this suggests, has persisted, though the forms in which such knowledge attains legitimacy change over time. Astrology enjoyed the prestige of an intellectual discourse practised by experts, and the authority of its practitioners is revealed in their habitual designation as *mathematici*. We might compare some contemporary discourses of prediction which have not (yet?) forfeited their intellectual credentials: economists too, for whom skill in mathematical modelling is essential, must be *mathematici*.[13] To cast a horoscope, an astrologer had to calculate the exact position of the heavenly bodies in relation to the precise time and the particular point on the globe at which the subject was born. Suetonius in his life of Augustus (94.12) recounts a story of how Augustus and Agrippa, on a retreat in Apollonia, visited an astrologer called Theogenes. Agrippa consults him first, and a great future is predicted. Augustus for a long time holds back and is unwilling to disclose the hour of his birth for fear he will be found to be less successful. Thereafter, Suetonius goes on to say, Augustus had such great faith in his destiny that he made his horoscope public, and struck a coin stamped with Capricorn, the sign under which he was born.[14] The anecdote may or may not be based on fact, and is clearly deeply complicit with Augustus' self-presentation,[15] but it gives a rare (and too brief) glimpse into the practice of an astrologer. Agrippa and Augustus are said to 'climb up' to the *pergula* of Theogenes, whom Suetonius describes as a *mathematicus*. Presumably this is an upper room or roof-terrace from which Theogenes can make precise observations of the stars which will provide the basis of his calculations of their position at a particular moment and particular place in the past. This was his work-space, a specialized site like the doctor's surgery, the laboratory, or the museum, which are the focus of much attention in current science studies for the understanding such venues can afford of knowledge production and knowledge

[12] Wallace-Hadrill 2005: 65.

[13] It was some time before our present travails with credit derivatives that John Kenneth Galbraith opined: 'The only function of economic forecasting is to make astrology look respectable.'

[14] The problematic association of Augustus with Capricorn is examined in Barton 1995.

[15] Cf. Barton 1994a: 40.

practice.[16] It would be good to know what calendrical records, charts, or even equipment would have been at the disposal of Theogenes here to help him establish the configuration of the heavens at the moment of his Roman visitors' births, or how they would have served to establish his professional authority.[17] The brevity of Suetonius' narrative probably does not do justice to the length of the consultation, nor the complex calculations Theogenes will have had to work through, still less the application of the astrological principles according to which the results of those calculations were to be interpreted— before the *mathematicus* was moved to prostrate himself at the great man's feet.

A decree which dates from AD 11 banning all diviners from private consultation (Cass. Dio 56.25.5) suggests that there were people in the twilight years of Augustus' reign with their eyes firmly fixed on the stars. Manilius' poem is a manifestation of this interest, as is Ovid's *Fasti*, which relates the stars to the Roman calendar—though conspicuously stripping out the astral determinism associated with the constellations[18]—and Germanicus' translation of Aratus' *Phaenomena*. But the *Astronomica* is, arguably, best seen as a late Augustan didactic counterpart to the *Georgica* of Virgil, which marked the beginning of the principate. The reference to the 'recent' disastrous loss of three Roman legions under the command of Quintilius Varus in the Teutoburg Forest in AD 9, for example, comes at the end of book 1 (896–902) in a discussion of comets as portents, which recalls the description of the portents after the assassination of Julius Caesar at the end of the first book of the *Georgics* (1.466–88).[19] Indeed, Manilius' apology for adding a fifth book to his poem could be seen as a homage to Virgil's four-book poem; in the first line of book 5, Manilius says 'at this point another would have finished his journey' (*hic alius finisset iter*).[20] One could push that didactic association a bit

---

[16] See Livingstone 2003. His Bibliographical Essay is especially helpful in navigating the extensive theoretical and applied research on both historical and contemporary 'venues' of science (2003: 186–223).

[17] For such an analysis of the Renaissance astrologer's work-space, see Grafton 1999: 22–37.

[18] See Herbert-Brown 2002.

[19] Cf. Volk 2009: 47–8.

[20] Given the licence Scaliger and Housman give us to compare Manilius with Ovid, it may not be unreasonable to draw attention also to the four-book cycle which comprises the *Ars Amatoria* and the *Remedia Amoris*, which also tropes its composition as a journey.

further. Seneca the Younger said of Virgil's poem that he wrote not to instruct farmers, but to delight readers (*Ep.* 86.15), and though some have tried, you would be hard-pressed to use it as a manual for farming. Housman once wrote to Robert Bridges, the then poet laureate: 'I adjure you not to waste your time on Manilius. He writes on astronomy and astrology without knowing either',[21] and in his introduction to his edition of book 1, he wrote: 'I defy anyone to cast a nativity from the information furnished in the poem as it stands',[22] and that is not simply because the poem as we have it is apparently incomplete. It is at least worth wondering whether the poem was written not to instruct would-be astrologers, but to delight readers, or at least, after the example of the *Georgics*, to offer them a world-view that arises out of the specialism it expounds.

The astrological determinism of the poem is such a world-view, of course, though one that will always have divided its readers, of whatever period.[23] But perhaps there is something left over for those of us fated not to be believers. The ancient observation of the heavens, and the techniques developed to make sense of those observations, those of the *mathematicus*, could be credited with the capacity to induce wonder and awe. At the very beginning of the *Astronomica*, Manilius speaks of the subject of his poem (1.1–4):

> carmine divinas artes et conscia fati
> sidera diversos hominum variantia casus,
> caelestis rationis opus, deducere mundo
> aggredior....

> By the magic of song to draw down from heaven god-given skills and fate's confidants, the stars, which by the operation of divine reason diversify the chequered fortunes of mankind . . . this is my aim.

Thus George Goold renders these lines in his Loeb translation.[24] The poet presents himself as in the act of drawing down to earth (*deducere*) through the power of *carmen*, song or incantation, godly skills (*divinas artes*), and the stars which are privy to fate that render

---

[21] Burnett 2007: 1.572. The letter is dated 25 Sept. 1924.

[22] Housman 1903–30: 1.lxii. For Scaliger's criticisms of Manilius' ignorance, cf. Grafton 1983–93: 1.200–3.

[23] For the philosophical objections to astrology in antiquity, see Long 1982; for the Renaissance debate, centring around Pico della Mirandola's *Disputationes adversus astrologiam divinatricem*, see Grafton 1997: 93–134.

[24] Goold 1992. Unless specifically attributed to Goold, the translations are my own.

diverse the different fortunes of mankind (*conscia fati / sidera*). The
sentence is a tricky one. Volk senses a difficulty in the fact that both
divinas artes, which she takes to be 'the science of astrology' and
conscia fati / sidera are both the object of *deducere*: 'While it is
possible to "draw the stars from heaven by means of a spell", one
cannot do the same thing with the "divine arts", and the sentence
becomes an actual zeugma that cannot be properly translated (see
also Lühr 1969: 17 n. 2)'.[25] Furthermore, the phrase *caelestis rationis
opus* could be in apposition to the action of diversifying the fortunes
of mankind 'by the operation of divine reason', which is how Goold
renders it; but, *pace* Housman, who states dogmatically that *opus* is in
apposition to *sidera casus variantia*, not to the actions suggested in
the verbs *deducere* and *aggredior*,[26] it might also, as Volk suggests,[27]
be associated with what the poet says here he is attempting to do in
his poem, 'a task involving divine reason'. Manilius would thus be
emphasizing a Stoic theme he makes much of, that the human race is
a microcosm partaking of the rationality of the cosmos, as he puts it
in 4.893–5, 'what wonder if men are able to understand the cosmos
since they have the cosmos within themselves and each one is in a
smaller likeness a copy of God?' (*quid mirum, noscere mundum / si
possunt homines, quibus est et mundus in ipsis / exemplumque dei
quisque est in imagine parva?*).

To some ears, 'reason' or 'rationality' as a translation in this context
will jar. Astrology these days is associated with the very opposite,
irrationality, perhaps most memorably so characterized by a great
modern analyst of the irrational, Theodor W. Adorno, in his classic
study of the *Los Angeles Times* astrology column, 'The Stars Down to
Earth'.[28] 'Reason' has a tendency to become a dense, monolithic term,
particularly in those teleological narratives that plot the convergence
of a single, unified Science towards a final Truth. As such, the term
resists analysis of how it might have come to take on the meanings it
has. To understand why it might have been invoked historically in
any specific circumstances, it is worth trying to see how a claim to
rationality is not independent of the practices that constitute a

---

[25] Volk 2002: 238. Lühr 1969: 73–111 surveys the use of the term *ratio* in the
Astronomica.
[26] Housman 1903–30 *ad loc.*: '*opus* ad *sidera casus variantia* per appositionem
adnexum est, non ad deducendi aggrediendive notionem'.
[27] Volk 2002: 238.
[28] Adorno 1994: 34–127 (*deducta sidera!*).

particular tradition of inquiry.[29] Why for Manilius might what he was involved in seem so compelling? *Ratio* is commonly used in Latin, like *logos* in Greek, of counting, of keeping accounts, of totting up the figures, and this seems relevant to how Manilius uses the term. A few lines later on, Manilius speaks of how heaven has given its blessing to his enterprise (1.10–11):

> iam propiusque favet mundus scrutantibus ipsum
> et cupit aetherios per carmina pandere census.

Goold translates: 'Now is heaven the readier to favour those who search out its secrets, eager to display through a poet's song the riches of the sky.' 'Riches' is, of course, one of the possible meanings of *census*, and Goold is following Housman's defence of Scaliger's emendation of *census* for the manuscripts' *sensus*; Housman glosses: '*census* pro opibus et diuitiis passim Manilius' ('Manilius uses *census* throughout for wealth and riches'). But for those seeking to discover what is hidden (*scrutari*, 10), what are revealed (*pandere*, 11) are *numbers*: the point about *census* is that it involves counting, whether heads or wealth.[30] Let us put to one side Housman's weary joke about Manilius' eminent aptitude for doing sums in verse, and recall once more that in Latin an astrologer was a *mathematicus*, an expert in calculation, as anyone trying to compute the past, present, and future positions of the stars had to be. For the greatest mathematicians of their times, the day job was often to be court astrologer, and this was no less the case for the astrologers at the court of Tiberius as it was for John Dee, the leading mathematician of the Elizabethan age, and astrologer to Elizabeth I. Astrology began to lose its intellectual credentials in the first half of the seventeenth century as a result of changes on a number of fronts. The gradual acceptance, in the teeth of fierce opposition, of Copernicus' heliocentric theory was one.[31] Another was the discovery of the telescope, which revealed the heavens to be rather different from what the naked eye suggests. Theories of matter cast doubt on the mechanisms that might underlie astral influence. But the *mathematici* themselves played a crucial role.

---

[29] A historical approach that links rationality with practice and tradition is developed in the work of Gadamer 1977, 1981; MacIntyre 1988.

[30] On *census*, and other economic metaphors in Manilius, see Glauthier in this volume.

[31] See now Biagioli 2006: 219–59.

The work of Pascal and Fermat saw the emergence in 1654 of the mathematics of probability, which transformed the process of reasoning with uncertainty.[32] It is no coincidence that the decline of astrology in the seventeenth century coincides with the rise of the insurance market.[33]

In a key passage in the poem, Manilius suggests that those born under Gemini have an inclination towards the study of poetry and the heavens, and it has been suggested that this is a self-portrait (4.152–60).[34] Lines 158–60 repay close attention:

> inveniunt et in astra vias numerisque modisque
> consummant orbem postque ipsos sidera linquunt:
> natura ingenio minor est perque omnia servit.

Those born under Gemini add up, reckon up (*consummant*) the *orbem*, the celestial sphere, *numerisque modisque*, which, happily in this context of composers of poetry, could refer to the rhythms and metres.[35] However, Scaliger, reported by Housman 1903–30 *ad loc.*, remarks 'by *numeris* he is including the arithmeticians, by *modis* the geometers' ('a *numeris* arithmeticos, a *modis* geometras censet'), *modus* being the unit of measurement a geometer would use. They 'leave the constellations behind them', as Housman explains, because their mathematical calculations allow them to conceptualize the whole celestial sphere, the *orbis*, including that which is invisible to us below the horizon, and so are able to predict when the constellations will rise before they actually do. That allows Manilus to say that 'nature yields to their genius and is at its service in all things' (160). The arts of the mathematician are at the very heart of Manilius' poem, and here he pays tribute to their power: they give a full *account* of the heavens—my best effort to get some purchase on that word

---

[32] Hacking 1975 is the fundamental study of the emergence of probability and statistical inference; see also Hacking 1990: 1–10. For a fascinating study of pre-mathematical discourses of probability and risk in Antiquity, the Middle Ages, and Renaissance, see Franklin 2001.

[33] Cf. Grafton 1999: 13: 'Insurance, which rested on statistical, rather than celestial, measurements, came into being only in the seventeenth century—and only after astrology and the other occult arts had lost their cultural value. In earlier periods, only the astrologer could use the best quantitative methods of the time to predict the future and offer useful counsels for averting risk and exploiting opportunities.'

[34] Cf. Volk 2002: 220.

[35] As Volk 2002: 236 suggests, the relationship of the poem to its subject matter 'is not arbitrary, but reflects an existential connection'.

consummant—and so grant us command over nature. A critical appreciation of the poem, then, rather than marginalize or make fun of its fascination with numbers, must (to extend that arithmetical metaphor in *consummant*) take that fully into *its* account.

Manilius on more than one occasion makes a point of the difficulty numbers present. In 3.31–4, they are amongst the difficult and obscure things he says he must wrestle with (*luctandum est*, 34). Each of the twelve signs of the zodiac comprises thirty degrees, and each of these degrees is of significance for determining the character at birth. When he is about to catalogue the so-called *damnandae partes*, the degrees under each sign which inflict harm, he comments (4.430–3):

> hae mihi signandae proprio sunt carmine partes.
> sed quis tot numeros totiens sub lege referre,
> tot partes iterare queat, tot dicere summas,
> perque paris causas faciem mutare loquendi?

These degrees I must now specify in fitting song. Yet who could so often express in metrical form so many numerals, go again over so many degrees, put into words so many totals, and vary the appearance of expression in dealing with like causes?

This proliferation of numbers is a given of his chosen subject, 'but this will bring with it a lack of charm, and that effort is wasted which the ear rejects' (*sed gratia derit, / in vanumque labor cedit quem despicit auris*, 434–5). 'Yet', he continues (436–8), 'as I report in song the laws of destiny and the sacred motions of heaven, I must speak in accordance with what is bidden: *it is not granted to me to fashion, only to point out, the pattern*':

> sed mihi per carmen fatalia iura ferenti
> et sacros caeli motus ad iussa loquendum est,
> nec fingenda datur, tantum monstranda figura.

Manilius executes a superb play here on *figura* and *fingenda*, which are etymologically linked. The pattern (*figura*) is not, as the word might seem to suggest, something that is *fingenda*, dreamed up, invented, or constructed; it is *monstranda*, there in the movement of the constellations to be pointed out and discovered. Manilius here expresses an attitude to number that has come to be known as 'mathematical realism', that mathematical entities, for example, numbers or geometrical shapes, exist independently of the human mind, and are not human constructs.[36] At one extreme, historical and in other ways too, we have the Pythagoreans, who believed that the world was generated by numbers, and the most famous ancient proponent of such mathematical realism was Plato, but it is a conviction still held by many mathematicians. Roger Penrose puts it succinctly: 'Like Everest, the Mandlebrot set is just there.'[37] It was Galileo who said that mathematics is the language with which God has written the Book of Nature,[38] but it might have been Manilius. He goes on to say 'to have shown the deity is more than enough: it will be he who grants authority to himself' (*ostendisse deum nimis est: dabit ipse sibimet / pondera*, 439–40), and continues 'nor is it right for the world to be dependent on words; in the reality it will be greater' (*nec fas est verbis suspendere mundum: / rebus erit maior*, 4.441–2).[39] Words only diminish it: *rebus erit maior*, it will be greater in the things themselves. *Fas*, here translated by 'right', is cognate with the verb 'to speak', and connotes a religious or ritualistic permission or prohibition on speaking. The suggestion of unutterability is piquantly associated with the idea that the universe is somehow dependent on *words*. The invocation of *res*, 'things', makes Manilius a realist, and for realists, mathematical relationships are discovered 'out there' rather than invented by the human mind. Numbers appear to be independent of space and time, in that mathematical relationships like '2 + 2 = 4' seem true regardless of where or when they are invoked. But if independent of space and time, where can these 'things' be said to exist? For figures like Manilius, or Galileo, the answer is obvious: in the mind of God. For Augustine, a test-case is infinity (*City of God* 12.19). Rejecting the 'blasphemy' that God does

---

[36] Abry 2006b: 301–2 notes how frequently Manilius uses the verbs *reddere* and *referre* of his own role of *representing* a reality that is 'out there'. For a detailed discussion of the divergent implications of the languages of 'discovery' and 'invention' in scientific discourses, see Kennedy 2002: 17–21.

[37] Penrose 1989: 95.

[38] Finocchiaro 2008: 183: 'Philosophy is written in this all-encompassing book that is constantly open before our eyes, that is the universe; but it cannot be understood unless one first learns to understand the language and knows the characters in which it is written. It is written in mathematical language, and its characters are triangles, circles, and other geometrical figures; without these it is humanly impossible to understand a word of it, and one wanders around pointlessly in a dark labyrinth.'

[39] Bentley suggested *splendescere* ('to shine out in words') for *suspendere* in the MSS, and this has been accepted by Housman and Goold. For a brief discussion, cf. Volk 2002: 243 n. 91. My reasons for preferring *suspendere* should be clear in the argument I present, and in the play between *pondera* and *suspendere* in 440.

not know all the numbers, Augustine ridicules the notion that God's knowledge extends only to a certain sum. He invokes the authority of Plato's *Timaeus* for the argument that God constructed the world by the use of numbers. But the result is paradoxical, and Augustine too resorts to the topos of inexpressibility:

> Never let us doubt, then, that every number is known to him 'whose understanding cannot be numbered' [Psalm 147: 5]. Although the infinite series of numbers cannot be numbered, this infinity of numbers is not outside of the comprehension of him 'whose understanding cannot be numbered'. And so, if what is comprehended in knowledge is bounded within the embrace of that knowledge, and thus is finite, it must follow that every infinity is, in a way we cannot express, made finite to God because it cannot be beyond the embrace of his knowledge (*profecto et omnis infinitas quodam ineffabili modo Deo finita est, quia scientiae ipsius inconprehensibilis non est*).[40]

Like other varieties of realism,[41] the mathematical finds resort to the notion of the divine difficult to avoid (Penrose, for example, avers that '[t]here is something absolute and "God given" about mathematical truth'[42]), even if those defenders of realism resistant to theism place God within scare-quotes and hasten to describe their language as 'metaphorical'—their version of the inexpressibility topos.[43] Manilius would certainly have had no truck with Reviel Netz's recent argument in *The Shaping of Greek Deduction* that mathematics is a painstakingly human construct that was hijacked by Plato for his metaphysical concerns.[44] Whatever one's take on the philosophical problem of mathematical realism, the language in which the workings of the cosmos are understood is that of mathematics, and for Manilius, these are the *divinas artes* 'brought down from the heavens by song' he spoke of in the opening line of the poem. His use of the phrase *carmine . . . deducere* (1.1–3) has been associated with a number of Virgilian uses: of 'singing a finely spun song' in the Callimachean tradition (*deductum dicere carmen*, *Ecl.* 6.5); of Hesiod's Orphic power to lead down the rigid ash trees from the mountain by singing (*cantando rigidas deducere montibus ornos*, *Ecl.* 6.71),

---

[40] Bettenson 2003: 496–7.
[41] Kennedy 2002: 101–5.
[42] Penrose 1989: 112.
[43] These arguments are pursued in greater depth in Kennedy forthcoming.
[44] Cf. Netz 1999.

which inspires Manilius' claim to be the first to move with these new songs Helicon and the woods nodding with their green tops (*primus-que novis Helicona movere / cantibus et viridi nutantis vertice silvas*, 1.4–5); and even of the magical power, associated with witches, to draw down the moon from the heavens with songs/spells (*carmina vel caelo possunt deducere lunam, Ecl.* 8.69).[45] However, Manilius gives a new and particularly apposite spin to this established trope, for *deducere* can also refer to the process of *deduction*, both in the broad sense and the more specifically mathematical. Towards the climax of the introduction to book 1, Manilius celebrates the capacity of human ingenuity (*sollertia*, 95) to overcome the obstacles of life on earth, but then proclaims that *ratio* 'did not impose a boundary or limit on things before it scaled the heavens and captured, by under-standing the causes, the innermost nature of things, and saw what anywhere exists' (1.96–8):

> nec prius imposuit rebus finemque modumque
> quam caelum ascendit ratio cepitque profundam
> naturam rerum causis viditque quod usquam est.

Ratio, in relating things to their causes, is superior to *sollertia* in allowing one to 'see' anything anywhere. Manilius initially focuses on terrestrial and meteorological phenomena which do not admit of visual inspection to determine their causes (clouds, thunder, snow, volcanoes, earthquakes, rain, and wind, 1.99–103). Explanation of these phenomena frees mankind of the superstition (*miracula rerum*, 103) that *sollertia* alone leaves one with, and thus 'wrests from Jupiter his lightning-bolt and power of thundering and attri-butes the noise to the winds and the fire to the clouds' (1.104–5). What *ratio* does is relate phenomena to their unseen causes, and the term applied to this process is *deducere*. Thus, 'after reason had referred each of these phenomena to its particular causes, it sought to understand, from on high, the neighbouring mass of the cosmos and to understand in the mind the heavens as a whole' (1.106–8):

> quae [sc. ratio] postquam in proprias *deduxit* singula causas
> vicinam ex alto mundi cognoscere molem
> intendit totumque animo comprendere caelum.

---

[45] Volk 2009: 186–7.

Apart from the shapes and names of the constellations (1.109), it 'set down the cycles they performed according to the specific laws governing their behaviour' (*quasque vices agerent certa sub sorte notavit*, 1.110). It is precisely such 'deductions' about the movement of the heavenly bodies that the *mathematicus* can establish. Thus in describing the characteristics of different signs of the zodiac in book 2, Manilius stipulates that you must not fail to ascertain, and to *deduce from their specific behaviour*, which signs are 'nocturnal' and which 'diurnal' (2.203–4):

> nec te praetereat nocturna diurnaque signa
> quae sint perspicere et *propria deducere lege.*

He goes on to explain that the terms 'nocturnal' and 'diurnal' do not mean that the signs perform their function by night or by day (2.205–8), but that under six of the signs the night is longer than the day and attains its greatest length, and under the other six, the opposite is the case (2.209–17). Manilius directs his reader to follow the mathematicians' procedures of measurement and calculation which permit them to deduce the 'laws' by which this is the case, the regular pattern which links the rising and setting of certain constellations with the shortening or lengthening of the day.

Thus in the phrase *carmine . . . deducere*, the actions of the poet are assimilated to those of the mathematician. If it is the case that the mathematical truths of the cosmos are ultimately independent of words, the poet's *numeri* and *modi* can provide a mediation. In 1.20–4, the poet says that two altars shine for him with lit flames, and that he prays at two temples surrounded by a double inspiration, of poetry and of the 'things' it sings of (*duplici circumdatus aestu / carminis et rerum*, 21–2). Just as the cosmos operates *propria . . . lege* that the mathematician can deduce (cf. 2.204), so with its immense sphere it resounds around the poet who sings to a fixed measure (*certa cum lege canentem / mundus et immenso vatem circumstrepit orbe*, 22–3)—the music of the spheres harmonizes with the poet's metre—although it 'scarce allows prose to be fitted to its constellations' (*vixque soluta suis immittit verba figuris*, 24).[46]

It is precisely on the sphere, as both a mathematical and an aesthetic object, that we must focus if we are to do justice to the *Astronomica*. Effectively, we must think of *two* concentric spheres:

---

[46] For this interpretation of 1.24, see Volk 2002: 240–1.

our world is a globe (a fact compellingly confirmed for us by astronomical observation, as Manilius argues in 1.206–10) poised within a
much larger sphere around which the constellations and the planets
track, and on which were projected the poles, the equator, and the
tropics, the so-called 'fixed circles of the sky' which Manilius describes in 1.561–665.[47] 'Earth' he says, 'has been allotted a hollow
space in mid-air, equidistant from every quarter of heaven's depths,
not stretched out into spreading plains, but formed into a sphere
which rises equally and equally falls at every point' (*sed condita in
orbem / undique surgentem pariter pariterque cadentem*, 1.202–5).
The aesthetic appeal of this two-sphere model has perhaps faded for
modern consciousness, but the first translation of book 1 of Manilius
into English by Edward Sherburne in 1675 went under the title *The
Sphere of Manilius*, and it is not hard to imagine that Manilius' image
of the world, as so many other aspects of his poem, might have been
more vividly present in a century of astronomical discovery which
ironically was struggling to free itself of the geocentric image of the
universe presented in Manilius. Apart from the gradual acceptance of
Copernican heliocentrism, the invention of the telescope and the
advances in observation it enabled led to the rejection of this vision
of the cosmos: in the 1780s, William Herschel's improvements to the
telescope allowed him to resolve the Milky Way into its constituent
stars and to develop the notion of deep space.[48] However, the aesthetic appeal of the two-dimensional celestial sphere has not entirely
faded, as a trip to Grand Central Station in New York and a look at
the ceiling there will attest. 'The sphere is the shape of nature',
Manilius avers (*haec est naturae facies*, 1.206); 'this shape stands
eternal and is most similar to that of the gods: in it there is nowhere
beginning or end, but it is alike over all its surface, identical at every
point' (*haec aeterna manet divisque simillima forma, / cui neque principium est usquam nec finis in ipsa, / sed similis toto ore sibi perque omnia
par est*, 1.211–13). But it is the celestial sphere that inspires in the
poet particular awe (1.529–38). The fact that the stars poised in
heaven do not fall to earth but take measured periods (*dimensa ...
tempora*, 530) to accomplish their orbits is not the work of chance,
but the arrangement of a great divine power: 'these then are the
constellations which embroider heaven with their even spread,

---

[47] Cf. Kuhn 1957: 1–99 and Volk 2009: 23–8.
[48] Cf. North 2008: 436–52.

panelling it with their fires into various designs. There is nothing loftier than them: they are the roof of the universe. It is within these limits the abode of nature we share is content to be held, embracing the lands and the sea that lie beneath. They all come into view and set with a concordant movement, where heaven ever sinks and, turning, rises again' (1.532–8):

> haec igitur texunt aequali sidera tractu
> ignibus in varias caelum *laqueantia* formas.
> altius his nihil est; haec sunt *fastigia* mundi;
> publica naturae *domus* his contenta tenetur
> finibus, amplectens pontum terrasque iacentis.
> omnia concordi tractu veniuntque caduntque,
> qua semel incubuit caelum versumque resurgit.

Manilius presents an image of the terrestrial sphere as a house (*domus*, 535) with the celestial sphere as its roof (*fastigia*, 534). The term *laqueantia* (533) suggests that the constellations are like the decorated panelling of a ceiling beneath that roof. However, that image does not fully do justice to the source of the sublimity it tries to capture, the regularity of the constellations' *movement* (*concordi tractu*, 537, echoes *aequali . . . tractu*, 532) as they rise and set.[49]

For Manilius, the celestial sphere is finite—and measurable. As for its size, the poet says (1.541–3):

> . . . docet ratio, cui nulla resistant
> claustra nec immensae moles caecive recessus;
> omnia succumbunt, ipsum est penetrabile caelum.

> . . . we learn from reason, reason that no barriers or huge masses or dark recesses withstand; all things yield to reason, and it can penetrate the sky itself.

This is Goold's rendering, but again I'm not happy with the translation 'reason' here, for Manilius immediately goes on to expound the

---

[49] Goold 1961 has noted a number of similarities between the *Astronomica* and the treatise *On Sublimity* attributed to Longinus, and has suggested that the two writers were moving in the same circles at Rome; as Katharina Volk has pointed out to me, some of these similarities had already been noted by Ellis 1899. Be that as it may, Manilius could benefit from a study of its aspirations to the literary sublime along the lines of the analysis of the Lucretian sublime carried out by Porter 2007. Recall that the greatest theorist of the sublime, Kant, wrote in 1755 a 'Universal Natural History and Theory of the Heavens', in which he postulated 'island universes' outside the Milky Way, and the theory (at odds with Manilius' view) of an infinite universe.

mathematics of the sphere, and give his own verse calculation of the value of π (1.545–7). 'Calculation' or even 'counting' seems more germane, for it is to this that all things bow down (*succumbunt*, 1.543). *Ratio*, calculation, allows one to penetrate to those places where physical travel is impossible, even the sky itself (1.543); as Manilius earlier said, it has the capacity to see everything everywhere (1.98). Although Manilius takes us on a trip to the stars,[50] let us restrict ourselves to the journey he takes us over the earth. The idea of the earth as a globe had become well established by the fourth century BC, and Eudoxus of Cnidos had crucially applied geometrical principles to its study.[51] By the third century BC, Eratosthenes may have calculated the size of the terrestrial sphere.[52] One effect of this, however, was to emphasize how narrow the limits of the known world, the *oikoumene*, were. The *oikoumene* was visualized as an island surrounded by Ocean, but (according to Macrobius in his commentary on Cicero's *Dream of Scipio* 2.9) the size of the globe suggested to Crates of Mallos in the second century BC that the world had room for three other such *oikoumenai*, which he called the *perioikoi*, the *antoikoi*, and the *antipodes*. Manilius may have been familiar with this idea; certainly he conjures up these antipodean places, which 'lie beneath our feet, but think themselves on top, because the ground deceives with its gradual curvature (*sub pedibusque iacet nostris supraque videtur / ipsa sibi fallente solo declivia longa*, 1.239–40).[53] In book 3, he takes us on a journey to the North Pole. Picking up on the argument in the first book that as you move across the surface of the earth, certain constellations do not rise above the horizon and that those living on the opposite side of the globe will see a completely different range of stars ('under which lies the other part of the globe which cannot be traversed by us', *altera pars orbis sub quis iacet invia nobis*, 1.377), he says that as you move north degree by degree, more constellations become invisible, concealed by the intervening curve of the earth; curious things also will happen to the length of the day. So, in a superb passage, he conjures up the scene were you able to walk over the perpetual snow to the North Pole and gaze up to the sky at that point. What you would see would be six

---

[50]   Cf. Volk 2002: 235–44.
[51]   North 2008: 73–9.
[52]   North 2008: 104–5 is sceptical.
[53]   On the antipodes in ancient thought, see Moretti 1994*a*.

constellations only, rotating around the sky and never disappearing beneath the horizon; a single day would last for six months before a single night of equal length (3.356–74). Similarly, you don't have to be physically there to work out the length of a standard hour at the equator (3.247–74), or the rate at which daylight at any latitude increases between midwinter and midsummer (3.443–82).

This evocation of the remote and inaccessible places of the world and of the regularity of the heavenly bodies can create a sense of wonder, but also serves an ideological function if read against the theme of the conquest of the world by the Romans so often invoked in the literature of the Augustan period. Jupiter's prophecy in the *Aeneid* promises to the Romans an empire without end, without boundaries of space or time (*his ego nec metas rerum nec tempora pono / imperium sine fine dedi*, 1.278–9). Closer in time to Manilius' poem, Ovid in the *Fasti* proclaims (2.683–4):

> gentibus est aliis tellus data limite certo:
> Romanae spatium est *urbis* et *orbis* idem.

To other nations is land given with a fixed boundary: the extent of Rome's *city* and *world* is the same.

This is just one of the numerous plays on *urbs* and *orbis* we find in this period. Such themes are there in Manilius too. In book 3, he catalogues the classic types of subject matter that won't be his theme in the present poem (23–6):

> Romanae gentis origo,
> quotque duces *urbis* tot bella atque otia, et omnis
> in populi unius leges ut cesserit *orbis*,
> differtur.

The origin of the Roman nation, the periods of war and peace as numerous as the consuls of the *city*, and how the whole *world* came under the sway of a single people, this is put off for the future.

The sphere in the abstract lacks any privileged point on its surface, but for many Roman writers the *orbis* is unashamedly Romano-centric, as when Livy asserts that Rome's imperial destiny is to be *caput orbis terrarum* (1.16.7), or in the recurrent theme of the praises of Italy and Rome in Varro's *Res rusticae* (1.2.3–8), in Virgil's *Georgics* (2.136–76), and in Vitruvius' *De architectura* (6.1.10–11). Often this vision of Rome is centripetal, as when Ovid in the *Ars amatoria* says you don't need to go off on a long journey to find the raw material for love-making, and, in a moment of calculation that is not quite Manilian, he remarks as he tots up the totty (1.55–6, 59):

> tot tibi tamque dabit formosas Roma puellas,
> 'haec habet' ut dicas 'quicquid in orbe fuit'.
> . . .
> quot caelum stellas, tot habet tua Roma puellas.

Rome will provide you with so many and such beautiful girls that you'll say 'this city has everything there is in the world' . . . as many stars as has the sky, so many girls does your own Rome have.

In contrast, Manilius' view of the Roman world seems centrifugal. Perhaps this has something to do with the circumstances under which it was composed. Towards the end of his long reign, Augustus may have been looking not to world domination but to defensible boundaries for the empire;[54] *differtur* in *Astronomica* 3.26, cited above, could suggest that it is not only the poetic topic that is put off for the future, but the imperial project itself. Enormous effort was going into cataloguing this empire, as Claude Nicolet has traced,[55] through mapping, census counts, and administrative organization, and this is reflected in works such as Augustus' own *Res gestae* or Strabo's *Geography*, or, more light-heartedly, as we have just seen, in Ovid's *Ars amatoria*, which see the acquisition of empire and the acquisition of knowledge as two sides of the same coin.[56] Manilius reflects this too, and astrology offers a typology of, and (if you believe in it) a causal explanation for, all the people you are ever likely to meet, anywhere, anytime. Indeed, they populate the pages of Manilius: there, associated with the astral influences that have made them what they are, you will find character-sketches of seamen, bustlers, charioteers, wantons, swineherds, browsers, effeminates, jugglers, hunters, dog-fanciers, hot-heads, drinkers, gardeners, farmers, archers, busybodies, musicians, priests, veterinaries, custodians, fowlers, snake-handlers, pearl-divers, torturers, swimmers, tragedians, plunderers, goldsmiths, executioners, horsemen, prowlers, fishmongers, and bear-tamers (5.32–709). In the

---

[54] Cf. Cass. Dio 56.33.5 and Tac. *Ann.* 1.11.4, though this does not emerge in Augustus' own *Res gestae*; cf. Cooley 2009: 218–19.

[55] Nicolet 1991.

[56] See in general the essays in König and Whitmarsh 2007, and Abry in this volume for how the *Astronomica* may reflect the imperial connotations of the Augustan building programme.

second half of book 4, Manilius offers a description of the world (585–710) and the distinctive characteristics of individual nations (711–43) before allotting countries to each sign (744–817); thus Italy is allotted to Libra, Spain, Gaul, and Germany to Capricorn. But the world he describes is the *oikoumene*, the *known* world. What about the 'unknown races of men' (*ignotae...hominum gentes*, 1.378) who populate the opposite side of the globe under different constellations? The imposition of limits, on knowledge no less than on empire, provokes a desire for what lies beyond: the knowledge that most excites us is the knowledge we do not *yet* have. Physically they may be restricted to the *oikoumene*, but in the climactic peroration to book 4 (866–935), he encourages his readers to recognize how the power of *ratio* allows them to transcend their physical limitations and at the same time invites them to make the leap of faith that will allow them to see that all is governed by fate (866–85). What use is it to search out the secrets of the universe with such subtle reasoning (*tam tenui...ratione*, 866), he asks, if the mind resists and fear banishes hope? He introduces an anonymous figure to voice this intellectual faintheartedness (869–72):

> 'conditur en' inquit 'vasto natura recessu
> mortalisque fugit visus et pectora nostra,
> nec prodesse potest quod fatis cuncta reguntur,
> cum fatum *nulla* possit *ratione* videri.'

'See', he objects, 'nature is buried in deep concealment and lies beyond our mortal gaze and ken; it cannot profit us that all is governed by fate, since the rule of fate cannot by any means be seen.'

So Goold translates, and *nulla...ratione* is normally rendered 'by any means'. But in the style of the diatribe, the interjected *inquit* signals that the imaginary interlocutor is introduced only to be put down with an ironic play on the very words he uses:[57] he says *nulla ratione*, but it is precisely *ratio*—crucially including the sense of 'mathematical calculation' that Manilius has been at pains to draw out in the poem—that allows the 'eyes of the mind' (*oculos...mentis*, 875) to perceive not simply the heavens but the gifts of the heavens (*perspicimus caelum, cur non et munera caeli?*, 876) that are associated with human rationality. The mind's eye can 'put together the

---

[57] See Wallach 1976: 6–7.

mighty mass of the universe from its component seeds' (that is, it can visualize the world at its most microscopic level, *seminibus... suis tantam componere molem*, 878); it can 'carry the offspring of heaven [mankind] through the places it was reared' (the mind's eye can traverse the heavens, *et partum caeli sua per nutricia ferre*, 879); and it can 'follow ocean's horizon and descend to the parts of the earth beneath, and inhabit the whole globe' (the mind's eye can take us anywhere in the world, *extremumque sequi pontum terraeque subire / pendentis tractus et toto vivere in orbe*, 880–1). This tricolon crescendo finds its climax in the power of mathematical *ratio* to realize Rome's faltering imperial fantasy. 'Now nature nowhere lies hidden from us; we have seen it in its entirety and are masters of the conquered sky' (*capto potimur mundo*, 883–4), an image that equates the acquisition of knowledge and the capture of empire. We are not masters of the heavens in any physical sense, but through *ratio* 'we see our creator, a part of whom we are, and approach the stars from whom we are born' (*nostrumque parentem / pars sua perspicimus genitique accedimus astris*, 884–5). As Augustine was to do four centuries later in *City of God*, Manilius finds in the spiritual dimension the sense of fulfilment that the secular version of Rome's imperial destiny frustrates. The theological aspect he sees as inseparable from his mathematical realism offers a transcendence of the boundaries of time and space that constrain Rome's historical aspirations.

Didactic poems are much given to explicit self-reflection on their scope and function—Manilius' to an even greater degree than his predecessors—so we can expect him to say more on this, and he does. The opening lines of book 3 (1–4) contemplate the novelty of his task:

> in nova surgentem maioraque viribus ausum
> nec per inaccessos metuentem vadere saltus
> ducite, Pierides. vestros extendere fines
> conor et ignotos in carmina ducere census.

Goold translates: 'As I rise to fresh heights and venture a task beyond my strength, fearlessly entering untrodden glades, O Muses be my guides. To widen your domains I strive, and to bring new treasures into song.' This looks like the usual imagery with which Manilius can emphasize his originality, and it would be easy to dismiss it as a hodge-podge of Callimachean clichés concocted by someone who freely admits he has taken on a task too great for him (*maioraque viribus ausum*, 1). But this is a poet we have just seen turning the familiar Augustan *recusatio* theme to a novel and profound use in 3.23–6,[58] and he is acutely aware that the claim of originality is not one to be lightly made. The Muses have sung every manner of theme, every path on the *approaches* to Helicon has been trodden, the streams are muddied that flow from its springs and cannot satisfy the thirst of the crowd that rushes *to what is familiar* to them (2.49–52):

> omne genus rerum doctae cecinere sorores,
> omnis ad *accessus* Heliconos semita trita est,
> et iam confusi manant de fontibus amnes
> nec capiunt haustum turbamque *ad nota* ruentem.

The manuscripts give *indignos... cantus* in 3.4, but 'bringing unworthy songs into my poems', apart from being self-effacing to the point of absurdity, hardly gives good sense. *Census*, again with the emphasis on counting as much as riches, is peculiarly appropriate to book 3, where the major theme is the determination of the degree of the ecliptic which is rising above the horizon at the moment of a nativity. Goold comments that 'this, the most important operation in the casting of a horoscope causes today's astrologer no trouble, but before the advent of clocks, atlases, and standard time account had to be taken of the varying lengths of daylight and darkness in different latitudes and different times of the year' (1992: 161). Book 3 is thus unusually dense in calculations, and it is the originality of bringing these calculations, heretofore *ignotos*, 'unfamiliar', into poetry, that is the substance of his boast. And his claim to have extended the domains of the Muses has a particular point in the context of the terrestrial and celestial spheres, for Manilius takes us to those parts of the world and the cosmos that lie beyond our physical presence, but not, thanks to mathematics, beyond our ken. The places of which he speaks are genuinely *inaccessos*, and remain beyond the capacity of normal human strength to penetrate (*maioraque viribus ausum*). It is precisely the combined power of mathematics and poetry that continues to drive our imagination and aspirations to go beyond the limits of the known.

---

[58] Compare also the echo of the opening words of Ov. *Met.* 1.1 (*in nova*) in 3.1, which juxtaposes a poem celebrating change with one celebrating permanence.

11

Census and commercium

Two economic metaphors in Manilius

Patrick Glauthier

At certain points throughout the course of the *Astronomica*, Manilius invites the student of astrology to consider the cosmos from an economic perspective.[1] This chapter traces Manilius' use of two particular economic metaphors, that of cosmic wealth (*census*) and that of celestial commerce (*commercium*). The *census* motif presents the *mundus* as a valuable commodity that can be catalogued, comprehended, and possessed. At the same time, it characterizes the acquisition of astrological knowledge as the accumulation of personal wealth. The language of *commercium*, however, stresses the fundamental interconnectedness of the world and underscores the mutual give and take that lies at the heart of the astrological poet's relationship with the cosmic sphere. As I hope to show, these images offer complementary, but also competing, intellectual frameworks for understanding the nature of the universe and what it means to engage in the study of the stars.[2]

[1] I would like to thank Steven Green and Katharina Volk for all the hard work that went into creating this volume. I would also like to express my thanks to everyone who attended the original conference and to those who participated in a graduate student conference at the University of Michigan in Feb. 2009, where material from this chapter was also presented.

[2] Baldini Moscadi 1991, Santini 1993, Calcante 2002: 56–7, 72, 90–3, and Landolfi 2003: 77–95 treat certain elements of Manilius' economic language and financial imagery. They do not, however, emphasize the importance of *census* and *commercium*. For Manilius' use of metaphor in general, see Scarsi 1987 and the contributions in this volume of Hübner and Kennedy. I refer the reader in particular to Kennedy for

The imagery of cosmic *census* occurs in the proems to books 1, 2, and 3 and in the programmatic finale of book 4. At the start of book 1, the poet declares his theme and then turns to Caesar: 'you who rule a world that obeys august laws and, yourself a god, earn the heavens that were granted to your father' (*qui regis augustis parentem legibus orbem / concessumque patri mundum deus ipse mereris*, 1.8–9). As others have seen, Manilius' language blurs the distinction between the celestial and human spheres.[3] Not only does the poet regularly use the vocabulary of rule, obedience, and law to characterize various cosmic interactions, the stars themselves and the cosmos as a whole are divine and follow the lead of an all-pervading divinity. But the astrologer then turns his attention to the cosmos itself: 'and now the universe favours those who investigate it more closely and it desires to reveal through song its ethereal riches' (*iam propiusque favet mundus scrutantibus ipsum / et cupit aetherios per carmina pandere census*, 1.11–12).[4] In the highly politicized context of a universe obedient to the laws of a cosmological emperor, we can understand *census* in an almost technical sense as an actual censor's list (*tabulae censoriae*).[5] The metaphor figures the universe as the cosmic equivalent of the Roman Empire and suggests that Manilius will play the role of the cosmic censor who records the names, places of residence, relations, occupations, and financial status of individual heavenly bodies. In fact, Manilius does something quite similar to this. The catalogues and computations that make up the *Astronomica* present a mass of social and economic data—what follows will be a veritable census of the stars.[6]

a complementary analysis of the *census* motif from the perspective of mathematics and counting rather than economics and wealth.

[3] On the proem to book 1 in general, see Schrijvers 1983; Flores 1982; Wilson 1985; Neuburg 1993: 243–57; Habinek 2005: 89–94; 2007: 231–5; Volk 2009: 185–94.

[4] It should be noted that *census* is Scaliger's emendation for *sensus*. It is defended by Housman and adopted by others, including Goold and Feraboli *et al*.

[5] See Hoppe 1906–12: 808.47–69. Thus the Elder Seneca, for instance, can tell someone to examine wills and 'probe the censor's lists' (*excutiat testamenta, scrutetur census, Controv.* 1.6.6).

[6] Manilius provides similar social and economic information for the inhabitants of the terrestrial sphere too, as Santini 1993 makes clear. From this perspective, the mundane financial/political implications of *census* contrast strikingly with the religious imagery that permeates the proem and that critics such as Wilson 1985: 297 n. 16 and Calcante 2002: 24–5 find in *pandere* (1.12) in particular. Some of the political implications of Manilius' project are discussed more generally in this volume

Of course, *census* frequently means little more than 'riches' or 'wealth'.[7] Manilius uses *census* in this sense elsewhere (e.g. 2.823, 3.72–3, 4.11, 172, 5.278, 369, etc.) and here too clearly characterizes the stars themselves, as well as knowledge of them, as valuable commodities. The context, however, points to something slightly more specific. *Scrutor* is the *vox propria* for 'probing' or 'sounding' the earth in the pursuit of precious metals. Lucretius, for instance, can speak of miners who search for veins of silver and gold as 'probing deeply the hidden places of the earth' (*terrai penitus scrutantes abdita*, 6.809). Elsewhere Manilius himself clearly plays on this sense of the word. In the system of cardinal points, lower mid-heaven 'governs wealth and probes the extent to which wishes are fulfilled with metals that are dug up and how much one is able to receive from that which is hidden' (*censusque gubernat, / quam rata sint fossis, scrutatur, vota metallis / atque ex occulto quantum contingere possit*, 2.823–5). Likewise, those born under the Dolphin hunt for shipwrecks and 'greedily probe the bottom of the [ocean's] sands' (*imas avidi scrutantur harenas*, 5.435; cf. 4.513). By extension, *scrutor* also takes as its object the metals for which one is searching. Thus Manilius can say of Capricorn: 'to search for hidden metals and to burn out from the veins of the earth the wealth that has been deposited there and to double up the material with sure hand—these activities will come from you' (*scrutari caeca metalla, / depositas et opes terrarum exurere venis, / materiamque manu certa duplicare erit a te*, 4.246–8).[8] From this perspective, at the beginning of the *Astronomica* the *mundus* seems to favour those who probe its depths (*scrutantibus*) in a search for its material or ethereal resources (*census*).[9] Although this scene dramatizes an essential theme of the poem, the fundamental

---

by Abry, Gale, Green, and Kennedy, the last of whom also highlights the numerical tone of *census* in the present passage.

[7] See Hoppe 1906–12: 809.28–810.68.

[8] Flores 1966: 91–5 discusses this passage in general and rightly notes that *scrutor* here refers to 'una generica attività di minatori' (92).

[9] For the use of *scrutor* and *census* at 4.867, see the discussion below. It should be kept in mind that *scrutor* also has connections with both extispicy and stargazing and that these connections may colour the present passage as well. On the one hand, Habinek 2007: 231–3 suggests that *scrutantibus* at 1.11 characterizes the *mundus* as a physical body eager for the sacrificial inspection of its entrails. This reading is supported by 4.909, where the astrologer 'probes heaven in its bowels' (*caelum scrutatur in alvo*), and texts such as Ov. *Met.* 15.137, where people can 'probe the minds of the gods through sacrificial entrails' (*mentesque deum scrutantur in illis* [sc.

connection between that which is up above and that which is down below, it also seems slightly out of place. At the literal level, Roman writers regularly criticize those who greedily probe (*scrutor*) the depths of the earth and dig below its surface.[10] In fact, this is a topos with which Manilius is familiar. In book 5 we hear that sowing seeds and reaping crops lead to great financial gain, 'which metal alone it were proper for men to know: then there would be no hunger, there would not be any starvation on earth' (*quod solum decuit mortalis nosse metallum: / nulla fames, non ulla forent ieiunia terris*, 5.276-7). Here the poet clearly laments man's unseemly penetration underground and its sad consequences.[11] At the beginning of the poem, then, Manilius transfers this topos from the literal sphere to the metaphorical sphere and, in the process, completely turns it upside down. In a remarkable act of 'common feeling' or *sympatheia*, the *mundus* itself willingly reveals its hidden riches to the astrologer. Instead of committing an act of violence against the natural world, Manilius finds himself living in a sort of astrological golden age when

---

fibris]). On the other hand, Ennius uses *scrutor* to refer to observation of the stars, albeit in a rather unfavourable way: 'no one looks at what is before his feet, they probe the tracts of heaven' (*quod est ante pedes nemo spectat, caeli scrutantur plagas*, *Fragmenta scenica* 244 Vahlen[2] = 187 Jocelyn). While Feraboli *et al.* 1996–2001: 2.351 *ad* 4.246 note Manilius' fondness for *scrutor* and observe its presence in Ennius, they do not mention its astronomical implications. These implications are recorded by Le Bœuffle 1987: 237, but he cites only Ennius and Ps.-Ausonius, *Opusc.* 22.3.7 Peiper for the usage. It is essential to recognize, however, that the Ennian line becomes proverbial (see Otto 1890: 274) and that *scrutor* often appears when the proverb is invoked. See Cic. *Rep.* 1.30, *Div.* 2.30, Sen. *Apocol.* 8.3, Plin. *HN* 18.252-3, August. *Conf.* 10.16.25, and Donat. *ad* Ter. *Ad.* 386, where the whole line is actually characterized as a common saying (*pervulgatum dictum*). Elsewhere Seneca himself can simply say that the part of philosophy devoted to the heavens 'probes the nature of the stars' (*naturam siderum scrutatur*, *Q Nat.* 2.1.1), and Pliny can play on both connotations of *scrutor* by claiming that it is madness to 'probe' the *extera* of the world as if its *interna* were already known (*HN* 2.4).

[10] For the use of *scrutor* in such contexts, see Sen. *Dial.* 5.33.1, *Clem.* 1.3.5, Plin. *HN* 33.2, Tac. *Germ.* 5.2, and the anonymous *Aetna* 276-7 (placed after line 257 by Goodyear). Note also the choice of words at Livy 35.36.6, Plin. *HN* 22.3, and Juvenal 5.95, an appropriately humorous adaptation. For the topos in general, see Sen. *Q Nat.* 1.17.5-6 and 5.15.

[11] Baldini Moscadi 1991 connects this passage with a golden-age topos of moral criticism. Santini 1993: 119 usefully compares 5.522-6, where the poet does not explicitly condemn searching below the ground for wealth, but his vocabulary seems strangely hostile and repeatedly suggests that such an activity inverts or turns upside down the natural order of things. For similar remarks on this passage, see Baldini Moscadi 1993: 94.

the wealth of the cosmos makes itself spontaneously available for consumption.[12]

This imagery returns in a striking way at the end of book 4. Here Manilius' interlocutor complains about the difficulty of probing the universe (*scrutari mundum*, 4.867) and bemoans the fact that nature itself has been hidden from view (*conditur . . . vasto natura recessu / mortalisque fugit visus*, 4.869–70). Manilius responds as follows:

> quid iuvat in semet sua per convicia ferri
> et fraudare bonis, quae nec deus invidet ipse,
> quosque dedit natura oculos deponere mentis?
> perspicimus caelum, cur not et munera caeli?
>
> *
>
> inque ipsos penitus mundi descendere census . . . . (4.873–7)[13]

What good is it to be borne against oneself in self-reproach and to cheat oneself of goods that god himself does not begrudge and to set aside the eyes of the mind that nature has given? We perceive the sky, why not the gifts of the sky as well? . . . and to descend deep into the very riches of the universe . . . .

Although the text is problematic, the meaning is clear: it is indeed possible to descend below the surface of the earth to find the precious metals of the cosmos. In what follows, Manilius explains that his own work has already brought to light these vast repositories of wealth, asserting 'now nature lies concealed nowhere; we have seen it in its entirety; we have captured and control the heavens' (*iam nusquam natura latet; pervidimus omnem / et capto potimur mundo*, 4.883–4). The entire passage places great weight on astrological knowledge from a fundamentally paradoxical point of view: astrological study

---

[12] This fits well with Manilius' treatment of the golden age in book 1 as interpreted by Romano 1979*b*. Landolfi 2003: 88–95 shows clearly that Manilius follows a similar pattern in his manipulation and reconfiguration of diatribe themes in general, including the condemnation of greed and the pursuit of wealth. Of course in the actual golden age, precious metals were unknown to man: 'at that time gold lived in the uninhabited mountains' (*tumque in desertis habitabat montibus aurum*, 1.75). For a look at some of the remarkable ways in which Manilius exploits Stoic *sympatheia*, see the contribution of Uden in this volume.

[13] Rossberg posits a lacuna after 876. As Housman 1903–30: 4.116 notes, there must have been at least one line that (1) contained a word on which the following infinitives depend and (2) itself contained an infinitive to which the -*que* in 877 joins *descendere*. Goold supplies, e.g. *mens humana potest propria discedere sede*, 'the mind of man has the power to leave its proper abode'.

may attempt to acquire the material resources of the cosmos, but intellectual mastery and economic possession quickly turn into physical and/or political domination. Elsewhere in the *Astronomica* the stars themselves control life on earth. Here the students of astrology appear to have robbed the stars of their natural resources and to have taken their place as the rulers of the natural world. From this perspective, Manilius' attempt at rethinking a familiar moral topos seems to falter.[14]

This paradox brings us to a slightly different use of *census*. At the start of book 3 the poet addresses the Pierides and makes the following declaration: 'I endeavour to extend your territories and to lead unknown riches into song' (*vestros extendere fines / conor et ignotos in carmina ducere census*, 3.3–4).[15] Manilius' astrological project suddenly looks like an act of imperial aggression. He will extend the borders of the Muses' territory by composing poetry on new themes, but he will also seize the possessions of his subject matter and lead them back to Rome in a sort of triumphal procession. Of course, the 'poetic triumph' is another literary commonplace (e.g. Verg. *G.* 3.10–11 and Prop. 3.1).[16] Although Manilius' use of *census* highlights the value of his project and situates him in an illustrious poetic tradition, it reifies the inherently dynamic nature of his subject and reduces the *mundus* along with cosmological study to the level of mere commodities. At the same time, the attentive reader may recall a passage from the prologue to book 2. While discussing the orderliness and interconnectedness of the universe as a whole, Manilius emphasizes that divine providence 'controls' or 'directs' the *census* of the cosmos and that, if it did not, the whole of existence would be thrown into chaos: 'the earth would not have its stability, the stars would not have their orbits, the heavens would wander without direction or stiffen from standing still' (*quod nisi . . . tantum mundi regeret prudentia censum, / non esset statio terris, non ambitus astris, / erraretque vagus mundus*

---

[14] Volk 2001 treats a similar paradox that creeps up in a number of Manilian passages, although Habinek 2007: 235 dismisses this sort of problem. For further discussions of various inconsistencies and/or ambiguities (real or apparent) in Manilius, see the contributions of Henderson, Mann, and Volk in this volume.

[15] *Census* is Unger's emendation for *cantus*. It receives a vigorous defence from Housman and is again adopted by Goold and Feraboli *et al.*

[16] Wilson 1985: 297–8 n. 17 and Volk 2001: 99–100 consider the triumphal implications of *deducere* at 1.3 and 2.127–8, respectively.

standove rigeret, 2.67–71).[17] The proper functioning of the *mundus*
depends, at least in part, on who or what administers its wealth.
Manilius' poetic triumph as depicted in book 3 seems to threaten
the very stability of the universe as configured in book 2. The topos,
then, is ill-suited to the subject at hand and even clashes with the
poet's own rhetoric. Nevertheless, Manilius insists on the financial
character of the cosmos and his work with almost blithe optimism.[18]

In opposition to the image of *census*, Manilius also promotes the
idea of celestial *commercium*. The metaphor occurs first in the proem
of book 2. The poet insists that man could not know the cosmos if he
were not himself divine,

> ni sanctos animis oculos natura dedisset
> cognatamque sibi mentem vertisset ad ipsam
> et tantum dictasset opus, caeloque veniret
> quod vocat in caelum sacra ad commercia rerum. (2.122–5)

> ... if nature had not given our minds sacred eyes and turned towards
> herself an intellect related to her and dictated so great a work, and if
> there did not come from the sky that which summons [us] into the sky
> to the sacred commerce of things.

These lines present a scene of astrological inspiration and initiation
that stands in the tradition of Hesiod, substituting of course *natura*
for the Muses. As a part of this drama, a mysterious heavenly power
summons Manilius to a special kind of *commercium*. The commerce
is sacred because the stars themselves are divine. That Manilius thinks
of this commerce as economic becomes clear from the following lines:
'Who could deny that it is impious to seize heaven against its will and,
having taken it captive, to lead it down to earth, as if to oneself?' (*quis
neget esse nefas invitum prendere mundum / et velut in semet captum
deducere in orbem?*, 2.127–8). The language of capture and triumph

---

[17] *Censum* is again Scaliger's emendation for *sensum* and is again adopted by
Housman, Goold, and Feraboli *et al.*

[18] Feraboli *et al.* 1996–2001: 2.245 interpret *census* here as indicating 'l'insieme
degli specifici calcoli astronomici e dei risultati concreti delle misurazioni cosmiche
globali cui il poeta si è dedicato.' Kennedy, in this volume, places a similar emphasis
on *census* in this line and notes that such a reading corresponds well with the
particularly dense mathematical subject matter of book 3. Without rejecting such
interpretations, I would simply point out that we need to take into account the
overriding influence of the poetic triumph topos in lines 3.1–4 and I would contrast
the use of *census* at 1.12 where the socio-political context allows Manilius to play the
role of the censor who computes and tabulates.

(*invitum, prendere, captum, deducere*) contrasts strongly with the idea of exchange and situates the entire episode squarely in the political and financial arenas.[19] But here Manilius programmatically refuses to participate in the traditional 'poetic triumph', choosing instead to engage in celestial commerce. Such language is not entirely without precedent. In the *Ars amatoria*, for instance, Ovid can boast of his inspiration (*est deus in nobis*) and declare that poets have commerce with the heavens (*et sunt commercia caeli*, *Ars am.* 3.549).[20] Manilius, however, thematizes this kind of language and deploys it within an intellectual framework where celestial commerce plays an essential role. Before we can see this clearly, we need to explore the nature of the metaphor itself.

The idea of celestial *commercium* is fundamentally grounded in the astrological minutiae of Manilius' work. Astrology creates meaning by considering the positions of different heavenly bodies relative to one another from the perspective of a specific point on earth at a specific moment in time. The astrologer must take into consideration the mutual influence that the heavenly bodies exert on one another and the different ways in which they interact—for Manilius, this means their patterns of *commercium*. This is not simply, and perhaps not even primarily, a metaphor. Although Manilius has little to say on the matter directly, his universe is fundamentally material and his signs influence one another through very real processes of physical interaction. We can therefore read the *commercium* motif as describing a literal exchange of physical goods between different corporeal entities. This makes perfect sense if we keep in mind the Stoicizing tendencies of Manilius' astrology.[21] Not only do the Stoics believe in a completely material universe, but Latin authors working in the Stoic tradition, Manilius included, regularly employ the *con-/com-* prefix to create technical terms that correspond to Stoic vocabulary built with

[19] Volk 2001 well discusses the passage and its triumphal language from various angles, although she does not broach the subject of *commercium*. Calcante 2002: 30 notes the tone of conquest and suggests that such language contributes to a topos he calls the 'eroicizzazione della scienza'.

[20] At *Tr.* 5.3.45, Ovid can also say that the gods have commerce among themselves (*sunt dis inter se commercia*). Different is Cic. *Tusc.* 5.66, where 'commerce with the Muses' (*cum Musis . . . commercium*) is glossed as commerce 'with human culture and learning' (*id est cum humanitate et cum doctrina*).

[21] See Volk 2009: 226–34 for overview of the relative importance of Stoicism for Manilius. In this volume, Habinek considers the influence of Stoic materialism on Manilius and shows the essentially physical nature of Manilius' cosmos.

the συν-/συμ- prefix (e.g. *consensus* for συμπάθεια).[22] *Commercium*, then, blends seamlessly with this sort of language and so becomes a philosophically loaded word that Manilius can deploy in a variety of astrologically significant contexts with a very literal meaning. In book 2, for instance, Manilius discusses the ways in which one can connect the signs of the zodiac by inscribing different geometrical shapes within their circle. An equilateral triangle connects signs in trine aspect (trigons), a square joins signs in quartile aspect (tetragons). But the poet stresses the importance of connecting the proper degree of each sign:

> his natura dedit communi foedera lege
> inque vicem affectus et mutua iura favoris.
> quocirca non omnis habet genitura trigonis
> consensum signis, nec, cum sunt forte quadrata,
> continuo inter se servant commercia rerum. (2.340–2, 345–6)[23]

To these nature has given treaties with common law and reciprocal affection and shared rights of goodwill. Wherefore not every nativity has agreement with the signs of the trigon, nor, when they happen to be quadrate, do they necessarily preserve among themselves their commerce in things.

The social and political metaphors that appear in this passage—treaties, laws, rights, agreement, or consensus—permeate Manilius' poem and belong to a long history of cosmological thinking.[24] Such

---

[22] Lapidge 1989 discusses the use of *con-/com-* prefixes at several points and notes certain Manilian usages within a broader discussion of Stoic elements in Manilius' cosmology (1393–7). By classifying Manilius' use of *commercium* under the heading of *consentire*, Le Bœuffle 1987: 101–2 suggests a similar connection between *commercium* and Stoicism. Note too how Scarsi 1987: 94 inadvertently characterizes the *sympatheia* that is the subject of the *Astronomica* as 'scambio mutuo tra macrocosmo e microcosmo'. It is interesting to observe that Seneca later exploits the potential Stoic colouring of *commercium* while talking about human relationships. At *Dial.* 9.4.4, for instance, he can say 'we have not shut ourselves up within the walls of one city but have sent ourselves forth to engage in commerce with the whole world and we have declared that the universe is our fatherland' (*nos non unius urbis moenibus clusimus sed in totius orbis commercium emisimus patriamque nobis mundum professi sumus*). For similar passages, see *Ben.* 7.17.1, *Dial.* 6.26.6, *Q Nat.* 3.27.11 and 5.18.4.

[23] For the fact that 2.343–4 = 2.318–19, see Housman 1903–30: 2.35. Editors since Scaliger have seen that the lines belong at 2.318–19.

[24] Lloyd 1966: 210–32 discusses such imagery in early Greek cosmological theory. For similar language in Lucretius, a clear model for Manilius, see Cabisius 1984–5; Fowler 1989: 145–50; Asmis 2008; and Lehoux 2006, a wide-ranging discussion on law and nature that touches on Lucretius and Manilius. Although Le Bœuffle 1987: 101–2

language emphasizes the harmonious and unfailing nature of the bond that connects certain signs, and underlines the parallelism between that which is up above and that which is down below. But as a heavenly phenomenon, *commercium* expresses something slightly different. Building off the Stoic and the political associations of *consensus*, *commercium* draws attention to the mutual influence that the signs exert on one another and highlights the natural give and take or back and forth that obtains between multiple signs at the physical level. It is precisely this shared interaction that requires the astrologer to investigate what a particular sign offers to and receives from another. In fact, only a few lines later, Manilius twice uses *commercium* to describe signs in sextile aspect as well. Although these signs do not exercise a particularly potent influence on the native—they have 'weak commerce' with one another and do not preserve 'reciprocal treaties with great agreement' (*debilia alternis data sunt commercia signis / mutua nec magno consensu foedera servant*, 2.358–9)—nevertheless, the poet emphasizes that even within such configurations male signs do respond to one another and female signs do engage in trade (*secum iungunt commercia mundi*, 2.382).[25] Celestial commerce plays an essential role in the construction of Manilius' cosmic society.

Throughout the poem, Manilius characterizes a wide variety of astrologically significant phenomena as commercial. At times, his language suggests that commerce plays a fundamental or even constitutive role in the cosmos. For instance, the pairs of signs that see, hear, love, and plot (the *videntia*, *audientia*, *amantia*, and *insidiantia*) come together according to their individual laws 'so as to conduct the sure commerce of things' (*quin etiam propriis inter se legibus astra / conveniunt, ut certa gerant commercia rerum*, 2.466–7). The phrase *certa commercia rerum* highlights the regularity and predictability of this celestial commerce, but it also suggests that certain patterns of exchange lie at the heart of all heavenly interactions: the heavenly bodies interact through trade. Manilius develops this idea elsewhere.

gives citations for, and briefly discusses, the astronomical and astrological uses of *consensus*, *societas*, and *commercium*, his citations for *commercium* come only from Manilius.

[25] Feraboli *et al.* 1996–2001: 1.323 try to find parallels for *commercia* and *foedera* in Virgil. But note the combination of *foedus* and *servare* at Lucr. 5.1025 (*pars servabat foedera*, 'part preserved their treaties') and 5.924 (*foedere naturae certo discrimina servant*, 'they preserve their differences by a fixed treaty of nature').

In book 4, after discussing the influences that the signs of the zodiac have on the native's character and professional life, the poet turns to the system of decans. Each sign is divided into three equal decans of ten degrees and each decan is then allotted to a specific sign. Manilius introduces the topic thus:

> sed nihil in semet totum valet: omnia vires
> cum certis sociant signis sub partibus aequis
> et velut hospitio mundi commercia iungunt. (4.294–6)

> But nothing thrives as a whole on its own: all ally their powers with certain signs under equal parts and, as if out of hospitality, bring together the commerce of the universe.

Since no sign is self-sufficient, every sign must form alliances and do business with other signs. But the phrase *mundi commercia* hints at a more significant role for celestial commerce in the construction of the Manilian cosmos: it is precisely this economic system that makes up the fabric of the *mundus* and that allows it to function smoothly. In some sense, these *commercia* are the *mundus* and the universe itself cannot be conceived outside an economic framework.[26]

This leaves us with one additional point to make about these processes of exchange. After discussing the geography of the known world and what signs influence what regions, Manilius reflects on the economic nature of international relations:

> sic divisa manet tellus per sidera cuncta,
> e quibus in proprias partes sunt iura trahenda;
> namque eadem, quae sunt signis, commercia servant. (4.807–9)

> Thus the earth remains divided through all the stars, and from them laws are to be drawn for the parts [of the earth] that belong to them; for they preserve the same commerce that the signs have.

The patterns of *commercium* through which the stars engage with one another up in heaven map on to the world down below. In fact, this kind of interaction describes the earth as a whole, from the level of geography to that of animal life—thus we hear of peaceful *commercia* between men and animals at 5.378–80 and 699–700. It is essential to

---

[26] Fowler 1989: 147 makes a similar point about Lucretius' *foedera naturai*: 'the genitive in *foedera naturai* is not simply possessive. The pacts the atoms make *are* nature, constitute the natural process.'

notice, however, that even though *iura* are drawn from the stars and patterns of *commercium* can be traced from the heavenly globe onto the terrestrial globe, the actual interaction between the human and divine spheres is not characterized by reciprocity or mutual influence. These two economic systems run parallel to one another, but the stars up above influence the world down below without getting anything in return.

This brings us back to the first occurrence of the *commercium* motif at 2.125. There the phrase 'sacred commerce of things' (*sacra commercia rerum*) seems to designate the sum total of interactions in heaven, on earth, and in between. But if those on earth do not trade with those in heaven, in what sense can anyone be said to participate in the *sacra commercia* of the universe? I would suggest that in one particular case human beings can in fact do business with the stars, through the study of astrology and the composition of astrological poetry. A few lines later Manilius makes the following declaration:

> sed caelo noscenda canam, mirantibus astris
> et gaudente sui mundo per carmina vatis,
> vel quibus illa sacros non invidere meatus
> notitiamque sui, minima est quae turba per orbem.
> illa frequens, quae divitias, quae diligit aurum,
> imperia et fasces mollemque per otia luxum. (2.141–6)

I will sing things for the sky to know, with the stars wondering in amazement and the heavenly sphere delighting in the songs of its own poet, or for those to whom the stars have not begrudged their sacred movements and knowledge of themselves, which is the smallest crowd on earth. [But] vast is that [crowd] that loves riches and gold, power and the *fasces* and soft luxury in one's spare time.

Manilius directs his own poem towards the cosmos itself. If the *mundus* reveals its wealth to the astrologer, the astrologer repays the *mundus* with his study of the cosmos and the composition of astrological *carmina*. But Manilius also sings for a small band of like-minded initiates and this group contrasts radically with the crowd of fools who pursue more ordinary forms of wealth and follow more traditional Roman career paths. This juxtaposition underscores the financial character of the poet's enterprise and, in context, comes close to portraying him as a sort of celestial merchant who sells his goods to a highly selective earthly clientele. From more than one perspective, then, the cosmos itself is essentially economic and so too is the astrological poet.[27]

A key passage in book 4 further confirms the financial basis of the relationship between poet and cosmos (4.387–407). When the student complains about the difficulty of his studies, Manilius insists that he will be appropriately compensated for his work (*pro pretio labor est*, 4.393). Manilius then encourages the student by returning to a familiar theme: 'but unless the mountains are mined, the gold will escape you and the earth, piled up above, will stand in the way of its own wealth' (*at nisi perfossis fugiet te montibus aurum,* / *obstabitque suis opibus super addita tellus*, 4.396–7). These lines once again figure astrological knowledge as a precious metal buried below the surface of the earth and unmistakably recall the celestial *census* of book 1 while looking forward to its dramatic reappearance at the end of book 4.[28] Manilius next denounces those who waste their lives in the pursuit of transient and meaningless goods—traders, mercenaries, gluttons, greedy heirs, etc. (4.398–405). The poet's moral indignation is topical. In fact, it renews a series of moral criticisms made at the very opening of the book where the poet complains about *luxuria* and criticizes those for whom 'the greatest reward that comes from wealth is to waste wealth' (*summum census pretium est effundere censum*, 4.11).[29] At the literal level, then, Manilius rejects human *census*, while at the metaphorical level he reconfigures astrological knowledge as the only form of wealth for which one may legitimately strive. But this

---

[27] Volk 2009: 207–8 treats this passage and its Callimachean resonances while analysing the ways in which Manilius connects himself with earlier Latin poets. It can also be usefully compared with Ov. *Fast.* 1.295–310. There Ovid celebrates astronomical and/or astrological poets for having brought knowledge of the stars to earth (*admovere oculis distantia sidera nostris*, 1.305) and sets them in opposition to a variety of figures, including those who pursue military/political careers (*officiumque fori militiaeve labor*, 1.302) and those who hunger after great riches (*magnarumque fames . . . opum*, 1.304). Among other things, this juxtaposition implies the financial worth of celestial literature and characterizes the celestial poet as a sort of interstellar trader who provides his readers with valuable goods. While such poets appear to do business with the community at large, Manilius' poets, at least in the proem to book 2, clearly cater to a narrower demographic. For more on the passage from the *Fasti*, see Green 2004: 135–44. Ovid's text should also be read against Manilius 4.152–61, a passage discussed briefly by Kennedy in this volume.

[28] Calcante 2002: 30, 36 notes in passing that this passage and the opening of book 3 emphasize the 'tesori' of nature.

[29] Landolfi 2003: 77–95 discusses the proem to book 4 and its relationship to the diatribe tradition.

precious commodity comes at a price: 'What will we give to the heavens? How great is the price at which everything is sold? Man must expend himself so that god may be able to be in him' (*quid caelo dabimus? quantum est, quo veneat omne? / impendendus homo est, deus esse ut possit in ipso*, 4.406–7). The cost is one's own investigation, represented as the devotion of the entire individual to astrological study, and the item for sale is communion with the cosmos, obtained through complete astrological understanding and symbolized as god's presence in man. As others have noted, Manilius's rhetoric here sounds almost mystical or Hermetic.[30] The choice of words, however, is significant. Although *impendendus* suggests perseverance and complete devotion to the task at hand, it also continues the financial language of the entire passage. A more literal translation would be: 'man must be *weighed out in payment*'.[31] This is a form of commerce, the very *sacra commercia* that figure so prominently in the proem to book 2.

As we have seen, Manilius presents the cosmos itself and astrological knowledge as valuable commodities. He also elaborates on the fundamentally commercial nature of the universe and the unique role played by the astrological poet within this economic system. By the beginning of the first century, it has become possible to view the world in fundamentally economic terms and to think about a variety of interactions and processes from an essentially economic perspective. The metaphors in question are not always consistent. Nevertheless, Manilius attempts to create a sort of parallel universe in which the financially conservative mindset of Roman morality can coexist with the quest for astrological gold.

[30] For a recent evaluation of possible Hermetic influences on Manilius, see Volk 2009: 234–9. As others have seen, the present passage bears a close resemblance to 2.105–8, where the *deus* is said to descend to man and actually to live in him.

[31] Note that Manilius makes the same demand of his student at the beginning of book 3: 'you must weigh out your mind out in payment' (*impendas animum*, 3.38).

Part IV

Didactic Digressions

12

Digressions, intertextuality, and ideology in didactic poetry

The case of Manilius

Monica R. Gale

How does didactic poetry define itself as a genre? It might be thought that the teacher-pupil constellation is in itself both necessary and sufficient to characterize a poem as didactic; but in fact ancient didactic poems will be seen to share a number of other formal features, notably their epic metre.[1] Amongst these further defining characteristics, the formal, 'set-piece' digression becomes increasingly prominent as the cumulative body of existing didactic material expands: as time passes, the pool of conventional topics from which didactic poets draw in constructing their digressions expands in both breadth and depth.

The classic instance is the Myth of Ages, which—because of its prominence in the Hesiodic archetype (*Op.* 106–201)—becomes a virtual sine qua non of all subsequent didactic poetry. As each successive poet places his own 'spin' on the Hesiodic model, the myth may be said to gain in complexity, to become encrusted (to change the metaphor) with layer upon layer of commentary, any or all of which may be regarded as legible 'between the lines' in all subsequent versions. Manilius' brief history of civilization at the

---

[1] For attempts to identify the defining characteristics of the genre, see esp. Pöhlmann 1973; Toohey 1996: 2–5; Volk 2002: 34–43; Gale 2005: 101–3; cf. also Dalzell 1996: 21–7.

beginning of *Astronomica* 1 follows upon reworkings of the myth by Empedocles, Aratus, Lucretius, Virgil, and Ovid, and no doubt also others unknown to us; it is my contention that all these earlier versions are potentially equally significant, though verbal echoes may tend to point the reader (or *some* readers) towards one or other in particular. Simultaneous with this 'complexification' of digressive material is a process of expansion: further topics become canonized or conventionalized as successive poets introduce new themes, to be imitated in their turn. Lucretius' Plague of Athens, notably, begets a vigorous progeny of plague narratives on its didactic successors.[2]

In part because of this process of accretion, the digression seems to lend itself particularly easily to the expression of a work's underlying ideology: I suggest that digressions are in their nature a locus of particularly intense intertextual engagement with other texts in (and beyond) the didactic tradition, and thus offer a clear opportunity for the poet to situate his own work within a range of (in a broad sense) political frameworks. My aim in this chapter is to illustrate this hypothesis with reference to three passages of Manilius' *Astronomica*: the aforementioned history of civilization; the digression at the end of book 1 on the premonitory functions of comets; and the brief series of vignettes of the four seasons towards the end of book 3.

It is widely recognized that Manilius' history of civilization draws extensively on the concluding section of Lucretius, book 5, and on the briefer account of the end of the Golden Age at *Georgics* 1.121–59.[3] If the reader bears in mind, however, that Virgil and Lucretius, in turn, are in dialogue not only with each other, but with earlier didactic poets, notably Hesiod and Aratus,[4] a more nuanced picture of Manilius' self-positioning begins to emerge. Indeed, a pointer towards such an interpretation is arguably embedded in Manilius' text, in the lines preceding the history of civilization proper, where the poet identifies the gods themselves as the ultimate source of astrological knowledge:

---

[2] Notably Verg. *G.* 3.478–566, Manilius, *Astr.* 1.864–91 (discussed below), Grattius, *Cyn.* 366–496.

[3] On Lucretian and Virgilian echoes in the proem to book 1, see esp. Effe 1971; Di Giovine 1978; Romano 1979*b*; Wilson 1985: 286–92; Liuzzi 1991–7: 1.111–25; Abry 1999*b*: 119–22; Habinek 2007: 236–7.

[4] On Lucretius and earlier didactic poetry, see Gale 2007*b*: 61–7; on Virgil and earlier didactic, Farrell 1991 and Gale 2000; cf. also Fakas 2001, on Aratus and Hesiod.

> quem primum interius licuit cognoscere terris
> *munere caelestum.* quis enim *condentibus illis*
> *clepsisset furto* mundum, quo cuncta reguntur?
> quis foret humano conatus pectore tantum,
> invitis ut dis cuperet deus ipse videri,
> sublimis aperire vias imumque sub orbem,
> et per inane suis parentia finibus astra?
> tu princeps auctorque sacri, Cyllenie, tanti;
> per te iam caelum interius, iam sidera nota. (*Astr.* 1.25–33)

The earth was first able to know this more intimately through the gift of the gods. For had they hidden it, who could have stolen knowledge of heaven, by which all things are ruled? Who of mere mortal understanding could have attempted so much, and desired, against the gods' will, to seem a god himself, to reveal paths on high and below the earth, and the stars obedient to their orbits through the void? You, god of Cyllene, were the first founder of this sacred art; through you, heaven and stars were first more intimately known.[5]

The counter-factual *condentibus illis,*[6] with the accompanying notion of *stealing* divinely guarded secrets—emphasized by the pleonastic *clepsisset furto*—may put us in mind of Hesiod's Prometheus, whose theft of fire motivated Zeus' double-edged gift of the first woman, Pandora:

> **κρύψε** δὲ πῦρ· τὸ μὲν αὖτις ἐὺς πάις Ἰαπετοῖο
> **ἔκλεψ**' ἀνθρώποισι Διὸς πάρα μητιόεντος. (Hes. *Op.* 50–1)

He [Zeus] hid fire: the noble son of Iapetus stole it again for men from wise Zeus.

> ὀνόμηνε δὲ τήνδε γυναῖκα
> Πανδώρην, ὅτι πάντες 'Ολύμπια δώματ' ἔχοντες
> δῶρον ἐδώρησαν, πῆμ' ἀνδράσιν ἀλφηστῇσιν. (*Op.* 80–2)

He [Hermes] called this woman Pandora, because all the gods who dwell on Olympus gave her a gift, this bane on men who eat bread.

For Manilius, the gift of the gods (*munere caelestum,* 1.26) is altogether more benevolent, consisting in the astrological knowledge which the poet goes on to depict at 1.106–12 as the highest

---

[5] Quotations from Manilius follow the Teubner text of Goold 1985; all translations are my own.

[6] The interpretation of Valvo 1978—who takes the phrase to suggest that Mercury did indeed 'steal' knowledge of the *mundus,* in the face of the other gods' hostility—seems very difficult to sustain, after *munere caelestum* at the beginning of the line.

achievement of *ratio*. Indeed, the entire culture-history may be said to invert the pattern of decline characteristic both of the Prometheus story and of the Hesiodic Myth of Ages: whereas Hesiod's primeval generation lived 'before that time without evil and without hard toil', for Manilius, 'primitive life before their time lacked *reason*',[7] and it is the gradual development of *sollertia* and *ingenium* that leads to the discovery of first practical and then theoretical arts. At the same time, the antithesis between *species* and *ratio* in line 67 recalls Lucretius' promise to reveal both the *species* and *ratio* of nature to his reader;[8] and this shift into a Lucretian frame of reference is confirmed by Manilius' subsequent suggestion (1.68–70) that early humans lamented when the sun[9] set, and were overjoyed at its return— a scenario which Lucretius ridicules, contrasting the vain fears which arise from astronomical speculation with the very real anxieties entailed by the harsh conditions under which the first human generations lived (Lucr. 5.973–83). Despite superficial similarities, then, Manilius' culture-history in certain respects inverts Lucretius' rationalized reworking of Hesiod, *as well as* the Hesiodic archetype: as emerges

---

[7] Πρὶν μὲν γὰρ ζώεσκον ἐπὶ χθονὶ φῦλ' ἀνθρώπων / νόσφιν ἄτερ τε κακῶν καὶ ἄτερ χαλεποῖο πόνοιο ('for before that time the tribes of men lived on the land without evil and without hard toil', *Op*. 90–1); *nam rudis ante illos nullo discrimine vita / in speciem conversa operum ratione carebat* ('for primitive life before their time lacked reason, and looked without discrimination on the outward appearance of things', *Astr*. 1.66–7). The close echo of Hesiod's opening phrase πρὶν μὲν γὰρ ζώεσκον... ἄτερ in Manilius' *nam... ante illos... vita / ... carebat* may again be seen as inviting the reader to make a comparison with the Hesiodic account specifically.

[8] *Hunc igitur terrorem animi tenebrasque necessest / non radii solis neque lucida tela diei / discutiant, sed naturae species ratioque* ('this mental anxiety and darkness must, then, be dispelled not by the rays of the sun and bright shafts of daylight, but by the outward appearance and inner workings of nature', Lucr. 1.146–8 = 2.59–61 = 3.91–3 = 6.39–41); *Astr*.1.67, *in speciem conversa operum ratione carebat* ('[the primitive human race] lacked reason, and looked without discrimination on the outward appearance of things'). Similarly Lucretian in flavour are *Astr*. 1.71–2, *nec ... / ... suis poterat discernere causis* ('they were not able to understand [natural phenomena] on the basis of their true causes'; cf. Lucr. 5.1185, *nec poterant quibus id fieret cognoscere causis* ('nor could they understand what caused this to happen') and 90, *semper enim ex aliis alias proseminat usus* ('for practice always brings forth one skill from another'; cf. Lucr. 5.1452–6, *usus... / paulatim docuit... / namque alid ex alio clarescere corde videbant*, 'practice taught them little by little... for they saw one thing after another grow clear in their minds').

[9] Or, retaining the transmitted text, the stars: Goold, following Breiter, emends the MS *amissis... sideribus* to the singular, positing a lacuna after line 69. While Goold's text brings Manilius slightly closer to Lucretius, my argument is not materially affected either way, since the echo is in any case conceptual rather than verbal.

particularly in lines 95–112, the triumph of *ratio* means something very different to the Stoicizing astrologer than to the Epicurean rationalist.[10] Like Lucretius in the proem to *De rerum natura* 3, Manilius' *ratio* ascends to heaven, and is able to 'see everything everywhere' (*viditque quod usquam est*, 1.98[11]); what it sees, however, is not atoms moving *sua sponte* in the void (Lucr. 3.33), but everything ordered and controlled by the *numen mundi*—the fateful power exerted by the stars (*Astr.* 1.111–12).

Paradoxically, inversion of Lucretius is further interwoven with inversion of Virgil's brief Myth of Ages in the *Georgics*, which itself echoes and partially inverts the Lucretian culture-history.[12] Manilius' opening *ante illos* (66) picks up Virgil's *ante Iovem* (*G.* 1.125) as well as its Hesiodic model, and Virgil, like Manilius, includes the naming of stars amongst the early discoveries prompted by need and developed through trial and error (*Astr.* 1.109 ∼ *G.* 1.137).[13] Falling

---

[10] On Manilius' conception of *ratio*, see Lühr 1969: 73–111; Reeh 1973: 162–7; Volk 2009: 219–21; cf. also Duncan Kennedy's discussion in this volume.

[11] Cf. Lucr. 3.17, *totum video per inane geri res* ('I see what is happening through the whole void'). For Lucretius, Epicurus' philosophy 'proclaims the nature of things' (*ratio tua coepit vociferari* / **naturam rerum**, Lucr. 3.14–5), while in Manilius' version personified reason 'scales heaven and seizes the fundamental nature of things' (*caelum ascendit ratio cepitque profundam* / **naturam rerum**, *Astr.* 1.97–8).

[12] On the intertextual framework of Virgil's culture-history, see Gale 2000: 61–7 (with further bibliography at n. 12). It is noteworthy that several of the Virgilian phrases echoed by Manilius simultaneously incorporate reminiscences of Virgil's Lucretian intertext: thus, the references to *usus* and *experientia* at *Astr.* 1.61, 83, and 90 recall both *G.* 1.133 *ut varias usus meditando extunderet artis* ('so that practice and thought might hammer out the various arts') and Lucr. 5.1452–6 (quoted in n. 8 above); *Astr.* 1.51 *primique per artem* ('first by their art') recalls both *G.* 1.122 *primusque per artem* ('[Jupiter] first by his art . . .') and Lucr. 5.10 *quique per artem* ('[Epicurus] by his art . . .'; the phrase occurs in the same *sedes* in all three cases); and Manilius' assertion that new discoveries were contributed to the common cause (*commune bonum*, 1.84) inverts both Lucr. 5.958 (early humans have *no* notion of a *commune bonum*) and *G.* 1.127 (the people of the Golden Age worked for the common good, *in medium quaerebant*). It will be evident that attempts—like those of Di Giovine 1978—to adjudicate *between* Lucretius and Virgil as 'sources' for the passage are in my view misguided. Again, Manilius' phrase *necdum etiam . . .* ('not as yet', 1.73) is—as Romano 1979b: 406 points out—typical of the technique of 'negative enumeration' characteristic of accounts of the Golden Age in general; but this need not prevent us from thinking *specifically*, in a context permeated by Lucretian and Virgilian echoes, of *G.* 2.539 (*necdum etiam audierant inflari classica*, 'they had not yet heard the blast of the war-trumpet') and/or Lucr. 5.953 (*necdum res igni scibant tractari*, 'they did not yet know how to work things with fire'); we might also recall Virgil's Aratean model, *Phaen.* 108 (οὔπω λευγαλέου τότε νείκεος ἠπίσταντο, 'they knew nothing as yet of bitter strife').

[13] Note especially the Manilian line-ending *nomina signis*, which recalls Virgil's *nomina fecit*, in the same *sedes*.

between these two echoes are two further striking instances, *Astr.*
1.79, where Manilius clearly signals the Virgilian connection by
quoting *G.* 1.123 almost verbatim, and 1.95, which recalls the famous
(and famously enigmatic) Virgilian motto *labor omnia vicit*:[14]

> sed cum longa dies *acuit mortalia corda*
> et *labor* ingenium miseris dedit...
>
> ...
>
> *omnia* conando docilis *sollertia vicit.* (*Astr.* 1.79–80, 95)

But when long ages had sharpened mortal hearts and toil had given the
poor souls ingenuity... Astuteness, quick to learn, overcame all obstacles with effort.

> curis *acuens mortalia corda*
> nec torpere gravi passus sua regna veterno
>
> ...
>
> tum variae venere artes. *labor omnia vicit*
> improbus et duris urgens in rebus egestas. (Verg. *G.* 1.123–4, 145–6)

[Jupiter], sharpening mortal hearts with care, did not allow his kingdom
to grow slothful in heavy idleness... then came the various arts. Toil
overcame everything—insatiable toil, and want, pressing when times
are hard.

In Manilius' hands, the slippery Virgilian phrase becomes unambiguously positive:[15] in conjunction with *conando*, Manilius'
omnia... docilis sollertia vicit has to mean 'astuteness overcame all
obstacles'. Surprisingly, perhaps, the Stoic Manilius[16] adopts at this
point something more like the rationalist tone of Lucretius, cutting
through the complexities and ambiguities of Virgil's (so-called) theodicy: time is ostentatiously substituted for Jupiter as the force that
'sharpened mortal hearts', and the advance of reason and scientific
knowledge culminates in the 'disarming' of Jupiter (*eripuit... Iovi
fulmen viresque tonandi / et sonitum ventis concessit, nubibus ignem,*

---

[14] The Virgilian phrase has been read both 'optimistically' ('toil overcame all
[obstacles]') and 'pessimistically' ('toil overwhelmed everything'): for discussion, see
esp. Wilkinson 1969: 134–43; Thomas 1988: 1.92–3; Jenkyns 1993; Gale 2000: 62–3.

[15] Cf. Effe 1971, who notes (398 n. 10) the further significant echo of the Virgilian
phrase at *Astr.* 4.932 *ratio omnia vincit* ('reason conquers all').

[16] Baldini Moscadi 1980: 13 argues that Manilius' vocabulary in this passage
suggests a specifically Stoic world-view, drawing particular attention to the conjunction of the terms *sollertia* and *ratio*, for which she cites parallels in the speech of
Cicero's Stoic spokesman in book 2 of the *De natura deorum*.

'[reason] wrested from Jupiter the lightning-bolt and the power to thunder, and assigned the sound to the winds and the fire to the clouds', 104-5). The latter image is particularly reminiscent of Lucretian gigantomachy (notably, 1.62-79 and 3.14-30, where Epicurus and his followers are depicted as launching an assault on the heavens); and of the Epicurean poet's mockery in *De rerum natura* 6 (esp. 387-422) of the notion that thunder and lightning are the weapons of the gods.[17] Yet, as we have already seen, Manilian *ratio* is in practice something very different from the synonymous concept so central to Lucretius' message: in the Stoic world-view, scientific rationalism and theism are in no way incompatible. The Stoic Jupiter is an aspect or manifestation of the all-pervasive divine *pneuma*, equated with Fate, Providence, and rationality; the god as traditionally conceived is either to be rejected as a poetic fable, or reinterpreted in allegorical terms.[18] Despite apparent similarities, then, Manilius' Lucretian language may prompt the reader to reflect on the distance as much as the similarities between the highly organized, deterministic cosmos depicted in the *Astronomica* and the far more chaotic, *ungoverned* universe of his Epicurean predecessor.

A fourth intertext which has been the focus of surprisingly little attention in relation to Manilius' poem is the *Phaenomena* of Aratus.[19] While verbal echoes are less in evidence, the educated ancient reader would surely have needed little prompting to call to mind the Greek poem—a work which seems to have been widely read by late Republican and Augustan *literati*[20]—in connection with a history of civilization set within a work on the stars and their influence on the human world. Like Manilius, Aratus emphasizes the gods' benevolence in making knowledge of the heavens available to mortals: particularly relevant here is Aratus' proem, where the poet celebrates Zeus' benign relation to the human world, self-consciously 'correcting' the Hesiodic emphasis on the god's arbitrary and unchallengeable might. Similarly, the Aratean Myth of Ages, while retaining the

---

[17] On gigantomachic imagery in Manilius, see further Volk 2001, 2009: 257-8; for Lucretius, see also Hardie 1986: 188-9, 209-13; Gale 1994: 43-5, 192-3; Clay 1997.

[18] For Stoic rationalization/allegorization of the gods of the traditional pantheon, see esp. Cic. *Nat. D.* 2.60-72.

[19] A notable exception is Abry 2007 (esp. 9-13 on Aratus' proem and the Myth of *Dike*); Abry's interpretation of the relationship between the two poets is, however, very different from that advanced here. Cf. also Volk 2009: 188-92.

[20] See e.g. Lewis 1992.

downward trajectory of its Hesiodic model, ends on a note of optimism: though *Dike* has left the earth, she is still visible and in a sense
available to human beings as a constellation in the heavens (*Phaen.*
133–6). Yet, while unambiguously benevolent, Aratus' gods remain
ultimately mysterious: as the poet observes at *Phaen.* 768–70, 'we men
do not yet have knowledge of everything from Zeus, but much still
is hidden'.[21] The *contrast* here with Manilius' self-revealing *deus*
(*Astr.* 1.28–33) is striking.

To recapitulate, then: I have argued that what has been called
Manilius' 'mosaic technique' (Lühr 1969: 171) of verbal and thematic
reminiscence serves in the passage in question as a means for the poet
to orientate himself against a range of didactic predecessors: the
history of civilization embodies a view of human development, and
of human beings' relationship with the divine, which bears both
similarities to and differences from not just a single model, but an
entire poetic tradition. In political as well as philosophical terms,
Manilius' stance is perhaps closest to that of Aratus, for whom the
benevolence of (Stoic) Zeus appears to correspond (as Schiesaro 1996:
20–4 has argued) to the benevolence of the quasi-divine Ptolemaic
monarchy. Something similar could be said of the universe depicted
by Manilius, in which Caesar (whether Augustus or Tiberius[22]) rules
the world *augustis legibus* (1.8) under the ultimate dominion of the
stars and their 'hidden laws' (*tacitis dominantia legibus astra*, 1.63).
Manilius' celebrated facility for 'doing sums in verse' is of some
relevance in this connection, as is the famous simile of the universe
as *res publica* (5.734–45), in which the emphasis lies on the orderly
allocation of the heavenly bodies to different ranks corresponding to
the class-divisions of Roman society.[23] His is a cosmos characterized
above all by *hierarchical* and *legible* (or rationally comprehensible)
order: the role of the *princeps* as guarantor of this order on earth
corresponds to the role of the stars as overriding 'rulers' of the world
and its human inhabitants. Recent work on Augustan ideology has
laid emphasis on the *princeps*'s reordering of and domination over

---

[21] Πάντα γὰρ οὔπω / ἐκ Διὸς ἄνθρωποι γινώσκομεν, ἀλλ᾽ ἔτι πολλὰ / κέκρυπται.

[22] For a full discussion of the dating of the poem and the identity of Manilius'
'Caesar', see now Volk 2009: 137–61 (with a brief review of earlier scholarship at 138–9).
Compare also Volk's Introduction to this volume, as well as the contribution by Enrico
Flores.

[23] On the *res publica* simile, see esp. Salemme 2000: 64–74 and Schindler 2000:
242–8.

time and space:[24] this ideological overlay supplements the Aratean combination of Stoic theology and Hellenistic kingship theory in Manilius' conception of both imperial rule on earth and divine rule over the cosmos as a whole. At the same time, Manilius advertises his departures from the pessimistic theology and anthropology of Hesiod (along with Virgil's more complex response to it), and from Lucretius' conception of a universe of randomly moving atoms, untrammelled by the rule of either the traditional gods or impersonal Fate.

The range of available intertexts in the conclusion to book 1 is somewhat narrower. Goold remarks of the book's final topic, comets and meteors, that its 'astrological relevance . . . is slight';[25] and this very tangentiality may encourage the reader to be on the lookout for 'relevance' at other levels. Such an expectation will soon be fulfilled by the very strong, indeed near-explicit, echoes of Lucretius' Plague of Athens (Lucr. 6.1138–1286)[26] and the finale to *Georgics* 1, which similarly ends in an account of the omens that foreshadowed the

---

[24] Notably by means of calendar reform, with the associated insertion of imperial anniversaries into the *fasti*, and the administrative reorganization of Rome and Italy, as well as symbolic representations of world-empire including the *Porticus Vipsania* (with its world map) and the *Porticus ad Nationes*. On these strategies, see esp. Nicolet 1991; Wallace-Hadrill 2005; Feeney 2007: 167–211; and (in relation to Manilius) Bajoni 2004 and the chapters by Abry and Kennedy in this volume.

[25] Goold 1977: 3; cf. Härke 1936: 63–8.

[26] The most striking echoes are the following (cf. Lühr 1973; Abry 1999*b*: 124): *qualis* **Erechtheos** *pestis populata* **colonos** / *extulit antiquas per* **funera** *pacis Athenas* ('Such a plague devastated the people of Erechtheus and sent forth the dead of ancient Athens in unwarlike funerals', *Astr.* 1.884–5) ∼ *haec ratio quondam morborum et mortifer aestus* / **finibus in Cecropis funestos** *redidit* **agros** ('once in the land of Cecrops a disease and a deathly air-current of this kind rendered the fields desolate', Lucr. 6.1138–9); *nec locus* **artis** *erat* **medicae** *nec vota valebant* ('no place was left for the art of medicine and prayer was powerless', *Astr.* 1.887) ∼ *mussabat tacito* **medicina** *timore* ('the art of medicine muttered in silent fear', Lucr. 6.1179); *funera derant* / *mortibus et lacrimae; lassus defecerat ignis* / *et* **coacervatis** *ardebant corpora membris* ('the dead lacked funerals and mourning; the weary pyres failed, bodies burned all heaped up together', *Astr.* 1.888–90) ∼ *nec mos ille* **sepulturae** *remanebat in urbe* ('nor did the customary burial practices continue to be observed in the city', Lucr. 6.1278), with the subsequent description of ad hoc funerals, and *confertos ita* **acervatim** *mors accumulabat* ('death piled them up, thrust together in heaps', Lucr. 6.1263). It is noteworthy that—once again (cf. n. 12 above)—Manilius selects details of the Lucretian account that are *also* echoed by Virgil in his version of the plague at the end of *Georgics* 3, in such a way that both predecessors may be simultaneously present to the reader's mind (cf. G. 3.549–50 for the failure of medicine, and 556–8, esp. 556 *catervatim . . . aggerat*, for Virgil's version of the heaped-up corpses and abandonment of funeral rites). The Virgilian intertext is also 'flagged' by the striking echo at 878–9,

Battle of Philippi. Most obviously, the finale seems concerned to *invert* the underlying message of its Lucretian intertext while *capping* the Virgilian model.[27] Lucretius' plague forms the conclusion, at one level, of the overarching argument of books 5 and 6 of the *De rerum natura*, that the world is governed by impersonal and mechanical forces, not by gods nor indeed quasi-divine stars (5.78–80). Manilius appropriates the plague as an example of the kind of disaster of which god, in pity, has forewarned humans; our problem is that we don't have sufficient trust in heaven (*nescimus credere caelo*, 1.905), whereas for Lucretius it is our ignorant and misguided *fear* of the gods that makes natural disasters into human tragedies (see esp. Lucr. 6.50–79).[28] For the Epicurean, it is crucial that we accept that meteorological and astronomical phenomena are *not* signs sent by the gods; for the Stoic, is it crucial that we accept that they *are*.

Manilius follows up his Plague of Athens with a longer section devoted to the disaster of the Saltus Teutobergensis, the Battles of Philippi and Actium, and the war against Sextus Pompey. Lines 896–913 are saturated with echoes of the Virgilian account, in the finale to *Georgics* 1, of the omens that followed the death of Julius Caesar and foreshadowed the subsequent conflict at Philippi:[29]

---

in the brief depiction of crop failure preceding the plague narrative proper: *sterilis inter sulcos defessus **arator** / ad iuga **maerentis** cogit frustrata **iuuencos*** ('the weary ploughman amidst the barren furrows confines his mourning oxen vainly under the yoke') ∼ G. 3.517–18, *it tristis **arator** / **maerentem** abiungens fraterna morte **iuuencum*** ('the ploughman goes sadly to unyoke the ox that grieves for its brother's death [sc. of the plague]').

[27] Cf. Bühler 1959: 492.

[28] As demonstrated by Steele Commager in an influential article (Commager 1957), Lucretius depicts the physical effects of the plague as exacerbated or even outweighed by its psychological consequences; for discussion of this psychologizing tendency throughout book 6, see also Jope 1989.

[29] The Virgilian intertext is already flagged in the opening lines of the Manilian finale, 874–7: ... *deus instantis fati **miseratus** in orbem / signa per affectus caelique incendia mittit; / numquam **futtilibus** excanduit ignibus aether, / **squalidaque** elusi deplorant **arva coloni*** ('god, in pity, sends the world tokens of impending doom through these moods and conflagrations of the sky; for heaven has never blazed with meaningless flames: farmers, cheated of their hopes, lament their unkempt fields'); cf. *G.* 1.466 (*ille etiam exstincto **miseratus** Caesare Romam*, 'he [the sun], too, in pity for Rome after Caesar's death'), 373–4 (*numquam **imprudentibus** imber / obfuit*, 'rain has never harmed men without warning') and 507 (*squalent abductis **arva colonis***, 'the fields are unkempt in the farmers' absence'). On Virgilian echoes in the finale as a whole, see Bühler 1959: 487–94; Landolfi 1990*b*.

quin et bella canunt ignes *subitosque tumultus*
et clandestinis surgentia fraudibus arma,
externas modo per gentes ut, *foedere rupto*
cum fera ductorem rapuit *Germania* Varum
*infecit*que trium legionum *sanguine campos,*
arserunt toto passim minitantia mundo
lumina, et ipsa tulit bellum natura per ignes
opposuitque suas vires finemque minata est.
ne mirere gravis rerumque hominumque ruinas,
saepe domi culpa est: nescimus credere caelo.
civilis etiam motus cognataque bella
significant. *nec plura alias* incendia mundus
sustinuit, quam cum ducibus iurata cruentis
arma Philippeos implerunt agmine campos,
vixque etiam sicca miles Romanus harena
ossa virum lacerosque prius super astitit artus,
imperiumque suis conflixit viribus ipsum
perque patris pater Augustus vestigia vicit. (*Astr.* 1.896–913)

These fires foretell wars, too, and sudden uprisings, and conflict arising from secret treachery; sometimes among foreign tribes, as when fierce Germany, breaking a treaty, carried off general Varus and stained the fields with the blood of three legions, threatening lights burned all over heaven and nature itself waged war with fire and ranged her own forces against us[30] and threatened of the end to come. Do not wonder at the calamitous ruin of men and their affairs: the blame is often ours; we do not know how to trust the heavens. Often, too, they foreshadow civil conflict and wars between kindred. At no other time did heaven display more flames than when armies sworn to follow their blood-stained leaders filled the plain of Philippi with their battle-lines, and the Roman soldier took his stand on sands scarcely dry, on the bones and dismembered limbs of warriors fallen in the previous conflict; when the might of empire engaged in battle against itself, and Father Augustus followed victoriously in his father's footsteps.

> ille etiam *caecos* instare *tumultus*
> saepe monet *fraudem*que et *operta tumescere bella*
>
> . . .
>
> hinc movet Euphrates, illinc *Germania* bellum;

[30] My translation follows the interpretation of Bühler 1959: 491 (so also Goold 1977: 77, with n. b) against Housman, who sees a reference here to cosmic cataclysm (taking *opposuit . . . suas vires* to indicate a war of nature against herself, and *finem . . . minata* to refer to the end of the world).

> vicinae *ruptis inter se legibus* urbes
> arma ferunt...
>
> ...
>
> nec fuit indignum superis, bis *sanguine* nostro
> Emathiam et latos Haemi *pinguescere campos*
>
> ...
>
> *non alias* caelo ceciderunt *plura* sereno
> fulgura. (Verg. *G.* 1.464–5, 509–11, 491–2, 487–8)

Often, too, he [the sun] warns that secret conspiracies threaten, that treachery and hidden wars are growing... On one side the Euphrates, on another Germany prepares for war; neighbouring cities break treaties and resort to arms... Nor did the gods above think it unfitting that Emathia and the broad fields of Haemus should be fertilized for a second time with Roman blood... At no other time have more lightning bolts fallen from a clear sky.

The Virgilian motif of doubling or repetition is crucial here. In *Georgics* 1.491–2, Virgil represents Philippi as a repetition of Pharsalus, fought on the same battlefield which is thus 'fertilized for a second time with Roman blood'. Manilius combines this notion with Virgil's glimpse into the far future, when the ploughman will unearth the huge bones and armour of fallen warriors (*G.* 1.493–7), and has the armies of Philippi trampling on the bones of the dead of Pharsalus; but he also caps Virgil by representing Actium as a further doubling of Philippi (*repetita ... rerum / alea*, 'affairs put once again at hazard', 915–16), while both Sextus Pompey and Augustus tread in their respective fathers' footsteps (913, 920–1).[31]

In ideological terms, the finale is more problematic than the proem, raising (if only to shelve it) the problem posed by the *value* of predicting the future in a wholly deterministic system,[32] and partially undercutting the overtly optimistic celebration of the *pax Augusta* through the troubling reference to the *clades Variana*. Yet, once again, the intertextual framework within which Manilius' finale is situated does appear to serve a squarely Augustan ideology. Here too, Lucretius' indifferent gods are replaced by a benevolent deity, who sends signs out of pity for mortal suffering (1.874–5): Manilius' *miseratus* reaches back through Virgil's use of the same verb at *G.* 1.466 to Aratus' ἐποικτείρουσα, in a somewhat similar but more

---

[31] Cf. Liuzzi 1995: 198, *ad* 904–26.
[32] Cf. Neuburg 1993: esp. 277–82; Volk 2009: 252–4.

optimistic context at *Phaen.* 412. Aratus, unlike Virgil, makes it clear that the signs sent by heaven are *useful* to mortals, if correctly interpreted; and generally speaking (with the caveats already mentioned), the uncertain and anxious tone of the Virgilian finale is carefully ironed out by Manilius, as death and disaster give way to Augustan peace:

> sed *satis hoc fatis fuerit: iam bella quiescant*
> atque adamanteis discordia vincta catenis
> aeternos habeat *frenos* in *carcere* clausa;
> sit pater invictus patriae, sit Roma sub illo,
> cumque deum caelo dederit non quaerat in orbe. (*Astr.* 1.922–6)

But let this be enough for the fates. May war now fall silent, and strife, closed up in prison and bound in adamantine chains, bear her bonds for ever. Let the Father of his Country be unconquered, and Rome under him, and when she has given a god to heaven, may she not miss him on earth.

>   *satis* iam pridem sanguine nostro
> Laomendonteae *luimus periuria Troiae*;
> iam pridem nobis caeli te regia, Caesar,
> invidet atque hominum queritur curare triumphos,
> quippe ubi fas versum atque nefas: *tot bella per orbem*
> tam multae scelerum facies . . .
>   . . .
>   saevit toto Mars impius orbe,
> ut cum *carceribus* sese effudere quadrigae,
> addunt in spatia, et frustra *retinacula* tendens
> fertur equis auriga neque audit currus habenas.
>   (Verg. *G.* 1.501–6, 511–14)

We have long since redeemed the perjury of Laomedon's Troy with our blood; the court of heaven has long begrudged you to us, Caesar, and complains that you care for mortal triumphs when right and wrong are overturned: so many wars throughout the world, so many forms of wickedness . . . Impious Mars rampages through the whole world, as when the chariots pour out from the starting-gate and gather speed from lap to lap, and the charioteer, tugging vainly on the bridle, is carried away by his horses; nor does his chariot heed the reins.

Virgil's despairing *satis iam pridem sanguine nostro . . .* (*G.* 1.501–2) is replaced by a much more confident *sed satis hoc fatis fuerit* (*Astr.* 1.922), as the wars which in the *Georgics* spread from Rome through

the entire *orbis* are to be lulled to sleep (*tot bella per orbem*, G. 1.505 ∼
iam bella quiescant, *Astr.* 1.922); and, in an image borrowed from the
Aeneid,[33] the *aeternos frenos* (literally, 'everlasting reins') confining
discordia are substituted for the Virgilian charioteer unable to control
the *retinacula* of his runaway chariot.

My final passage, *Astr.* 3.625–65, has attracted less attention from
commentators than the proem and finale to book 1. Goold, following
Housman, once again dismisses it as a 'terminal ornament', unrelated
to the themes of the book.[34] I will argue, again, that this 'poetical
description of the changes occurring at the mid-points of the four
seasons' (in Goold's words) gains in point if read against similar
passages in the works of other didactic poets. Indeed, descriptions
of the seasons are almost as common and prominent a theme for the
didactic digression as the Myth of Ages; like the latter, they originate
in the *Works and Days*, and can be closely connected with the
ideological stance of the poems in which they occur. Hesiod himself
offers descriptions of winter (the month Lenaion, *Op.* 504–35) and
high summer (582–96), both quite closely related to the central
themes of labour, religious observance, and relations between the
sexes. At midwinter, the north wind and snow bring misery on man
and beast alike; but even at this wretched time of year, the farmer
must wrap himself up and go out to work. Only the *parthenos*,
pampering herself in an inner chamber, appears exempt: the theme
of the Prometheus myth—that idle females were sent as burden on
hard-working men—is thus implicitly continued. In high summer,
women are just as problematic, since they become sexually excited
just at the time when men are at their weakest.[35] Otherwise, this is an
idyllic time, offering a brief pause in the never-ending cycle of labour:
even at this season, though, the pious farmer does not forget the gods,
offering them a libation of wine and water as he enjoys his picnic in
the shade. Aratus follows the Hesiodic precedent with brief asides on
summer and winter as dangerous times for sailors (*Phaen.* 149–55,
287–99) and a passage on signs used to forecast summer and winter
weather, particularly in relation to agriculture (1064–1103). These

---

[33] Compare Jupiter's prophecy of the binding of *furor*, *Aen.* 1.294–6, esp. *centum
vinctus aenis* / . . . *nodis* ('bound with a hundred knots of bronze'); Manilius' *ada-
manteis . . . vincta catenis* ('bound in adamantine chains') goes one better.
[34] Goold 1977: p. lxxxi.
[35] On the gender-discourse of the *Works and Days*, cf. Zeitlin 1996; esp. 57–72.

three passages can be linked to the theme of Zeus' benevolence discussed earlier, given that the god's role as controller of the weather is specifically related in the proem to agricultural seasons (7–9) and elsewhere to his good will (or that of the closely associated deity Night) towards sailors struggling at sea (408–30, 758–77). Both Lucretius and Virgil, finally, celebrate spring as a time of procreation and renewed growth; we also have, in *De rerum natura* 5 (737–47), a kind of tableau of the seasons represented by appropriate deities, winds, and personifications of the weather. Lucretius' Venus has, of course, been a focus for much controversy; but one might reasonably characterize her, without too much oversimplification, as a personification of Epicurean pleasure and of nature in its creative aspect. What is initially represented as the work of a deity is progressively revealed as the product of impersonal natural forces; similarly, the procession in book 5 is (somewhat paradoxically) designed to demonstrate that regular recurrence is a natural phenomenon which does *not* call for the intervention of gods.[36] Virgil's response to Lucretius is complex, here as elsewhere: the praise of spring (*G.* 2.323–45) opens with Jupiter as sky god fertilizing mother earth; but this positive image has intratextual connections with other parts of the poem where the god seems less favourably disposed to human endeavours, notably the earlier evocation of 'rainy spring' (1.313–34) in which he wields the thunder and lightning which will *destroy* the farmer's crops.[37]

Manilius' lines on the spring equinox contain clear echoes of both Lucretius' proem and Virgil's Praise of Spring;[38] but my concern here is with the digression as a whole in relation to the tradition just sketched. What seems most immediately striking in the Manilian lines when read in this context is their reference to Rome's imperial ambitions and to seasonal campaigning more generally, alongside the more conventional mention of agriculture and sailing. In summer, 'bloody wars are waged by fierce Mars' (*tunc et bella fero tractantur Marte cruenta*, 3.632), and the northern lands of Scythia and Germany are no longer defended by frozen or marshy ground; in winter, conversely, campaigning comes to a halt (*condita castra*, 641). In

---

[36] On the tableau of the seasons, see further Gale 1994: 81–3; on Venus, see esp. Clay 1983: 82–110, 226–34; and Gale 1994: 208–23 (with further bibliography at n. 2).

[37] On these passages, see further Gale 2000: 67–71.

[38] See e.g. Rösch 1911: 73–4; Liuzzi 1991–7: 3.140–1; Feraboli *et al.* 1996: 1.290–1; Abry 1999*b*: 123.

this context, the application of the adjective *concordia* (648) to the
equal length of day and night at the equinox seems loaded, as does the
vocabulary of victory and coercion used both of the stars' 'control'
over seasonal change, and of the 'conflict' between day and night
(*cogit*, 638; *coercet*, 647; *victas . . . vincere*, 660; cf. *pari cum foedere*,
659). Hints can be found here, once again, at a parallel between the
divine and the imperial order: as Rome holds sway over the earth, so
the stars hold sway over the seasons. It is no doubt significant in this
context that Capricorn (the constellation of winter solstice) and Libra
(the constellation of the autumn equinox) were the star-signs of
Augustus and Tiberius respectively.[39] Under Capricorn, war is laid
to rest and nature is for a while at peace (641–3); under Libra, the vine
gives up its fruits and the earth receives the seed of next year's crop
(662–5). We may perhaps detect an allusion to *pax Augusta* and the
agricultural renewal with which it is so commonly associated in both
literature and iconography.[40] As a small point in support of this
reading, we might note that the same verb, *quiesco*, is applied to the
impending pacification of the world under Augustus in the closing
lines of book 1 (*iam bella quiescant*, 1.922), and to nature's 'rest' at the
solstice (*natura . . . paulum . . . quiescit*, 3.643), in both instances at
the line-end.

   I have suggested—in conclusion—that Manilius' so-called digressions, and those of didactic poetry in general, are anything but
irrelevant to the central themes of the poems in which they appear.
I hope to have shown, moreover, that such passages gain in depth of
meaning if read as members of a series; as focuses for dense intertextual engagement, they may, and commonly do, serve as a means
for these poems to orientate themselves against each other, in terms
both of literary filiation and of ideological stance. In Manilius' case, all

---

[39] More strictly, the *moon*-signs of the two *principes*. Alternatively, the passage
may be taken to refer to Augustus alone, at whose birth the sun was—probably—in
Libra and the moon in Capricorn (so Volk 2009: 153). Compare also 2.507–9 for
Capricorn as the birth-sign of Augustus, and 4.773–7 for Libra as the birth-sign of
both Caesar (Augustus or Tiberius?) and Rome itself; on these passages, see Habinek
2007: 239 and Volk 2009: 146, 157–9. On the details and ideological importance of
Augustus' horoscope, see further Barton 1995 and Volk 2009: 146–53.

[40] For the fertility theme in Augustan discourse and iconography, see e.g. Zanker
1988: 172–83; Galinsky 1996: 90–121. It is perhaps significant, in this connection, that
the Capricorn motif appears on Augustan gems, coins, and other artefacts in conjunction with symbols of both fertility (the cornucopia) and world-domination: see
Barton 1995: 48–51.

three of the digressions which I have examined may be seen to contribute to the image of the cosmos as an ordered, legible (or perhaps 'calculable'[41]), and law-bound whole, coordinate with the imperial rule of Augustus and/or Tiberius, whose rule on earth is represented as parallel to—if ultimately subordinate to—that of the stars that, for Manilius, govern the fates of all.

---

[41] On the ideological significance of number and calculation in the *Astronomica*, see the chapter by Kennedy in this volume.

13

Cosmos and imperium

Politicized digressions in Manilius' Astronomica

Josèphe-Henriette Abry

As the reader will have undoubtedly noticed, the title of this contribution is meant to pay a (double) tribute.[1] The first is to Philip
Hardie's influential 1986 book, *Virgil's Aeneid:* Cosmos *and* Imperium. For a long time I have had the strong feeling that this title,
underlining important cosmological aspects of Virgil's epic, could just
as well be suited to Manilius' *Astronomica*, even though the works
differ considerably in their content. The starting point is, more or less,
the same: two major poems, dealing with natural philosophy, which
share a common literary model, the *De rerum natura* of Lucretius,
and intend to disclose correspondence between the natural universe
and events or beings in the human world through the medium of a
poet privy to the secrets of the universe. But at the beginning of our
era, Manilius no longer needed to tell the story of the creation of what
was to become Rome and the genesis of the Augustan world. Nearly
thirty years had elapsed since the *Aeneid*, and the dramatic struggle
between cosmic forces of order and disorder, which lasted for some
years after Actium, had been replaced by a new and evolving political

---

[1] This is a revision of the oral version of the chapter, provided by the author prior
to the conference and just before her untimely death. Though the overall argument
concerning the three digressions is that of Abry, she was not able to make use of some
of the most useful recent bibliography, especially Geiger 2008. Nor was she able to
exemplify her view that Manilius makes use of Agrippa's Map. The revision has been
undertaken by Steven Green, who trusts that he has kept as close as possible to the
spirit of Abry's argument.

system, which developed new ideological themes diffused through different media: coinage, literature, and, most importantly, architecture. And here comes my second tribute: some years ago, when I came across Paul Rehak's 2006 work, *Imperium and Cosmos: Augustus and the Northern Campus Martius*, the link between both scholarly books became obvious:[2] the 'cosmic setting' that Hardie had analysed with regard to Virgil's *Aeneid* was also relevant to major elements of the architectural programme that Augustus had set up during the second part of his reign. Both the changes that the old historical parts of Rome underwent (the recreation of the Forum Romanum, the architectural alterations on the Palatine Hill, the creation of the Forum Augustum) and the complete transformation of the Campus Martius with the Mausoleum, the Horologium, and the Ara Pacis—all this was part of a united vision which expressed Augustus' desire to create a new world capital, highlighting imperial and monarchical themes, with some structures specially designed to reproduce or represent the cosmological aspects of the Augustan ideology. At that time, I also realized that some of the digressions in the *Astronomica*, which I had hereto been working on separately,[3] might be closely intertwined and might be in dialogue with monuments of Augustan Rome. It is this political reading of three Manilian digressions that I am pursuing in the current chapter.

THE MILKY WAY (1.761–804) AND
THE FORUM AUGUSTUM

In the long digression on the Milky Way (120 lines in all), the climax is reserved for the catalogue of *fortes animae* who are allowed to stay in that region as a reward for their accomplishments in life. First come Greek heroes belonging to Homeric epic, Greek statesmen, philosophers, or historical figures such as Solon, Plato, Socrates, Themistocles, and Alexander the Great (1.761–76); then follow the *Romani viri* (1.777–804), who are mainly political figures. The

---

[2] Rehak 2006: xv himself acknowledges this debt.
[3] See Abry 2000, 2006a.

heavenly population is thus a double constituency, Greeks and Romans (one-third/two-thirds), fictitious alongside historical figures.

Obviously, the sources of this excursus are literary and the influence of both Plato and Cicero is felt in the four lines which introduce the enumeration (1.758–61):

> an fortes animae dignataque nomina caelo
> corporibus resoluta suis terraeque remissa
> huc migrant ex orbe suumque habitantia caelum
> aetherios vivunt annos mundoque fruuntur.[4]

Perhaps the souls of heroes, outstanding men deemed worthy of heaven, freed from the body and released from the globe of the Earth, pass hither and, dwelling in a heaven that is their own, live the infinite years of paradise and enjoy celestial bliss. (Translation from Goold 1992)

These lines are also strongly reminiscent of Virgil, *Aeneid* 6.756–892, where Anchises shows to Aeneas the pageant of Roman heroes who are waiting in the Underworld to come to life and realize their destinies.[5] But it is surprising how little attention has been given to the possibility that Manilius' list of Roman heroes might have been influenced by the Forum Augustum, especially as such a connection has already been entertained with regard to the works of Virgil, Horace, and Livy.[6]

In Virgil's case, this issue is complicated: we just do not know how long the construction of the Forum lasted, though the consensus is

---

[4] The similarities with Cicero's *Somnium Scipionis* have already been noticed by Baldini Moscadi 1981: 54: 'L'espressione *corporibus resoluta* può richiamare alla mente *corpore laxati* (*Somn.* 16), come *terra remissa / huc migrant ex orbe* richiama *ex hominum uita migrandum est* (*Somn.* 15). Ma soprattutto mi sembra significativo il v. 761 *aetherios uiuunt annos mundoque fruuntur* se confrontato con *Somn.* 13: *omnibus qui patriam conseruauerint, adiuuerint, auxerint, certum esse in caelo ac definitum locum ubi beati aeuo sempiterno fruantur.*'

[5] Landolfi 1990*a*: 89–92 has collected the main similarities between Manilius and Virgil. Similar lists of heroes are found in Verg. *G.* 2.169–70, *Aen.* 8.630 ff., *Culex* 362 ff. and were common in schools of rhetoric both before (Cic. *Parad.* 1, 2, Prop. 3.3–9) and after Augustus' reign (Landolfi 1990*a*: 91–3).

[6] For a recent brief discussion of a connection between the Forum Augustum and Manilius, see Geiger 2008: 189–91; for a connection with the pageant of heroes in Virgil's sixth book, see esp. Harrison 2006: 178–83; for a connection with Hor. *Carm.* 1.12, see e.g. Geiger 2008: 51 and S. J. Harrison, 'Horace and the Monuments' (an unpublished paper delivered at the Leeds International Classical Seminar, May 2009); for a connection with Livy, see Luce 1990.

that it started rather late, around 12 or 11 BC[7] and that the Forum was opened for general use some time before the dedication of the Temple of Mars Ultor (2 BC). The chronology makes it very unlikely that Virgil would have seen the Forum when he was writing *Aeneid* 6: at best he might have heard about it or have taken part in discussions about the programme of the future building.[8] By contrast, Manilius was certainly able to see the Forum and the Temple of Mars Ultor after they had been completed; but there is not the faintest hint inside the text itself[9] and, furthermore, the programme of Manilius' list is rather different. Despite continuing excavation work on the site, we are still unsure as to the number and identity of the notable characters whose statues adorned the long galleries on both sides, but it is most unlikely that Greek epic heroes or statesmen would have stood there.[10] The same could be said for the figures belonging to the mythological period of Roman history, the *Horatia proles*, Scaevola, Cloelia, and Horatius Cocles, who are not included in Virgil's pageant either.[11]

And yet it is worth asking the question, because Manilius' digression seems very close to the ideological thrust of the Forum display.[12] With every historical figure residing in the Milky Way, Manilius accounts briefly for his or her presence, in a few words which are reminiscent of literary sources as well as the *elogia* inscribed under every statue. He underlines the exemplary virtues or deeds that made each one eternally famous: here comes *Brutus . . . / conditor* (1.786),

---

[7] See Spannagel 1999: 79, although the overall programme must have been discussed and planned at an earlier stage.

[8] According to Putnam 1986: 330, the plans for the Forum could date from 27 BC (cf. Geiger 2008: 53–9, who proposes a date just before 19 BC), construction might have begun in 12/11 BC, and the inauguration took place in 6 BC. It is just as plausible, perhaps, that the influence worked the other way round: that Virgil helped to inspire Augustus, or that both artefacts were indeed inspired by a shared imperial rhetoric.

[9] Unlike e.g. Ov. *Fast.* 5.563–6.

[10] For speculation about the number and identity of the statues in the galleries, see Spannagel 1999: 257 and Geiger 2008: 117–62. As a rough figure, there would appear to have been about ninety statues, for about a third of which we have fragmentary inscriptional evidence from *elogia*. Scholars agree, however, that there is no evidence of Greek individuals forming part of this collection.

[11] In the case of Cloelia, however, it is worth remembering that there is sufficient evidence for the presence of women in the Forum display; see Geiger 2008: 112–15, 131–3.

[12] On a more general level, we might well ask whether any listing of Roman heroes in the early years AD could have ignored the Emperor's innovative visual display of Roman heroes in his Forum. Geiger's instinct might be right here: that it would have been 'impudent' and 'foolhardy' to have ignored it (2008: 189).

Papirius ultor (1.786), Corvinus (whose statue stood in the Forum[13]) *commilitio volucris... adeptus / et spolia et nomen* (1.782–3); here come two famous *triumphatores, tertia palma / Marcellus Cossusque prior de rege necato* (1.787–8), i.e. A. Cornelius Cossus,[14] who triumphed in 437 BC for having killed the king of Veii, Lars Tolumnius, and M. Claudius Marcellus, who defeated Viridomarus in 222 BC at Clastidium.[15] There are several other heroes besides.[16] Moreover, it is worth noting that many of the heroes in Manilius' list played an important historical role during the Republic and belonged to *gentes* that were part of the imperial family in Manilius' time, such as *victorque nefandi / Livius Hasdrubalis socio per bella Nerone* (1.790–1), both of whom belonged to the ancestors of Augustus' stepsons.[17] To individual names Manilius also added whole *gentes*, many of whose members were dignified with a statue in the Forum, such as *Claudi magna propago / Aemiliaeque domus proceres, clarique Metelli* (1.795–6).[18] Last but not least, there was the *proles Iulia* whose members were standing not only in the niches of the left semicircle but also in the left gallery.[19]

[13] Gell. 9.11.10: *statuam Corvino isti divus Augustus in foro suo statuendam curavit; in eius statuae capite corvi simulacrum est rei pugnaeque quam diximus monumentum.* See also Spannagel 1999: 321; Geiger 2008: 141.

[14] See Spannagel 1999: 139 n. 321; Geiger 2008: 139–40.

[15] Verg. *Aen.* 6.855. See also Spannagel 1999: 139 n. 323; Geiger 2008: 134.

[16] E.g. M. Furius Camillus (*Astr.* 1.784; Spannagel 1999: 185 n. 628; Geiger 2008: 140–1), L. Papirius Cursor (*Astr.* 1.786; Geiger 2008: 141–2).

[17] These two men, C. Claudius Nero and M. Livius Salinator, are often mentioned together for their victory over Hannibal's younger brother near the Metaurus (207 BC); cf. Val. Max. 2.9.6. For the possible inclusion of Nero in the gallery, see Geiger 2008: 152. Spannagel 1999: 322–3 thinks that Livius could be meant by the fragmentary *elogium* no. 20; see also Geiger 2008: 151.

[18] Many Claudii were very likely to have had a statue in the Forum: Ap. Claudius Caecus, C. Claudius Pulcher (cons. 177, cens. 178), Ap. Claudius Pulcher (cons. 143, cens. 136), besides M. Claudius Marcellus and C. Claudius Nero; see Spannagel 1999: 321; Geiger 2008: 142–3, 152. The same can be said of the Aemilii: M. Aemilius Lepidus (cons. 187, cens. 179), M. Aemilius Lepidus (cons. 87), M. Aemilius Lepidus the triumvir; see Geiger 2008: 151–2. Manilius seems to have had personal links with the latter *gens*, which was very close to the imperial family; see Scarcia in Feraboli *et al.* 1996–2001: 1.xviii–xix. The Metelli might also have been dignified with statues, either Q. Caecilius Metellus Numidicus (Geiger 2008: 153–4), L. Caecilius Metellus (Spannagel 1999: 322 n. 423), or Q. Caecilius Metellus Macedonicus (Geiger 2008: 153).

[19] According to Zanker's plan (1988: 194), the Iulii occupied seven niches in the northern semicircle; Spannagel thinks that this number could be much higher and that the statues of the Iulii (*lato sensu!*) not only filled the fourteen niches of the semicircle around Aeneas but also the northern gallery; see Spannagel 1999: chs. 3.4 and 3.5; Geiger 2008: 129–37.

As with the Forum Augustum, the Milky Way memorializes not only dignitaries from the Roman Republic but also their most recent heirs in the imperial family. At the climax of the enumeration, Manilius highlights the two most important founder figures of the city, namely Augustus (1.800) and Quirinus (1.801). Augustus, whom Manilius hailed as *patriae princepsque paterque* at the beginning of the work (1.7)—precisely the title given to him on the occasion of the dedication of the Temple of Mars Ultor and inscribed under the *quadriga* standing in the middle of the Forum—appears as the climactic outcome of Roman history.[20]

In summary, if no word in Manilius' excursus connects it directly with the Forum Augustum, it is clear that there is a strong parallelism between them in terms of individual detail and overall imperial thrust. If one accepts the connection, it does not follow that one should agree with Geiger 2008: 190 that the differences in the Manilian list represent a subtle form of criticism of the choices made by Augustus for his Forum. It would be more fitting to think in terms of dynamic engagement with and appropriation of the Augustan monument. As Harrison 2006: 182–3 notes, the list of heroes in Virgil's pageant includes characters, not found in the Forum Augustum, whose stories are ones of suffering and violence (such as Brutus executing his sons). Virgil may well have adapted the list found in the Forum so that it ties in with a central theme of his epic, namely the grievous cost of empire (Verg. *Aen.* 1.33). We might adopt a similar line of enquiry when considering Manilius' appropriation of the Augustan monument. As the theme of his poem transcends the mortal (let alone Roman) world, and as he is dealing with the timeless realm of the Milky Way, it is fitting that his list of heroes should take on a broader cultural and temporal perspective: notable figures from both Greece and Rome are there, from the world of myth right up to the present times.[21] But Manilius still leaves sufficient opportunity for

---

[20] At this point, there is an apparent lacuna between lines 801 and 802 which has been variously filled by modern editors. However, given the potential interaction with the Forum Augustum, it would be very tempting here to locate a reference to Aeneas, otherwise conspicuous by his absence from the list; these climactic lines would then draw attention to the three figures that were given particular prominence among the heroes in the Forum; for which, see Zanker 1988: 201–10; Geiger 2008: 61.

[21] Manilius might be envisaging his Milky Way as a sort of mirror of all the notable collections of Greek and Roman statues; see Geiger 2008: 13–24 for public statues of Greek political figures. Particularly interesting is the collection at the Serapeion in

a Roman (imperial) reader to take pride in this: after all, the Romans occupy about two-thirds of the list![22]

In both the Forum Augustum and the Milky Way of Manilius, Roman heroes achieve timeless memorialized status by virtue of their mortal accomplishments in serving their homeland either as statesmen or, more often, as courageous warriors. The Milky Way is a kind of gigantic and collective catasterism of Roman history: in the heavens as in the Forum the *summi viri* remain models, *exemplaria* of the virtues which Roman worthies displayed all along the centuries and which secured their consecration; and Augustus' celestial apotheosis is already registered in the heavens as his supernatural character is stressed in the Forum (1.799–803). When he was planning the Forum, Augustus wanted the virtuous examples of the past glories to remain forever and inspire the coming generation (cf. Suet. *Aug.* 31.2). The same can be said of Manilius' enumeration: Roman history, which gave birth to the new *imperium* over the world, is engraved in the cosmos as it is on earth, in Rome's architecture, and all Romans can meditate on it as they walk along the Forum's galleries or gaze up at the starry sky.

TEMPORAL CALCULATIONS (3.443–82)
AND THE HOROLOGIUM AUGUSTI

I have discussed elsewhere the fact that book 3 of the *Astronomica* is almost entirely dedicated to the issue of time.[23] Dealing with the difficult computation of the horoscope (3.203–509), Manilius has to explain why day length varies all around the earth according to the

Memphis where, as in Manilius, city leaders and philosophers are located together (Geiger 2008: 23–4).

[22] It would be wrong to suggest that the Emperor would have been opposed to the mingling of Greek and Roman heroes in one list. Though there is no evidence for statues of Greek heroes in the Forum Augustum, Augustus did place there two paintings of Alexander the Great by the famous painter Apelles (Plin. *HN* 35.27, 93–4), which would naturally have invited comparison with some of the Roman statues (Geiger 2008: 142). Moreover, one might argue that the very process of 'adding' to the list of heroes is one sanctioned by the Emperor himself; cf. Suet. *Aug.* 31.5, Cass. Dio 55.10.3, and see further Geiger 2008: 163–78.

[23] See Abry 2006a.

season (3.225–40) and the latitude (3.301–84). To be able to calculate precisely the specific moment of a birth, an astrologer needs a uniform measure of time (the equinoctial hour). He must then know timetables of the rising times of the signs (*anaphorai*) according to the main latitudes (3.385–442); these will also help to reckon the length of life allotted to everyone (3.560–617). In order to make clear the underlying notions of mathematical astronomy, the poet indulges in his first digression on the variations of time starting from the equatorial region, where night and day each last twelve hours all year long, all the way to the poles, where the year consists of one day and one night lasting six months each. The computation of the horoscope, then, gives the poet the opportunity for a meditation on every form of time, be it cosmic time, or the span of life allotted to every man, or the signs which rule every portion of time (*chronocratores*, 3.510–59). The poetic description of tropic signs at the end of book 3, therefore, is not simply a terminal ornament imitating Lucretius' description of the seasons (Lucr. 5.737–47), but a lively epilogue taking the reader back to the familiar activities which peacefully follow one another as the seasons go by.[24]

Against the background of this strong thematic unity within the book, however, 3.443–82 look like a digression. In the previous section Manilius has put into verse two tables which an astrologer must learn by heart in order to reckon the rising times (in stades and in hours) for every zodiacal sign. But suddenly he digresses, providing the reader with a third table, one that summarizes at what rate the daylight increases or decreases between midwinter and midsummer. This issue, of no help to an astrologer, has nothing to do with the main section on the computation of the horoscope. It is a second digression, shorter than the excursus about the latitudes, and although Manilius does not offer any specific information, it is possible to find out the origin of this table. It rests on the ratio 15/9 between daylight (*M*, the longest day, 15 hours) and night (*m*, the shortest night, 9 hours) for a place, unspecified by Manilius, but one which was considered in antiquity to be the latitude of the Hellespont or of an area south of Rome, and, roughly speaking, of Rome herself;[25] the increments of light are reckoned according to the Babylonian System B.[26] The interesting point is that Manilius

---

[24] Compare the discussion by Gale in this volume.
[25] Neugebauer 1975: 711 n. 26.   [26] Ibid. 722–3.

previously used the other system (A) for the rising times supposedly occurring at Alexandria; so there has been a change in his sources, a change of which he might not have been aware. This new table has at least two characteristics: in the general table of the *klimata* of the *oikoumene*, this *klima* is positioned exactly at the centre, with three *klimata* south of it, three *klimata* north of it; secondly, from the winter to the summer solstice, the increments of the length of the day follow a simple mathematical progression of ½ hour, 1 hour, 1½ hours, and, again 1½ hours, 1 hour and ½ hour, in other words, $^{1}/_{12}$ (30'), $^{1}/_{6}$ (60'), ¼ (90'), ¼ (90'), $^{1}/_{6}$ (60'), $^{1}/_{12}$ (30'). Obviously, the source at the origin of this table wanted to show that Rome stood at the centre of the inhabited world and that time passed there with the most perfect regularity, as mathematical progression shows.

Manilius was obviously fond of mathematical astronomy, for both personal reasons (though the many mistakes he makes show that he was not a specialist) and poetic ones: the way he describes the sky in the polar regions and the dancing shadows of light and night all around the earth suggest a fascination on the poet's part. Nevertheless, in light of Manilius' ideological focus here, it is worth considering what connection this digression might have with the Horologium that Augustus built on the Campus Martius.[27] Buchner's seminal theory that the Horologium was a daily time-keeping device in the form of a giant sundial has given way in more recent times to the view that the obelisk was in fact a solar meridian, an astrological instrument to mark the progress of the solar year through the signs of the zodiac.[28] If we accept this, the Horologium might certainly have aroused among the learned Romans a strong interest in its scientific background: why does an hour vary according to the seasons, why is it different in every place, what is the *ratio* of the increments of daylight? If these are some of the issues that the Romans

---

[27] I first asked this question in Abry 2006a: 167: 'la fascination pour les jeux d'ombre et de lumière à la surface de la terre, l'intérêt pour les questions scientifiques et philosophiques que soulèvent l'espace et le temps, sont sans doute propres à l'auteur des *Astronomiques*: il y revient trop souvent pour que l'on n'y voie pas un trait de sa personnalité, et le seul fait qu'il ait fait de ce thème l'axe poétique du chant 3 est significatif. Mais sa sensibilité a vraisemblablement été nourrie par la construction du *Solarium Augusti*, par le spectacle constant et profondément poétique des ombres qui glissent sur le sol, par les discussions scientifiques qui ont nécessairement accompagné cette réalisation fondée tout entière sur la notion de latitude.'

[28] For the history of the debate, which was animated in particular by the German scholars Buchner 1982 and Schütz 1990, see now Heslin 2007: 2–6.

contemplated as they were walking through the Campus Martius, answers to these questions are to be found in Manilius' digressions in book 3. The symbolic function of the Horologium is generally agreed: this was a monument which emphasized the control that the Emperor—and, by, extension Rome—held over time itself.[29] At a more directly scientific and intellectual level, Manilius' digression can be seen to intimate the same affinity between Rome, centre of the world, and the workings of time.

ZODIACAL GEOGRAPHY (4.585–743) AND THE MAP OF AGRIPPA

The main digression in book 4 is unusually large: 159 lines plus a lacuna. Before presenting the chapter on 'zodiacal geography'—the influences that the zodiacal signs exert on the different parts of the earth[30]—Manilius describes the *orbis terrarum*. Starting from the columns of Hercules, the reader is afforded the opportunity of a cruise around the Mediterranean Sea, with its many associated islands; he may also catch a glimpse of the seas outside the *oikoumene*, understand what the three continents are, and even receive ethnographical information on the characteristics of the many peoples living in the inhabited world.

This is in fact the first complete description in Latin of the inhabited world which has come down to us;[31] it is most likely earlier than Strabo's work by about ten years.[32] It was, however, written not simply for the sake of describing exotic lands and people, but in order to highlight Europe as a continent, at the head of which stand Italy and Rome, close to the heavens (4.681–95). In the same way, the zodiacal geography is devised to highlight the sign of Libra under

---

[29] More precisely, it may have represented Augustus' newly acquired custody over time in the form of the Roman calendar; see Heslin 2007: 5–6.

[30] On this topic, see now De Callataÿ 2001.

[31] We can only speculate now on what might have been contained within the lost geographical works of authors such as Cornelius Nepos and Varro of Atax; for Roman geographical writing before Manilius, see e.g. Dueck 2000: 122–6.

[32] The dating of Manilius is typically placed *c*.9–16 AD; for the history of the debate, see Volk's introduction to this volume as well as the contribution of Flores. Strabo's work can be given tentative date parameters of *c*.18–24 AD; for discussion, see Dueck 2000: 145–51.

which Rome was founded and a Caesar born who now rules the entire world (see 4.769–77). It has, then, a strong political thrust, with Rome and the Princeps representing its climax.

The length of this digression, and indeed its very presence in a work which otherwise deals only with natal (genethlialogical) astrology, demands attention. Although it is clear that Manilius is influenced by literary sources,[33] it is at least plausible that he was also influenced by the technical work undertaken by M. Vipsanius Agrippa as part of his (so-called) Map.[34]

A map of the world was apparently commissioned by Agrippa, a man whose foreign military campaigns and technical expertise put him in a prime position to conceive a detailed and visual representation of the *orbis terrarum*. Unfinished at the time of his death in 12 BC, it was completed by Augustus and erected on the wall(s) of the portico named after Agrippa, the Porticus Vipsania, situated on the western part of the Campus Agrippae. No remains of the Map have come down to us, and our knowledge of its existence comes primarily from Pliny the Elder. At *HN* 3.16–17, Pliny attributes to Agrippa both a visual representation of the world and technical notes (*commentarii*), though it is not clear what relationship there was between them: are we dealing with two quite separate pieces of Agrippan 'scholarship', with the notes informing the Map, or were the two more closely integrated, perhaps in the form of a Map with technical annotations? Whatever the precise relationship between the two, Pliny testifies regularly in his work to his use of Agrippa's calculations, especially for length and breadth measurements for provinces.[35]

It is widely believed that this publicly displayed Map was designed to emphasize Rome's dominance and centrality in the world as well as the *pax Augusta*, thus forming part of a number of Augustan building projects which subtly linked Rome with the world.[36] Nevertheless, the technical details gleaned from Pliny also point to a work of diligence and painstaking attention to accuracy. Consequently, there remains

---

[33] For likely sources, see e.g. Goold 1977: lxxxix–xc; De Callataÿ 2001: 36–9.

[34] For general discussions, see esp. Dilke 1985: 41–53; Nicolet 1991: 98–114; Trousset 1993. Strictly speaking, no ancient source specifically refers to a 'map', but Pliny certainly suggests a visual representation: *orbem terrarum urbi spectandum* (*HN* 3.17). For this reason, I find unconvincing the view that Agrippa's work was in fact a monumental inscription; see Brodersen 1995: 268–85.

[35] For references and discussion, see esp. Dilke 1985: 44–52.

[36] See e.g. Nicolet 1991: 110–14; Favro 2005: 224–5.

lively open debate as to the shape and scientific objectivity of Agrippa's Map. Earlier theories of a single circular or rectangular Map, represented on one wall of the Porticus Vipsania, have recently given way to a more 'Mediterranean-centric' model, whereby the Northern, Southern, and Eastern parts of the Empire were represented over the space of three walls of the Porticus.[37]

Without any real information about the shape and style of the Map, it is of course difficult to determine with any certainty the influence it had on Manilius. Still, the question is worth posing, not only because Manilius' is the Roman geographical description closest in time to Agrippa's Map, but also because interaction between literary geography and the Agrippan monument has already been suggested for his near-contemporary, Strabo.[38] Certain features of Manilius' description, taken together, might provide a tentative case for suggesting that our author is drawing information from a 'scientific', visual representation such as Agrippa's Map.[39]

First, there is an underlying left–right orientation to Manilius' description which might suggest a two-dimensional visual reference.[40] This impression is felt particularly in the poet's description of Sardinia as a 'footprint' (*vestigia plantae*, 4.631). Much like the way that Italy is often visualized as a boot with heel, Manilius' familiar description suggests that he is tapping into a popular visual impression, rather than inviting the reader to construct a novel mental image.[41] In terms of specific detail too, the Map of Agrippa looks a likely source for Manilius. The detailed focus on seas and winds (4.589–657), and on a whole host of minor islands (4.630–41), might tie in with the painstaking work of Agrippa, whose exposure to a world outside Italy was primarily as a naval man.[42] In fact, in the

---

[37] For the history of the debate, see Nicolet 1991: 102–6; Trousset 1993.

[38] See Dueck 2000: 127–9.

[39] Abry, who had intended to provide detail for the connection in a revised version of the paper, notes in the parentheses of the oral version of her paper 'I'll gather the details which can prove that Manilius had a map under his eyes.' In the more tentative argument that I (Steven Green) present here, therefore, it is possible that I am doing Abry an injustice.

[40] Cf. *dextra* (4.598), *laeva* (602), *dextram* (604), *laeva* (608), *laevum* (613), *laevaque* (621).

[41] Sallust (*apud* Gell. 13.30.5) would also appear to have a visual reference in mind when he likewise describes Sardinia *facie vestigii humani*.

[42] For the apparent detail of Agrippa's Map, which included information about seas and islands, see Nicolet 1991: 106–9.

middle of an otherwise impersonal descriptive section about the seas, Manilius unexpectedly focalizes the world through the experiences of a sailor (4.619–27, esp. *navita*, 619): is this simply poetic *variatio*, or might this be an allusion to the naval outlook of his Agrippan source? A final point of contact is that both Manilius and the Map of Agrippa draw attention to a world outside the *orbis Romanus* to include places like Parthia and India.[43]

CONCLUSION

In the three monuments described, Augustus undertook to display some of the most important imperial themes of his reign. The Forum Augustum provided a visual representation of the ancestral Roman virtues of which the Principate of Augustus was the climax; the Horologium symbolized the power over time of the Emperor/Rome; the Map of Agrippa memorialized growing Roman *imperium*. The three Manilian digressions discussed above might be seen to act as a commentary on these monuments and reveal the parallel between the heavens and the new political order, or rather, between cosmos and imperium.

---

[43] See esp. Nicolet 1991: 101, who describes Agrippa's Map as 'truly geographic' and notes that Parthian territory was included (specifically Spasinou Charax). Nicolet 1991: 101–2 surmises that the Map contained 24 regions, 19 corresponding to those under Roman rule, and 5 outside, which included Parthia and India.

14

A song from the universal chorus

The Perseus and Andromeda epyllion

James Uden

In the proem to book 2 of the *Astronomica,* Manilius sets out to fashion a place for himself in literary history.[1] When he comes to discuss astronomical poetry, he says that others have described the stars, and he lists constellations and their myths that constituted the typical *materia* of his poetic forebears. But he distinguishes his work from theirs, because, as he says, 'in their songs, heaven is nothing but a story, and earth has composed the universe on which it depends'.[2] Of course, Manilius also introduces mythical elements into his account of the stars, though he could justly claim to have devoted more space to the technical aspects of astronomy than previous poets had done. But the issue here is primarily philosophical, as a strategic verbal correspondence demonstrates. For these 'myth-centred' astronomical poets (of which Aratus is the most influential example), the constellations are, as Manilius put it in the sentence immediately previous, 'dependent on chance occurrences' (*pendentia casibus,* 2.35). That is to say, the existence and form of these constellations are presented in other poems as the result of the individual details of the catasterization myths. This perverted vision of the universe

---

[1] I would like to thank the organizers of the conference for their invitation to participate and comments on my chapter. Particular thanks must go to Katharina Volk, who first guided me through the *Astronomica* with such a sure hand. Dunstan Lowe and Suzanne Saïd kindly read a draft and offered helpful suggestions.

[2] *Astr.* 2.37–8: *quorum carminibus nihil est nisi fabula caelum / terraque composuit mundum quae pendet ab illo.* I use Goold's 1985 text of the *Astronomica.*

reverses the 'correct' view: the universe does not 'depend' on the myths which 'earth composes'; it is earth, rather, that 'depends' on the universe.[3] The very first example given by Manilius of a path already trodden by the poets to which he objects is the Perseus and Andromeda myth: 'some have spoken of Perseus, freeing Andromeda and her grieving parents from the penalty' (2.28–9). No doubt, this myth had a special appeal for astronomical poets beholden to cata-sterization stories since every major figure in the story became a star, producing, as Goold put it, a 'group portrait among the stars of the sky'.[4] Given his objections, though, when Manilius himself crafts an epyllion based on the Perseus and Andromeda story in his fifth book, we should expect a rather different take on the tale.

A mythological epyllion[5] may seem like an accommodating entry point into Manilius' often esoteric poem for readers more conversant with the intertextual *commercia* of Augustan poetry than with the sacred *commercia* of the stars. But this is an anomalous epyllion, and its idiosyncrasies are the focus of my reading here. The moments for which the myth was best known, especially that stunning mid-air reversal whereby Perseus, flying overhead, falls in love with Andro-meda at first sight, are downplayed by Manilius. His concerns are more universal. Indeed, it is the universe which plays the largest role in this epyllion, as Manilius systematically replaces human or mytho-logical characters from previous retellings of the myth with elements from the personified natural world. The sea, the birds, the breeze—these are Manilius' central protagonists, and the sympathetic picture of a dynamic, thunderously alive natural world is a fitting counter-point to Manilius' image elsewhere in the poem of the universe that surrounds and controls us. The epyllion may not further Manilius' didactic project in any literal sense, but we ought not ask it to do so. Rather, it is a kind of 'figurative space', where themes and motifs from the poem can be explored and recombined in new, metaphorical forms. In one specific sense, though, the epyllion does positively advance Manilius' ideas and, indeed, corrects other 'myth-centred' astrological poets' misconceptions about the correct relationship of *fabulae* to the stars. Through intratextual connections to surrounding sections describing the astrological influences of signs in the Perseus–Andromeda constellation group, Manilius tendentiously refigures

---

[3] See Volk 2002: 221–2.   [4] Goold 1959: 10.
[5] On the question of genre, see below.

the story as a myth which 'hangs from the stars', and, finally, not the other way around.

AN ANOMALOUS EPYLLION

Manilius offers an outline of the Perseus–Andromeda myth in book 1 of the *Astronomica,* which will later be filled in with imaginative detail in book 5—just like the constellations themselves, whose shapes, Manilius says, appear to us only in outline (*linea*), leaving the details to be filled in by the human imagination (1.456–73). The account of the myth he gives in book 1 is quite different in its emphases from that in book 5; reading sequentially, it will join other texts in the mythic tradition in forming the background against which to judge Manilius' epyllion later in the work. As Manilius is describing the constellations of the Northern skies, he arrives at the Andromeda constellation group:

> . . . Cepheusque et Cassiepia
> in poenas sinuata suas iuxtaque relictam
> Andromedan, vastos metuentem Pristis hiatus,
> ni veterem Perseus caelo quoque servet amorem
> auxilioque iuvet fugiendaque Gorgonis ora
> sustineat spoliumque sibi pestemque videnti. (1.354–60)[6]

> [There lie] Cepheus and Cassiopeia,
> looking up at the penalty she caused, and at Andromeda,
> abandoned nearby, dreading the vast gaping jaws of the monster,
> if Perseus should fail to maintain his old love in heaven and bring
> assistance, and hold up Medusa's head, which must be avoided—
> a boon to Perseus but destruction to anyone who sees it.

Certainly, elements of the myth are taken for granted here. We must remember, for example, that the 'penalty' in question, Andromeda's exposure to the sea monster, is the result of Cassiopeia's boast to exceed the beauty of the Nereids, a boast which incurred the wrath of Neptune. According to the traditional story, Neptune then demanded

---

[6] This passage presents textual difficulties. *Sinuata* is Watt's emendation for the MS *signata* (1994: 451). Since Bentley, editors have also omitted line 357 (*expositam ponto deflet scopulisque revinctam*) as unnecessary and clumsy in its construction (see Housman 1903–30 *ad loc.*).

that Andromeda be exposed to the sea monster as expiation for her mother's sin.[7] But the essential elements are here, and Perseus' love (*amor*, 358) is conspicuously foregrounded.

The amatory emphasis is consistent with what was, for ancient readers, the most popular and influential retelling of the Perseus and Andromeda myth: Euripides' tragedy, the *Andromeda*.[8] Although this play only survives in fragments, the *Andromeda* was extremely popular in antiquity and owed much of its popularity to its unusually positive treatment of the love theme between Perseus and Andromeda. Aristophanes, in his extended parody of the tragedy in his *Thesmophoriazusae,* takes Perseus' exuberant professions of love as a primary target.[9] Fragments of *Andromeda* tragedies by Sophocles, Livius Andronicus, Ennius, and Accius all survive. It is clear from Accius' version, in particular, that the domestic drama of Perseus' later conflict with Andromeda's suitors was a large part of the story, as it is in Ovid's account of the myth (*Met.* 4.663–5.249).[10] No doubt the popularity of Euripides' play affected perception of the myth itself, which came to be identified with its amatory theme. The myth is referred to in shorthand as the 'romance of Andromeda and Perseus' (τοῖς Ἀνδρομέδας τε καί Περσέως ἔρωσιν) in Heliodorus (*Aeth.* 4.8.3), and Perseus and Andromeda appear as frequent exempla of mythological lovers in Greek epigram and Roman elegy.[11]

---

[7] Apollod. 2.4.3; Hyg. *Fab.* 64.

[8] The fragments of the *Andromeda* are most conveniently presented in Bubel 1991 and Collard *et al.* 2004: 133–68. On the Perseus myth and parallel stories in other traditions, the magisterial, 3-vol. work of the late 19th-cent. folklorist Edwin Hartland (1894–6) is a treasure trove of comparative material, to be read now with Ogden 2008. The story of Perseus and Andromeda was a very frequent subject of ancient wall paintings and other art; see Schauenburg 1960, Phillips 1968, and on the reception of the myth in Victorian art and literature, Munich 1989.

[9] The parody of the work is at *Thesm.* 1008–124; Perseus' professions of love are parodied at 1098–1124. See Moorton 1987; Sfyroeras 2008.

[10] Fragments 65, 66–7, 68–9, 73, 74, 76, and 78 Warmington clearly indicate the domestic focus of Accius' *Andromeda*. Astronomical elements in fragments of the *Andromeda* tragedies are also tantalizing; perhaps the astronomical frame of Manilius' poem served to underline a focus already present in the tradition. Euripides' play seems to have begun with a description of night driving its chariot across the sky (fr.114 Collard *et al.*); this is imitated by fr. 118 Warmington of Ennius' *Andromeda*, and fr. 62 of Accius' play describes the moon.

[11] Voss 1972: 424. On the reception history of the play in antiquity, and ancient readers' preoccupation with the tragedy's amatory theme, see Gibert 1999–2000; Klimek-Winter 1993: 105–8.

The first and most striking element of Manilius' version of the Perseus and Andromeda myth is that it is missing its second half. This is the only substantial narrative account of the myth which ends as soon as Andromeda is freed from the rock, omitting entirely Perseus' conflict with Andromeda's other suitors. The incidents in the first stages of the myth are also greatly abbreviated; Cassiopeia's boast about her beauty, for example, which provides the impetus for the entire story, is merely and vaguely described as *dirorum culpa parentum*—'the sin of dreadful parents'—at 5.540. Manilius neglects opportunities granted by his previous models to introduce further plot information about Andromeda's plight. In Ovid's version, when Perseus flies onto the scene, he asks the bound Andromeda, rather tauntingly, to 'open up' (*pande*) her name, and that of her country, and why she is in chains (*Met.* 4.680–1). By contrast, in Manilius, Perseus is like a didactic poet whose task is already complete: he merely 'learnt the cause (*causam cognovit*, 574) of her penalty'.[12] But the most memorable scene from Euripides' play seems to have been that in which Perseus abruptly falls in love at first sight.[13] Such, at least, is the inference from parodies which attribute to Euripides' audiences repeat occurrences of Perseus' abrupt affliction: so Aristophanes has Dionysos say that longing (πόθος) suddenly struck his heart with great vehemence upon reading Euripides' *Andromeda* (*Ran.* 52–3), and Lucian depicts an entire audience of Abderites afflicted by a sudden erotic madness after witnessing a performance of Euripides' *Andromeda* (*Hist. conscr.* 1). While Manilius' retelling is not altogether devoid of erotic motifs,[14] his handling of this famous point in the myth demonstrates the striking degree to which he has minimized the amatory element. Here is the pivotal moment:

---

[12] Cf. Verg. *G.* 290: *felix qui potuit rerum cognoscere causas*.

[13] As Gibert 1999–2000: 76 notes, the phrase 'fall in love'—εἰς ἔρωτα πίπτειν—has its first attestation in Greek in the fragments of the *Andromeda* (fr. 138). Since Perseus was first afflicted with love while flying in on his winged sandals (fr. 124), the phrase must originally have had very literal connotations indeed. Ovid nicely brings this out in his version: the hero is so transfixed by his first sight of Andromeda that he 'almost forgot to flap his wings in the air' (*Met.* 4.676–7).

[14] So note the familiar equation of death with marriage (545–8); the conventional elegiac topos of the *militia amoris* (571–2, quoted below); and the very Ovidian *supplicia decent* motif (553–4). In Ovidian mood, Perseus also envies the chains that bind Andromeda (572–3); cf. *Met.* 4.678–81.

isque, ubi pendentem vidit de rupe puellam,
deriguit, facie quem non stupefecerat hostis,
vixque manu spolium tenuit, victorque Medusae
victus in Andromeda est. (5.569–72)

When he saw the girl hanging from the rock,
he stiffened—he whom even his enemy had not stunned.
Scarcely did he hold his prize in his hand,
and the conqueror of Medusa was conquered in the presence of
Andromeda.

He stiffened? Manilius' use of the verb *deriguit* (570)—which means
'to become stiff or rigid usually through fear or sim'—is novel in an
amatory context.[15] There is rhetorical point, of course, in the man
holding the head of Medusa himself hardening. Indeed, the simple
form of the verb, *rigesco*, is used by Ovid to describe those turned to
stone at the sight of Medusa's head (*Met.* 5.209). There is playful
irony in another reversal, too. In Euripides' version, Perseus, on
seeing Andromeda for the first time, likens her to a statue carved
from stone;[16] here, instead, it is Perseus who undergoes a stony
hardening in their first erotic encounter. What is most fascinating
about these rhetorical plays, though, is not the ironic reversals themselves so much as the fact that they are substituted here in place of the
romantic sequence which readers, familiar with other sources, must
have been awaiting at that pivotal point in the story. In this ostensibly
romantic scene, Manilius has used the strange, distancing expression
in Andromeda, as if avoiding direct contact between the two lovers
even syntactically: Perseus is overcome, not by Andromeda's amatory
or grammatical agency, but 'in her presence'.[17] Indeed, unlike in
the *linea* of the myth in book 1, at no point in the epyllion is the
literal language of love used of Perseus and Andromeda, nor do
the characters at any point address each other in direct speech. For
Murgatroyd, Perseus in Manilius' account is portrayed as a 'sympathetic character, a combination of the warrior and the lover, with

[15] *OLD* s.v. *derigesco*. Sexual overtones cannot be completely excluded; on the
sexual sense of the adjective *rigidus*, see Adams 1982: 46, 103.

[16] Eur. *Andr.* fr. 125; cf. Ov. *Met.* 4.675. The same comparison is made by Achilles
Tatius, complete with intertextual 'capping': on the basis of her beauty, he says, one
would think Andromeda a statue, but given her chains and the approaching sea monster,
a better comparison would be a tomb (3.7.2).

[17] *In Mario . . . victum* at 4.45 similarly means, apparently, 'conquered in the
presence of Marius'.

warmth infused by the latter component' (1994: 428).[18] The lover and his warmth, are, though, precisely the elements de-emphasized by Manilius.

At lines 587–92, Manilius turns to Andromeda and apostrophizes his character. 'Unlucky maiden (*infelix virgo*)', he begins, 'what a look you had on your face then, even though you were subject to such a great champion!' (5.587–8). The author's direct apostrophe of a central character, especially perhaps a female one, is a conceit of which Roman poets were very fond. *Infelix virgo* is, however, as specific an intertextual signpost as one could ever want. The phrase is the tie that binds the influential neoteric epyllion of Calvus to those who would imitate it. Virgil, Ovid, and the author of the hyper-neoteric *Ciris* all signal their allegiance to Calvus' epyllion by repeating this very phrase.[19] Whether modern critics would classify the Perseus–Andromeda episode as an epyllion or not (and it is a notoriously speculative genre),[20] Manilius' text itself clearly signals its allegiances to the neoteric epyllion and situates itself in the ranks of Calvus' literary progeny. But note the swerve. Part of what distinguished the epyllion (especially in its Roman incarnation) from the epic proper was the way in which erotic themes were promoted from side interest to main stage.[21] Manilius' version of the neoteric epyllion, on the other hand, largely eliminates the domestic drama of the myth by omitting the half of the story dealing with the betrothal and the suitors, and downplays the myth's pivotal erotic moments. For Crump 1931: 22–3, the interest in human as opposed to divine characters is also a distinctive characteristic of the epyllion genre. But in this epyllion, there is curiously little at stake, least of all mortality. Despite the narrator's claim at the denouement that Perseus won a place in the stars for himself and Andromeda as a 'reward' (*mercedem*, 618), the fact that the epyllion is placed in the midst of an explication of the Perseus-Andromeda constellation group means

---

[18] Cf. also Landolfi 1993 and 1996, for whom Manilius' account of Perseus' reversal captures a sense of 'le pieghe dell'animo umano' (1996: 83).

[19] Calvus, fr. 20 Hollis; Verg. *Ecl.* 6.47, 52; [Verg.] *Ciris* 71, 167, 517; Ov. *Met.*10.443–4 (describing Myrrha, the subject of another neoteric epyllion, Cinna's *Zmyrna*). Cf. also Val. Flac. 6.490–1. For the epyllion as the characteristic genre of the neoterics, see Lyne 1978: 172–4.

[20] Kroll 1924: 199 assumes in his comments on the passage that the episode should be regarded as an epyllion; Voss 1972: 432–3 argues otherwise. Romano 1980: 232 describes the episode, instead, as 'un momento evolutivo nella storia del genere'.

[21] Crump 1931: 22; Merriam 2001: 142–3.

that we are always aware that every character in the story—hero, maiden, monster, 'dreadful parents'—already has a place in the stars.

Manilius' 'unerotic' epyllion is a generic anomaly, but the absences at its core thematize a central element of Manilius' deterministic universe. For what, after all, would a love story *mean* in the *Astronomica*, which describes precisely the omnipotent control of the universe over the lives and emotions of human agents? Love is not exempt from astral control, as Manilius makes clear in those passages in which he describes the constellations that influence individuals' *coniugia*.[22] In Manilius' world, reason, not love, conquers all, a point underlined by Manilius' pointed recasting of the famous Virgilian tag *omnia vincit Amor*.[23] It is the universe to which the drama of human existence belongs and, accordingly, in the figurative space of the epyllion, it is the personified universe which is envisioned experiencing all the pity and fear of the Perseus and Andromeda story. If Manilius' epyllion seems short of human drama, it is only because it has been displaced onto the universe, which, at least according to the *Astronomica*, is properly seen as generating that drama in the first place.

THE UNIVERSAL CHORUS

In lines 558–66, after describing the scene of Andromeda hanging from the rocks, Manilius describes a succession of mourners who come to pity and console the endangered girl:

> te circum alcyones pinnis planxere volantes
> fleveruntque tuos miserando carmine casus
> et tibi contextas umbram fecere per alas.   560
> ad tua sustinuit fluctus spectacula pontus
> assuetasque sibi desit perfundere rupes,
> extulit et liquido Nereis ab aequore vultus
> et, casus miserata tuos, roravit et undas.

---

[22] 2.836–40, 924–6; 3.120–1. Nowhere does Manilius say directly that love is controlled by the stars, although, of course, it follows necessarily from his views, and this is the implication of other lines (4.157; the possibly spurious line 2.518).

[23] 4.931–2: *perspice vires, / quas ratio, non pondus habet: ratio omnia vincit* ('observe the power which reason has, not matter: reason conquers all').

ipsa levi flatu refovens pendentia membra   565
aura per extremas resonavit flebile rupes.

Halcyons circling on the wing mourned for you,
and wept for your misfortunes in plaintive song,
and cast shade for you, weaving together their wings.
The sea stemmed its waves to watch your spectacle,
and neglected to break upon the usual cliffs.
The Nereids raised their faces from the surface
of the sea, and moistened even the waves.
The breeze itself, warming your limbs with its gentle breath,
resounded tearfully throughout the farthest reaches of the cliffs.

Manilius' imagistic vision of the natural world in sympathy with
Andromeda has not escaped comment from previous readers. Voss,
for example, places Manilius' passage in a line stretching from the
lament of nature in the pastoral myth of Daphnis through Greek
epigram and Latin elegy to the *Metamorphoses* of Ovid, but remarks
that nowhere else in ancient literature is the motif as rich and detailed
as here.[24] What has not previously been emphasized, though, is the
extent to which such personification of the natural world deliberately
and self-consciously occupies the structural place of human or
mythological characters in previous versions of the myth. In Euripides' play, Andromeda, still tied to the rock, is consoled by the
chorus, composed of Ethiopean maidens, who, as we know from the
fragments, are friends and presumably of the same age as Andromeda. In one of the surviving fragments, Andromeda speaks of her
'longing for mourning with her friends' (σὺν φίλαις γόου πόθον); in
another, she asks them to 'suffer with her' and offers a commonplace
on the pleasure of sharing tears with other people.[25] Occupying their
place in Manilius' account is a chorus of halcyons, whose lamenting
and weeping replace that of the chorus of maidens. By describing
their bird calls in the language of human art—their cries are a
'plaintive song' (*miserandum carmen*) at line 559—Manilius implicitly likens them to previous (human) mourners in the tragic

---

[24] Voss 1972: 417. The specific influence of Aeschylus' *Prometheus Bound* is also
perceptible here. Particularly close to Manilius' present passage is the second song of
the chorus (398–435), composed of daughters of Ocean, who describe the lamenta-
tions of the personified earth for the chained Prometheus.

[25] Fr. 117–20 Collard *et al.* Ov. *Met.* 4.691–5 depicts the bound Andromeda
accompanied by her grieving parents, 'both unhappy, but more justly, her mother'
(692).

Andromeda tradition. It has been suggested (by Powell 1919: 134) that a fragment surviving from an anonymous Hellenistic Andromeda epyllion might have provided Manilius with inspiration for his image of the halcyons here. Noonan comments: 'If the words *alcyones ...planxere* in Manilius 5.558 quote *Papyrus Chicaginiensis [Collectanea Alexandrina* 85] Col.ix.13 ([ἀ]λκυονίς χήρα), then Manilius has entirely missed the effect of χήρα = "bereft" or "widowed" and of the pathetic, single sea-bird, who may represent Alcyone' (1991: 332). But Manilius' move from a single halcyon to a chorus of lamenting halcyons makes perfect poetic sense if we read his scene as deliberately evoking the chorus of sympathetic maidens in Euripides' tragedy. Underlining the theatrical connotations of the scene, Manilius memorably describes the sea itself as pausing to watch the tragic tableau, the *spectacula* (561) of the girl and her avian chorus.

Contributing to the company of mourners from the personified natural world is the breeze, *aura*, which comforts Andromeda and resounds around the cliff face (565–6). Here, too, we are made aware of the substitution by Manilius of elements of the natural world for characters in previous versions of the story. Scaliger, no less, suggested that this *aura* was a reminiscence of the nymph Echo, Andromeda's interlocutor in the first scene of Euripides' *Andromeda*.[26] The key word here is *resonavit*, from a verb which means not only 'to resound', but also, commonly and specifically, 'to echo'.[27] The breeze's 'tearful' (*flebile*) echo, then, replaces the mythological Echo of Euripides, who repeated the heroine's cries of woe in the beginning of Euripides' *Andromeda*. The exception to the substitution of human and mythological figures for the natural world is the Nereids, sea nymphs who come to pity Andromeda's misfortune at lines 563–4. As Flores 1966: 24 first pointed out, the description of the sea nymphs is highly reminiscent of the description of the Nereids in another influential neoteric epyllion, Catullus 64.[28] But their inclusion in this

---

[26] Scaliger's note reads: 'Alludit ad Tragoediam Euripidis, in qua Echo inducitur Andromedam consolans. Vide Aristophanem Thesmopho-riazousais' (1579: 287). Flores 1966: 24 suggests instead that the Nereids (see below) are more likely to be a reminiscence of Euripides' Echo.

[27] *OLD* s.v. *resono* 1. Cf. esp. Verg. *Ecl.* 1.5; Prop. 1.18.31; Varro, *Rust.* 3.16.12. As Feraboli *et al.* 1996–2001: 2.535 point out, *resonabilis* is an epithet of Echo in Ovid's *Metamorphoses* (3.358).

[28] Catull. 64.14–5. Biondi 1981: 112 further notes that the beginning of 5.565, describing the breeze (*ipsa levi flatu . . .*), recalls (or, better, 'echoes') the beginning of

sequence is still remarkable, because in the usual story, it is precisely the Nereids' rage at Cassiopeia's claim to exceed them in beauty that inspired Neptune to flood Cepheus' land in the first place.[29] Still, if we remember their rage in former accounts, Manilius' presentation of them as mourners becomes an even more powerful image of sympathy for the chained girl, in an epyllion where the feelings of family, friends, and lover are strikingly downplayed.

Equally striking is the way in which the sea itself is promoted to the role of central character in Manilius' epyllion. The anger of Neptune, the driving force in the myth in other retellings, is here displaced onto the personified ocean, who assumes Neptune's central characteristic: it is *infestus*, 'hostile' (a kind of stock epithet, repeated at 541–2 and 549), and *vesanus*, 'out of its mind' (543). The flood at the outset of the story is represented as the result of the hostility, not of Neptune, but of the sea itself. Perseus is thus called to wage a 'war against the sea' (*bellum ponti*, 575), which fights back with its 'battle line of waves' (*agmine fluctus*, 580), and Andromeda herself is 'the sea's booty' (*praeda maris*, 592). Indeed, grandiosely, moving beyond the needs of the plot, the flood is represented as a universal catastrophe. It submerges 'every shore' (*totis cum finibus / incubuit*, 541–2); the 'shipwrecked earth is afloat' (*fluitavit naufraga tellus*, 542); 'what was kingdom was now sea' (*quod erat regnum pelagus fuit*, [514]).[30] The sea threatens to engulf everything—even Manilius, whose metaphors at this point become distinctly watery. In describing the figure of Andromeda, chained before the hostile sea, he says that the folds of her robe 'flowed away' (*defluxere*, 556) from her upper arms. The strands of her hair 'were poured' (*effusi*, 557) over her shoulder blades.

Moreover, although Manilius does, in accordance with the traditional myth, depict a fight between Perseus and the sea monster, his descriptions continue to centre, fixedly, on the sea. The battle is an elemental conflict which threatens the stability of the sea as an

---

Catull. 64.9 (*ipsa levi facit . . .*). Here, too, there is also a link to the *Prometheus Bound*: the odd image in Manilius of the Nereids moistening the very waves recalls that play's description of the daughters of Ocean, who moisten their cheeks with 'wet streams' of tears (ῥαδινὰν λειβομένα ῥέος παρειὰν / νοτίοις ἔτεγξα παγαῖς, *PV* 401–2).

[29] See e.g. Enn. fr. 125 Warmington; Apollod. 2.4.3.

[30] As Feraboli *et al.* 1996–2001 point out, this last phrase recalls Ovid's description of the primeval great flood engulfing the entire world (*Met.* 1.291–2).

element:[31] the back of the monster 'consumes the sea' (*consumunt pelagus*, 585), and the mountains, the crags, and the very ocean itself quake at its approach (585–6). At 604, the monster is said to 'drip the sea on the stars' (*pontumque exstillat in astra*), a bizarre collocation that nonetheless clearly evokes the image of stars drenched in the sea, an image typical of representations of cosmic cataclysm.[32] The defeat of the monster is strikingly depicted as his reabsorption into the sea (5.609–10), and the resolution of the epyllion is described, in its final words, as restoring normality to the sea: Perseus 'alleviated the ocean' (5.618). This theme of elemental conflict finds expression elsewhere in the *Astronomica* in a variety of contexts. Amidst the recounting of Rome's military battles at the end of book 1, Manilius says that 'nature herself waged war against us' (1.902). In the second book, Manilius talks of the 'eternal wars between men and beasts' (2.528), and even the climatic changes in the year are described grandiosely as a war waged between the seasons (2.422–3). As I have suggested so far, the epyllion need not be seen to illustrate directly elements of Manilius' didactic programme; instead, the epyllion is a figurative space, where central ideas of the work can be re-explored in altered or metaphorical forms, displaced onto the looser canvas of myth. Astrology, Manilius tells us, is the *ratio* which uncovers the *latitantis robora mundi*—'the brute force of the hidden universe' (4.363). Thus, as a counterpoint to his astrological discussions, Manilius has inserted a tale which portrays the *robora* of a suddenly visible, suddenly personified, crying, hostile, warring *mundus*. Its power over us is different from, but analogous to, that of the tyrannical constellations which determine our destinies.

The same may be said of Manilius' image of the natural world mourning for the bound Andromeda. This scene is more than simply an instance of the poetic fancy of the world in sympathy with our emotions. For Manilius, it is an emotional world. The constellations above us which determine our fates are themselves locked in

---

[31] The paper of Lowe 2004 on the sea monster as a 'symbol for terrestrial disturbance' is particularly suggestive here.

[32] See esp. Luc. 1.72–6; Sen. *Thy.* 867–8. F. Jones 1984, troubled by the startling image of the sea being 'dripped' onto the stars (the verb is *exstillat*, which is 'always used for liquids moving downwards by force of gravity'), argues for the lectio facilior, *extollit*. But such 'anti-gravitational' reversals of water flow are a stock adynaton in evocations of cosmic disorder: see Dutoit 1936: 16–18, 92–4; Mastronarde 2002 *ad* Eur. *Med.* 410–11.

relationships of love and hate. Moreover, the Stoic concept of συμπάθεια, of universal interconnectedness, is, to Manilius, not poetic fancy, but a vital part of his world-view. Of course, it is not part of his philosophy that nature literally sympathizes with human individuals—after all, humans 'hang from' the stars, not the other way around. But Manilius' replacement of human or mythological actors from the myth with sympathetic natural ones recasts, within the imaginative space of the epyllion, Manilius' world picture of humans dwarfed by a dynamic, emotional universe.

PREDICTIVE INTRATEXTUALITY

We saw at the beginning of this chapter that Manilius objected to previous 'myth-centred' astrological poets, for whom the existence and form of constellations is presented as the result of the individual details of the catasterization myths. Manilius' extended treatment of one of these myths will be an important test case for how his own approach differs. He places the epyllion in the midst of his description of the typical personalities of those born under the astrological influence of the extra-zodiacal constellations, the *paranatellonta*. Four of the constellations described—Cepheus, Cassiopeia, Andromeda, and Cetus—belong to characters in the Perseus and Andromeda episode. As we have already noted, the individual personalities and motivations of these characters are not at all emphasized in the epyllion, their narrative place having been largely taken over by personified representations of elements of the natural world. But the episode in fact engages with these descriptions of the astrological influences of its characters' constellations in subtle and surprising ways. In the Perseus and Andromeda episode, various themes, ideas, words, and phrases from the descriptions of the *paranatellonta* recur, but always twisted or applied to unexpected referents. This gives the text a certain kind of predictive logic, since ideas 'predicted' in one section of the poem will reoccur in a later section of the poem, but it is the predictive logic of astrology: oblique, riddling, enigmatic. Thus, if only within the rhetoric of the work itself, the 'correct' relationship between the stars and the myths has been briefly achieved. The stars are not a result of the myth; rather, the myth is a realization, at least textually, of the influences of the stars.

The links are perhaps clearest in the section devoted to those born under the astrological influence of Cassiopeia's constellation (5.504–37), the section immediately preceding the Perseus and Andromeda episode. As in the other descriptions of astrological influence, the section describes the typical personalities of those born under the sign in a series of interlocking images: those born under Cassiopeia will be workers of gold and jewels (504–9); thus they will produce the trophies of war (510–15) and jewellery for personal adornment (516–19). To provide the materials for this they may also be miners (521–34) or traders in precious metals (535–8). None of these themes or ideas will recur unchanged in the Perseus and Andromeda episode. But the ways in which these activities are described will certainly find resonances later. So, for example, the description of personal beautification reads, presciently, like the fetishistic binding of a beautiful object:

> perque caput ducti lapides per colla manusque
> et pedibus niveis fulserunt aurea vincla. (5.518–19)

> Stones have been spread over head and neck and hands
> And golden bonds have glittered on snow-white feet.

Manilius' enumeration of parts of the body over which stones have been *ducti* ('extended/dragged/led as prisoners') gives the sense of gradual imprisonment or engulfment by stones rather than beautification, and *vincla* is strained as a word for jewellery. If this is an odd way to describe a woman putting on jewellery, the nightmarish imagery Manilius employs will be realized at a literal level in the picture he presents of Andromeda chained to the rock in the epyllion. There, the stones (*lapides*) have become the crags (*cautes*, 5.550) to which she is shackled and the *vincla* have assumed their literal signification of 'chains' (551). Andromeda's neck, equally, is described as 'snow-white' (*nivea*, 554). Later, in a further, bizarre realization of the Cassiopeia constellation's astral influence on the text of the epyllion, when the sea monster arrives to devour her, its coils (*orbis*, also 'orbit') will surge from the sea in 'enormous necklaces' (*immensis torquibus*, 584).[33]

---

[33] The description of miners in this section, who 'upend all nature and turn the world upside down' (524), is reminiscent of moralistic condemnations of mining elsewhere (cf. e.g. Plin. *HN* 33.2, and see Glauthier in this volume). But it also employs the imagery of cosmic cataclysm that will recur in the description of the Cetus in the epyllion. Indeed, the specific image of the sea being 'dripped on' the stars (*exstillat*, 604) is foreshadowed in line 528, when Manilius says that the man searching for gold in the sands will 'thoroughly drench the shore, dripping (*stillantia*) with a new sea'.

Links may equally be drawn between the Cepheus section (449–85) and the Perseus and Andromeda episode. Those born under the influence of Cepheus' sign will be stern fathers (449–56); or they will assume the *role* of stern fathers (457); or—moving from the idea of social roles to that of theatrical roles—they will write tragedy and 'delight in the appearance of crime and in the upheaval of affairs' (460–1)—perhaps even in Cepheus' own family tragedy (469); or they will write comedy, like Menander (470–6), or act on the stage (477–85). The most obvious intratextual 'prediction' in this section is that relating to Cepheus' family tragedy. Less than seventy lines after it is predicted that tragedies featuring Cepheus will be written, Cepheus' own family tragedy is written into the text: but with the notable irony that the familial element of the tale is severely downplayed, and Cepheus himself is never actually mentioned by name. Yet the idea of acting and role-playing does find reminiscences in the Perseus and Andromeda episode. So the literal *spectacula* the poet will compose for the stage in 471 will become the metaphorical *spectacula* of the chained Andromeda in line 561, a theatrical show for the audience of the elements. Andromeda, like an actress, will preserve amidst her trials her composure (*vultus*, 553), the guardian of her appearance (*custos . . . figurae*, 555).

Immediately after the Perseus and Andromeda episode, Manilius describes the personalities of those born under Andromeda's sign (619–30) and Cetus' sign (656–92). Having noted the way in which earlier descriptions of the constellations found correspondences (albeit oblique ones) in the epyllion, we have a keener expectation for elements of the epyllion to be mirrored when the other constellations in the constellation group are described in later sections. Echoes there certainly are, but the interpretive jolts here are even more pronounced, as Manilius has deliberately exchanged characters' roles from the epyllion. So, the lives of those born under Andromeda will revolve around punishment, but they will not be prisoners like Andromeda—they will be the executioners. Other signs 'surge' (*consurgere*); but Andromeda's, specifically, 'surges from the sea' (*surgentis ponto*, 619), like the sea monster, the 'bearer of punishment and sea' (*poenam pelagusque ferentem*, 591).[34] Where Andromeda's ordeal was repeatedly and tendentiously called a punishment (*poena*)

---

[34] The coils of the sea monster 'surge' at 5.584 (*hinc vasti surgunt . . . orbes*). *Consurgere* is the *vox propria* for the rising of the *paranatellonta* (cf. 5.175, 270, 656).

in the epyllion,[35] those born under Andromeda will instead be dispensers of punishment (*poenaeque minister*, 620). The image of grieving mother and father that was replaced in the epyllion by the image of the grieving *mundus* makes its displaced appearance here, but reversed: the Andromedan executioner will stand by as mothers prostrate themselves on the threshold of the jail, and fathers long for a last kiss and to feel their dying child's last breath (621–4). Lest the irony of these reversals escape the student of the poem, Manilius formulates it explicitly: those born under Andromeda's sign are the kinds of people who could 'have watched the girl herself hanging from the rocks' (627–8).

A similar ironic reversal exists in the anomalously violent description of fishing, the typical profession of those born under Cetus' sign. The violent imagery in the passage clearly recalls the menace brought by the 'hostile sea' in the epyllion, but now it is the sea itself which suffers violence. These fishermen will bring slaughter and wounding (*caedes et vulnera*, 658) to fish. Emphasizing the fact that the sea now suffers Andromeda's fate, the fishermen's nets are described as 'chains' (*vincula*, 660), which 'imprison' (*carceribus claudent*) and 'bind in shackles' (*compede nectent*, 662) the seals caught in them. The 'bloody waves' that the Cetus shot to heaven in the epyllion (604) are now the bloody waters of the ocean savaged by trawlers (666). The sea monster 'vomits out' the sea as it threateningly approaches the shore (582); in a pathetic reversal, shoals of dead fish 'vomit out' their moisture as they decompose on the shore (680). As before, the ties between epyllion and constellation are readily perceptible, but they are tangled, and Manilius seems particularly keen to point out, through textual reminiscence or explicit commentary, the irony of their reversals.

Manilius' task in writing the *Astronomica*, which is guided by fate as much as anything else in the universe (4.118), is immense—a totalizing account of the rational system through which the entire universe forms an ordered whole. According to Manilius' own description of his task, he must 'sing the very shape of nature, and describe the entire universe in its own image' (1.120–1). The representation of this system in verse necessarily identifies, to a certain extent, the text with the universe of which it aims to be a faithful

---

[35] Andromeda's sufferings are called a *poena* no less than five times in the episode: see lines 540, 546, 553, 574, 591.

mimesis. Indeed, Manilius seems to encourage the sense that his poem, which he audaciously claims is sung in harmony with the music of the spheres, is a cosmic mirror of the universe.[36] If the poem is, then, truly a reflection of the systematized universe, it too is a kind of rational system. In the universe, once this system is understood, then it will 'grant sure paths for foreseeing one's fate' (3.45). By analogy, the complex intratextual connections between different sections of the work also acquire a certain astrological logic, whereby motifs, images, and phrases from earlier points in the work are systematically recalled and developed later in the poem. In effect, the poem 'predicts' its own future, at the only level possible in this textual κόσμος—in text.

The correspondences between the *paranatellonta* and the epyllion are an ideal test case. As we have seen, words and phrases from the sections describing the influences of the Andromeda constellation group reappear when the myth about these figures is told in the epyllion, but always in a way that is oblique and riddling, frequently replacing metaphorical for literal signification, applying similar ideas to dissimilar characters, and so on. Yet this is exactly what we would expect. 'The appearance of one sign deceives us', says Manilius. 'It obscures its own powers and hides its influences' (4.306–7). 'The truth' is, rather, in the 'manifold windings of things' (4.304), or, indeed, like Andromeda herself, tangled in the 'chains of things' (4.394). The textual relationship between the account of the *paranatellonta* and the epyllion reflects precisely the kind of astrological *ambages* which necessarily confront the reader of the stars. Yet, in another sense, these echoes occur in precisely the correct order. As we have already seen, Manilius distinguished himself in the proem of book 2 from earlier, 'myth-centred' astrological poets, for whom the presence and form of the constellations were presented as the result of the individual details of the catasterization myths. Manilius' objection was that the earth 'hangs' from the universe, and not the other way around. Now, when we see elements in the epyllion realizing elements in the sections describing astrological influence, tendentiously, the myth is refigured as the product of astrological influence. Truly, then,

---

[36] At 1.22–3. Volk 2002: 234–44 analyses the ways in which text and universe are identified with each other in Manilius. Cf. at 236: 'The relationship between *carmen* and *res* is not arbitrary, but reflects an existential connection: just as the poem about the universe is itself part of the universe it describes (being, like everything, a product of fate), it is also, in a sense, a microcosm of the macrocosm, sharing the same (musical) structure.'

does Manilius achieve the 'different take' on the tale implicitly promised in book 2. His most startling innovation in the Perseus and
Andromeda epyllion is the way in which the myth is made to accord
philosophically with Manilius' deterministic view of the universe. By
virtue of the astrological network of intratextual connection, finally,
the sky has composed the *fabula,* and not the other way around.

LEFT HANGING

In the dying phrases of Manilius' epyllion, Andromeda, freed by
Perseus from her chains, finds immortality in the stars—in chains.
The 'hanging maiden', as she is repeatedly called in Manilius (5.552,
569, 628), becomes the constellation now commonly known as the
'chained maiden', hanging immortal and immobile in the night sky.
Andromeda's 'hanging' gives her a certain iconic status in Manilius'
text. The word 'to hang' (*pendere*) is used very commonly in Manilius, both to mean literal suspension and metaphorical dependence.[37]
The earth, as we have seen, 'hangs' on the stars. Our end 'hangs' on
our beginning. Given the frequently reiterated difficulty and importance of Manilius' task as a didactic poet, we ourselves, as readers,
depend (from *pendere,* 'to hang') on Manilius, though his fate 'hangs'
as much as ours, just like the audience 'hanging' on the sight of a
tightrope walker, 'hanging' on a rope to the sky.[38] Hanging, then, with
its implications of reliance on something above us and outside of our
control, may well be the poem's dominant metaphor. I have stressed
that the epyllion should not be read directly as part of Manilius'
didactic programme. But, finally, it is suggestive that Manilius has
taken as his subject the 'hanging' girl, whose immobility and subjec-
tion to the forces of the natural world could stand for our experience
as readers, our experience as objects of astrological influence, or
indeed for all humanity, subject to universal forces which we cannot
control, and can only with difficulty come to know.

[37] Cf. Hübner 1984: 225–7 and in this volume.
[38] 5.652–5, describing the constellation Engonasin. The journey to the sky is a
frequent figure in Manilius for the poet's composition of his song: Volk 2002: 225–34.
For the tightrope walker as a metaphor for the author, see Faber 1979.

Part V

Reception

15

Augustus, Manilius, and Claudian

Enrico Flores

Until the beginning of the nineteenth century, it was the *communis opinio* among scholars that Manilius' *Astronomica* was composed in the Augustan age, specifically in the final years of the emperor's reign.[1] In particular, Johann Müller (called Regiomontanus from Königsberg, his birthplace),[2] Joseph Scaliger,[3] and Richard Bentley[4] gave strong support to this hypothesis: to each of them we owe an edition of Manilius, with the last two being true monuments of classical philology. The same opinion was shared by Michael Du Fay in the introduction (*De vita Marci Manilii*) of his edition *in usum Delphini* of 1679,[5] and by Alexandre Guy Pingré, who could assert in his French edition of 1786[6] that 'Manilius écrivoit sous Auguste; c'est une vérité qui n'est plus révoquée en doute' (Introduction, p. vii).

---

[1] Compare the discussion by Katharina Volk in the Introduction to this volume.

[2] He was a famous astronomer who, perhaps in 1472 or 1473, in Nuremberg printed an edition of Manilius. On certain peculiarities of the *editio Regiomontana*, see Kleingünther 1907: 42 ff.

[3] See his three editions the first of which was published in Paris in 1579, the second in Leiden in 1600, and the third after his death in Strassburg in 1655. Vossius, too, denying what he had previously defended, came to the conclusion that 'Legenti enim Manilium, iterum, iterumque omnia Augusti temporibus videntur convenire' (Vossius 1662: *Liber alter qui est de poetis Latinis*, 36).

[4] In the preface to his edition of Manilius (p. xiii), published in London in 1739 with the help of the editor's nephew, who had the same name, Richard, and actually wrote the preface. On all the early edns., see also A. Cramer 1893.

[5] Du Fay 1679, an edition with a bad text and a bad commentary, especially if compared with the excellent work of Scaliger.

[6] Pingré 1786. This is a superb edition, resting on the best contributions of its predecessors and conspicuous because in the *Introduction* (pp. xix–xxxviii), all the previous editions published until 1786 are submitted to examination and discussion.

In 1815, however, Karl Lachmann initiated a scholarly revolution by coming to the resolute conclusion that Manilius composed the poem under Tiberius.[7] This opinion was reiterated by the same author with greater force in his *Observationes criticae* (1815). The debate about the date then rested for a long time, because most of the critics still preferred the traditional opinion: for example, Jacob conformed to it in his 1846 edition,[8] where he developed and completed the argumentation of Jacob 1832–6.

It was Berthold Freier who recognized for the first time the great value of Lachmann's point of view and himself came out in support of the Tiberian date, even if in his 1880 dissertation 'non ab erroribus satis cavit Freierus; plus semel indicia Tiberianae aetatis deprehendere sibi visus est, ubi nulla essent', as Felice Ramorino writes (1898: 327).

Here I have briefly portrayed the history of the poem's attribution to the Augustan and Tiberian periods, respectively, and should add that, from the end of the nineteenth century until now, the *querelle* between the defenders of each hypothesis has remained open, and that 'in the middle' there remains still to mention one notable scholar, A. E. Housman, who was persuaded that the *Astronomica* was started in the Augustan age and continued after Augustus' death, in the following age, under Tiberius.[9]

As for my own opinion, I have covered this in my essay entitled 'Augusto nella visione astrologica di Manilio ed il problema della cronologia degli *Astronomicon* libri' (= Flores 1960–1), where I make the case that the poem, dedicated to Augustus, was composed in the last five years of Augustus' life (from AD 9 to 14).[10] In what follows, I discuss a passage from Claudian's *In Rufinum* 1, with the purpose of demonstrating that the poet is thinking about specific lines from Manilius' fourth book, which, I maintain, allude to Augustus as the living emperor.

Claudian's poem is an invective against Flavius Rufinus, the Roman statesman whose evil machinations are described as wreaking

---

Sometimes it can be naïve; see e.g. 'Nous croyons qu'on peut supposer que ce poëme n'a pas été achevé: il n'a pas été publié; il est resté inconnu jusqu'au règne de Constantin; il s'est trouvé alors en la possession de Julius-Firmicus-Maternus . . .' (Introduction, p. viii).

[7] *De aetate Manilii*, Göttingen 1815 (= Lachmann 1876: 42–5).

[8] Jacob 1846: xvi–xvii: Manilius would have completed his fourth book during Augustus' life, 'quintum tamen librum sub Tiberio scriptum esse probabile est'.

[9] See Housman 1932: lxix ff.

[10] This view is now confirmed by Volk 2009: 137–61.

havoc in the Roman Empire in the last decade of the fourth century
AD. Claudian imagines Rufinus as being instigated by the Fury Megaera, as part of a general plan of the Furies to interrupt the peace
brought about by the reign of Theodosius and plunge the world
into chaos. At one point in the narrative, Claudian has Megaera
address Iustitia, who under Theodosius has taken her abode on
earth, and invite her to return to the sign of Virgo, situated between
Leo and Libra:

> linque homines sortemque meam, pete sidera, notis
> autumni te redde plagis, qua vergit in Austrum
> Signifer: aestivo sedes vicina Leoni
> iam pridem geminaeque vacant confinia Librae. (1.363–6)

Leave the world of men; that lot is mine. Mount to the stars, return to
that well-known tract of autumn sky where the zodiac dips towards the
south. The space next to the summer constellation of Leo, the neigh-
bourhood of twin Libra has long been empty.[11]

The crucial verses are 365–6, with *geminaeque vacant*. This reading
was first argued for by Heinsius in 1650, who suggested *geminae*
(accepted by the most recent editors, Hall 1985 and Charlet 2000)
as a replacement for *gelidae* on the basis of the edition that appeared
in Vicentia 1482, of the *Excerpta Florentina* (after 1482), and, perhaps, of the *Excerpta Gyraldina* (after 1523); Heinsius also preferred
vacant, offered by a pair of manuscripts, to the *cessant* or *cessent* of
the remaining codices.

It is right to be sceptical of *gelidae*, as Antonella Prenner explains in
her excellent commentary on Claudian: the adjective *gelidae*

suscita qualche perplessità, in quanto la Bilancia, essendo la prima
costellazione del ciclo autunnale, non è in genere portatrice di un clima
particolarmente freddo ... La scelta dell'aggettivo *geminus* ... potrebbe
trovare le sue ragioni, oltre che nella più ovvia semantica del doppio in
relazione ai due piatti, anche nella raffinata erudizione e memoria lette-
raria del poeta. La costellazione della Bilancia era, in effetti, un concetto
astronomico di acquisizione relativamente recente per i romani, e che
non ebbe rilievo presso i greci, dal momento che questa parte del
cielo veniva considerata come un'appendice della costellazione dello

---

[11] Translations of Claudian are adapted from Platnauer 1922, those of Virgil come
from Fairclough and Goold 1999, and those of Manilius from Goold 1992.

Scorpione, le cui grandi chele venivano paragonate per la loro forma proprio ai piatti di una bilancia. (2007: 355)

We may compare a passage from the proem of Virgil's *Georgics*, where the poet, speaking to Octavian, makes a prophetic announcement that there will be a place for the emperor reserved in the sign of Libra (1.32–5):

> anne novum tardis sidus te mensibus addas,
> qua locus Erigonen inter Chelasque sequentis
> panditur (ipse tibi iam bracchia contrahit ardens
> Scorpios et caeli iusta plus parte reliquit).

Or whether you add yourself as a new star to the lingering months, where, between the Virgin and the grasping Claws, a space is opening (lo! for you even now the blazing Scorpion draws in his arms and has left more than a due portion of the heaven!).

Compare what Manilius has to say on the matter (4.542–50):

> Erigone surgens, quae rexit saecula prisca
> iustitia rursusque eadem labentia fugit,
> alta per imperium tribuit fastigia summum,
> rectoremque dabit legum iurisque sacrati
> sancta pudicitia divorum templa colentem.
> sed, cum autumnales coeperunt surgere Chelae,
> felix aequato genitus sub pondere Librae.
> iudex examen sistet vitaeque necisque
> imponetque iugum terris legesque rogabit.

At her rising Erigone, who reigned with justice over a bygone age and fled when it fell into sinful ways, bestows high eminence by bestowing supreme power; she will produce a man to direct the laws of the state and the sacred code, one who will tend with reverence the hallowed temples of the gods. When autumn's Claws begin to rise, blessed is he that is born under the equilibrium of the Balance. As judge he will set up scales weighted with life and death; he will impose the weight of his authority upon the world and make laws.

Note also what Manilius says later in the same book (4.773–7):

> Hesperiam sua Libra tenet, qua condita Roma
> orbis et imperium retinet discrimina rerum,
> lancibus et positas gentes tollitque premitque,
> qua genitus Caesar melius nunc condidit urbem
> et propriis frenat pendentem nutibus orbem.

Italy belongs to the Balance, her rightful sign: beneath it Rome and her sovereignty of the world were founded, Rome, which controls the issue of events, exalting and depressing nations placed in the scales: beneath this sign was born the emperor, who has now effected a better foundation of the city and governs a world which hangs on his command alone.

Virgil and Manilius both record the moment when Libra definitely made its entrance into the zodiac as the twelfth sign; they also demonstrate that Libra was closely linked to Augustus' person, by virtue of being the sign of his birth[12] and, besides that, the sign of Rome and of Italy. It is clear from Manilius 4.549 that Augustus is envisioned as a man who will rise as an impartial judge of life and death, setting the standard for justice.

As for Virgo, the sign between Leo and Libra to which Claudian's Iustitia is told to return is in Manilius likewise associated with sovereignty and justice. In the previous centuries, called *saecula prisca*, the sign of Erigone or Virgo had been chosen as the place of justice, but she famously abandoned this place in the era of decadence. These refined ideas coming from Manilius could have given Claudian the notion of the right location for justice: the sign of Virgo. However, in the following verses (372–3), Iustitia replies to Megaera, announcing Honorius' accession to the throne with the words *iamque aderit laeto promissus Honorius aevo / nec forti genitore minor nec fratre corusco* ('soon shall come Honorius, promised of old to this fortunate age, brave as his father Theodosius, brilliant as his brother Arcadius'). Thanks to Honorius' future action, justice will be ensured and his enemies will come under his yoke: *sub iuga venturi reges* (375). What immediately comes to mind is Manilius 4.550 (*imponetque iugum terris*)[13]—but there, we are under Libra.

To sum up, Claudian uses for justice the same ideas as Manilius does in describing both signs, Virgo and Libra. Similarly, when describing Honorius with the words *qui subiget Medos, qui cuspide proteret Indos* ('who shall subdue the Medes and overthrow the Indians with his spear', 374) etc., Claudian also makes use of all the ideas that Manilius had recognized for a birth under the sign of Virgo:

---

[12] See Flores 1960–1: 9 ff.

[13] In addition, the verb *vergit* of *In Rufinum* 1.364 comes from Manilius 1.655, as shown by Prenner 2007: 354.

alta per imperium tribuit fastigia summum ('bestows high eminence by bestowing supreme power', 4.544).

For this reason I do not see how, as Antonella Prenner suggests (2007: 356; see also 353–4), there might be 'una velata polemica del poeta verso il governo appena passato nelle mani dei giovani *principes*'. A lack of justice, if it really existed, might be suggested here by the word *vacant* and, from Claudian's supposed perspective, it would concern the very brief moment between Theodosius' death in January 395 and the consolidation of Honorius' position in the western Empire. Honorius was very young at that time—about ten years old—but already when he was eight years old, he had been named *Augustus* and celebrated with enthusiasm by Claudian in 372–3 (cf. above). The fact that Honorius, at the time when he was still rising to the throne, could already enjoy the title of *Augustus*, makes it more likely that Claudian is deliberately re-echoing verses written by Manilius in praise of the first Augustus. We can conclude, moreover, that the final section of *In Rufinum* 1 was composed after Theodosius' death and after Honorius' hold on power had been confirmed thanks to the actions of general Stilicho. This happened immediately after Rufinus' death, in November 395.

In conclusion: (*a*) Claudian is alluding to Manilius' description of Virgo and Libra as signs associated with justice and rule; (*b*) since in Manilius, at least Libra and generally the concepts of justice and rule are associated with Augustus, it is especially fitting that Claudian uses these allusions in the celebration of Honorius, the 'new' Augustus; (*c*) if Claudian believed that Manilius was talking about Augustus (not e.g. Tiberius), this is an additional indication that Manilius wrote indeed under Augustus.

16

Renaissance receptions of Manilius' anthropology

Caroline Stark

An anthropology, that is, a history of the development of mankind, can reveal a number of underlying conceptions about the nature of man, his relationship to God and to Nature, and the role of knowledge in society.[1] At the time of Poggio Bracciolini's rediscovery of Manilius' *Astronomica* and Lucretius' *De rerum natura* in 1417,[2] an ongoing debate over the condition of man was generating renewed interest. A number of notable humanists, including Petrarch, Facio, Manetti, and Pico della Mirandola,[3] responded to what they perceived as the Christian medieval tradition of the condition of man, as exemplified by Pope Innocent III's treatise on the misery of the human condition.[4] The

---

[1] I would like to thank the editors Steven Green and Katharina Volk; the other contributors, esp. Stephan Heilen; and Verity Harte, Christina S. Kraus, Giuseppe Mazzotta, and Celia E. Schultz for their thoughtful comments and suggestions.

[2] Poggio Bracciolini (1380-1459) rediscovered both of these texts during the Council of Constance 1414-18; for the textual history of these authors, see Reeve 1983 and Maranini 1994 for Manilius, and Gordon 1962; Fleischmann 1971; Reeve 1980*b*, 2005, 2006, 2007 for Lucretius.

[3] Francesco Petrarca (1304-74), *De remediis utriusque fortunae* (1360); Bartolomeo Facio (*c*.1405-57), *De excellentia ac praestantia hominis* (*c*.1447); Giannozzo Manetti (1396-1459), *De dignitate et excellentia hominis* (*c*.1453); Giovanni Pico della Mirandola (1463-94), *Oratio* (written in 1486 but published posthumously); for more on this literature and the debate over the condition of man, see Gentile 1920; Garin 1938; Di Napoli 1956; Kristeller 1972; Trinkaus 1973; Craven 1981: 21-45; Trinkaus 1983: 372-96; Dougherty 2008: 114-51.

[4] Pope Innocent III (Cardinal Deacon Lotario da Signa, *c*.1160-1216; *De miseria humanae conditionis*, *c*.1195) offered to write a companion work on the dignity of man. His failure to complete the projected companion work provoked many later humanist

humanists drew not only from the patristic exegetic tradition of the 'creative' man in Genesis but also from classical attitudes towards man.[5] The rediscovery of Lucretius' and Manilius' anthropologies, with their powerful assertions of man's capacity to develop the technical and political arts and to master his environment, further fuelled the debate.[6] One aspect of the relationship between God and man that was a particular point of contention was the issue of free will.[7] Astrology, which implies a predictable and knowable future, was the obvious target for proponents of man's free will.[8] Renaissance astrological poets responded to this criticism by attempting to demonstrate the compatibility of free will with astrology. With this background in mind, I would like to examine the reception of Manilius' anthropology in the works of two fifteenth-century Renaissance astrological poets, Lorenzo Bonincontri (1410–c.1491) and Giovanni Pontano (1429–1503). After looking at how Manilius sets out the role of knowledge in his anthropology, I will examine how Bonincontri and Pontano engage with Manilius' anthropology, in particular his ideas on the role of knowledge, in their effort to reconcile the astrological world-view with the Christian notion of man's free will.

responses, particularly from Facio and Manetti, who responded with a praise of man's dignity in an attempt to redress the negative conception of the condition of man particularly characteristic of the 11th and 12th cents.; see Howard 1954, 1966. Although the theme of the dignity of man also had its patristic and medieval predecessors, the combination of the usual Christian arguments (the immortality of the soul, man made in God's image) with classical ideas and rhetoric marked in the humanists' eyes an improvement on the genre; see Trinkaus 1973: 141; 1983; Goddard 1991*b*: 252.

[5] Two passages of great importance were Genesis 1: 26—that man was made in God's image ('creative' man, thus, is seen as made in the image of God the creator)— and 1: 28—that man has dominion over the animals; see Trinkaus 1983. In addition to patristic exegesis, there was also a tradition of creative retellings of the creation story in Genesis; see Robbins 1912; Evans 1968; Couffignal 1980; Grant 2004.

[6] Cf. Garin 1938: 105. Despite the scaling back of the early claims of Burckhardt 1860 and Cassirer 1927 that these humanist writings marked a significant departure from the Christian medieval tradition of man, there remains strong evidence of the impact of classical anthropologies and of the reconciliation of those conceptions of man with Christian conceptions of man; see Trinkaus 1973, 1983, 343–403; Blair and Grafton 1992: 538; Gambino Longo 2004: 262.

[7] The debate over man also involved other contentious issues such as the immortality of the soul and creation *ex nihilo*.

[8] Two major critics of astrology were Coluccio Salutati (1330–1406) in *De fato et fortuna* (1396) and Pico della Mirandola in his *Disputationes adversus astrologiam divinatricem* (1494); see Thorndike 1923–58: esp. vol. 4; Garin 1976; Trinkaus 1970: 51–102; Poppi 1988; Trinkaus 1989; Rabin 2008; as for their ancient counterparts, Barton 1994*a*: 52–7.

MANILIUS' ANTHROPOLOGY

Manilius' anthropology in book 1 of his poem is itself a complex text that addresses many themes: the idea of a culture hero; man's divine origin; the role of *ratio* and *labor* in man's development; the role of fate; historical recurrence; and the value of astrology. The primary purpose of Manilius' anthropology is to praise astrology as the culmination of man's achievement. However, Manilius is not entirely clear about how man obtains his astrological expertise. In fact, the poet presents three different types of knowledge in man's mastery of astrology: revealed, inspired, and acquired.

Manilius first presents astrology as a gift from the gods (*munere caelestum*, 1.26; *caeli munere*, 2.115), a 'revealed' knowledge. Mercury as 'culture hero' establishes the art of astrology among men:[9]

> quem primum interius licuit cognoscere terris
> munere caelestum. quis enim condentibus illis
> clepsisset furto mundum, quo cuncta reguntur?
> quis foret humano conatus pectore tantum,
> invitis ut dis cuperet deus ipse videri,
>
> . . .
>
> tu princeps auctorque sacri, Cyllenie, tanti;
> per te iam caelum interius.... (*Astr.* 1.25–9, 30–1; cf. Lucr. 5.1041–54).

Deeper knowledge of heaven was first granted to earth by the gift of the gods. For who, if the gods wished to conceal it, would have cunningly stolen the secret of the skies by which all things are ruled? Who of but human understanding would have attempted so great a task as to desire against heaven's wish to appear a god himself... You, God of Cyllene, are the first founder of this great and holy science; through you man has gained a deeper knowledge of the sky.[10]

By asserting that astrological knowledge is given to man by the gods, Manilius counters claims of overreaching and theft, criticisms that

---

[9] Manilius' Renaissance readers, esp. Bonincontri (see discussion below), equated Mercury with Hermes Trismegistus. For the influence or 'shared tradition' of the *Corpus Hermeticum* with Manilius, see Vallauri 1954; Valvo 1956; Salemme 2000: 21–6; Volk 2009: 234–9.

[10] All texts are from G. P. Goold's 1985 Teubner edition of Manilius' *Astronomica*, Heilen's 1999 edition of Bonincontri's *De rebus naturalibus et divinis*, and Soldati's 1902 edition of Pontano's *Urania*. Transcriptions of Bonincontri's 1484 commentary on Manilius are my own; translations of Manilius are adapted from Goold's 1977 Loeb edition; for all translations, I have favoured a literal translation for clarity.

often accompany 'culture heroes' such as Prometheus. Manilius dismisses the very notion of theft or understanding without divine consent: *condentibus illis* (1.26), *invitis dis* (1.29).[11] Contrary to Lucretius' deliberate use of gigantomachic imagery in his depiction of a defiant Epicurus confronting heaven (Lucr. 1.62–79), Manilius is eager to assert that astrological knowledge is neither impious nor sacrilegious (1.28–9, 2.127–8) by depicting man as a probing investigator of nature (4.905–10).[12] Instead, not only does the poet claim repeatedly that the gods are willing for man to achieve an understanding of the heavens, Manilius even goes so far as to declare that the gods demand it. God does not just offer himself (*non invidet, recludit, offert*) but summons and even compels us to understand: *inculcat, doceat, cogat, vocat* (4.915–20). Ultimately, Manilius is able to dismiss any charges of impiety or overreaching by asserting man's divine origin:

> quis caelum posset nisi caeli munere nosse,
> et reperire deum, nisi qui pars ipse deorum est?
> (2.115–16; see also 4.893–7)

Who could know heaven except by the gift of heaven, and who could discover god, unless he were himself part of the gods?

By making this claim, he explains why returning to heaven is man's natural apogee and why heaven is so willing to disclose its secrets. Rather than overturning or challenging heaven's power, Manilius' man fulfils his ultimate purpose by turning his mind to the skies. Man's knowledge of the heavens is his crowning achievement (1.106–12, 2.107–10, 4.901–10).[13]

Manilius refers to astrology in language that suggests that it is a sacred knowledge known only by a select few who are 'chosen' by the

---

[11] Cf. Valvo 1978: 112, 115–20. Even if Mercury 'stole' the art of astrology and is the Promethean benefactor of civilization's arts to mankind, as Valvo claims, Mercury's motivations are not sinister according to Manilius (1.35–7, 4.866–935). Astrological knowledge increases man's admiration of heaven. For a thought-provoking discussion of allusions to magical or subversive language as part of a larger unresolved tension in Manilius between pious and impious approaches to cosmology or contrasting world-views, see Volk 2001; 2009: 264–5. See also the discussion in this chapter of Pontano's use of this passage.

[12] Habinek 2007: 232–3 takes this characterization a step further in assigning a religious role to this investigator—a *haruspex* examining the entrails of the body of the universe.

[13] See also Lühr 1969; Effe 1971; Salemme 2000: 59–60.

gods or fate.[14] In other words, astrology is an 'inspired' knowledge that is a combination of celestial forces and divine favour.[15] Nature first inspires the minds of kings who start the process of civilization (*domuere feras gentes*, 1.43) that enables astrology to develop.[16] Manilius uses words like *dedit vires, reclusit, dignata movere* (1.40–41) to suggest divine intervention in the natural course of things. Then, after an indeterminate amount of time, astrological knowledge is granted to priests, who secure heaven's favour by supplication and are only then 'initiated' into the art of astrology.[17] The presence of god actually inflames (*accendit*, 1.49) the mind of the priests. In this passage Manilius implies a mutual desire and action on the part of man and on the part of the gods. Man's seeking of knowledge must meet with heaven's willingness to disclose that knowledge.

After narrating the start of civilization and rise of astrology, Manilius flashes backwards in time to the early stages of man, presenting astrology as an art developed over time: an 'acquired' knowledge.[18] The

---

[14] Manilius makes it clear that both the poet and his audience are similarly chosen by fate: *Astr.* 2.137, 143–4, 149. Manilius exerts the full power behind the concept of poetic/prophetic *vates* by claiming to worship at the two altars of *carmen* and *res* (1.20–4); see Newman 1967: 115–22; Volk 2002: 209–24; Habinek 2007: 234–5; for the use of *vates* in Augustan and later Latin literature, see Newman 1967; Jocelyn 1995; Lovatt 2007.

[15] Although heaven is visible to all and would therefore seem accessible to all, as Manilius argues at 4.915–22, only a select few understand its secrets. Rather than merely pointing out that few achieve what is seemingly available to all, Manilius implies a more causal relationship between heaven and the attainment of astrological knowledge. Only a small segment of men is 'inspired' or able to win heaven's favour. Manilius suggests that multiple factors are at work: celestial forces in the form of astrological predisposition (e.g. those born under the sign of Erigone, 4.191–6, 545–6) or of auspicious astrological conditions (e.g. the conditions for the undertaking of his poem, 1.10–13) and divine favour, evident in both the selection and the ultimate granting of knowledge. Thus, it would seem that for Manilius, ability and predisposition in man must meet with auspicious astrological conditions and divine favour. This contradiction will be discussed further in what follows.

[16] Manilius here alludes to the role of 'wise men' in the formation of early societies as well as to a divine impetus behind them, an idea often attributed to Posidonius (Sen. *Ep.* 90) but one which could equally stem from the tradition of the Seven Sages; see Snell 1952; Fehling 1985.

[17] Cf. Valvo 1978: 118; Volk 2001: 110–11; 2009: 257, cf. 70, 258, who read *vinxere* (1.48) as an act of violence. In this section, Manilius suggests the opposite: the gods are bound by reciprocity and choose to reward the priests' life-long piety. The *OLD* is right to connect this line with moral, emotional, or other ties, e.g. Cic. *Att.* 10.7.1.

[18] This form of knowledge and this section of Manilius' anthropology have attracted the most attention from scholars; see esp. Sikes 1923; Vallauri 1954; Lühr 1969; Di Giovine 1978; Romano 1979b; Flammini 1990, 1993; Salemme 2000: 56–64.

poet marks different stages in man's development, emphasizing both
a latent, inherent ability that develops gradually out of necessity and a
steadfastness and determination to overcome all obstacles along the
way.[19] Manilius stresses early man's initial ignorance, his lack of reason
and ability to see patterns and causes in nature (*nullo discrimine, ratione
carebat*), and his susceptibility to his emotions (*stupefacta, maerens,
laeta*) (1.66–72).[20] In describing man's subsequent development of the
technical arts, Manilius deploys the traditional topos of defining the past
by contrast to the present (1.73–6). Manilius attributes early man's
ignorance to his complacency: *se quisque satis novisse putabant* (1.78).
Only time (*longa dies*), hard work (*labor*), and experience (*sagax usus*)
awaken man's *ingenium, sollertia*, and ultimately his *ratio* (1.73–98). As
many scholars have remarked,[21] Manilius' sentiment echoes that in
Virgil's *Georgics* when Jupiter ends the severe sloth (*gravi veterno*) of
early man and introduces relentless toil (*labor improbus*) and oppres-
sing need (*urgens egestas*) to mankind (*G.* 1.121–46).[22] However,
Manilius does not lament the passing of this earlier time as that of a
Golden Age[23] or a time of natural abundance; instead, he celebrates
man's ability to adapt to his environment and overcome all obstacles—it
is not *labor* that conquers all things (*G.* 1.145), but *sollertia* (*Astr.* 1.95)
and *ratio* (4.932).[24] Manilius narrates the history of early man in order
to illustrate man's nascent ability to comprehend and master his circumstances, which culminates in his coming to understand himself
through understanding the universe.

Manilius similarly underscores man's relentless pursuit of astrological knowledge over time. As in other areas, time, hard work, and
experience perfect the art of astrology (1.53–65). In both passages

[19] Modern scholars have questioned Manilius' attribution of the impetus behind
progress and the arts, whether it is to Democritean χρεία or to Posidonian λόγος; see
Romano 1979*b*; Flammini 1990; Salemme 2000: 57–64.

[20] Cf. Lucr. 5.958–61; see also Sikes 1923: 172–81; Lühr 1969; Romano 1979*b*.

[21] Effe 1971; Romano 1979*b*; Habinek 2007: 237.

[22] See *Astr.* 1.79 with *G.* 1.123, also noted by Habinek 2007: 237; for *labor improbus*
and its manifold interpretations, see esp. Altevogt 1952; Wilkinson 1969: 132–8; Effe
1971; J. S. Campbell 1982; Thomas 1988: 1.92–3; Gale 2000: 143–95.

[23] There are two references to what could be called a Golden Age in Manilius
(4.542–6, 5.276–9), both of which could be merely remnants of imitation or, as Abry
2007 has argued, deliberate responses to Aratus; see esp. the conflation of Erigone
with Astraea, *Astr.* 4.542–6 and *Phaen.* 98–136. See also Baldini Moscadi 1991, who
attempts to reconcile Manilius' contradiction of technological progress in book 1 with
ethical regress in book 5.

[24] Baldini Moscadi 1980; Flammini 1993.

Manilius emphasizes the third form of knowledge which derives from man's active role in his own development—only great effort sustained over long periods of time has led to this present moment in which man, as master of the conquered sky, can rise to the stars (4.883–5).[25]

Modern scholars have noted an inconsistency in Manilius' thought: he presents astrological knowledge both as accessible to all (4.893–7, 915–22) but also as a sacred knowledge bestowed only upon a select few (2.137, 143–4, 149), as a divine gift and as the final moment in the evolution of human civilization.[26] The apparent contradiction has been attributed to his astrological subject matter, to his philosophical sources, or to an unresolved 'self-contradiction'.[27] Regardless of which explanation one chooses, Manilius' ambiguity provided a model for his Renaissance imitators.[28] Bonincontri and Pontano exploit this dual aspect of Manilius' anthropology to address the predominant issue in the debate between free will and astrology: given the existence of astrological knowledge, to what extent is man responsible for his actions?

RENAISSANCE RECEPTIONS

Lorenzo Bonincontri's relationship to Manilius is extensive.[29] He engaged with the *Astronomica* not only analytically by lecturing on Manilius in Florence and by writing a commentary on the *Astronomica*, but also poetically, as is evident especially in the three books of his *De rebus naturalibus et divinis* (c.1475).[30]

---

[25] *Iam nusquam natura latet; pervidimus omnem / et capto potimur mundo nostrumque parentem / pars sua perspicimus genitique accedimus astris* ('now nowhere does nature remain unknown; we have surveyed all and are masters of the conquered sky; as its own part, we perceive our creator, and begotten (of heaven), we ascend to the stars', *Astr.* 4.883–5).

[26] Di Giovine 1978: 399; Salemme 2000: 59–60.

[27] Vallauri 1954: 147–51; Neuburg 1993: 276–82; Volk 2002: 204–9. See also the contributions by Volk and Mann in this volume.

[28] For an analysis of the 16th-cent. treatment of the origin of astrology that involves a similar tension between revealed and acquired astrological knowledge, see Bokdam 1987: 57–72.

[29] See the work of Soldati 1906; Landucci Ruffo 1965; Verde 1974; Roellenbleck 1975: 49–62; Hübner 1980; Maranini 1994: 181–4; Field 1996; Heilen 1999, 2000.

[30] See the discussion in Soldati 1906: 157; Haskell 1998: 508 n. 34. I refer to this work by the title given in Heilen's 1999 edition, *De rebus naturalibus et divinis*

All three forms of Manilian knowledge (revealed, inspired, and acquired) come together in Bonincontri's story of Endymion in book 2. Bonincontri presents a euhemeristic interpretation of the myth of Endymion[31] that draws, as has been noted, from a tradition already present in Pliny, Fulgentius, and Boccaccio.[32] Endymion is no longer merely a handsome shepherd who attracts the attention of the moon: he is now one of the early astronomers. For Bonincontri, therefore, the myth represents mankind's pursuit of astrological knowledge. Bonincontri even identifies with Endymion at the end of the passage.[33] In addition, it is through the portrait of Endymion's courageous perseverance and ultimate triumph that Bonincontri demonstrates his belief in the compatibility of astrology and human freedom.

Like Manilius, Bonincontri counters charges of impiety and overreaching by claiming that astrological knowledge is a gift from the gods.[34] Endymion is given knowledge of the moon's movements and secrets by divine consent: *humano licuit comprendere sensu* ('he was *allowed* to understand with his human faculty', DRND II.2.178). Several scholars have noticed the Lucretian language in this passage, particularly *mundi moenia* (*DRND* II.2.179), an allusion to the defiant Epicurus of Lucr. 1.73.[35] Even so, the true spirit of this passage is

---

(hereafter *DRND*). Since Bonincontri wrote three books of the same title to Lorenzo de' Medici, I distinguish the three books to Ferdinand of Aragon as *DRND* II. For more on *DRND* I to Lorenzo, see Heilen's chapter in this volume.

[31] See Agapiou 2005: 44–5, 199–220, for the euhemeristic tradition of Endymion in antiquity and in the Renaissance.

[32] Plin. *HN* 2.9, Fulg. *Myth.* 2.16, Boccaccio, *Genealogie* 1.4.16; Soldati 1906: 186–91; see also Roellenbleck 1975: 58; Haskell 1998: 509.

[33] *Sed me Luna vocat caeli ad sublimia et orbes* ('but the moon urges me to the heights and circuits of heaven', *DRND* II.2.190).

[34] See also Bonincontri's 1484 commentary on Manilius: *Cum Poeta noster dicat Deum illam divinis revelasse sacerdotibus* ('since our Poet says that God revealed that (science) to divine priests', 2ᵛ); *Vere eni(m) astrologia est ars divina quoniam a deo hominibus revelata* ('for truly astrology is a divine art since it was revealed to men by God', 3ᵛ); and on line 1.26: *quia b(e)n(e)ficio deor(um) astrologia est nobis revelata* ('since astrology was revealed to us by the favour of the gods', 6ʳ). Although Goddard's focus is on the three earlier hexameter books (*c.*1469–72) dedicated to Lorenzo de' Medici, *DRND* I, she points out the importance of Manilius (which holds true for his later books to Ferdinand, *DRND* II) in Bonincontri's claim that 'astronomy, as the science of the heavens, is a God-given gift which reveals to its scholars a deeper knowledge and understanding of God' (1991*a*: 38). Bonincontri, like Manilius, identifies the original culture hero of astrology as Mercury (*DRND* II.2.392–401, 451–60), and in his commentary on Manilius, he equates Mercury with Hermes Trismegistus (6ᵛ).

[35] Cf. Haskell 1998: 511–12.

not Lucretian but Manilian. Endymion is not overreaching or challenging heaven with his knowledge, but, like Manilius' everyman, he
achieves astrological knowledge with the help of heaven. Unlike
Lucretius' extolling of Epicurus, Bonincontri is careful not to over-
state Endymion's breakthrough and emphasizes the limitations of his
understanding: *humano sensu* (*DRND* II.2.178).[36] Man is granted
knowledge of the heavens, but only to the extent of his limited
capacity to understand.[37]

Bonincontri's Endymion resembles the inspired priests in Manilius' anthropology, a connection the poet makes explicit in his commentary on *Astr.* 1.54 by linking Hebrew[38] and Egyptian priests to the
story of Endymion:

> Et pret(er) hebreos (et) egyptios legimus q(uod) Endimion xxx annis
> p(er) mo(n)tes nagatus [*lege* vagatus] <est> ut lune figuras posset
> adinvenire (7ᵛ).[39]

---

[36] Cf. *Astr.* 1.145–6. Euhemeristic interpretations of culture heroes like Prometheus, Icarus, and Phaethon often served as monitory symbols of man's overreaching, particularly against astrology and other claims of sacred knowledge.

[37] Bonincontri makes this clear at the beginning of his commentary on Manilius,
where he divides philosophy into three kinds: 'divine, mathematical, and natural' (i.e.
theology, mathematics, and natural philosophy). The limitations of man's intellect
circumscribe his understanding of the first and last kinds (2ʳ), but Bonincontri places
astrology in the second: *Secundum vero genus quod (et) astrologiam co(m)plectitur . . .
quod mathematicum nu(n)cupamus totu(m) scientificu(m) est* ('but the second kind,
because it also includes astrology about which we are about to discuss which we call
mathematical, is entirely scientific', 2ᵛ). Bonincontri's belief in the interconnectedness
of astronomy and astrology also explains his interpolated lines in book 1: *Qui sua
disposuit p(er) temp(or)a, cognita ut essent / Omnibus (et) mundi facies celumq(ue)
supernum* ('who arranged the appearance of heaven and the sky above in special
cycles of time that they be known to all', 1.38–9, 6ᵛ).

[38] Bonincontri mentions several times in this section that the Hebrew prophets
and patriarchs knew astrology and thus could also be the early kings and priests in
Manilius' anthropology; see esp. 6ᵛ–7ʳ.

[39] See also Bonincontri's comment on Endymion in his unpublished commentary
on *DRND* at II.2.151: *Endymona: hic philosophus primus apud Graecos lunae formas
admiratus, cum eius varios motus vidisset, triginta annis observasse haec dicitur,
antequam quicquam veri de eius motu et formis invenisset* ('Endymion: he was the
first philosopher among the Greeks who wondered at the shapes of the moon, when he
had seen her different movements; he is said to have observed these things for thirty
years before he discovered anything true about her movement and phases', cod. Vat.
Lat. 2845, 105ᵛ). The text for the 1484 Manilius commentary was copied from cod. Vat.
Ottob. Lat. 1706, which contains the correct reading *vagatus* (18ʳ) but also omits the
finite verb <est>, which is merely a diagnostic conjecture. My thanks to Wolfgang
Hübner and to Stephan Heilen for discussing this passage with me and to Heilen for
providing the readings from both cod. Ottob. Lat. 1706 and cod. Vat. Lat. 2845.

And besides the Hebrews and Egyptians we read that Endymion wandered through the mountains for thirty years in order to discover the phases of the moon.

Like the priests in their supplications to the gods, Endymion spends long hours in devotion to his goddess, the moon. Endymion is *fervidus* (*DRND* II.2.155) like the *fervida* stars he seeks and like the priests, who are inflamed by the divine *numen*'s presence (*Astr.* 1.49).[40] While Bonincontri does not exclude the role of direct divine influence, his Endymion also shows signs of a certain celestial predisposition for astrology. Endymion's relentless devotion to the moon is remarkably similar to Bonincontri's discussion later in book 2 of men under the planetary influence of Mercury.[41] Mercury can have both negative and positive effects, depending on his appearance with other planets. For example, with Saturn, the sleeplessness he causes can be a symptom of man's insatiable desire for gold as well as for knowledge.[42] However, these celestial forces can be overturned or mediated and directed towards the good, as Bonincontri makes clear in describing the two paths, and hence the two choices, before men under Mercury's influence.[43] They can either fall victim to their carnal desires and be led to Tartarus, or they can ascend to heaven after living a life of piety, devoted to the arts (*DRND* II.2.442–50).[44] Despite stellar or planetary influence on the body, Bonincontri strongly asserts the will of the mind to choose the ultimate path (*DRND* II.2.442–4). In this way, he reconciles his astrological beliefs

---

[40] Bonincontri's Endymion portrays characteristics of 'hot melancholy'; see the discussion in this chapter.

[41] See esp. *DRND* II.2.404–60; Endymion also bears resemblance to men who are born under the sign of Erigone in Manilius, *Astr.* 4.191–6, 545–6.

[42] *Hic premit insomnes duro dare tempora lucro; / impellitque homines naturae discere mores, / Saturni hospitio si fulserit astrave signet* ('if he (Mercury) should shine in the quarters of Saturn or should mark the stars, this one vexes sleepless men to give time to toilsome profit and drives men to learn the precepts of nature', *DRND* II.2.404–6).

[43] The similarity to Ficino's 'hot melancholy' is striking; see e.g. *De vita libri tres* 1.4.1–9, 1.5.17, 1.6.11–28. Although Ficino's *De vita* was written in 1478–80 and the *editio princeps* appeared in 1489, his ideas are adumbrated in earlier works; for discussions of melancholy and the influence of Saturn, see Klibansky *et al.* 1964; Culianu 1987: 46–52.

[44] Cf. *DRND* II.2.183–90, where Bonincontri describes the path of Endymion and his fellow pursuers of knowledge, including himself.

and man's free will.[45] This explains why Bonincontri emphasizes that Endymion's yearning for knowledge has nothing to do with a desire for wealth.[46] While Endymion exhibits the characteristics of a man under Mercury's planetary influence (his passion and his sleeplessness, *fervidus insomnis* (*DRND* II.2.155)), he directs his energies not to accumulating wealth but to investigating the heavens. Endymion, thus, chooses the path to heaven. For Bonincontri, astrological predisposition coupled with will and right living provides the necessary conditions for divine inspiration that enable man to ascend to heaven and attain astrological knowledge.[47]

The route to heaven is not an easy one, however. As for Manilius' everyman, Endymion's understanding of the moon comes only after much effort over a long period of time.[48] In lines 173–5, drawing on both the Virgilian and Manilian passages already mentioned, Bonincontri distinguishes the initial skill from the perfected art.[49]

---

[45] Bonincontri explains this further at the beginning of his commentary on Manilius, by claiming that celestial forces act on *materia* but that the intellect (being the divine part in man) is able to overcome these influences (3^v–4^r); see the discussion in Soldati 1906: 152–3, who quotes this passage and a letter to Bonincontri from Ficino that addresses his reconciliation of Providence, Fate, and man's Free Will (Ficino, *Opera* 1576: 1.2, 750). Bonincontri is not entirely consistent, as earlier in that same section he claims that the stars only signify but do not bring about what will happen: *dicamus ergo sidera non facere sed significare* ('therefore we may say that the stars do not cause but indicate (future things)', 3^v).

[46] *Non illi studium gemmae, non divitis auri / cura fuit, sed sancta deum perquirere templa / et superum flammas et fervida sidera caeli* ('that one had no desire for jewels, no care for precious gold, only to seek out the sacred sanctuaries of the gods and the fires of heaven and the burning stars of the sky', *DRND* II.2.156–8); cf. *DRND* II.2.412–13: *hic etiam cupidos auri rerumque novarum / esse animos hominum cogit, vigilare iacentes* ('this one also urges the hearts of men to be desirous of gold and of new things and those who are lying in repose to stay awake').

[47] *Hic caelo dignus superas et scandere sedes* ('this man is worthy of heaven and to ascend to the upper seats', *DRND* II.2.450). Bonincontri's belief that only pious men can enter the sanctuaries of heaven and attain astrological knowledge is also evident in Ficino's letter to Bonincontri: 'You are accustomed often to say, Lorenzo, that ungodly men are never able to become true astrologers; which, indeed, also seems to me to be very true. For if heaven is the sanctuary of God himself, it is fitting that impious men be driven far away from heaven and heavenly secrets' (Ficino, *Opera* 1576: 1.2, 787, also mentioned by Goddard 1991a: 38).

[48] *Tantum illi studium longaevi temporis acre / attulit* ('that one's ardent exertion of so many years helped him so much', *DRND* II.2.177–8).

[49] Flammini 1993 views *sollertia* as the skill that drives mankind's technical advancement, but it is *ratio* that allows man to ascend. This distinction is also used to separate man's reason from an animal's instinct, or *sollertia*; see e.g. Cic. *Off.* 1.157, *Nat. D.* 2.48.123.

Endymion's *sollertior usus* conquers all things, but his *labor* and *studium* perfect it.[50] Time, hard work, and experience give Endymion both the desire and the strength (*velle et vim*, DRND II.2.174–5) to understand and to pursue his art to perfection. Bonincontri emphasizes Endymion's courageous perseverance in investigating the heavens, demonstrated not only in the great lengths he goes physically in tracking the movements of the moon but also mentally in his tireless effort over so many years. It is the extreme physical and mental exertion (*labor* and *sollertia*) on his chosen virtuous path that earns for Endymion both his knowledge and entrance to heaven. His example leads the way to those who would follow: *haec via sublimes animos ad sidera vexit* ('this path has carried exalted minds to the stars', DRND II.2.183).

For Bonincontri, then, astrological knowledge not only furthers man's understanding of God and of celestial influences but also gives him the tools to act. It is in man's power to act and not merely be acted upon that Bonincontri most clearly celebrates man's freedom.

Manilius' anthropology was taken up in a different way by Giovanni Pontano, a friend of Bonincontri and a fellow member of the academy in Naples, who wrote several astrological works, most notably the *De rebus coelestibus* (1494), a technical treatise on astrology, and *Urania* (1476–80), an astrological poem in five books closely modelled on Manilius' *Astronomica*.[51] In *Urania*, Pontano discusses the divine forces that act upon mankind, attributing much of man's astrological knowledge to a culture hero or to celestial influences (revealed and inspired knowledge). In his anthropology, however, which is both the culmination of the creation story and the conclusion of the first book, Pontano takes Bonincontri's Endymion a step further and celebrates man's active role in shaping his own destiny.

---

[50] *Omnia sed postquam vicit sollertior usus / et labor et studium, quod perficit omnia, velle et / vim dedit* ('but after more skilful experience conquered all things, both hard work and enthusiasm, which perfects all things, gave him the will and the strength', DRND II.2.173–5); in his Manilius commentary, Bonincontri draws from a number of different sources to explain the concept of *sollertia* and *labor*, including the aforementioned passage in Virgil's *Georgics* and *sollertia* in Lucretius. Bonincontri stresses the experimental quality of *sollertia* as well as the idea that *labor* is both the condition of man and a necessary component in striving to attain wisdom (8ᵛ–9ʳ).

[51] See Soldati 1906; Toffanin 1938; Tateo 1960; De Nichilo 1975; Hübner 1980; Kidwell 1991; Haskell 1998. While Pontano addresses the subject of free will in other works (esp. *Aegidius, Charon, De fortuna*), this discussion focuses on Pontano's use of Manilius' anthropology to reconcile astrology with man's free will in his *Urania*; cf. Goddard 1991*b*.

For most of book 1, Pontano emphasizes the role of revealed and inspired knowledge in mankind's pursuit of astrological wisdom. In the proem he stresses the importance of the astrological knowledge which his poem offers by describing the powerful divine forces that set events in motion and affect actions on earth (*Urania* 1.1–7). With divine inspiration and with the aid of Mercury, Pontano intends to take his son Lucio on a celestial journey through the heavens (cf. Manilius, *Astr.* 1.13–15, 2.58–9, 136–44).[52] As in Manilius, Mercury acts as the culture hero or 'instructor' of astrological knowledge. Mercury, the grandson of *coelifer* (heaven-bearing) Atlas, will teach Pontano's son the known arts of astrology: *notas puerum puer instruet artis* (*Urania* 1.30–1).

Later in book 1 in his description of planetary influences, Pontano presents Saturn and Mercury both as culture heroes and as the celestial forces behind the development of the agricultural and industrial arts. After describing Saturn's appearance and characteristics, Pontano narrates the story of his expulsion from heaven and refuge in Latium, where he introduces the art of agriculture to men (*Urania* 1.705–26).[53] Likewise, after discussing Mercury's ancestry, attributes, and patronage over the sacred arts (*Urania* 1.105–37), Pontano describes Mercury's planetary influence on earth in conjunction with the moon. Mercury brings about the arts of seafaring, medicine, war, and jurisprudence (*Urania* 1.137–62). By combining mythology with astrology, Pontano highlights not only the historical moment of these gods as culture heroes but also their continuing influence on earth as planets.

In book 2, Pontano develops Mercury's role in Manilius' anthropology by incorporating all three forms of knowledge in order to demonstrate how they work together in mankind's development. Pontano's Mercury acts as the impetus behind mankind's achievement in the technical and cultural arts and as the culture hero of astrological knowledge. Pontano qualifies heaven's importance, however, by emphasizing man's role in his own development. Mercury, impressed by the skilful industry (*sollers Industria, Urania* 2.436) of mankind in the agricultural arts, decides to help man progress to the next stage of his development. Through the constellation Gemini, Mercury 'inspires' and instructs mankind: *traxit, accessit* (*Urania* 2.443–4). Once the process towards the noble arts (*bonae artes*,

---

[52] For Manilius' use of this metaphor, see esp. Volk 2001.
[53] Cf. Verg. *Aen.* 8.319–23.

Urania 2.446) has begun, Mercury himself reveals the arts of astrology, rhetoric, and writing to man (*Urania* 2.451–4, 485–6). Man's achievement not only reaffirms his divine origin but also wins heaven's approval and aid (*Urania* 2.457–61).[54] As in Manilius' anthropology, mankind develops the arts of civilization with time, reason, and experience: *ratio, doctrina, ingenium, usus* (*Urania* 2.442–7, 455–61). Beyond this, however, man also receives divine help and inspiration. For Pontano as for Manilius, then, man's progress is a collaborative effort between man and heaven.

Pontano assigns man the ultimate responsibility for his own actions in the story of creation at the end of book 1. Pontano begins his creation story with a council of the gods and narrates a 'mini' anthropology in the form of God's plan for mankind (*Urania* 1.951–69). Man will have part of the divine within him (*Urania* 1.952–4).[55] In Jupiter's prophecy, Pontano attributes all positive aspects of man's development to his divine part: it is the divine part of man that founds cities, establishes law, assigns names to things, follows what is right, fights against what is wrong, avoids dangers, and lives honestly (*Urania* 1.955–67). In this way, Pontano clearly assigns responsibility for the good and evil in man: all good is from God, all evil is man's own making.[56] Man chooses to act according to his better nature (the divine part of himself) or not and, therefore, is responsible for his actions.

For Pontano, as for Manilius, astrological wisdom frees man from his ignorance, fear, and superstition (*Urania* 1.679–96, *Astr.* 1.96–112) and brings him closer to God and to his origin (*Urania* 1.962–7, 2.457–61).[57] Most importantly, however, for Pontano, astrological expertise

---

[54] Pontano also addresses Mercury's 'gift' of the noble arts to mankind. While Mercury acts on his own initiative in helping mankind, the gods approve of his actions and benefit as a result: *unde et honos superis et victima creverit aris* ('whence increased both honour for the gods and sacrificial victims for the altars', *Urania* 2.473); see the discussion above.

[55] *Tum condere membra / cura sit, aetherios divini seminis haustus / apta haurire animos coelesti e fomite ductos* ('then let it be a care to fashion members suitable to gather minds which have drunk ethereal draughts of divine seed from heavenly tinder', *Urania* 1.952–4).

[56] See also *De mundi creatione* 111–12: *quodque decet bona cuncta deo iustumque piumque/ascribis, nostrae sed mala nequitiae* ('and it is fitting that you ascribe justice and piety and all good things to God but bad things to our wickedness', Soldati 1902, *Carmina* II, 231); see Trinkaus 1985: 453.

[57] For Manilius, Bonincontri, and Pontano, man's divine origin necessitates both his quest for astrological knowledge and his ultimate celestial return.

empowers mankind to act (*Urania* 4.636–42).[58] Without astrological knowledge (cf. *Astr.* 1.66–72, 103–5), man can fall victim to circumstances and to his senses, but with astrological knowledge, man's reason and will can overturn celestial predisposition and influence.

In his anthropology, Pontano focuses almost entirely on man's gradual acquisition of knowledge. By eliminating a culture hero from the anthropology itself and instead emphasizing mankind's self-motivated and self-propelled progress, Pontano further asserts man's responsibility for his actions.[59] Despite man's potential because of his divine nature, at his creation he is without any natural advantage: his corporeal weakness—*corpore debilis ipso* (*Urania* 1.1127)—leaves him vulnerable until he acquires the arts of civilization. Man is born naked, poor, and needy: *nudus, inops, dura egestas* (*Urania* 1.1128).[60] Yet despite this, man is born with great hope, *spe ingenti* (*Urania* 1.1127), and an inherent ability to adapt to his environment and overcome all obstacles.

For Pontano, man's initial acquisition of knowledge, particularly of the basics of survival such as food and shelter, comes not only from necessity, but also through observing and learning from nature, *formica monstrante* (*Urania* 1.1138).[61] In contrast to his preceding narration of bees and their divine vigour, *divinum vigorem* (*Urania* 1.1118),[62] creatures who already understand the arts of civilization as if by natural instinct, man develops the technical and political arts only with time, hard work, and experience: *ipsa dies, multusque*

---

[58] *Saepe tamen vis firma animi, resque extera, lexve / alternant fata, aut genio adversatur egestas* ('nevertheless, often a powerful force of mind, and external action, or law changes destined events, or want opposes natural inclination', *Urania* 4.636–7), noted also by Tateo 1960: 25. In *Urania* 4.636–42, Pontano responds to the controversial opening of *Astr.* 4.1–118, esp. 108–18 (cf. *Urania* 1.697–703). Hints of man's assertion of will over nature also appear in Manilius' allusions to magic, e.g. *Astr.* 1.1–6, 92–4; see Baldini Moscadi 1980; Volk 2009: 246–8.

[59] Goddard 1991*b*: 256. Cf. Tateo's thought-provoking assertion that Pontano moves towards an Epicurean materiality in his *Urania* (1960: 74–5).

[60] Cf. Lucr. 5.222–7, Plin. *HN* 7.1, Lactant. *De opificio Dei* 3.1–2, even Virgil's *egestas* in *G.* 1.146; see also Tateo 1960: 77; Goddard 1991*b*: 253–5.

[61] Cf. *exemplo monstrante viam* ('with imitation showing the way', *Astr.* 1.62).

[62] Pontano not only alludes to the bees in Virgil's *Georgics*, as Hübner 1980: 58–9 and others have mentioned, but also engages with the 'misery of man' topos by pointing out man's natural disadvantages in contrast to other animals. Instead of lamenting man's wretched state, however, Pontano celebrates his adaptability and ingenuity.

labor . . . pervigil usus (*Urania* 1.1139–40)—the same factors so crucial to man's development in Manilius' anthropology.

Like Manilius, Pontano also relies on divine intervention to explain
man's jump from complacency about being able to satisfy basic needs
to his rapid development of technology and of the political and social
arts. Instead of a culture hero, however, the sudden appearance of fire
helps bring about the development of the arts (cf. *Urania* 1.105–62,
705–26, 2.433–76). Fire is the divine gift, *divini muneris* (*Urania*
1.1149), that instigates mankind's development.[63] Although fire initially arouses fear, over time man realizes its potential. In addition to
launching the technical arts of metallurgy, agriculture, and architecture, fire is also the stimulus for social progress.[64] Man no longer lives
a solitary existence but learns to interact and to communicate. Pontano's fire, therefore, is proof of the cooperation between heaven and
mankind in human development, but, by reducing heaven's role to
the occurrence of a natural phenomenon or to chance, Pontano shifts
the focus entirely to man's responsibility and actions.

Unlike in Manilius, the summit of Pontano's anthropology is not
astrology but poetry—*carmen* over *res*, and, therefore, an individual's
achievement of astrological knowledge comes with the responsibility
to share it for the improvement of society.[65] Pontano narrates man's
triumph over nature and ultimate ascendance to God not in his
anthropology but in God's speech to all the gods before his creation,
as a prophecy or assertion of divine Providence.[66] For Manilius, man
has at last achieved the point at which he can ascend to heaven by
virtue of his astrological knowledge. For Pontano, however, this
moment is deferred to a time yet to be realized.

---

[63] Pontano's choice of fire is consistent with the long poetic tradition starting with
Hesiod of Prometheus as the culture hero who steals fire for man. Pontano's equivo-
cation on this matter—he attributes fire to lightning or man's striking of flint (cf.
Verg. *Aen.* 1.174–6)—and the absence of a culture hero (like Prometheus) point to an
almost Lucretian determination to make man wholly responsible for his development
(cf. Lucr. 5.1091–1101).

[64] Vitruvius also highlights the social element in the discovery of fire (*De arch.*
2.1.1–2).

[65] See Trinkaus 1983: 365–9 for Pontano's interest in rhetoric and its role in
society.

[66] '*Sic placitum, sic nostra fluant certo ordine fata.*' / *dixit et ingentem nutu
concussit olimpum* ('"Thus it is settled, thus let our decrees proceed in fixed succession." He spoke and shook great Olympus with a nod', *Urania* 1.968–9).

Drawing upon Manilius' anthropology, Bonincontri and Pontano re-concile the astrological world-view with the Christian notion of free will by explaining mankind's capacity to attain astrological knowledge, by establishing limits to astrological knowledge, and finally, by reaffirming man's ability to shape his own destiny through an assertion of reason and will. Both Bonincontri and Pontano stress man's inherent potential to achieve astrological knowledge (whether due to his divine origin, an astrological predisposition, or divine nature). For Bonincontri and Pontano, man's attainment of astrological knowledge is a cooperative effort between mankind and heaven: man's reason and hard work must meet with heaven's willingness and aid. In his anthropology, Pontano especially celebrates man's autonomy and ability to triumph over all obstacles without divine help or influence. Bonincontri and Pontano also argue for astrology's place as a science. By narrating the methods and process of achieving astrological knowledge (time, hard work, and experience), Bonincontri and Pontano not only establish astrology's limits, fallibility, and scope but also separate the true practitioners or astrological scientists, like Endymion, from superstitious fortune-tellers. Finally, Bonincontri and Pontano repeatedly claim that man's reason and will can overturn astrological predisposition and celestial influence. Therefore, the existence of astrological knowledge does not curtail man's actions, but rather empowers and informs his choices.

The Renaissance reception of Manilius' anthropology in the astro-logical poetry of Bonincontri and Pontano thus centres around one of the most controversial issues of the fifteenth century: man's free will. Bonincontri, in the story of Endymion, and Pontano, in the concep-tion, birth, and development of man in *Urania*, draw on Manilius' three forms of knowledge to argue that man is ultimately responsible for his actions. It is Manilius' strong assertion of man's ability to overcome all obstacles with time, hard work, and experience that forms the cornerstone of both Bonincontri's and Pontano's response to criticism of the astrological world-view.

17

Lorenzo Bonincontri's reception of Manilius' chapter on comets (*Astr.* 1.809–926)

Stephan Heilen

The Italian humanist Lorenzo Bonincontri da San Miniato (Laurentius Bonincontrius Miniatensis, 1410–*c*.1491)[1] is known to classicists primarily as the first commentator on Manilius. After the text of the *Astronomica* had been rediscovered by Poggio Bracciolini in 1417, Bonincontri held the first public lectures on Manilius. This was in the 1470s in Florence (Field 1996), where Bonincontri enjoyed a lively intellectual exchange with Marsilio Ficino, Luigi Pulci, and other humanists.[2] We know from contemporary sources that Bonincontri's lectures attracted huge audiences from all parts of Italy.[3] Since the typical and most important literary product of university lecturing in the Middle Ages and the Renaissance were commentaries (Buck 1975: 8), it is no surprise that Bonincontri, too, published his lecture notes along with his recension of the Manilian text. This work was printed in 1484.[4]

---

[1] The most complete and still authoritative account of Bonincontri's life and works is that of Soldati 1906: 105–98. See further Caroline Stark's contribution to this volume.

[2] See Soldati 1906: 126–7, 152–3; Heilen 1999: 9–10; and—on Bonincontri and Pulci—Bessi 1974.

[3] Cf. Paolo Cortese, *De hominibus doctis* 5 (ed. Ferraù 1979: 183–4): *Laurentius Miniatensis, qui nuper est mortuus, quoquo modo potuit et poemata scripsit et historiam, sed hunc sublimius astronomica scientia sustulit, in quo genere ita laboravit et praestitit, ut esset ex tota Italia ad eum concursus. Atque is primus ex omnibus Manilium poetam ex adito erutum in lucem revocavit.*

[4] Marcus Manilius, *Astronomica cum commento Laurentii Bonincontri*, Rome [printer of Manilius], 26.X.1484. On this edition (henceforth: E), see Heilen 1999: 198–202, 296.

It remained authoritative throughout the Renaissance, until it was replaced, in 1579, by Joseph Justus Scaliger's vastly improved text with commentary.

What is less well known about Bonincontri is that he left numerous other writings as well. His literary productions in Latin include historiographical works, biographies, philosophical and astrological treatises, commentaries, annual predictions (*Vaticinia*), and letters, as well as three large poems: a late work in elegiac distichs and lyric metres on the Christian calendar[5] and two earlier hexametrical poems, each having the title *De rebus naturalibus et divinis*, for which he drew inspiration from Lucretius, Virgil, and Manilius. The latter two poems are didactic, comprising three books each, and they form a unit, despite their dedication to different rulers, Lorenzo de' Medici (I.1–3) and the King of Naples, Ferdinand of Aragon (II.1–3).[6] They were completed some time before 1475, when Bonincontri started lecturing in Florence, and earned him the coveted title of *poeta laureatus*, conferred upon him by the Roman Academy of Pomponius Laetus in 1484 (Tournoy-Thoen 1972). To the benefit of modern scholarship, Bonincontri also left a complete, hitherto unedited commentary on his altogether six books on things natural and divine. The autograph of this commentary is lost, but one manuscript copy is preserved in cod. Vat. lat. 2845, which can be dated c.1525–30 (Heilen 1999: 136–59, 261–2).

The poetic passage that interests us is the finale of Bonincontri's first book dedicated to Lorenzo de' Medici, which is devoted to comets (I.1.474–591). It is instructive to compare this Neo-Latin imitation with the ancient Roman model, taking into account also Bonincontri's respective commentaries. The relevant passages are, then, four:

1. *Astr.* 1.809–926.
2. Bon. comm. ad *Astr.* 1.809–926.[7]
3. Bon. *De reb. nat. et div.* I.1.474–591.[8]
4. Bon. comm. ad I.1.474–591.[9]

---

[5] *Fastorum siue Dierum solemnium Christianae religionis libri IIII*, written 1484–91, ed. princ. 1491.

[6] See the critical edition by Heilen 1999. Of the second poem an uncritical early modern edition exists (ed. princ. 1526, repr. 1540, 1575).

[7] Cod. Vat. Ottob. lat. 1706 (henceforth: **O**), fo. 95^v–101^v = **E**, fo. <37>^{v}–<40>^{r}.

[8] Ed. Heilen 1999: 376–83.

[9] Cod. Vat. lat. 2845, fos. 13^v–15^v. This section will be edited in this chapter (see commentary on I.1.474–591, pp. 301–10).

The first three texts will now be discussed in chronological order. The last will be edited as part of the line-by-line commentary at the end of this article and referred to in the following discussion when needed. Note, however, that the second half of Bonincontri's commentary on I.1.474–591 is missing because of the loss of one leaf in the autograph. This loss is truly regrettable because the verses in question (I.1.534–591) contain contemporary allusions and brief autobiographical information. In all likelihood Bonincontri gave precious additional information on all this in his commentary.[10]

Manilius' chapter on comets (1.809–926) is well-known thanks to various scholars' analyses, some of which are published in this volume.[11] Therefore it requires only a brief summary. Four parts can easily be distinguished: the first and last are short, introduction (809–16) and peroration (922–6), respectively. In between lie the two main sections, the first being devoted to explaining the nature and origin of the phenomenon of comets (817–75) and the other to interpreting their significance (876–921). Broadly speaking, we can characterize these two sections as 'physical' and 'astrological'. Among the three explanations that Manilius offers, the Aristotelian view comes first (817–66),[12] namely that comets are meteorological phenomena that take place in the earth's atmosphere, where occasionally dry vapour exhaled by the earth is ignited and becomes visible as a short-lived fire. Thanks to Aristotle's authority, this was the dominant theory from antiquity to the Renaissance.[13] The second explanation in Manilius' doxography is astronomical (867–73), that comets are eternal celestial bodies attracted to and then released by the Sun, so as to become visible only rarely, when they are close to the Sun. The only extant parallel from ancient literature is of later date,

---

[10] On the loss of this section, see n. 72 below.

[11] See the contribution of Duncan F. Kennedy (on *Astr.* 1.896–902) and Monica R. Gale's discussion of the intertextual allusions to Virgil, Lucretius, and other models in *Astr.* 1.876–9, 887–91, 896–909, 922–6. Earlier contributions will be quoted *suis locis.*

[12] Cf. Arist. *Mete.* A 7 344a5–345a10. This is by far the longest of the three explanations, not least because it includes a typology of comets (1.831–51).

[13] See Jervis 1985 and van Nouhuys 1998. In order to understand the extraordinary longevity of Aristotle's cometary theory, it is essential to appreciate the fact that to challenge it requires us to challenge Aristotle's cosmology as well (Jervis 1985: 13), and even to destabilize the structure of early modern university learning, which was based on the coherent philosophical system of Aristotle (see Gindhart 2006: 250–1 for interesting remarks on a 17th-cent. scholar who feared the outbreak of 'Chaos').

a brief remark in Plin. *HN* 2.94, which does not shed any light on Manilius' source. I tend to agree with Montanari Caldini 1989: 4–17, who thoroughly discusses the source problem of *Astr.* 1.867–73, that this second explanation is an extension of the Chaldaean radio-solar theory according to which the movements of the planets are caused by the attraction of the Sun. This theory had a broad reception in Rome (see e.g. Vitr. 9.1.11–14 and Plin. *HN* 2.59–60), and it was easy to replace the planets in it with comets, probably under the influence of a Pythagorean cometary theory reported by Aristotle (*Mete.* A 6 342b29–35). Lastly, Manilius briefly proposes the theological and providential explanation that comets are god's warnings to mankind (874–5).

Since Manilius' previous chapters were devoted to the fixed stars and the circles of the sky, while the final peroration envisages the earthly matters of the Roman Empire, the chapter on comets with its broad treatment of Aristotle's meteorological explanation serves as a *descensus* which leads the reader, at the end of the first book, down from heaven to earth.[14]

The significance of comets (876–921) is, according to Manilius, various but negative without exception: blighted fields (877–9), plagues (880–95), and wars (896–921). Our poet gives altogether six examples of historical disasters, the earliest being the famous plague of Athens in 430 BC (884–91). The other examples are wars from recent Roman history, first the disaster of Varus at Teutoburg Forest in Germany (AD 9, 898–903) and then the most important battles of the civil wars (906–21): Philippi (42 BC), Pharsalus (48 BC), Actium (31 BC), and the destruction of Sextus Pompeius (36/35 BC).

Interestingly, only the first three of the six disasters that Manilius mentions are more or less explicitly connected to the appearance of comets, and not one of these cases can actually be confirmed either through the testimony of historical records or by way of backward computation based on the periodicity of comets known to modern astronomers. We owe this insight to John Ramsey's *Descriptive Catalogue of Greco-Roman Comets* (2006, 2nd edn. 2008), which contains masterly analyses of all potentially relevant phenomena

---

[14] See Hübner 1984: 242–68, esp. 248–52. On the section *Astr.* 1.777–805, which precedes the chapter on comets, see Josèphe-Henriette Abry in this volume.

reported in Graeco-Roman, Mesopotamian, Chinese, and Korean sources.[15]

The preserved evidence indicates that Manilius was the first ancient author to interpret comets as signs or causes of plague.[16] Different explanations have been proposed: Hübner 1984: 251 interprets the evidence as a phenomenon of literary imitation, with Manilius combining the ends of the two 'dark' or pessimistic books of Virgil's *Georgics*, that is, of the first (comets signifying war) and the third (the plague of Noricum).[17] Ramsey (2006: 192, cf. 97 n. 122) instead concludes that it was presumably as a result of two historical comets, that of 426 BC, which coincided with the second, severe outbreak of the plague at Athens, and that of 87 BC (Halley's), which accompanied a severe plague at Rome, that comets came to acquire, by Manilius' day, their reputation as harbingers of plagues. These two explanations do not necessarily exclude one another.

We now turn to Bonincontri's imitation of Manilius. The first book *De rebus naturalibus et divinis* was dedicated to Lorenzo de' Medici in 1475, and for various reasons it must have been completed a few years before that date, probably in the early 1470s. The section on comets (I.1.474–591, the text is reproduced below) forms, as in the case of Manilius, the end of Bonincontri's first book, but it is not a *descensus* from heaven to earth. Bonincontri rather develops his chapter on comets out of a discussion of earthly things, namely the regular pattern of the seasons and its potential disturbances (474–84). They both

[15] The three comets (or similar phenomena) mentioned by Manilius are: (1) 1.880–6 (Athenian plague), cf. Ramsey 2006: 191–2, object 1a: not a comet or a meteor (Ramsey emphasizes that Manilius does not make an explicit claim that a comet actually foreshadowed the Athenian plague; see also his discussion on pp. 56–9 of object 3, 426 BC, which certainly was a comet); (2) 1.898–900: AD 9 (the *clades Variana*), cf. Ramsey 2006: 132–4, object 31 (uncertain); (3) 1.907–9: 42 BC (Philippi), cf. Ramsey 2006: 205–7, object 17a (not a comet; maybe meteors?). While there is no comet clearly mentioned as such by Manilius and confirmed by other records, a comet did appear in February/March 32 BC, i.e. some 18 months before the Battle of Actium, which Manilius mentions in 1.914–18, though without explicitly asserting that this battle was foreshadowed by a comet (Ramsey 2006: 125–6, object 27).
[16] This distinguishes Manilius' chapter from other poetic accounts of plagues. See esp. Lucr. 6.1138–1286, Verg. G. 3.440–566, Ov. Met. 7.523–613, and their analyses by Grimm 1965. On comets and plague in *Astr.* 1.874–95, see further Lühr 1973 and Landolfi 1990*b*.
[17] Hübner 1984: 251 n. 380 points out that the *tertium comparationis* for comets and war is the Martial heat, while the *tertium comparationis* for comets and plague is the Latin term *faces* which denotes the comets as well as the torches used for fire burials.

depend on celestial causes: the orderly succession of the seasons with their Aristotelian qualities (either warm or cold mixed with either dry or humid) is determined by the astronomical course of the Sun and lets life on earth prosper according to a natural rhythm of coming to be and passing away. On rare occasions, however, celestial disturbances occur, which violently confuse the regular pattern of the seasons and thereby cause sickness among plant and animal life on earth, and even earthquakes and similar disorders of inanimate nature. Bonincontri concludes this introductory, general explanation with a historical example (485–93) drawn from Manilius (1.884–91), the plague of Athens.[18]

In a second step Bonincontri provides details concerning the physical causes (494–542), beginning with the assertion that different celestial disturbances have different earthly consequences (494–503). In the extant section of the commentary on his poem, Bonincontri specifies that he is thinking of three kinds of disturbances, namely solar eclipses, comets, and conjunctions of the upper planets Saturn, Jupiter, and Mars.[19]

These disturbances are the inscrutable will of God, part of the clearly defined order with which he replaced the primordial chaos (509–15, esp. 513 *certo ordine*). This divine order is impenetrable (510 *occultum est*) and has positive consequences (516–22), but also negative ones (523–35): among the latter, comets rank first. They allegedly originate from dry smoke that is ignited by the rays of the Sun, Mars, or Mercury (525–6)—in other words, by those three celestial bodies that were thought to exceed in dry heat—and they affect both the animate and the inanimate nature. Bonincontri's reference to the planets[20] is important because otherwise it would be unclear why he speaks of celestial, that is, supralunar causation (496, 503) while following Aristotle's explanation of comets as meteorological phenomena that originate from dry earthly exhalations and take place in the upper air. The ultimate cause of comets is the planets:[21] this justifies their inclusion in one astronomical category together with the solar eclipses and planetary conjunctions that are

---

[18] Bonincontri's account of this plague is similarly introduced (I.1.485 *qualem per populos*, cf. *Astr.* 1.884 *qualis Erectheos*) and of almost exactly the same length.

[19] The Latin original is quoted in my commentary on p. 302 (ad v. 499).

[20] I am using this term in the ancient and early modern sense, including the five true planets and the two luminaries (Sun and Moon), as opposed to the fixed stars.

[21] See Bonincontri's prose explanations quoted on pp. 302–3 in the commentary on v. 525.

mentioned only in the prose commentary.[22] In the poem, Bonincontri focuses exclusively on what he calls the most violent and devastating of these three types of disturbances, comets (481). Despite their rare appearances we can, in view of their dire consequences (war, rebellion, murder, plague, famine), only pray to be spared (536–42). The religious note of these lines leads back to the explicit remarks on the divine will in 509–15, thereby emphasizing the unity of this second section (494–542).

The third major section (543–82) is devoted to two contemporary examples: the comets of 1456 and 1472. It is convenient to display the elements of this section in tabular form:

543–6: the comet of 1456.
547–52: shape and appearance of both comets (1456/1472).
553–71: effects of the comet of 1456:
- earthquake [5 December 1456]
- plague
- death of Bonincontri's wife and children
- death of King Alfonso I of Naples [27 June 1458]
- wars of succession [1458–1464]
571–7: warning to Lorenzo de' Medici.
578–82: danger of war with the Ottoman Empire.

Apart from a few lines (547–52) in which both comets are mentioned, this section is exclusively about the comet of 1456. Bonincontri associates that comet with a whole series of dreadful events in Naples, where he lived at the time, events that in his view matched the catastrophic dimensions of the plague of Athens. This is no surprise because he personally lost everything: his wife, his children, and his king, whom he considered a just ruler and whose armies he had commanded in the field (554–6, 563–6, 576–7).

This traumatic experience was probably a reason, maybe even *the* reason, why Bonincontri became so deeply interested in Manilius. The events following the comet of 1456 must have convinced him that Manilius' astrological teaching was true, that it deserved close study in order to learn from it, and that it would be a worthy undertaking to write a new didactic poem incorporating the astrological wisdom of the ancients into the Christian world-view. The

---

[22] See again my commentary on p. 302 (ad v. 499).

Ciceronian maxim *historia magistra vitae* (Cic. *De or.* 2.36) is, generally speaking, an important motive of the humanists of the Renaissance (Harth 1970: 166; Landfester 1972), and Bonincontri makes it
clear in his address to Lorenzo de' Medici (570–2) that one can and
should learn from history in order to be prepared for the future: the
war of succession that Ferdinand of Aragon had to fight in the kingdom of Naples at age 35 after the death of his father, King Alfonso I,
might be a lesson for the even younger Lorenzo de' Medici who may
wish to be prepared against similar events in Florence after the recent
death of his own father, Piero di Cosimo de' Medici.[23] As a side-effect,
this reasoning also helps to advertise Bonincontri as a personal,
indispensable adviser to the young and little-experienced leading
man in Florence, and thereby possibly to have Bonincontri's ban
from Tuscany lifted.[24]

In this context his gross flattery of Lorenzo de' Medici in the final
lines of the first book (588–91) deserves a closer look. These lines are
an obvious imitation of Manilius' address to the emperor Augustus
in the proem of the *Astronomica*: compare v. 591 *dant animos
mentemque movent ad tanta canenda* with *Astr.* 1.10 *das animum
viresque facis ad tanta canenda.* But there is reason to suspect that
Bonincontri added these lines (588–91), which are somewhat clum-
sily connected to the previous lines,[25] rather late, during or after the
appearance of the comet of 1472 to which they allude and which
Bonincontri explicitly calls a recent foreboding (*praenuntia nuper
visa mali*).[26] His original plan was probably to have the first book,

---

[23] Lorenzo was born on 1 January 1449 and became ruler of Florence after Piero
died on 2 December 1469.

[24] He had been exiled as a young man in 1432 together with other citizens of San
Miniato as the result of a failed conspiracy against the supremacy of Florence. For
details, see Soldati 1906: 119.

[25] See the tautological use of *at* and *sed* (588) and the immediate succession of two
concessive thoughts (583–7, 588–91).

[26] Compare the similar, more easily datable case in Bonincontri's *Vaticinium anni
1491* (Rome: Stephanus Plannck; *GW* no. 4912). This annual prediction, which was
dedicated to the Roman cardinal Raphael Riarius, is the latest historical evidence of
Bonincontri still being alive. The *Vaticinium* opens with a poem in elegiac distichs. In
lines 21–6, a recent comet of unclear significance is mentioned: *exortus nuper boreali
parte cometes / infecit Pisces Marte oriente mari / . . . / exitus in dubio est: nequeo
discernere; vestrum / arbitrium solvat dirimat atque litem!* From records preserved in
Chinese, Japanese, and Korean sources we know that this comet, which appeared in the
northern constellation Cygnus, was observed from 31 December 1490 to 11 February
1491. See Kronk 1999: 290–1, s.v. C/1490 Y1 and also Hasegawa 1979: 260–1, 263;

after the third section on contemporary examples (543–82), end with a fourth and last section (583–7) on a more profound, religious note, because it is there that he expresses in Christian terms the third explanation offered by Manilius (1.874–5), namely, that God sends comets as a warning to mankind. Comparing the ends of the other five books *De rebus naturalibus et divinis* one finds that they all speak directly of God, of the final judgement, or of the soul's return to its heavenly abode.[27]

One could object that the comet of 1472 was mentioned once before, in lines 547–52, where Bonincontri distinguished between the comets of 1456 and 1472. But on closer inspection that passage, too, seems to be a later addendum because it obscures the otherwise clear and linear development of Bonincontri's thought. I assume that the poet's original idea was to speak of only one contemporary comet, that of 1456, just as he mentions only one ancient example: these two are linked to each other both by the overall gravity of the disasters that followed as well as by the specific occurrence of plagues.[28] This gives a well-balanced structure of a central theoretical section (494–542) surrounded by two sections (474–93, 543–82) that include one example each, the whole being followed by a short theological résumé. If this analysis is correct, Bonincontri imitated the structure of Manilius' chapter at multiple levels: in its overall location at the end of the first book, in its division into four main sections, and in the brief extension—exactly five lines—of the respective last sections (*Astr.* 1.922–6/Bon. I.1.583–7). When a new comet appeared in 1472, Bonincontri must have yielded to the temptation of expanding and updating his poem: certainly a way of capturing his addressee's attention, but artistically detrimental in so far as the unity of the

---

Hasegawa 1980: 84; Zhou *et al.* 1997: 1553; I. P. Williams *et al.* 2004: 1179–80. Since Bonincontri's *Vaticinium* is dated 10 February 1491, the author probably wrote his distichs while the comet was still visible, anticipating the reader's retrospective view by saying *nuper* ('recently'; compare the above–quoted *praenuntia nuper visa mali* referring to the comet of 1472). C/1490 Y1 remained an evening object throughout its apparition. Whenever it was visible above the north-eastern horizon in the West, Mars was rising in the East (hence, *Marte oriente mari* in the above quotation).

[27] The only exception is arguably book II.2, whose last section is devoted to the star of Venus, but even there the final verses express the hope for a peaceful world without greed, which is in keeping with Christian values.

[28] Note that Bonincontri says nothing about the effects of the comet of 1472, which remain to be seen. In other words, only the comet of 1456 presents a set of empirical data that can reasonably be compared to ancient cases.

original composition suffered from the addition of lines 547–52 and 588–91.[29]

We now turn to Bonincontri's commentary on Manilius, which is of interest not only in regard to the chapter on comets but more broadly speaking as the first modern commentary on the *Astronomica*. It originated in the late 1470s, after the completion of Bonincontri's poem *De rebus naturalibus et divinis*, from a plethora of notes that Bonincontri made in the margins of his personal copy of the 1474 Bologna edition of Manilius while lecturing in Florence.[30] This working copy, which was still known to Angelo Maria Bandini in the late eighteenth century, is now lost (Maranini 1994: 182). But we can easily get an idea of what the original commentary on Manilius might have looked like from preserved autographs of Bonincontri's commentaries on other texts, such as the pseudo-Ptolemaic *Centiloquium* and the *Sphaera* of John of Holywood (Johannes de Sacrobosco), both extant in cod. Vat. lat. 3379 (photographs in Heilen 1999: 43–4, 157–9). The margins of Bonincontri's lost copy of the Bologna edition of Manilius must have been similarly covered with tiny handwritten notes. Some years after Bonincontri's Florentine lectures, these notes on Manilius were copied by a negligent or incompetent scribe[31] into the preserved codex Vat. Ottob. lat. 1706, in order to provide the printer of the 1484 edition with a readable manuscript. Bonincontri, who was over 70 at the time, revised the codex Ottobonianus as well as he could and corrected many mistakes, but more than a few remained unnoticed and made their way into the printed version of 1484.[32] Needless to say,

---

[29] This interpretation of lines 547–52 and 588–91 develops a hint in the right direction given by Soldati 1906: 158–9.

[30] The *editio princeps* by Regiomontanus had been printed in Nuremberg in 1473. See the first two entries in the complete list of editions of the *Astronomica* in Maranini 1994: 350–64.

[31] There is reason to believe that this scribe was a cleric, presumably at the service of cardinal Raphael Riarius (1451–1521), whose protégé Bonincontri was during his last years and to whom he dedicated the commentary on Manilius. See, for instance, what may be an instance of 'monastic corruption' (Ogilvie 1971) on fo. 96[v] of cod. Ottob. lat. 1706, where *ingenitum* (*Astr.* 1.817) is corrupted to *in gemitu*, a nonsensical reading that may be a subconscious borrowing from Psalm 6: 6 *laboravi in gemitu meo* (possibly facilitated by *spirante* in the Manilian line).

[32] See e.g. the nonsensical reading *conatus* for *cometae* quoted below in the commentary to v. 550. For a detailed analysis, see Heilen 1999: 191–7. Note that sometimes the lemmata in the commentary are different from the readings of the text because the scribe of the codex Ottobonianus must have overlooked some of Bonincontri's numerous corrections of the readings of the 1474 Bologna edition, on which

the typesetter added further mistakes. These editorial circumstances ought to be kept in mind when dealing with Bonincontri's commentary, which should be used preferably in the manuscript version of the codex Ottobonianus.[33] A last step in Bonincontri's commenting activity on Manilius dates from the time after 1484: one of the about thirty surviving copies of the printed edition, BNCF Inc. B 3 no. 11 (Florence),[34] was Bonincontri's personal copy in which he continued his earlier habit of adding marginal notes.[35] However, even if all the marginal notes seem ultimately to go back to Bonincontri, not all of them were written by his own hand.[36]

Bonincontri's commentary on Manilius is a typical product of its time, based on the philological-historical method that was being developed by the humanists. Among the philological elements are, besides explanations of grammatical problems and etymologies, numerous conjectures, which were partly accepted by editors like Housman, Goold, and others.[37] A less commendable aspect of Bonincontri's textual criticism was his interpolation of some verses (*Astr.* 1.38–9 and 2.631) in passages that he considered lacunose.[38]

---

he was working. See e.g. *Astr.* 1.845 where O and E (for these sigla see n. 7 above) both read *messes* (this is the reading of all the incunabula editions), but Bonincontri's commentary is on *menses* (= consensus codd. GLM; modern editors prefer Bentley's conjecture *menta*).

[33] Another reason for this is that O preserves Bonincontri's habit of underlining the lemmata. This helpful visual distinction between lemmata and commentary was given up by the typesetter of 1484 (E), which makes the printed version difficult to read.

[34] On this copy, see Heilen 1999: 203–10, 296. For the full list of all preserved copies, see Heilen 1999: 200.

[35] See above on the copy of the Bologna edition of 1474.

[36] See the discussion in Heilen 1999: 203–10. Other scholars' remarks on this problem are generally short and partly wrong (Soldati 1906: 151 n. 2; Field 1996: 210 n. 15; Giorgetti 2002: 207). A possible yet uncertain explanation of the evidence is that Bonincontri, and maybe also students who followed his Roman lectures on Manilius in the 1480s, left notes on the margins of two or even more copies of the edition of 1484 and that someone, either before or after Bonincontri's death, ordered a copyist to transcribe all these notes into one copy (BNCF Inc. B 3 no. 11).

[37] In Manilius' chapter on comets, see 1.850 *exiliunt* and 1.851 *ardua* (cod. Ottob. fo. 98^r = ed. 1484 fo. 38^v). Both conjectures were accepted by Housman 1932; Fels 1990; and Goold 1998.

[38] In O, *Astr.* 1.38–9 is on fos. 14^v–15^r, with the respective commentary on fo. 16^r (in E all this is on fo. 6^v): *hic duo deerant versus, videlicet qui sua disposuit* [E: *dispoit*] *per tempora: bene, cum a deo omnia sint perfectissime ordinata ad perfectionem humanj generis, quod ostendit dicens 'omnibus'. Astr.* 2.631 is on O fo. 136^v (= E fo. 55^r): *Magnus erit geminis amor et concordia duplex*; the commentary reads (ibid.): *Concordia duplex: quia Geminorum signum est duarum similium formarum.* In his personal copy of E

Much of the commentary is devoted to the quotation of literary sources and parallels, for instance—in our chapter on comets—remarks on Manilius' imitation of Lucretius' account of the Athenian plague (*Astr.* 1.884–91 ~ Lucr. 6.1138–1286). The range of sources used by Bonincontri is limited to ancient Latin authors and some Greek authorities in Latin translation, such as Aristotle and Ptolemy. Like his contemporaries, Bonincontri was unaware of the fact that a few texts and the doctrines contained therein, especially the *Centiloquium* attributed to Ptolemy, were actually of later, Arabic origin.[39] This accounts, for example, for Bonincontri's erroneous belief that the ninefold typology of comets which was widespread in the Renaissance went back to Ptolemy.[40] Only rarely does Bonincontri abandon the stereotypical structure of commenting lemma by lemma in order to insert brief autobiographical, theological, geographical, or other *excursus*.[41]

Like other humanistic commentators, Bonincontri combines his exegetical purpose with practical goals by envisaging the relevance of ancient texts for his own time. This attitude leads him, in our specific context, to compare ancient reports on comets to contemporary apparitions. It is interesting to see which comets Bonincontri deems worthy of being mentioned in his commentary on *Astr.* 1.809–926. The relevant passages are four:[42]

(BNCF Inc. B 3 no. 11) Bonincontri made a handwritten addendum (fo. 55ʳ): *concordia duplex* quia saturnus in utroque signo fortis est. nam in libra habet exaltacionem et in aquario domicilium. ergo ambo sunt triplicitatis aeree, ambo masculina diurnaque [cf. *Astr.* 2.150–4 and 2.221–2] et ad formam hominis figurata [cf. *Astr.* 2.155–7 and 2.529]. For the unprecedented juncture *concordia duplex,* cf. *concordia discors* (Hor. *Epist.* 1.12.19, Luc. 1.98) and *discordia demens* (Verg. *Aen.* 6.280, Sil. 9.288, Val. Fl. 2.204). The removal of these two interpolations (*Astr.* 1.38–9 and 2.631) by later scholars accounts for small gaps in the verse numbering of our modern edns.

[39] The *Centiloquium* is an Arabic collection of one hundred astrological sentences (*Kitāb al-Thamara*), which received a commentary in around AD 922 in Egypt by Abū Jaʿfar Aḥmad ibn Yūsuf ibn Ibrāhīm al-Dāya. It is highly likely that Aḥmad ibn Yūsuf is also the author of the collection. See the authoritative study by Lemay 1978. On the Greek and Latin translations that circulated under the titles Καρπός and *Liber fructus* or *Centiloquium,* see Lemay 1978: 99–106 and Rinaldi 1999.

[40] The actual origin of this typology remains to be investigated. See Jervis 1985: 17.

[41] In this respect his method is clearly different from e.g. Filippo Beroaldo's commentary on the *Metamorphoses* of Apuleius (see Krautter 1971) or Machiavelli's *Discorsi sulla prima deca di Tito Livio,* where the work of the ancient author forms little more than the starting point for independent reasonings of the commentator (Buck 1975: 19).

[42] All quotations are from cod. Vat. Ottob. Lat. 1706 (O), fos. 95ᵛ–101ᵛ. On this manuscript's superiority over the printed edition (E), see pp. 287–8 above.

1. Fo. 96^v (ad *Astr.* 1.816): comet of AD 1456

breuissimum spatium, quo fulgeant, adnotatum est vij dierum, Longissimum uero Lxxx^{ta} [cf. Plin. HN 2.90],[43] *ut fuit ille cometes, qui nostra memoria anno 1456 apparuit biduo* [item E, corrige *biennio*] *ante Alfonsi Regis Aragonij mortem.*

2. Fo. 96^v (ad *Astr.* 1.816): comet of 44 BC[44]

unum [sc. *sidus*] *apparuit initio potentatus diuj Augustj non multo post obitum Cęsaris. Vulgus credidit Cęsaris animam in cęlum translatam, fluxitque vij diebus ex parte septentrionis et oriebatur xi^a diej hora clarum omnibus terris et conspicuum* [cf. Plin. HN 2.94]. *cuius significatio bona. Non tantum felix Octauianj imperio, sed etiam christi aduentu.*

3. Fo. 97^v (ad *Astr.* 1.833): comets of 87 BC, 49 BC, and AD 1264[45]

hic vocatur dominus Ascone, qui apparuit Octauiano consule ciuilj bello Cesaris et pompej: et nostro tempore [i.e., AD 1264],[46] *quo Carolus venit in regno Neapolitano.*

4. Fo. 97^v (ad *Astr.* 1.846): comet of 44 BC[47]

hic est, quj Augusti apparuit temporibus, et habet faciem humanę similem, lucentem. significat pacem et tranquillitatem. ceteri omnes econtra.

---

[43] Plin. HN 2.90: *brevissimum quo cernerentur spatium VII dierum adnotatum est, longissimum <C>LXXX* [emend. Harduin]. These data—respectively 7 and 80 days— are also referred to by Bonincontri in his commentary on the pseudo-Ptolemaic *Centiloquium*, sent. 100 (cod. Vat. lat. 3379, fo. 113^v): *ad minus per 7 dies, ad plus per Lxxx^{ta}* (without reference to Pliny, cf. the similar case of Bonincontri's contemporary Matteo dell'Aquila, *Tractatus de cometa atque terraemotu*, cod. Vat. Barb. Lat. 268, fos. 12^v–13^r (ed. Figliuolo 1990: 50): *Nam, ut huius rei observatoribus placuit, minus septem et amplius diebus octuaginta durare eidem* [i.e. *cometae*] *non licet*).

[44] See Ramsey and Licht 1997, as well as Kronk 1999: 22–4 and Ramsey 2006: 106–24, object no. 26.

[45] On the comets of 87 and 49 BC, see Ramsey 2006: 93–106, objects nos. 24–5; on that of AD 1264, see Kronk 1999: 218–22.

[46] See Jervis 1985: 24–7, with references to the discussions of this comet by Aegidius (Giles) of Lessines, Henry Bate, Gerard de Silteo, Giles the Dominican, and Vincent of Beauvais (with further secondary literature). Giovanni Pontano describes this comet thus in his commentary on the 100th sentence of the pseudo-Ptolemaic *Centiloquy* (Venice 1519, fo. 92^r): *Anno millesimo ducentesimo sexagesimo quarto à natali Christi die, mense Augusto, crinita stella in orientis cœli parte uisa est, quæ ab ortu ipso ad medium cœlum crines diffunderet, fulsitque circiter mensibus tribus, nec ante desijt uideri, quàm Vrbanus Pontifex Maximus diem obijt*. Pontano's commentary will be quoted again, commentary on vv. 547–52 (p. 304).

[47] See n. 44 above.

These quotations show that Bonincontri's interest focuses, in antiquity, on the comet of 44 BC which is mentioned twice (texts 2 and 4). This is the so-called *sidus Iulium*, which appeared at the funeral games of Julius Caesar and was interpreted by the future emperor Augustus as a good omen (therefore Manilius omits it). Bonincontri emphasizes that it appeared for only seven days (text 2) and belonged, among the various categories of comets, to the only good one, while that of 1456 was allegedly visible for a period of eighty days (text 1), the longest period possible, and had disastrous consequences. Bonincontri drew these minimum and maximum figures of respectively seven and eighty days of visibility from Pliny (*HN* 2.90). The application of the (unemended) Plinian figure of eighty days to the comet of 1456 is an exaggeration on Bonincontri's part, as is clear from the numerous preserved contemporary records.[48] They show that the comet of 1456 could be observed from the second half of May[49] to the first half of July, which makes for a maximum visibility of about fifty–sixty days. Note that most contemporary observations of the comet started no earlier than in June, and even the day-by-day records of the Florentine astronomer Paolo dal Pozzo Toscanelli (1397–1482) cover only the period from 8 June 1456 until the comet's disappearance on 8 July 1456.[50] Bonincontri's exaggeration shows how gruesome the comet of 1456 had, in his perception, proven to be, so as to justify juxtaposing it as the worst comet ever to the most benign comet ever, that of 44 BC.

Interestingly, he says nothing about the comet of 1472. This is noteworthy because more than a decade had gone by since the author wrote lines 547–52 and 588–91 of his first book to Lorenzo de' Medici. At that time, soon after the appearance of the comet in January 1472, one could hardly say anything certain about its future effects. By 1484, however, any such effects should, from an

---

[48] See esp. Thorndike 1958: 225–33; Jervis 1985; and further literature quoted in the commentary on vv. 547–52.

[49] The earliest observation that I know of is dated 15 May 1456. It was made by Giovanni Cambio, Florence; see Figliuolo 1988–9: 1.18. The next observation is dated 18 May 1456. It was made by Matteo dell'Aquila in his *Tractatus de cometa atque terraemotu*, Cod. Vat. Barb. Lat. 268, fo. 5ᵛ. See the edition of Figliuolo 1990: 42 who wrongly renders *quintodecimo kl. iunii* as 'il 17 di maggio'. The Chinese saw the comet first on 27 May (Hunger *et al.* 1985: 59).

[50] This may, however, be due to the unusually rainy spring of AD 1456, on which see Figliuolo 1988–9: 1.4. See further the commentary on v. 563.

astrological point of view, long have taken place.[51] The fact that Bonincontri says nothing about this comet reinforces our earlier impression that—unlike the comet of 1456—the one of 1472, despite its being more recent, never came to play an important, permanent role in Bonincontri's thinking. The references to it in lines 547–52 and 588–91 must have been due to a passing interest prompted by the occasion.

There are two historical details that Bonincontri did not know and that might arguably have led him to a different choice for his ancient example in the poem. Modern analysis of Graeco-Roman, Mesopotamian, and East Asian sources, combined with what we know about the periodicities of all major comets, reveals that there was no comet preceding the first outbreak of the Athenian plague in 430 BC (Ramsey 2006: 191–2, obj. 1a). Hence, this example used by both Manilius and Bonincontri seems inappropriately chosen. A much better candidate was available to Bonincontri from a passage in Pliny that he does quote in his commentary on Manilius, though in a somewhat garbled fashion (text 3 above). The words *qui apparuit Octauiano consule ciuilj bello Cesaris et pompej* (O fo. 97^v = E fo. 38^r) are a contamination of two separate records transmitted by Plin. *HN* 2.92: *sed cometes <non>numquam* [emend. Kroll] *in occasura parte caeli est, terrificum magna ex parte sidus atque non leviter piatum, ut civili motu Octavio consule iterumque Pompei et Caesaris bello.* Bonincontri was almost certainly quoting from memory, and this led him all the more easily to commit a mistake which persists among certain modern scholars, namely to confuse the name *Octavius* in that passage, referring to the consul of 87 BC, with the more famous *Octavianus*, future emperor of Rome, and thereby to refer that whole passage to the period of civil wars in the 40s BC.[52] If Bonincontri had correctly realized that Pliny was speaking of two different *terrifica sidera*, and that the first of these was the comet of 87 BC, which appeared during the Marian-Cinnan war, when a severe plague killed thousands in Rome, he might well, for his poetry, have preferred that Roman example to the foreign plague of Athens. Had he, in addition, known that the comet of 87 BC was the same celestial object that appeared in AD 1456, the one whose periodicity would be discovered

---

[51] See the commentary below on v. 555.
[52] For bibliographical references regarding this mistaken view and conclusive arguments against it, see Ramsey 2006: 99–100.

in the eighteenth century by Edmond Halley and give rise to the now famous designation of 'Halley's comet', Bonincontri would probably have stylized the return of the comet of 87 BC in his own time as a perfect example of the validity of the maxim *historia magistra vitae*.

To sum up, Bonincontri in his poem follows Manilius in several regards: by discussing comets at the end of the first book, by envisaging only cases of negative significance (despite his knowledge of the positive *sidus Iulium* revealed in his commentary on the *Astronomica*; see above texts 2 and 4), by considering comets as harbingers of plague, by omitting details concerning the astrological technique of interpreting comets based on their shapes and orbital parameters, and by referring, instead, to both historical and contemporary examples. But there are also differences, for instance, the fact that Manilius discusses various types of comets (1.831–51), while Bonincontri does not,[53] or that Manilius offers three different explanations of the nature and origin of comets (1.817–75) without giving explicit preference to any of them,[54] while Bonincontri adopts both the first and third of these, which in fact are not incompatible. Note also that Manilius gives six examples of historical disasters signified by different comets, while Bonincontri attributes roughly the same number of contemporary disasters to a single comet, that of 1456.[55] This autobiographically motivated concentration on one comet in the original version of the first book to Lorenzo de' Medici is all the more significant in view of the fact that both Manilius and Bonincontri, while emphasizing the general rarity of comets (*Astr.* 1.813, 1.816; Bon. I.1.536), personally lived in times that were unusually rich in such phenomena. By the late 1460s Bonincontri had personally witnessed five comets (1433, 1449/50, 1456, 1457 I, and 1457 II),[56] and he described the one of 1402 in his *Annales*.[57] Besides, Italian

---

[53] At least not in his poem; see, however, the references to his prose works in the commentary below on v. 525.

[54] I follow Montanari Caldini 1989: 19 in disagreeing with scholars—like Lühr 1969: 59 and Reeh 1973: 138—who think that Manilius gives preference to his third and last option.

[55] See the tabular analysis of I.1.553–71 on pp. 298–9 above.

[56] See the reports on all these comets (plus that of 1472) by Toscanelli, analysed by Jervis 1985: 43–69, esp. 56–66. See further the commentary below on Bon. I.1.547–52. On the comet of 1402, see Jervis 1985: 37–42.

[57] Bon. *Ann.* 10 ad ann. 1402 (Muratori 1732: 88C): *Cometes illis diebus ingens exortus est. De quo Galeatius nuntiatus, ex cubili per manus suorum deductus, quum eam Cometem conspexit, 'gratias', inquit, 'ago Deo, quòd mortis meæ signum Cælo*

history of the fifteenth century is an endless series of wars between the various powers among which the peninsula was divided, civil wars, so to speak, with Bonincontri commanding the troops of one of the contending parties, the King of Naples. In other words: there was a plethora of both recent comets and wars, especially civil wars, available for a close imitation of Manilius' list of examples in 1.896–921. But our Renaissance poet decided to focus on the one comet that deprived him of everything that had made his Neapolitan exile bearable.[58]

The most important point of comparison, however, is another one. In the aforementioned doxography of *Astr.* 1.817–75, the last and shortest explanation offered by the ancient poet (1.874–5) envisages the possibility that a benevolent god who feels pity for mankind sends warning signs of impending doom. This is a welcome opportunity for Bonincontri (I.1.585–7) to incorporate the significance of comets into his Christian world-view, which similarly subordinates celestial events and their meaning to the will of God. In order adequately to determine the theological and structural differences between those two ways of introducing the concept of a warning god, a closer look at each of the two passages is needed.

How could Manilius envisage an explanation like 1.874–5 *seu deus instantis fati miseratus in orbem / signa per affectus caelique incendia mittit*? They are irreconcilable with his otherwise rigid determinism and have, therefore, caused considerable perplexity among scholars.[59] Montanari Caldini is probably right in referring the reader to a parallel in the *Corpus Hermeticum*: ἐπὰν οὖν μέλλῃ τι τῷ κόσμῳ συμβαίνειν, οὗτοι φαίνονται κτλ., 'if something is about to happen to the cosmos, these (comets) appear etc.'[60] Regardless of the indisputable general differences between Manilius' emphasis on a rational, self-sufficient human approach to the cosmos and the typically Hermetic emphasis on divine revelation, the passage quoted proves that *Astr.* 1.874–5 is not a unique astrological concept in antiquity. Manilius may well have drawn it from the influential manual attributed to

---

cunctis innotescere voluit'; paulloque post morbo invalescente mortuus est. Bonincontri's *Annales* cover the years 903–1458 (until the death of King Alfonso). Only the tenth and last book was ever printed.

[58] For details regarding Bonincontri's exile, see Soldati 1906: 119.

[59] See the overview given by Montanari Caldini 1989: 18–19.

[60] *Corp. Herm.* fr. 6.16 (Stob. 1.21.9, p. 1.189 W.). This text and the whole problem of *Astr.* 1.874–5 is discussed masterly by Montanari Caldini 1989: 21–30. See also Vallauri 1954: 157.

the Egyptian King Nechepso and his High Priest Petosiris (second/ first century BC) which seems to have been his source for other passages, too (esp. *Astr.* 1.40–50), and which certainly treated comets.[61] The doxography in *Astr.* 1.817–75 would then cover all three cultures that contributed to the rise of astrology in the ancient world, Greek (1.817–66), Chaldaean (1.867–73), and Egyptian (1.874–5). And the inconsistency of including a Hermetic element that was, strictly speaking, incompatible with Manilius' philosophical attitude, would have been mitigated by the fact that comets pertain to universal astrology,[62] whose rules may be different from those of genethlialogy (i.e. individual astrology), which occupies most of the *Astronomica* and to which the Roman poet applies his rigid determinism.[63]

Bonincontri, who at no point discusses Manilius' inconsistency, adapts lines 1.874–5 with two modifications: he replaces the emphasis on the pity of God (*miseratus*) with the divine warning's terrifying quality (*tremore*), and while Manilius treats comets here (1.875) and throughout the whole chapter (1.809–926) as signs, Bonincontri equally consistently treats them as efficient causes.[64] Both discrepancies find their explanation in peculiar features of the latter's Christian faith, that is, in the concept of *liberum arbitrium*, in its relevance for moral behaviour, and in its consequences for salvation in the afterlife. A first hint in this direction is given by Bonincontri himself in his commentary on *Astr.* 1.874–5, which he interprets thus: *vt homines abstineant a vitiis* [!] *dat eis per comętas signa euentus rerum futurarum, qui solet ex eorum apparitione comprehendj.*[65] Human morality is, in his view, exempt from the otherwise inescapable impact of comets on the material world. Catastrophes like plagues and earthquakes come about with certainty once a critical disturbance of the celestial environment has occurred. But these

---

[61] See Nechepso and Petosiris, frr. 6, 9, 10, and 11 in Riess 1891–3. See further Keyser 1994. For an updated account of what we know about the pseudepigraphic manual of Nechepso and Petosiris, including a much enlarged list of fragments (fr. +32 is on comets), see Heilen (forthcoming).

[62] As the Hermetic fragment just quoted (*Corp. Herm.* fr. 6.16) rightly emphasizes (κήρυκες καθολικῶν ἀποτελεσμάτων).

[63] This point is rightly emphasized by Montanari Caldini 1989: 29.

[64] Cf. *Astr.* 1.875 *signa*, 1.892 and 1.907 *significant*, 1.893 *minantur*, 1.896 *canunt*, 1.903 *minata est*; Bon. I.1.481 *generat*, 482 *causa*, 484 *generant*, 499 *generantur*, etc. The difference is most obvious with regard to diseases: compare *Astr.* 1.892 *talia* [sc. *morbos*] *significant* with Bon. I.1.484 *generant morbos*.

[65] Bon. comm. ad *Astr.* 1.874 *miseratus* (O fo. 99ᵛ). See also Bonincontri's comments on I.1.510 *occultum est* quoted in the commentary *ad loc.*

very catastrophes have an intrinsic potential of bringing about some
good by shaking man's sinful arrogance, by teaching him a lesson that
will make him tremble (I.1.586-7), by urging him to do penitence and to
make proper use of his free will, the only thing that matters for salvation.
In this sense, the terrifying warning of the Christian God ultimately
operates in the interest of man and is an expression of similar pity to
the one that motivates the—seemingly—more benign god of Manilius.

Of more difficult interpretation is the relationship between comets
and wars. In vv. 523-6 Bonincontri asserts in general terms that God
sends comets which, in their turn, bring about war, and in v. 544 a
specific comet, that of 1456, is said to have stirred up large wars. Are
such wars divine punishment for human sins?[66] One might read vv.
536-42 and 578-82 thus, but Bonincontri piously abstains from
theodicy questions (cf. v. 510 *occultum est*). Be this as it may, the
more important question is whether an expression like v. 544
bellorum motus excivit implies a mechanical, inexorable causation
of wars by comets or whether this is a poetically concise expression
denoting that there had been an opportunity for men to heed a divine
warning and abstain from *bella nefanda* (I.1.577), but they had
neglected to take to heart the admonition. Bonincontri's view seems
to be that, even if God sends, for whatever reason, a comet with the
potential to stir up war by physically 'heating up' human minds,[67]
man always has the option to resist the temptation to give in to fury
and commit slaughter in accordance with the maxim attributed to
Thomas Aquinas which aptly captures the late medieval and Renaissance attitude towards astrology: *astra inclinant, non necessitant.*[68] In

---

[66]   There was a widespread belief that the series of disasters that occurred in 1456 was
not only signified by the comet but ultimately a divine punishment for sexual perver-
sion, esp. sodomy (Figliuolo 1988-9: 1.28; cf. 1.156, 1.169). Right after the earthquake of
5 December 1456, which was seen as a consequence of the comet's appearance,
processions were organized throughout southern Italy, asking God to forgive the sinners
for the vice of sodomy (ibid. 28). The typical shape of a comet was by many interpreted
as a divine rod of correction (Gindhart 2006: 51: 'Zuchtrute Gottes').

[67]   See vv. 525-6 on the ignition of comets by hot planetary rays, esp. those of Mars,
and their psychological effects described in v. 538 *populosque agitare furentis*. For an
interesting, somewhat later example of how early modern writers explained the
physical action of comets on the humoural pathology of man, see Gindhart 2006:
59, who paraphrases and quotes from a German treatise from 1619: 'Der heiße Dampf
trocknet die Luft und die Körpersäfte aus und führt so insbesondere bei Cholerikern
zu *Zorn/Neid/Mord/Krieg vnnd Blutvergiessen*.' See also ibid. 231.

[68]   Bonincontri subscribes to this maxim in the final lines of his second poem
(II.3.1106-16): *ast hominum mentes nullo succumbere possunt / incursu caeli vario,*

his concluding remarks on line 100 (concerning comets) of the pseudo-Ptolemaic *Centiloqium*, written in 1477, Bonincontri explicitly asserts this freedom of choice, which limits comets to being—at least with regard to human affairs—signs rather than causes: *An* ['whether'] *autem isti cometes sint predictorum cause et an impediant arbitrij libertatem magna questio est. Vnde cum fide catholica sentientes dicamus cometas magis signa esse futurorum accidentium quam illorum causas. Vnde bene, pie, Iuste, sancteque uiuentes non timent stellarum aut Cometarum influxus, quoniam in anima rationalj non possunt quicquam operarj: bene ergo dicitur et scriptum est 'A signis cęlj nolite metuere'* [Jer. 10: 2].[69] The seeming contradiction between the final words of this quotation and vv. I.1.585–7 of the poem finds its explanation in whether one focuses on things that are subject to the free will or on such things that are not.

In sum, the remarkable structural difference between the chapters on comets in the two authors is this: while Manilius' Hermetic remark on the role of comets to convey warnings sent by the gods is inconsistent with the rest of the *Astronomica* and is confined to just the two lines 874–5, it becomes the prominent Christian key note on which the first book of Bonincontri was originally supposed to end (I.1.585–7).[70]

---

sed libera cunctis / libertas, quocumque velint, deducere mores. / vis tamen immensa est, hominum quae comprimit artus / et cui vix possunt pauci subsistere contra. / sed quidam valuere tamen, quis iusta fuere / pectora etc. See also his commentary on II.3.942 *est animus* (cod. Vat. lat. 2845, fo. 138ᵛ), where he asserts that *stellas significare nobis, earum dispositionem non facere, sed inclinare. bene profe[c]ta 'a signis cęlj nolite timere'*.

[69] Cod. autogr. Vat. lat. 3379, fo. 114ʳ. For the biblical quotation, compare the previous note.

[70] I am grateful to John T. Ramsey for his helpful comments on an earlier version of this contribution.

APPENDIX

L. Bonincontri, *De rebus naturalibus et divinis* I.1.474–591
Text and commentary[71]

Quae si lege data labuntur mensibus anni
nec variata suis alternent tempora formis,   475
servabit natura modum propriumque recursum;
sin secus alternis variaverit omnia signis
et permutatis assurgat mensibus annus,
omnia seminibus corruptis nata resurgent
et mortale genus morbis vexabitur aegris.   480
quos non ulla magis generat violentia caeli,
non alia fiunt causa manifestius alto,
ni calor ingruerit diri nocuique vaporis,
qui subitos generant morbos pestesque tremendas:
qualem per populos legimus Pandionis olim,   485
qua moribunda virum ceciderunt corpora passim
strataque per terram languebant, ipsaque morbo
tabida; nulla malo poterat medicina valere,
non artes medicae, non ulla piamina curae;
non pater auxilium nato natusve parenti,   490
non dulcis coniunx poterat moribunda marito
ferre manum, sed quisque malo depressus acerbo
ad terram moriens animam fundebat in ictu.
  Non possum tibi cuncta modis exponere certis,
quae generat natura parens referatque per annos.   495
namque poli specie variata vertitur ipsum,
quod caeli lumen recipit, qualemque reportant
nata polum, talem reddunt in luminis oras.
hinc clades fiunt dirae, generantur et inde
morborum species variae pestesque luesque   500
et pecudum mortes, messique inimica resurgunt
corpora reptilium: nam sic quaeque impia fiunt,
caelesti faciente malo flammisque perortis.
haec prius infectant terras, ventique furentes
concipiunt caeli tabem portantque per auras,   505
quaque meant, generant morbos, nam tractus ad ima

---

[71] For *apparatus criticus* and *loci similes*, see Heilen 1999: 376–83. Compared with
that full edition, the distinction by paragraphs is here slightly modified to reflect the
above analysis.

spiritus ille gravis vitalia membra veneno
degravat et leti causas mortalibus affert.
sic placitum superis—causas ne quaere doceri;
occultum est. placuit caelestia semina et astra   510
perpetuas afferre vices motusque sinistros.
haec species rerum forma faciente suprema
omnigenumque genus pecudum certo ordine reddunt,
qui super impositus, ne sic sine lege iacerent
omnia vel mixtis volitarent orbibus astra.   515
hinc herbae innumerae, frondes et pabula laeta,
arboris omne genus virgultaque consita ripis
bracchia submissae spargunt pendentia terrae;
hinc etiam volucres implent concentibus auras
garrulaque in tignis nidum sibi fingit hirundo;   520
hinc tauri brutumque genus flammaeque volantes
in lucem venere suam caelique sub axem.
ille etiam diros portantes bella cometas
ignibus accendit variis flammisque coruscis
aut calido Martis radio solisque rotatu   525
Cyllenique facis fluxu siccoque vapore.
hinc validi perflant boreali a cardine venti
aequora turbantes et culmina summa domorum
arescuntque lacus et flumina pervia cursu
labi nativis desistunt fontibus; hinc est,   530
quod virides pereunt frondes et montibus herbae,
pabula siccantur pecudumque miserrima mortis
fit clades macieque feras tabescere cernes.
pascua quid mirum si caelo infecta venenum
sunt miseris morti et dedunt animalia quaeque?   535
qui quamquam raro apparent, quod noxia portant
tempora et immutant placidissima saecula pacis
bellorum excessu populosque agitare furentis
compertum primosque dari mucrone secandos
et regum mortes varias pestemque famemque,   540
optandum tamen a superis, ne claustra resolvant
aëreamque domum flammis ferventibus ullis.
     Unus et ille, tuo qui fulsit tempore, quantos
bellorum motus excivit! et omnibus ingens
iniectus pavor unus erat, qua peste necandos   545
fata parent miseros, reges quos tradere morti.
(+) vidimus (heu nimium dictu lacrimabile) binas
(+) ardentes caelo stellas caudisque refusis
(+) scintillare faces et longo albescere tractu:

(+) fronte prior succensa comam referebat ab ortu, 550
(+) altera sed maior, quae fumida cuspide caelum
(+) sulcabat, late radios fundebat in alto.
post subito exarsit terris violentior ignis,
quo cecidere duces antiquae gentis et ipse
Alfonsus, pacis pignus placidaeque quietis, 555
non aliter belli cupidus quam pacis amore.
heu quantum non fanda lues cladesque secuta est
illius extremam noctem, qua concidit ictu
Lucanus Samnisque simul, nec Tuscia parvo
tacta malo, sed quaeque domus turrisque superba 560
ad terram prostrata gravi cum pondere lapsa est
milia multa virum convolvens corpora tectis.
quos terrae ingentis motus pestisque secuta est:
nulla domus luctu caruit; mihi (pro dolor) ipsi,
quos geminos dederat partu Caecilia natos, 565
heu moriens secum condit miseranda sepulcro.
nec tamen omne malum miseris hac peste remotum,
nam bellis concussa quies populique rebelles
impia funestis sumpserunt arma maniplis.
Alfonsi regis mortem quae bella secuta, 570
ipse vides: vidisse iuvet, vir maxime, ne quid
aut sit inexpertum vel non satis ante paratum.
tu vero, ne quid desit Tuscisque tibique,
prospicito, nam quanta dedit qualesque procellas
bellorum rabie, qui fulsit ad alta cometes 575
sidera! nos miseros! nam perdimus omnia, postquam
heroes vertere manus ad bella nefanda.
nonne vides Ligures omnes ad bella paratos,
armari classem Venetam Teucrumque petentem
Italiam totisque animis petere arma, ferocem 580
insultare solo nec non oriente subacto
Hesperiam properare gradu Romaque potiri?
    Haec etsi caeli fluxu reserata feruntur
aëreamque domum flammant labentibus annis,
attamen omnipotens fulgentibus addidit astris 585
eventus rerum varios documenta virorum
humanos motura animos mentesque tremore.
(+) At me sed quamquam terrent ostenta nefandi
(+) sideris et flammae nec non praenuntia nuper
(+) visa mali, tua mi virtus et facta parentum 590
(+) dant animos mentemque movent ad tanta canenda.

In the following commentary, Bonincontri's own, hitherto unpublished comments on I.1.474–591 are included completely as far as they are extant (I.1.474–533) in the only preserved copy of the lost autograph, cod. Vat. lat. 2845 (**V**).[72] Due to the poor quality of this copy, several emendations are needed. In such cases, the manuscript reading will be indicated in square brackets after my emendation. I did not correct purely orthographical matters.

474 *quae*] sc. *quattuor anni tempora.* **478** cf. Bon. comm. (Vat. lat. 2845, fo. 14ʳ, sine lemmate): *non quod menses mutentur, sed illorum mensium qualitates in calido et frigido, sicco et humido.* **480** cf. Bon. comm. ad *mortale* (Vat. lat. 2845, fo. 14ʳ): *dicit ypocras* [i.e. Hippoc. *Aphorisms* 3.1]: *mutationes temporum maxime generant <morbos>.* The full aphorism reads in the Greek original: αἱ μεταβολαὶ τῶν ὡρέων μάλιστα τίκτουσι νουσήματα, καὶ ἐν τῇσιν ὥρῃσιν αἱ μεγάλαι μεταλλαγαὶ ἢ ψύξιος ἢ θάλψιος, καὶ τἄλλα κατὰ λόγον οὕτως. **485–93** the Athenian plague: cf. *Astr.* 1.884–91 and Lucr. 6.1138–1286. See further Bon. comm. ad v. 485 (Vat. lat. 2845, fo. 14ʳ⁻ᵛ): *De hac pestilentia quę fuit athenis Titus Lucretius in ultimo sui operis aperte dicit* [cit. Lucr. 6.1138–40] *et subdit* [cit. Lucr. 6.1144–54]. *deinde ponit quę signa erant illis lętalia dicens* [cit. Lucr. 6.1182–11; fo. 14ᵛ] *et cętera que sequuntur.* **487** *ipsaque*] sc. *terra* (cf. *Astr.* 1.894–5). **489** *non ulla piamina curae*] cf. Plin. *HN* 2.92 *non leviter piatum*

---

[72] This manuscript preserves numerous comments on the first half of I.1.474–591, but nothing on the second. In view of the autobiographical relevance of that second half it is unlikely that Bonincontri did not comment on it in his lost autograph. Note also that there is circumstantial evidence that the copy in Vat. lat. 2845 originated as a result of the Sack of Rome in 1527. The original (Bonincontri's autograph) must have been in very bad condition by that time. And we know for certain that the original was a handwritten copy of the poem itself on whose margins Bonincontri had added numerous notes which were then copied into two different manuscripts, Vat. lat. 2844 (the poem) and Vat. lat. 2845 (the commentary). The copy of the text (Vat. lat. 2844) is complete, but the very copying activity and the continued manœuvring of the original, now lost manuscript over days and weeks may have caused the material loss of a few leaves after their poetic content had already been copied. Note that there are two gaps of similar extension (56 and 75 lines respectively) in the commentary on the following book, between I.2.374 and I.2.431 and between I.2.710 and I.2.786. This indicates that in each of the three cases one leaf got lost, with *c.*28–30 lines per page (cf. e.g. another autograph of Bonincontri, cod. Vat. lat. 3379, fo. 9ʳ, with 29 lines on one page, reproduced by Heilen 1999: 158, fig. 33). Note also, with regard to the first large gap which is at issue here (I.1.534–91), that fo. 15ᵛ of Vat. lat. 2845 is, except for the first three lines, blank, and so is the whole following leaf (fo. 16ʳ⁻ᵛ). This strongly indicates that the copyist was aware of the loss of one leaf and left enough blank space to copy the missing leaf's marginal notes as soon as he would find it. However, the intended supplement was never made.

(a passage quoted by Bonincontri in his commentary on Manilius; see p. 292 above). **491** *dulcis coniunx* = Verg. *G.* 4.465 and *Aen.* 2.777 (both times in the context of death). **499** cf. Bon. comm. ad *hinc clades* (Vat. lat. 2845, fos. 13ᵛ–14ʳ): *pestilentię terremotus diluuiaque fiunt aut propter solares eclipses uel cometarum apparitiones uel* [fo. 14ʳ] *propter coniunctiones planetarum superiorum Saturni Iouis et Martis, et cum mutantur in signis de una in aliam triplicitatem, de quibus albumaβar in libro de magnis <coniunctionibus> dicit.* In this prose survey the solar eclipses naturally come first because the regular pattern of the seasons is based on the course of the Sun. For a brief explanation of Abū Maʿšar's (AD 787–886) astrological theory of the Great Conjunctions, esp. the change of triplicity alluded to by Bonincontri, see Yamamoto and Burnett 2000: 1.582–4 or Heilen 2005: 312–15. A famous, roughly contemporary example of an epidemic disease explained with a conjunction of the upper planets is Fracastoro's *Syphilis* (ed. princ. 1530), on which see Heilen 2008. **500** cf. Bon. comm. ad *variae* (Vat. lat. 2845, fo. 14ᵛ): *nam cum coniunctiones* [correxi; gᵉˢ (= generationes) V, debuit scribere ₉ᵉˢ] *et eclipses fiunt in signis ad effigiem hominum figuratis, no[s]cent hominibus; si in ariete tauroque, animalibus; et sic secundum signorum naturam hominibus et locis pręcipue tali signo subiecti[o]s, in quibus fuit talis coniunctio uel eclipsis.* **504–8** cf. Bon. comm. (Vat. lat. 2845, fo. 14ᵛ, sine lemm.): *Optimam subiecit poeta rationem, cum aer inficitur a malis constellationibus et nos attrahimus ipsum aera ita infectum* [*in fenum* V]. **510** cf. Bon. comm. ad *occultum est* (Vat. lat. 2845, fos. 14ᵛ–15ʳ): *nolite sapere plus quam oportet sapere* [Rom. 12: 3]. *quis es tu, dicit scriptura, qui inquiris sensum dei? ordine enim di*[fo. 15ʳ]*uino fatalis series texitur* [*fat. ser. tex.* = Boeth. *Cons.* 4.6.13], *quę etsi nobis occulta sunt, que eueniunt, tamen—ut dicit Caius Manilius de apparitione cometarum, deus per signa apparentia nobis indicat, quid sit futurum in his inferioribus, dicens:* [cit. *Astr.* 1.865–6] *et post multas causa<s> generationis ipsorum dicit:* [cit. *Astr.* 1.874–83; 1.896–7]. **525** cf. Bon. comm. ad *Martis* (Vat. lat. 2845, fo. 15ʳ): *cometas eβe siccos* [*succos* V] *uapores; ideo siccitatem ualidam significant, terrę- motus et pestilentiam et regum mortes et populorum rebelliones. gen- erantur a solis radijs Mercurijque et Martis in isto aere uicino spere ignis et significant, quę Manilius dicit. ipsarum 9 sunt species, ut dicit Ptholomeus. uide de his in Plinio de naturali historia* [cf. Plin. *HN* 2.89–94 and Serv. *ad Aen.* 10.272]. As to the importance of Sun, Mars, and Mercury, cf. Bon. comm. ad *Astr.* 1.814 (**O** fo. 96ʳ) about the *radios solis Mercurij et Martis qui sunt causa generationis cometarum potissima.* As to the nine kinds of comets, Bonincontri lists their names ibid. ad *Astr.* 1.833 (**O** fo. 97ᵛ): *de quibus Tolomeus in fine centiloquij ponit viiij species et eorum nomina videlicet dominus Ascone, Veru, Miles, Trabs, dolium, matuta, Rosa, pertica, et tenaculum*; he further characterizes each of these types in his autograph commentary on Sent. 100 of the *Centiloquium*, cod. Vat. lat. 3379, fo. 113ʳ⁻ᵛ. The true origin of this typology, which was in the Renaissance generally yet wrongly accepted as Ptolemaic, remains to be investigated. **527-33** cf. Bon. comm. (Vat. lat. 2845, fo. 15ᵛ, sine lemm.) *Ponit poeta Cometarum uarios eße effectus, minanturque [minantur quę **V**], cum apparent, his locis, ubi caudas extendunt, et plerumque apparent a parte [aperte **V**] septentrionali XI signis a sole distantes [distantibus **V**].* After this entry the rest of Bonincontri's commentary on the first book is lost. **543** *ille*] marginal notes preserved in the MSS. **UM** explain that this is the comet of 1456, that the one described in 551-2 is the comet of 1472, and that the following lines from 553 onwards are about the first comet's (1456) effects. All marginal notes of the MSS. are edited in Heilen 1999. *tuo ... tempore*] see n. 23. **547-52** These lines were probably added by Bonincontri at a later date, together with vv. 588-91. On the comets of 1456 and 1472, see the contemporary records from European, Arabic, and East Asian sources quoted and discussed by Kronk 1999: 273-6, 285-9; as well as earlier contributions by Celoria 1885*a* and *b*; Celoria 1894; Thorndike 1923-58: 4.413-37; Thorndike 1958; Abel and Martens 1956 (esp. 71-86, where Johannes de Vesalia's treatise on the comet of 1472 is edited); Lhotsky and Ferrari d'Occhieppo 1960; Jervis 1985; Hunger *et al.* 1985: 59, 62; Figliuolo 1988-9: 1.198-210; Figliuolo 1990; Heitzer 1995 (with plates); and Figliuolo 1997: 61-3. While most of the observational records of fifteenth-century comets have a qualitative, descriptive style, more quantitative observations were exceptionally made by Paolo dal Pozzo Toscanelli (1397-1482), Georg Aunpeck of Peuerbach (1423-61), and Regiomontanus (i.e. Johannes Müller from Königsberg in Bavaria, 1436-76). On each of these astronomers, see the respective chapters in Jervis 1985. Particularly important is Toscanelli: his extant autograph *Immensi labores et graves vigilie magistri Pauli de Puteo Toscanello super mensura comete* (Bibl. Naz. Florence, Banco Rari 30) contains the earliest systematic cometary observations in Western history, day-by-day positions plotted on star maps, treating comets as if they were celestial bodies (Jervis 1985: 127; cf. Hunger *et al.* 1985: 62). Jervis further emphasizes (1985: 67) that 'the phenomenon which shows the greatest variation in this series of observations and which, therefore, may have been the phenomenon of greatest interest to him [= Toscanelli] at this time, probably for astrological reasons, was the length and direction of the comet's tail'. It is tempting to wonder whether Bonincontri knew Toscanelli personally, but there is no evidence for any contact between the two scholars. Another observer was a close friend of Bonincontri, Giovanni Pontano (1429–1503); see Rinaldi 2004 and Caroline Stark's contribution to this volume. Pontano's profound interest in all kinds of astrological lore, which was probably instilled in him by Bonincontri, led the former to write, just as Bonincontri did at the same time (1477), a commentary on the pseudo-Ptolemaic *Centiloquium* (ed. pr. Venice 1519), which contains the following description of the comets of 1456 and 1472 (fo. 91^v, ad *Sent.* 100): *Nobis adolescentibus insignis etiam cometes ad orientem in Cancri Leonisque regi<o>nibus multis diebus fulsit, tantæ longitudinis, ut amplius quàm duo cœli signa comæ suæ tractu occuparet. Eum secuta est Alphonsi regis mors, quæ Aemiliam, Sabinam, Campaniam uniuersumque regnum Neapolitanum et longo et graui bello implicauit. Secuta est et pestilentia aliquanto diuturnior. Annis his superioribus cometes alius tenui primo capite, comaque admodum breui conspectus est, mox miræ magnitudinis factus ab ortu deflectere in septentrionem cœpit, nunc citato motu, nunc remisso, et, quod Mars Saturnusque uterque repedabat, auersus ipse prægrediente coma ferebatur, donec ad ipsas arctos peruenit. inde cum primum Saturnus ac* [fo. 92^r] *Mars recto cursu pergere cœperunt, in occasum iter flexit, tanta celeritate, ut die uno ad triginta gradus emensus sit, atque ubi ad Arietem ac Taurum peruenit, uideri desijt. Hic et dies plurimos fulsit, et qui initio breuior uisus est, adeo creuit, ut quin<qua>ginta gradus atque etiam amplius occuparet.* (Pontano goes on to describe one more comet, that of AD 1264; see n. 46.) For details concerning the comets of 1456 and 1472, see the following separate entries on v. 550 and vv. 551–2. **549** on the length of both comets' tails, see Pontano (above ad vv. 547–52), esp. *tantæ longitudinis etc.* (1456) and *adeo creuit etc.* (1472). **550** The orbital parameters of the comet of 1456 have been computed many times; the authoritative reconstruction is that of Yeomans and Kiang, quoted by Kronk 1999: 275. Some of the contemporary records deserve to be quoted here. When Georg Aunpeck of Peuerbach first observed the comet from Vienna during the night of 9/10 June 1456, it was 10° long, extending from 6° Gemini (head), latitude 19°, to 26°

Taurus (tip of the tail), latitude 22° (Jervis 1985: 89). In other words, it was rather close to the ecliptic and visible in the east before dawn. During the following weeks, it moved further eastwards in the direction of the zodiacal signs, dragging its tail behind it. After its perihelion on 9 June and its conjunction with the Sun on 17 June 1456 the comet was observed in the west after sunset (Jervis 1985: 61; Kronk 1999: 273, 275). Altogether, its progress from Taurus to Virgo covered *c.*108° (see the table in Celoria 1885*a*: 67–8). It attained its most northernly declination of +41° (apparent) on 16 June 1456 (Kronk 1999: 275). For day-by-day data on the comet's longitude and latitude from 8 June to 8 July 1456, see Toscanelli's observations assembled by Jervis 1985: 62. They are 'the most valuable set of observations made during this apparition' (Kronk 1999: 273). Since the comet was first seen in the east (Bon. v. 550: *ab ortu*, misinterpreted by Haskell 1998: 512 n. 39) with its tail pointing westwards, the west was the geographical area that would, according to astrological cometary theory, be struck by disaster. Cf. Bon. comm. ad *Astr.* 1.897 (cod. Ottob. fo. 100ᵛ): *ex cauda comętę cognoscitur, ubi malum, quod ab eo portenditur, sit futurum, et quomodo et quando, a signo et parte celj, in qua apparuerit. nam vbi crines suos iaculatur, ibi erit eius cometae [conatus cod. Ottob., item ed. 1484] effectus.* (Cf. Ptol. *Tetr.* 2.9 and see also Plin. *HN* 2.92 *referre arbitrantur, in quas partes sese iaculetur aut cuius stellae vires accipiat quasque similitudines reddat et quibus in locis emicet;* interestingly Manilius in his section on the significance of comets (1.876–921) does not give any comparable information on the divinatory technique to be employed). It was observed only later, in the 1530s, that a comet's tail is always directed away from the Sun (the first European to report in print the antisolar nature of comet tails was Girolamo Fracastoro; see Yeomans 1991: 29; cf. Gindhart 2006: 219). This was a significant advance in cometary theory that would eventually replace the superstitious belief that the tail is a kind of divine finger pointing to the region of the comet's influence (Jervis 1985: 121, 128). **551–2** The comet of 1472, which was observed from 21 December 1471 to 21 February 1472 (Kronk 1999: 285), was the most impressive of the fifteenth century (Kokott 1994: 18). Its orbital characteristics were entirely different from that of 1456 because it moved quickly from Libra against the succession of the zodiacal signs to Aries, covered an impressive latitudinal distance (from its most southerly declination of +3° on 12 December to its most northerly declination of +76° on 22 January; Kronk 1999: 288–9) and approached the earth very closely (0.0696 Astronomical Units on 22 January; Kronk 1999:

285), thus producing an astonishing (seeming) growth in size. The last two characteristics explain Bonincontri's words *maior* and *in alto*. Compare, for the size, Pontano (above ad vv. 547–52: *miræ magnitudinis*), for the latitude, the brief treatise *De cometis* transmitted under the name of Johannes Regiomontanus, which, however, is probably a false attribution, the true author being an anonymous physician of Zurich (Jervis 1985: 114–17). This text says that the comet of 1472, when its longitude fell in the middle of Cancer, reached its greatest distance from the ecliptic, 77°: *Ubi cum esset in medio Cancri, maxime distabat ab orbe signorum 77 gradibus, & tunc inter duos polos zodiaci & aequinoctialis, ibat usque ad interpedes Cephei* (see Jervis 1985: 118 and 195, appendix D). The description of the comet given in *De cometis* is confirmed by other contemporary reports like Toscanelli's (see the Latin text with Engl. translation in Jervis 1985: 65–6) and by modern computation (ibid. 120 and Kronk 1999: 285–9). **553–69** The year 1456 was later remembered as one of many catastrophes. Jacobo Sannazaro, for instance, who was born in that period, thought that since he was 'sotto infelice prodigio di comete, di terremoto, di pestilenzia, di sanguinose battaglie nato', it was his destiny to experience an ardent yet unanswered love which would lead him to consider suicide (quoted from his autobiographical passage in *Arcadia*, Prose 7, on which see Mauro 1955: 5–6). **555** King Alfonso I died on 27 June 1458. Cf. Bon. *Ann.* 10 ad ann. 1458 (Muratori 1732: 162A–B): *Alphonsus Aragon extremo mensis Junii moritur in Peninsula Ovi* [i.e. Castel dell'Ovo, Naples], *paullo ante Solis occasum.* [. . .] *Fuit Alphonsi mors IV. Calendas Julii* [this is correct only by exclusive reckoning], *religiosa atque suavis.* As to the two-year distance between the comet's appearance and the king's death, see (e.g.) Jacobus Angelus of Ulm, who asserts in his treatise on the comet of 1402 (discussed by Jervis 1985: 37–42) that the effects of a comet need not be immediate but may lag behind the appearance by as much as six years (ibid. 41; see also Gindhart 2006: 187 and 200, who quotes examples from seventeenth-century authors who connected comets to historical events that followed the celestial phenomena by up to twenty years or even preceded them by one to three years). The connection between the comet of 1456 and King Alfonso's death in 1458 was favoured by the fact that both events occurred in the same month of the respective years, June. Note also that in the days following the earthquake of 5 December 1456 (on which see below), itself believed to be a result of the comet, a rumour originated that King Alfonso had been struck so badly by the news of the enormous damage as to make him fall seriously ill. Enea Silvio Piccolomini, the future 'humanist pope' Pius II, upon learning of King Alfonso's sickness, commented thus in a letter to the Holy Roman Emperor Frederick III (28 Dec. 1456): *si moriatur tantus rex (quod absit), non frustra cometam vidimus* ('if such a great king were to die—may it not happen!—then we did not see the comet in vain'). For details, see Figliuolo 1988-9: 1.189–90. The view that the comet of 1456 had caused or announced the death of King Alfonso in 1458 as well as the earthquake of 1456 (see next entry) was held until the seventeenth century; see, for example, Gindhart 2006: 178 on Kepler's *De cometis*. **557-62** On Sunday, 5 December 1456, around 4 a.m., an earthquake devastated large parts of the kingdom of Naples. It came to be considered the big earthquake *per antonomasiam*, and a new metonymy for 'earthquake' was coined: *Santa Barbara* (the patron saint of 5 December). While the immediately following reports on this event by contemporaries stayed, on the whole, within realistic limits, the number of victims was in later decades absurdly exaggerated: Matteo Palmieri in his *Annales* spoke of some 70,000, Angelo di Tummolillo of more than 100,000. The true number was probably around 15,000. Exaggerated scenarios of the area affected and the number of inhabitants killed were commonly accepted by seismologists until the 1980s. The recent reassessment of what actually happened was possible thanks to the extremely detailed and conscientious account provided in 1457 as an official court report by Giannozzo Manetti (1396–1459). Unlike the same author's famous programmatic text of Renaissance humanism, *De dignitate et excellentia hominis*, his manuscript report on the earthquake of 1456 soon fell into oblivion. Figliuolo 1988-9 provides an exhaustive, up-to-date analysis of the earthquake of 1456 based on all available historical sources plus an assessment within the seismo-tectonic situation of the southern Apennine range by three seismological experts. From his detailed analysis of 198 localities with indication, in each single case, of the number of inhabitants, of casualties due to the earthquake, and of fires, it appears that in Naples (locality #110, Figliuolo 1988-9: 1.106, sources: ibid. 2.108–19), where Bonincontri lived, the number of victims was comparatively low (*c*.100), with an intensity of 8 on the Modified Mercalli Scale. In certain other localities in the interior the intensity was 11 and almost 100 per cent of the population were killed by the collapsing houses in which they were sleeping. Bonincontri, who was at the time a military commander at the service of King Alfonso I, describes the earthquake also in his *Annales*. Note that this account contains a story about King Alfonso I that does not seem to deserve credence: *Anno Salutis 1456 quinta die Decembris in aurora ingens terræmotus in Regno Neapolitano factus est, multasque obruit Civitatum Ædes, Neapoli trecentas, Nolæ quinquaginta, quasdam etiam funditus evertit, Arejanum, Alifium, Apicium, Trojam pæne totam, Alphonso Rege Sanseverini demorante in solemnitate Missarum, qui quum omnes fugerent, solus Deo fidens, genibus uti erat flexis, ante Altare permansit. Ego autem cum ceteris aufugi, ne tectorum ruina opprimerer* (Muratori 1732: 159A–B). As to the localities mentioned by Bonincontri, see the detailed analyses of damages and casualties in Figliuolo 1988–9: 1.104–8 and 2.47–160, nos. 5 (Alife), 9 (Apice), 11 (Ariano Irpino), 110 (Napoli), 112 (Nola), 186 (Troia). Figliuolo 1988–9: 1.138 argues from the alleged time of day and the well-known itinerary and whereabouts of King Alfonso in late 1456 that Bonincontri's account here cannot be true and seems to be motivated either by gratitude towards the late king or by the desire to please his son and successor, Ferrante (1423–94). Be this as it may, the story of the intrepid, exemplary sovereign was recounted by various historians until the end of the sixteenth century (ibid. 1.138–41, with Ferrante assuming—in some accounts—the role of the royal protagonist) and gave rise to pictorial representations such as the one in Figure 17.1 of King Ferrante (*sic*) kneeling and praying during the earthquake. **558** *illius*] sc. *cometae*, not *Alfonsi*. The comet was visible only at night, while the king died in the late afternoon (see above on v. 555). **559–60** Tuscany was not affected by the earthquake (see the map of the macroseismic field attached to Figliuolo 1988–9), but the earlier hurricane of 23 August 1456 (see next entry) caused severe damages: Matteo Palmieri in his *Annales* (also known as *Historia florentina*) speaks of very large trees uprooted, collapsed buildings and towers, etc. (ed. Scaramella 1905–16: 176–7). **563** *pestisque*] i.e. *pestis quoque*. Meteorologically speaking, 1456 was an unusually inclement year in Italy, extraordinarily rainy and humid, with a devastating hurricane in central Italy in August and a very cold winter (Figliuolo 1988–9: 1.3–5). These were favourable conditions for the development of agents of sickness (ibid. 1.11). Various treatises on the plague of 1456 are reviewed by Figliuolo 1988–9: 1.189–97. The plague continued into 1457 (cf. Palmieri, *Annales* ad annum), and it may have been only then, after the earthquake (as the text says), that Bonincontri lost his family. **565–6** Caecilia was Bonincontri's first wife. On their happy marriage, see Pontano's dedication of the first book of his *Parthenopeus* to Lorenzo Bonincontri; on their deaths in 1456 and (probably) 1491, see Pontano's respective funerary epigrams (*Tumuli*

Figure 17.1. King Ferrante (sic) praying during the earthquake of 1456. Ms. Ital. 1711 (Giuniano Maio, *De maiestate*), fo. 19ʳ. Bibliothèque Nationale de France, Paris. Reproduced by permission.

1.7 and 1.25). **570** cf. below v. 577. Alfonso I was succeeded by his legitimate son Ferdinand (also called Don Ferrante, 1423–94) in 1458. However, it was only after a long war of succession against John of Anjou that Ferdinand was able to re-establish his authority in the kingdom (1464). The worst setback was his defeat in the battle of Sarno (July 1460), inflicted upon him by the Angevins and the Neapolitan rebel barons (here: *heroes*; cf. Ijsewijn and Sacré 1998: 378). **579–82** This may be an allusion to the Venetian-Ottoman war AD 1463–79 when the Turks became for the first time a real danger on Italian soil through their raids in the Friuli lands controlled by the Venetian Republic. Note also that Pope Sixtus IV (1471–84) tried, right after his election, to organize a new crusade against the Ottoman Turks, but his ambition to forge a coalition of the European powers failed. Only a small fleet equipped with the support of Venice and Florence actually set sail for Smyrna in 1472 but returned soon afterwards without having achieved anything note-worthy. The Turkish invasion of southern Italy in 1480 was still in the future when Bonincontri finished his poem. **579** *Teucrumque*] the identification of the Turks (*Turci*) with the Trojans (*Teucri*) was ac-cepted by many contemporaries, including the Turkish Sultan Mehmed II (r. 1451–80) himself, who was steeped in classical culture and claimed that the capture of Constantinople (1453) was a belated revenge for the sack of Troy. See the anthology of contemporary texts and documents edited with scholarly commentary by Pertusi 1976; as well as Spencer 1952; Schwoebel 1967; and Meserve 2000. **582** *potiri*] conative infinitive. There had been a body of prophetic literature promising that Constan-tinople would fall to Islam before the End of the World. Often these prophecies linked the fall of the Byzantine capital (cf. 581 *oriente subacto*) to the fall of Rome. Mehmed II seems to have been planning to invade Italy and conquer Rome in fulfillment of these ancient pro-phecies, but his premature death prevented him from realizing this plan. **585** *omnipotens*] for God as the ultimate cause of comets, cf. vv. 509, 512, and esp. 523. **588–91** were probably added on a later date, together with vv. 547–52 (see pp. 285–6 above). Cf. (for the sense) *Astr.* 1.876. Earlier members of the Medici family had accomplished memorable deeds (*facta*), esp. Cosimo il Vecchio (1389–1464), who came posthumously to be called *pater patriae*. Young Lorenzo, instead, can at this point of his career only be praised for his *virtus*. Rather than of military prowess (Roman 'manliness'), the poet seems here to be thinking of Christian virtue, esp. peaceful politics: compare vv. 555–6 (on King Alfonso I), the verbal imitation of *Astr.* 1.10 (concerning the emperor Augustus), and what has been said on pp. 295–6 above about *liberum arbitrium*.

Bibliography

Abel, A., and Martens, M. (1956) 'Le Rôle de Jean de Vésale, médecin de la ville de Bruxelles, dans la propagande de Charles le Téméraire', *Cahiers Bruxellois*, 1: 41–86.

Abry, J.-H. (1993a) 'Le Nil: réflexions sur les vers III 271–274 des *Astronomiques*', in Liuzzi (ed.), *Manilio fra poesia e scienza* (Galatina: Congedo), 195–210.

——(1993b) 'Manilius et Germanicus, une énigme historique et littéraire', *REL* 71: 179–202.

——(1999a) 'Manilius et Julius Firmicus Maternus, deux astrologues sous l'empire', in N. Blanc and A. Buisson (eds.), Imago antiquitatis: *Religions et iconographie du monde romain. Mélanges offerts à Robert Turcan* (Paris: De Boccard), 35–45.

——(1999b) 'Présence de Lucrèce: Les *Astronomiques* de Manilius', in R. Poignault (ed.), *Présence de Lucrèce* (Tours: Centre de Recherches A. Piganiol), 111–28.

——(2000) 'Une carte du monde à l'époque d'Auguste: Manilius, *Astronomiques*, IV, 585–817', in A. Bonnafé, J.-C. Decourt, and B. Helly (eds.), *L'Espace et ses représentations* (Lyon: Maison de l'Orient Méditerranéen), 83–112.

——(2003) 'Manilius', in R. Goulet (ed.), *Dictionnaire des philosophes antiques*, 4 (Paris: CNRS Éditions), 248–54.

——(2005) 'La Sphéricité de la terre: Un poète aux prises avec la démonstration (Manilius, *Astronomiques* I, 173–235)', *Pallas*, 69: 247–60.

——(2006a) 'L'*Excursus* sur les latitudes (Manilius, *Astronomiques*, 3, 301–384)', *Pallas*, 72: 149–70.

——(2006b) '*Sed caelo noscenda canam . . .* (*Astr.*, 2. 142): Poésie et astrologie dans les *Astronomiques* de Manilius', in C. Cusset (ed.), *Musa docta: Recherches sur la poésie scientifique dans l'antiquité* (Saint-Étienne: Université de Saint-Étienne), 293–333.

——(2007) 'Manilius and Aratus: Two Stoic Poets on Stars', *LICS* 6.01. (http://www.leeds.ac.uk/classics/lics/volumes.html#6; accessed Feb. 2010).

Adams, J. N. (1982) *The Latin Sexual Vocabulary* (Baltimore: Johns Hopkins University Press).

Adorno, T. W. (1994) *The Stars Down to Earth and Other Essays on the Irrational in Culture* (London: Routledge).

Agapiou, N. (2005) *Endymion au carrefour: La Fortune littéraire et artistique du mythe d'Endymion à l'aube de l'ère moderne* (Berlin: Mann).

Algra, K. (1999) 'The Beginnings of Cosmology', in A. A. Long (ed.), *The Cambridge Companion to Early Greek Philosophy* (Cambridge: Cambridge University Press), 45–65.

——*et al.* (eds.) (1999) *The Cambridge History of Hellenistic Philosophy* (Cambridge: Cambridge University Press).

Allen, J. (1994) 'Academic Probabilism and Stoic Epistemology', *CQ* 44: 85–113.

Altevogt, H. (1952) *Labor improbus, eine Vergilstudie* (Münster: Aschendorff).

Anderson, W. S. (1960) 'Discontinuity in Lucretian Symbolism', *TAPA* 91: 1–29.

Annas, J. (1992) *Hellenistic Philosophy of Mind* (Berkeley, Calif.: University of California Press).

Arthur, E. P. (1983) 'The Stoic Analysis of the Mind's Reaction to Presentations', *Hermes*, 111: 69–78.

Asmis, E. (2008) 'Lucretius' New World Order: Making a Pact with Nature', *CQ* 58: 141–57.

Bajoni, M. G. (2004) 'Gli *Astronomica* di Manilio come rappresentazione politica dello spazio celeste', *Latomus*, 63: 98–107.

Bakhouche, B. (1996) *Les Textes latins d'astronomie: Un maillon dans la chaîne du savoir* (Louvain: Peeters).

Baldini Moscadi, L. (1980) 'Magia e progresso in Manilio', *A&R* 25: 8–14.

——(1981) 'Il poeta fra storia e ideologia: Manilio e le guerre civili', in *Cultura e ideologia da Cicerone a Seneca* (Florence: Le Monnier), 39–69.

——(1986) 'Manilio e i poeti augustei: Considerazioni sul proemio del II e del III libro degli *Astronomica*', in *Munus amicitiae: Scritti in memoria di Alessandro Ronconi*, 1 (Florence: Le Monnier), 3–22.

——(1991) 'Il mito adombrato o l'età dell'oro ritrovata (Manilio, *Astr.* 5.270–92)', *Prometheus*, 17: 173–85.

——(1993) 'Caratteri paradigmatici e modelli letterari: Manilio e i paranatellonta dell'Aquarius', in Liuzzi (ed.), *Manilio fra poesia e scienza* (Galatina: Congedo), 79–94.

Baldwin, B. (1987) 'Dating Manilius' *Astronomica*', *Maia*, 39: 101–3.

Barnes, J. (1993) 'Meaning, Saying and Thinking', in K. Döring and T. Ebert (eds.), *Dialektiker und Stoiker: Zur Logik der Stoa und ihrer Vorläufer* (Stuttgart: Steiner), 47–61.

Barnouw, J. (2002) *Propositional Perception: Phantasia, Predication and Signs in Plato, Aristotle, and the Stoics* (Lanham, Md.: University Press of America).

Barton, T. (1994*a*) *Ancient Astrology* (London: Routledge).

——(1994*b*) 'Astrology and the State in Imperial Rome', in N. Thomas and C. Humphrey (eds.), *Shamanism, History and the State* (Ann Arbor: University of Michigan Press), 146–63.

——(1994c) *Power and Knowledge: Astrology, Physiognomics and Medicine under the Roman Empire* (Ann Arbor: University of Michigan Press).

——(1995) 'Augustus and Capricorn: Astrological Polyvalency and Imperial Rhetoric', *JRS* 85: 33–51.

Beard, M., North, J., and Price, S. (1998) *Religions of Rome. Vol. 1: A History* (Cambridge: Cambridge University Press).

Bechert, M. (1900) 'Prolegomena in M. Manilii *Astronomica*', *CR* 14: 296–304.

Beck, R. (2007) *A Brief History of Ancient Astrology* (Malden, Mass.: Blackwell).

Bentley, R. (1739) *M. Manilii Astronomicon* (London: Woodfall).

Bessi, R. (1974) 'Luigi Pulci e Lorenzo Buonincontri', *Rinascimento*, 14: 289–95.

Bettenson, H. (2003) *St Augustine:* Concerning the City of God against the Pagans (London: Penguin).

Biagioli, M. (2006) *Galileo's Instruments of Credit: Telescopes, Imagery, Secrecy* (Chicago: University of Chicago Press).

Bickel, E. (1910) 'De Manilio et Tiberio Caesare', *RhM* 65: 233–48.

Biondi, G. G. (1981) 'Catullo in Manilio? (Nota a Catullo 64, 14)', *Orpheus*, 2: 105–13.

Black, M. (1962) *Models and Metaphors: Studies in Language and Philosophy* (Ithaca, NY: Cornell University Press).

Blair, A., and Grafton, A. (1992) 'Reassessing Humanism and Science', *JHI* 53: 535–40.

Blum, R. (1934) *Manilius' Quelle im ersten Buche der Astronomica*. Diss. Berlin.

Bokdam, S. (1987) 'Les Mythes de l'origine de l'astrologie', in *Divination et controverse religieuse en France au XVIe siècle* (Paris: École Normale Supérieure de Jeunes Filles), 57–72.

Boll, F. (1903) *Sphaera: Neue griechische Texte und Untersuchungen zur Geschichte der Sternbilder* (Leipzig: Teubner).

——and Gundel, W. (1924–37) 'Sternbilder, Sternglaube und Sternsymbolik bei Griechen und Römern', in W. H. Roscher (ed.), *Ausführliches Lexikon der griechischen und römischen Mythologie*, 6 (Leipzig: Teubner), 867–1071.

Bonadeo, A. (2004) *Iride: Un arco tra mito e natura* (Florence: Le Monnier).

Bonincontri, L. (1484) *Astronomicon cum commento Laurentii Bonincontrii Miniatensis* (Rome: no publ.).

Bouché-Leclercq, A. (1899) *L'Astrologie grecque* (Paris: Leroux).

Breiter, T. (1907–8) *M. Manilius:* Astronomica, 2 vols. (Leipzig: Dieterich).

Brind'Amour, P. (1983a) *Le Calendrier romain: Recherches chronologiques* (Ottawa: Éditions de l'Université d'Ottawa).

——(1983b) 'Manilius and the Computation of the Ascendant', *CP* 78: 144–8.

Brind'Amour, P. (1989) 'D'où l'on peut apercevoir Canope: Remarque critique sur le vers 217 des *Astronomiques* de Manilius', *EMC* 8: 355–6.

Brisson, L. (1996) *Einführung in die Philosophie des Mythos. Vol. 1: Antike, Mittelalter und Renaissance* (Darmstadt: Wissenschaftliche Buchgesellschaft; English trans. 2004, *How Philosophers Saved Myths*).

Brittain, C. (2001) 'Rationality, Rules and Rights', *Apeiron*, 34: 247–67.

——(2002) 'Non-Rational Perception in the Stoics and Augustine', *OSAPh* 22: 253–308.

Brodersen, K. (1995) *Terra Cognita: Studien zur römischen Raumerfassung* (Hildesheim: Olms).

Brunschwig, J. (1986) 'The Cradle Argument in Epicureanism and Stoicism', in M. Schofield and G. Striker (eds.), *The Norms of Nature: Studies in Hellenistic Ethics* (Cambridge: Cambridge University Press), 113–44.

Brunt, P. A. (1975) 'Stoicism and the Principate', *PBSR* 43: 7–35.

Bubel, F. (1991) *Euripides, Andromeda* (Stuttgart: Steiner).

Buchner, E. (1982) *Die Sonnenuhr des Augustus* (Mainz: Philipp von Zabern).

Buck, A. (1975) 'Einführung', in A. Buck and O. Herding (eds.), *Der Kommentar in der Renaissance* (Bonn-Bad Godesberg: Boldt), 7–19.

Bühler, W. (1959) 'Maniliana', *Hermes*, 87: 475–94.

Burckhardt, J. (1860) *Die Cultur der Renaissance in Italien: ein Versuch* (Basel: Schweighauser).

Burnett, A. (2007) *The Letters of A. E. Housman*, 2 vols. (Oxford: Clarendon Press).

Buxton, R. (1999) *From Myth to Reason?: Studies in the Development of Greek Thought* (Oxford: Oxford University Press).

Cabisius, G. (1984–5) 'Social Metaphor and the Atomic Cycle in Lucretius', *CJ* 80: 109–20.

Calcante, C. M. (2002) Miracula rerum: *Strategie semiologiche del genere didascalico negli* Astronomica *di Manilio* (Pisa: Edizioni ETS).

Campbell, G. (2002) 'Lucretius and the Memes of Prehistory', *LICS Discussion Paper* 1. (http://www.leeds.ac.uk/classics/lics/volumes.html#Discussion; accessed Feb. 2010)

——(2003) *Lucretius on Creation and Evolution: A Commentary on* De Rerum Natura *Book Five, Lines 772–1104* (Oxford: Oxford University Press).

Campbell, J. S. (1982) 'The Ambiguity of Progress: *Georgics* I, 118–159', *Latomus*, 41: 566–76.

Cassirer, E. (1922) *Die Begriffsform im mythischen Denken* (Leipzig: Teubner; repr. in id., *Wesen und Wirkung des Symbolbegriffs* (Darmstadt: Wissenschaftliche Buchgesellschaft, 1956), 1–70).

——(1925) *Philosophie der symbolischen Formen II: Das mythische Denken* (Berlin: Bruno Cassirer; rev. repr. in id., *Gesammelte Werke*, 12, ed. Birgit Recki (Darmstadt: Wissenschaftliche Buchgesellschaft, 2002)).

——(1927) *Individuum und Kosmos in der Philosophie der Renaissance* (Leipzig: Teubner).

Celoria, G. (1885*a*) 'Sull'apparizione della Cometa di Halley avvenuta nell' anno 1456', *Astronomische Nachrichten*, 2645/111: 65–72.

——(1885*b*) 'Sulla Cometa dell'anno 1472', *Astronomische Nachrichten*, 2668/112: 49–54.

——(1894) 'Sulle osservazioni di comete fatte da Paolo dal Pozzo Toscanelli e sui lavori astronomici suoi in generale', in Gustavo Uzielli, *La vita e i tempi di Paolo dal Pozzo Toscanelli. Ricerche e studi* (Rome: Ministero della Pubblica Istruzione), ch. 6 (repr. of Celoria's chapter alone: *Pubblicazioni del Reale Osservatorio Astronomico di Brera in Milano*, 55, Milan 1921).

Charlet, J.-L. (2000) *Claudien: Poèmes politiques (395–8)* (Paris: Les Belles Lettres).

Christiansen, H. (1908) 'Que–que bei den römischen Hexametrikern (bis etwa 500 n.Chr.'), *Archiv für Lateinische Lexikographie*, 15: 165–211.

Clay, D. (1983) *Lucretius and Epicurus* (Ithaca, NY: Cornell University Press).

——(1997) 'Lucretius' Gigantomachy', in K. A. Algra, M. H. Koenen, and P. H. Schrijvers (eds.), *Lucretius and his Intellectual Background* (Amsterdam: North-Holland), 187–92.

Collard, C., Cropp, M. J., and Gibert, J. (2004) *Euripides: Selected Fragmentary Plays* (Oxford: Oxbow Books).

Commager, H. S. (1957) 'Lucretius' Interpretation of the Plague', *HSCP* 62: 105–18 (repr. in Gale (ed.) *Oxford Readings in Classical Studies: Lucretius* (Oxford: Oxford University Press, 2007), 182–98).

Connolly, J. (2001) 'Picture Arcadia: The Politics of Representation in Vergil's *Eclogues*', *Vergilius*, 47: 89–116.

Connors, C. (1998) *Petronius the Poet: Verse and Literary Tradition in the Satyricon* (Cambridge: Cambridge University Press).

Conte, G. B. (1994) *Latin Literature: A History*, tr. J. B. Solodow (Baltimore: Johns Hopkins University Press; Italian 1987).

Cooley, A. E. (2009) Res Gestae Divi Augusti: *Text, Translation, and Commentary* (Cambridge: Cambridge University Press).

Costanza, S. (1984) 'Appunti sulla fortuna di M. Manilio Astr. I 13 in Germanico, in Calpurnio Siculo e in Tertulliano', *Vichiana*, 13: 26–48.

——(1987) 'Ci fu un sesto libro degli *Astronomica* di Manilio?', in *Filologia e forme letterarie: Studi offerti a Francesco Della Corte*, 1 (Urbino: Quattro Venti), 223–63.

Couffignal, R. (1980) *Le Drame de l'Eden: Le Récit de la Genèse et sa fortune littéraire* (Toulouse: Association des Publications de l'Université de Toulouse-Le Mirail).

Courtney, E. (2009) 'Housman and Manilius', in D. J. Butterfield and C. A. Stray (eds.), *A. E. Housman: Classical Scholar* (London: Duckworth), 29–43.

Cramer, A. (1882) *De Manilii qui dicitur elocutione*. Diss. Strasburg.

——(1893) *Über die ältesten Ausgaben von Manilius' Astronomica* (Ratibor: Riedinger).

Cramer, F. H. (1954) *Astrology in Roman Law and Politics* (Philadelphia: American Philosophical Society).

Craven, W. G. (1981) *Giovanni Pico della Mirandola, Symbol of his Age: Modern Interpretations of a Renaissance Philosopher* (Geneva: Droz).

Crump, M. M. (1931) *The Epyllion from Theocritus to Ovid* (Oxford: Blackwell).

Csapo, E. (2005) *Theories of Mythology* (Malden, Mass.: Blackwell).

Culianu, I. P. (1987) *Eros and Magic in the Renaissance*, tr. Margaret Cook (Chicago: University of Chicago Press).

Dalzell, A. (1996) *The Criticism of Didactic Poetry: Essays on Lucretius, Virgil, and Ovid* (Toronto: University of Toronto Press).

Dams, P. (1970) *Dichtungskritik bei nachaugusteischen Dichtern*. Diss. Marburg.

Dawkins, R. (1976) *The Selfish Gene* (New York: Oxford University Press).

De Callataÿ, G. (2001) 'La Géographie zodiacale de Manilius (*Astr.* 4, 744–817), avec une note sur l'*Énéide* virgilienne', *Latomus*, 60: 35–66.

DeNardis, V. S. (2003) Ratio omnia vincit: *Cosmological, Political and Poetic Power in the* Astronomica *of Manilius*. Diss. New York University.

De Nichilo, M. (1975) *I poemi astrologici di Giovanni Pontano: Storia del testo* (Bari: Dedalo Libri).

Dennett, D. C. (1990) 'Memes and the Exploitation of Imagination', *Journal of Aesthetics and Art Criticism*, 48: 127–35.

Denningmann, S. (2005) *Die astrologische Lehre der Doryphorie: Eine soziomorphe Metapher in der antiken Planetenastrologie* (Munich: Saur).

Detienne, M. (1981) *L'Invention de la mythologie* (Paris: Gallimard; English trans., *The Creation of Mythology*, 1986).

Di Giovine, C. (1978) 'Note sulla tecnica imitativa di Manilio', *RFIC* 106: 398–406.

Dilke, O. A. W. (1985) *Greek and Roman Maps* (Baltimore: Johns Hopkins University Press).

Di Napoli, G. (1956) '"Contemptus mundi" e "dignitas hominis" nel Rinascimento', *Rivista di Filosofia Neoscolastica*, 48: 9–41.

Dougherty, M. V. (ed.) (2008) *Pico della Mirandola: New Essays* (Cambridge: Cambridge University Press).

Dueck, D. (2000) *Strabo of Amasia: A Greek Man of Letters in Augustan Rome* (London: Routledge).

Du Fay, M. (1679) *M. Manilii Astronomicon* (Paris: Leonard).

Dumont, J-P. (1978) 'Mos geometricus, mos physicus', in *Les Stoïciens et leur logique: Actes du Colloque de Chantillly, 18–22 septembre 1976* (Paris: J. Vrin), 121–34.

——(1989) 'La Stoïcienne d'Herculanum: Un regard au vestiaire des thermes', in *Du Banal au merveilleux: Mélanges offerts à L. Jerphagnon* (Fontenay-St. Cloud: ENS Fontenay), 63–75.

Dutoit, E. (1936) *Le Thème de l'adynaton dans la poésie antique* (Paris: Les Belles Lettres).

Effe, B. (1971) 'Labor improbus: Ein Grundgedanke der Georgica in der Sicht des Manilius', *Gymnasium*, 78: 393–9.

——(1977) *Dichtung und Lehre: Untersuchungen zur Typologie des antiken Lehrgedichts* (Munich: Beck).

Ellis, R. (1899) 'The Literary Relations of "Longinus" and Manilius', *CR* 13: 294.

Eriksson, S. (1956) *Wochentagsgötter, Mond und Tierkreis: Laienastrologie in der römischen Kaiserzeit* (Stockholm: Almquist & Wiksell).

Evans, J. M. (1968) *Paradise Lost and the Genesis Tradition* (Oxford: Clarendon Press).

Faber, M. (1979) *Angels of Daring: Tightrope Walker and Acrobat in Nietzsche, Kafka, Rilke and Thomas Mann* (Stuttgart: Akademischer Verlag Hans-Dieter Heinz).

Fairclough, F. R., and Goold, G. P. (1999) *Virgil: Eclogues, Georgics, Aeneid I–VI* (Cambridge, Mass.: Harvard University Press).

Fakas, C. (2001) *Der hellenistiche Hesiod: Arats Phainomena und die Tradition der antiken Lehrepik* (Wiesbaden: Reichert).

Fantham, R. E. (1985) 'Ovid, Germanicus and the Composition of the *Fasti*', *Papers of the Liverpool Latin Seminar*, 5: 243–81.

Farrell, J. (1991) *Vergil's Georgics and the Traditions of Ancient Epic: The Art of Allusion in Literary History* (New York: Oxford University Press).

Favro, D. (2005) 'Making Rome a World City', in K. Galinsky (ed.), *The Cambridge Companion to the Age of Augustus* (Cambridge: Cambridge University Press), 234–63.

Feeney, D. C. (2007) *Caesar's Calendar: Ancient Time and the Beginnings of History* (Berkeley, Calif.: University of California Press).

Fehling, D. (1985) *Die sieben Weisen und die frühgriechische Chronologie: Eine traditionsgeschichtliche Studie* (Berne: Lang).

Fels, W. (1990) *Marcus Manilius: Astronomica/Astrologie* (Stuttgart: Reclam).

Feraboli, S., Flores, E., and Scarcia, R. (1996–2001) *Manilio: Il poema degli astri (Astronomica)*, 2 vols. (No pl.: Mondadori).

Ferraù, G. (1979) *Pauli Cortesii De hominibus doctis* (Palermo: Il Vespro).

Ficino, M. (1959) *Opera Omnia: Photographic Reproduction of the Basel Edition of 1576*, 1.2, ed. P. O. Kristeller and M. Sancipriano (Turin: Bottega d'Erasmo).

Ficino, M. (1989) *Three Books on Life*, ed. C. V. Kaske and J. R. Clark (Binghamton, NY: Center for Medieval and Early Renaissance Studies).

Field, A. (1996) 'Lorenzo Buonincontri and the First Public Lectures on Manilius (Florence, ca. 1475–78)', *Rivista dell'Istituto Nazionale di Studi sul Rinascimento*, 36: 207–25.

Figliuolo, B. (1988–9) *Il terremoto del 1456*, 2 vols. (Altavilla Silentina: Edizioni Studi Storici Meridionali).

——(1990) *Matteo dell'Aquila*, Tractatus de cometa atque terraemotu *(Cod. Vat. Barb. Lat. 268)* (Salerno: Pietro Laveglia Editore).

——(1997) *La cultura a Napoli nel secondo Quattrocento: Ritratti di protagonisti* (Udine: Forum).

Finocchiaro, M. A. (2008) *The Essential Galileo* (Indianapolis, Ind.: Hackett).

Flammini, G. (1990) 'La *Praefatio* agli *Astronomica* di Manilio', in C. Santini and N. Scivoletto (eds.), *Prefazioni, prologhi, proemi di opere tecnico-scientifiche latine*, 1 (Rome: Herder), 29–64.

——(1993) 'Manilio e la "sollertia" nella storia delle acquisizioni tecnico-scientifiche: *Astron.* 1, Praef. 66–95', in Liuzzi (ed.), *Manilio fra poesia e scienza* (Galatina: Congedo), 185–94.

Fleischmann, W. B. (1971) 'Lucretius', in P. O. Kristeller (ed.), *Catalogus Translationum et Commentariorum: Mediaeval and Renaissance Latin Translations and Commentaries*, 2 (Washington, DC: Catholic University of America Press), 349–65.

Fletcher, G. B. A. (1973) 'Manilius', *Durham University Journal*, 65: 129–50.

Flores, E. (1960–1) 'Augusto nella visione astrologica di Manilio ed il problema della cronologia degli *Astronomicon* libri', *AFLN* 9: 5–66.

——(1966) *Contributi di filologia maniliana* (Naples: L'Arte Tipografica).

——(1982) 'Dal fato alla storia: Manilio e la sacralità del potere augusteo fra poetica e ideologia', *Vichiana*, 11: 109–30.

——(1993) 'Aspetti della tradizione manoscritta e della ricostruzione testuale in Manilio', in Liuzzi (ed.), *Manilio fra poesia e scienza* (Galatina: Congedo), 9–19.

——(1995) 'Il poeta Manilio, ultimo degli augustei, e Ovidio', in I. Gallo and L. Nicastri (eds.), *Aetates Ovidianae: Lettori di Ovidio dall'antichità al rinascimento* (Naples: Edizioni Scientifiche Italiane), 27–38.

——(1996) 'Gli *Astronomica* di Manilio e l'epicureismo', in G. Giannantoni and M. Gigante (eds.), *Epicureismo greco e romano*, 2 (Naples: Bibliopolis), 895–908.

Fontanella, F. (1991) 'A proposito di Manilio e Firmico', *Prometheus*, 17: 75–92.

Fowler, D. P. (1989) 'Lucretius and Politics', in M. Griffin and J. Barnes (eds.), *Philosophia Togata: Essays on Philosophy and Roman Society* (Oxford: Oxford University Press), 120–50.

Fraenkel, E. D. M. (1942) 'The Stars in the Prologue of the *Rudens*', *CQ* 36: 140–4 (repr. in id., *Kleine Beiträge zur klassichen Philologie*, 2 vols. (Rome: Edizioni di Storia e Letteratura, 1964), 2.40–1).

Franklin, J. (2001) *The Science of Conjecture: Evidence and Probability before Pascal* (Baltimore: Johns Hopkins University Press).

Frede, M. (1983) 'Stoics and Skeptics on Clear and Distinct Impressions', in M. Burnyeat (ed.), *The Skeptical Tradition* (Berkeley, Calif.: University of California Press), 65–93 (repr. in id., *Essays in Ancient Philosophy* (Minneapolis: University of Minnesota Press, 1987), 151–76).

——(1994) 'The Stoic Notion of a *lekton*', in S. Everson (ed.), *Language* (Cambridge: Cambridge University Press), 109–29.

——(1999*a*) 'On the Stoic Conception of the Good', in K. Ierodiakonou (ed.), *Topics in Stoic Philosophy* (Oxford: Clarendon Press), 71–94.

——(1999*b*) 'Stoic Epistemology', in Algra *et al.* (eds.), *The Cambridge History of Hellenistic Philosophy* (Cambridge: Cambridge University Press), 295–322.

——(2005) 'Sur la Théologie stoïcienne', in G. Romeyer-Dherbey and J.-B. Gourinat (eds.), *Les Stoïciens* (Paris: J. Vrin), 213–32.

Freier, B. (1880) *De M. Manilii quae feruntur Astronomicon aetate*. Diss. Göttingen.

French, R. (1994) *Ancient Natural History: Histories of Nature* (New York: Routledge).

Friedlaender, P. (1941) 'Pattern of Sound and Atomistic Theory in Lucretius', *AJP* 62: 16–34.

Gadamer, H.-G. (1977) *Philosophical Hermeneutics* (Berkeley, Calif.: University of California Press).

——(1981) *Reason in the Age of Science* (Cambridge, Mass: MIT Press).

Gain, D. B. (1970) 'Gerbert and Manilius', *Latomus* 29: 128–32.

Gale, M. R. (1994) *Myth and Poetry in Lucretius* (Cambridge: Cambridge University Press).

——(2000) *Virgil on the Nature of Things: The Georgics, Lucretius, and the Didactic Tradition* (Cambridge: Cambridge University Press).

——(2005) 'Didactic Epic', in S. Harrison (ed.), *A Companion to Latin Literature* (Malden, Mass.: Blackwell), 101–15.

——(2007*a*) 'Introduction', in Gale (ed.), *Oxford Readings in Classical Studies: Lucretius* (Oxford: Oxford University Press), 1–17.

——(2007*b*) 'Lucretius and Previous Poetic Traditions', in S. Gillespie and P. R. Hardie (eds.), *The Cambridge Companion to Lucretius* (Cambridge: Cambridge University Press), 59–75.

——(ed.) (2007*c*) *Oxford Readings in Classical Studies: Lucretius* (Oxford: Oxford University Press).

Galinsky, K. (1996) *Augustan Culture: An Interpretive Introduction* (Princeton: Princeton University Press).

Gambino Longo, S. (2004) *Savoir de la nature et poésie des choses: Lucrèce et Epicure à la renaissance italienne* (Paris: Champion).

Garani, M. (2007) *Empedocles* Redivivus: *Poetry and Analogy in Lucretius* (New York: Routledge).

Garin, E. (1938) 'La "Dignitas Hominis" e la letteratura patristica', *La Rinascita*, 1: 102–46.

——(1976) *Zodiaco della vita: La polemica sull'astrologia dal trecento al cinquecento* (Rome: Laterza).

Garrod, H. W. (1911) *Manili Astronomicon Liber II* (Oxford: Frowde).

Gebhardt, E. (1961) 'Zur Datierungsfrage des Manilius', *RhM* 104: 278–86.

Geer, R. M. (1964) *Epicurus: Letters, Principal Doctrines, and Vatican Sayings* (Indianapolis, Ind.: Bobbs-Merrill).

——(1965) *Lucretius: On Nature* (Indianapolis, Ind.: Bobbs-Merrill).

Geiger, J. (2008) *The First Hall of Fame: A Study of the Statues in the Forum Augustum* (Leiden: Brill).

Gentile, G. (1920) *Giordano Bruno e il pensiero del rinascimento* (Florence: Vallecchi).

Gibert, J. (1999–2000) 'Falling in Love with Euripides (*Andromeda*)', *ICS* 24–5: 75–91.

Gillespie, S., and Hardie, P. R. (eds.) (2007) *The Cambridge Companion to Lucretius* (Cambridge: Cambridge University Press).

Gindhart, M. (2006) *Das Kometenjahr 1618: Antikes und zeitgenössisches Wissen in der frühneuzeitlichen Kometenliteratur des deutschsprachigen Raumes* (Wiesbaden: Reichert).

Giorgetti, L. (2002) 'Da Giorgio Trapezunzio a Luca Gaurico intorno a Tolomeo', *Roma nel Rinascimento*, 201–11.

Goddard, C. P. (1991*a*) *Epicureanism and the Poetry of Lucretius in the Renaissance*. Diss. Cambridge.

——(1991*b*) 'Pontano's Use of the Didactic Genre: Rhetoric, Irony and the Manipulation of Lucretius in *Urania*', *Renaissance Studies*, 5: 250–62.

Goold, G. P. (1954) 'De fonte codicum Manilianorum', *RhM* 97: 359–72.

——(1959) 'Perseus and Andromeda: A Myth from the Skies', *PACA* 11: 10–5.

——(1961) 'A Greek Professorial Circle at Rome', *TAPA* 92: 168–92.

——(1977) *Manilius:* Astronomica (Cambridge, Mass.: Harvard University Press).

——(1983) 'The Great Lacuna in Manilius', *PACA* 17: 64–8.

——(1985) *M. Manilii Astronomica* (Leipzig: Teubner).

——(1992) *Manilius:* Astronomica, 2nd edn. (Cambridge, Mass.: Harvard University Press).

——(1998) *M. Manilii Astronomica*, 2nd edn. (Stuttgart: Teubner).

——(2000) 'Housman's Manilius', in A. W. Holden and J. R. Birch (eds.), *A. E. Housman: A Reassessment* (Basingstoke: Macmillan), 134–53.

Gordon, C. A. (1962) *A Bibliography of Lucretius* (London: Hart-Davis).

Grafton, A. T. (1983–93) *Joseph Scaliger: A Study in the History of Classical Scholarship*, 2 vols. (Oxford: Clarendon Press).

——(1997) *Commerce with the Classics: Ancient Books and Renaissance Readers* (Ann Arbor: University of Michigan Press).

——(1999) *Cardano's Cosmos: The World and Works of a Renaissance Astrologer* (Cambridge, Mass.: Harvard University Press).

Graham, D. (2006) *Explaining the Cosmos* (Princeton: Princeton University Press).

Grant, E. (2004) *Science and Religion, 400 B.C. to A.D. 1550: From Aristotle to Copernicus* (Westport, Conn.: Greenwood Press).

Green, S. J. (2004) *Ovid Fasti I: A Commentary* (Leiden: Brill).

——(2006) 'Lessons in Love: Fifty Years of Scholarship on Ovid's *Ars Amatoria* and *Remedia Amoris*', in R. K. Gibson, S. J. Green, and A. R. Sharrock (eds.), *The Art of Love: Bimillennial Essays on Ovid's Ars Amatoria and Remedia Amoris* (Oxford: Oxford University Press), 1–20.

Gregory, A. (2001) *Eureka! The Birth of Science* (Cambridge: Icon).

Grimm, J. (1965) *Die literarische Darstellung der Pest in der Antike und in der Romania* (Munich: Fink).

Griset, E. (1931) 'Manilio poeta augusteo (Appunti sulla divinizzazione d Augusto)', *MC* 1: 49–58.

Gundel, W. (1936) *Dekane und Dekansternbilder: Ein Beitrag zur Geschichte der Sternbilder der Kulturvölker* (Glückstadt: Augustin).

——(1949) 'Paranatellonta', *Pauly-Wissowa*, 18.2.2: 1214–75.

Guthrie, S. E. (1993) *Faces in the Clouds: A New Theory of Religion* (New York: Oxford University Press).

Habinek, T. N. (2005) *The World of Roman Song: From Ritualized Speech to Social Order* (Baltimore: Johns Hopkins University Press).

——(2007) 'Probing the Entrails of the Universe: Astrology as Bodily Knowledge in Manilius' *Astronomica*', in J. König and T. Whitmarsh (eds.), *Ordering Knowledge in the Roman Empire* (Cambridge: Cambridge University Press), 229–40.

——(2010) 'Tentacular Mind: Stoicism, Neuroscience, and the Configurations of Physical Reality', in B. Stafford (ed.), *Neuroscience and the Humanities: A Field Guide to a New Academic Field* (Chicago: University of Chicago Press).

Hacking, I. (1975) *The Emergence of Probability: A Philosophical Study of Early Ideas about Probability, Induction and Statistical Inference* (Cambridge: Cambridge University Press).

——(1990) *The Taming of Chance* (Cambridge: Cambridge University Press).

Hahm, D. (1977) *The Origins of Stoic Cosmology* (Columbus, Ohio: Ohio State University Press).

Hahm, D. (1989) 'Posidonius' Theory of Historical Causation', *ANRW* 2.36.3: 1325–63.

Hall, J. B. (1985) *Claudii Claudiani Carmina* (Leipzig: Teubner).

Hamblenne, P. (1984) '*Eādem naue . . .* ou un brin d' "hagiographie" plinienne (*Nat.*, 35, 199)', *RBPh* 62: 16–29.

Hankinson, R. J. (1988) 'Stoicism, Science and Divination', in id. (ed.), *Method, Medicine and Metaphysics: Studies in the Philosophy of Ancient Science* (= *Apeiron* 21.2) (Edmonton: Academic Printing and Publishing), 123–60.

——(1998) *Cause and Explanation in Ancient Greek Thought* (Oxford: Clarendon Press).

Hardie, P. R. (1986) *Virgil's* Aeneid: Cosmos *and* Imperium (Oxford: Oxford University Press).

Härke, G. (1936) *Studien zur Exkurstechnik im römischen Lehrgedicht (Lukrez und Vergil), mit einem Anhang über Manilius*. Diss. Würzburg.

Harrison, S. J. (2006) 'The Epic and the Monuments: Interactions between Virgil's *Aeneid* and the Augustan Building Programme', in M. J. Clarke, B. G. F. Currie, and R. O. A. M. Lyne (eds.), *Epic Interactions: Perspectives on Homer, Virgil, and the Epic Tradition* (Oxford: Oxford University Press), 159–84.

Harth, D. (1970) *Philologie und praktische Philosophie: Untersuchungen zum Sprach- und Traditionsverständnis des Erasmus von Rotterdam* (Munich: Fink).

Hartland, E. S. (1894–6) *The Legend of Perseus: A Study of Tradition in Story, Custom and Belief*, 3 vols. (London: Nutt).

Hasegawa, I. (1979) 'Orbits of Ancient and Medieval Comets', *Publications of the Astronomical Society of Japan*, 31: 257–70.

——(1980) 'Catalogue of Ancient and Naked-Eye Comets', *Vistas in Astronomy*, 24: 59–102.

Haskell, Y. (1998) 'Renaissance Latin Didactic Poetry on the Stars: Wonder, Myth, and Science', *Renaissance Studies*, 12: 495–522.

Heath, M. F. (1985) 'Hesiod's Didactic Poetry', *CQ* 35: 245–63.

Heilen, S. (1999) *Laurentius Bonincontrius Miniatensis: De rebus naturalibus et divinis. Zwei Lehrgedichte an Lorenzo de' Medici und Ferdinand von Aragonien* (Stuttgart-Leipzig: Saur).

——(2000) *Concordantia in Laurentii Bonincontri Miniatensis carmina* De rebus naturalibus et diuinis (Hildesheim: Olms-Weidmann).

——(2005) 'Lorenzo Bonincontris Schlußprophezeiung in *De rebus naturalibus et divinis*', in K. Bergdolt and W. Ludwig (eds.), *Zukunftsvoraussagen in der Renaissance* (Wiesbaden: Harrassowitz), 309–28.

——(2008) 'Fracastoros Götterversammlung im Krebs (Syph. 1,219–246)', in S. Heilen *et al.* (eds.), *In Pursuit of Wissenschaft: Festschrift für William M. Calder III zum 75. Geburtstag* (Hildesheim: Olms), 143–76.

——(forthcoming) 'Some Metrical Fragments from Nechepso(s) and Petosiris', in J.-H. Abry *et al.* (eds.), *La Poésie astrologique dans l'Antiquité.*

Heitzer, E. (1995) *Das Bild des Kometen in der Kunst: Untersuchungen zur ikonographischen und ikonologischen Tradition des Kometenmotivs in der Kunst vom 14. bis zum 18. Jahrhundert* (Berlin: Gebrüder Mann).

Henrichs, A. (1974) 'Die Kritik der stoischen Theologie im *P. Herc.* 1428', *CErc* 4: 5–32.

Herbert-Brown, G. (2002) 'Ovid and the Stellar Calendar', in ead. (ed.), *Ovid's* Fasti: *Historical Readings at its Bimillennium* (Oxford: Oxford University Press), 101–28.

Herrmann, L. (1962) 'Hypothèse sur L. et M. Manilius', *AC* 31: 82–90.

Heslin, P. J. (2007) 'Augustus, Domitian and the So-Called Horologium Augusti', *JRS* 97: 1–20.

Hesse, M. B. (1966) *Models and Analogies in Science* (Notre Dame, Ind.: University of Notre Dame Press).

Hiatt, A. (2008) Terra Incognita: *Mapping the Antipodes before 1600* (Chicago: University of Chicago Press).

Hicks, R. D. (1925) *Diogenes Laertius:* Lives of Eminent Philosophers, 2 vols. (London: Heinemann).

Hoppe, H. (1906–12) 'Census', *TLL* 3: 806.62–812.60.

Housman, A. E. (1903–30) *M. Manilii Astronomicon Libri*, 5 vols. (London: Richards).

——(1932) *M. Manilii Astronomica. Editio minor* (Cambridge: Cambridge University Press).

Howard, D. R. (1954) *The Contempt of the World: A Study in the Ideology of Latin Christendom, with Emphasis on Fourteenth Century English Literature.* Diss. University of Florida.

——(1966) *The Three Temptations: Medieval Man in Search of the World* (Princeton: Princeton University Press).

Howe, D., and Rowland, I. D. (1999) *Vitruvius: Ten Books of Architecture* (Cambridge: Cambridge University Press).

Hübner, W. (1975) 'Die Paranatellonten im Liber Hermetis', *Sudhoffs Archiv*, 59: 387–414.

——(1980) 'Die Rezeption des astrologischen Lehrgedichts des Manilius in der italienischen Renaissance', in R. Schmitz and F. Krafft (eds.), *Humanismus und Naturwissenschaften* (Boppard: Boldt), 39–67.

——(1982) *Die Eigenschaften der Tierkreiszeichen in der Antike: Ihre Darstellung und Verwendung unter besonderer Berücksichtigung des Manilius* (Wiesbaden: Steiner).

——(1984) 'Manilius als Astrologe und Dichter', *ANRW* 2.32.1: 126–320.

——(1988) 'Religion und Wissenschaft in der antiken Astrologie', in J.-F. Bergier (ed.), *Zwischen Wahn, Glaube und Wissenschaft: Magie,*

324   Bibliography

Astrologie, Alchemie und Wissenschaftsgeschichte (Zurich: Verlag der Fachvereine), 9–50.

——(1989) *Die Begriffe 'Astrologie' und 'Astronomie' in der Antike: Wortgeschichte und Wissenschaftssystematik, mit einer Hypothese zum Terminus 'Quadrivium'* (= Akademie der Wissenschaften und der Literatur Mainz, Geistes- und sozialwissenschaftliche Klasse, Abhandlungen 1989.7) (Stuttgart: Steiner).

——(1990) 'Uranoscopus: Der verstirnte Sterngucker', *RhM* 133: 264–74.

——(1993) 'Manilio e Teucro di Babilonia', in Liuzzi (ed.), *Manilio fra poesia e scienza* (Galatina: Congedo), 21–40.

——(1995*a*) *Die Dodekatropos des Manilius (MANIL. 2,856–970)* (= Akademie der Wissenschaften und der Literatur Mainz, Geistes- und sozialwissenschaftliche Klasse, Abhandlungen 1995.6) (Stuttgart: Steiner).

——(1995*b*) *Grade und Gradbezirke der Tierkreiszeichen: Der anonyme Traktat De stellis fixis, in quibus gradibus oriuntur signorum*, 2 vols. (Stuttgart: Teubner).

——(1997) 'Antike Kosmologie bei Dante', *Deutsches Dante-Jahrbuch*, 72: 45–81.

——(1998) *Claudii Ptolemaei opera quae exstant omnia. Vol. 3.1: ΑΠΟΤΕΛΕΣΜΑΤΙΚΑ* (Stuttgart: Teubner).

——(1999) 'Manilius III', *Neuer Pauly*, 7: 819–21.

——(2002) 'Decani e paranatellonta del segno zodiacale dei Pesci', in Marco Bertozzi (ed.), *Aby Warburg e le metamorfosi degli antichi dèi: atti del convegno 24–26 settembre 1998 a Ferrara* (Modena: Panini), 63–85.

——(2006*a*) 'Die vier Sterne des Dreiecks (Triangulum)', in *Antike Naturwissenschaft und ihre Rezeption*, 16: 109–24.

——(2006*b*) '*Vir gregis*: Imitations structurelles de Virgile dans les *Astronomica* de Manilius', *Pallas*, 72: 137–48.

——(2007) 'The Tropical Points of the Zodiacal Year and the *Paranatellonta* in Manilius' *Astronomica*', in C. Burnett and D. G. Greenbaum (eds.), *The Winding Courses of the Stars: Essays in Ancient Astrology* (= Culture and Cosmos, 11) (Bristol: Culture and Cosmos), 87–110.

——(2010) *Manilius: Astronomica Buch V*, 2 vols. (Berlin: De Gruyter).

Hunger, H. *et al.* (1985) *Halley's Comet in History* (London: British Museum).

Hunziker, R. (1896) *Die Figur der Hyperbel in den Gedichten Vergils: Mit einer einleitenden Untersuchung über Wesen und Einteilung der Hyperbel und ausführlichen Indices* (Berlin: Mayer & Müller).

Hurley, D. (2001) *Suetonius: Divus Claudius* (Cambridge: Cambridge University Press).

Hutchinson, G. O. (2006) *Propertius: Elegies Book IV* (Cambridge: Cambridge University Press).

——(2009) 'Read the Instructions: Didactic Poetry and Didactic Prose', *CQ* 59: 196–211.

Ierodiakonou, K. (1999) (ed.), *Topics in Stoic Philosophy* (Oxford: Clarendon Press).

Ijsewijn, J., and Sacré, D. (1998) *Companion to Neo-Latin Studies. Part II: Literary, Linguistic, Philological and Editorial Questions*, 2nd edn. (Louvain: Leuven University Press).

Inwood, B. (ed.) (2003) *The Cambridge Companion to the Stoics* (Cambridge: Cambridge University Press).

——and Gerson, L. P. (1997) *Hellenistic Philosophy: Introductory Readings*, 2nd edn. (Indianapolis, Ind.: Hackett).

Ioppolo, A.-M. (1990) 'Presentation and Assent: A Physical and Cognitive Problem in Early Stoicism', *CQ* 40: 433–49.

Jacob, F. (1832–6) *De M. Manilio poeta* (Lübeck: Programm St. Katharinenschule).

——(1846) *M. Manili Astronomicon libri quinque* (Berlin: Reimer).

Jenkyns, R. (1993) '*Labor improbus*', *CQ* 43: 243–8.

Jervis, J. L. (1985) *Cometary Theory in Fifteenth-Century Europe* (Dordrecht: D. Reidel).

Jocelyn, H. D. (1995) '"Poeta" and "Vates": Concerning the Nomenclature of the Composer of Verses in Republican and Early Imperial Rome', in L. Belloni, G. Milanese, and A. Porro (eds.), *Studia Classica Iohanni Tarditi Oblata* (Milan: Vita e pensiero), 19–50.

Jones, A. (2003) 'The Stoics and the Astronomical Sciences', in B. Inwood (ed.), *The Cambridge Companion to the Stoics* (Cambridge: Cambridge University Press), 328–44.

Jones, F. (1984) 'A Note on Manilius 5.604', *AClass* 27: 139.

Jope, J. (1989) 'The Didactic Unity and Emotional Import of Book 6 of *De Rerum Natura*', *Phoenix*, 43: 16–34.

Jung, C. G. (1978) 'Das Zeichen der Fische', in id., *Gesammelte Werke*, 2nd edn., 9.2 (Olten: Walter), 81–103.

Kennedy, D. F. (2000) 'Making a Text of the Universe: Perspectives on Discursive Order in the *De Rerum Natura* of Lucretius', in A. Sharrock and H. Morales (eds.), *Intratextuality: Greek and Roman Textual Relations* (Oxford: Oxford University Press), 205–25 (repr. in Gale (ed.) *Oxford Readings in Classical Studies: Lucretius* (Oxford: Oxford University Press, 2007), 376–96).

——(2002) *Rethinking Reality: Lucretius and the Textualization of Nature* (Ann Arbor: University of Michigan Press).

——(2006) 'Atoms, Individuals and Myths', in V. Zajko and M. Leonard (eds), *Laughing with Medusa: Classical Myth and Feminist Thought* (Oxford: Oxford University Press), 233–52.

——(forthcoming) *Antiquity and the Meanings of Time* (London: I. B. Tauris).

Kerényi, K. (1923) 'De teletis Mercurialibus observationes II', *EphK* 47: 150–64.

Kerferd, G. B. (1978) 'What does the Wise Man Know?', in J. M. Rist (ed.), *The Stoics* (Berkeley, Calif.: University of California Press), 125–36.

Keyser, P. T. (1994) 'On Cometary Theory and Typology from Nechepso-Petosiris through Apuleius to Servius', *Mnemosyne*, 47: 625–51.

Kidwell, C. (1991) *Pontano: Poet and Prime Minister* (London: Duckworth).

Kießling, A., and Heinze, R. (1898) *Quintus Horatius Flaccus. Vol. 1: Oden und Epoden*, 3rd edn. (Berlin: Weidmann).

Kingsley, P. (1995) *Ancient Philosophy, Mystery, and Magic: Empedocles and Pythagorean Tradition* (Oxford: Oxford University Press).

Kleingünther, H. (1907) *Textkritische und exegetische Beiträge zum astrologischen Lehrgedicht des sogenannten Manilius* (Leipzig: Fock).

Klibansky, R., Panofsky, E., and Saxl, F. (1964) *Saturn and Melancholy: Studies in the History of Natural Philosophy, Religion, and Art* (New York: Basic Books).

Klimek-Winter, R. (1993) *Andromedatragödien: Sophokles, Euripides, Livius Andronikos, Ennius, Accius* (Stuttgart: Teubner).

Kokott, W. (1994) *Die Kometen der Jahre 1531 bis 1539 und ihre Bedeutung für die spätere Entwicklung der Kometenforschung* (Stuttgart: Verlag für Geschichte der Naturwissenschaften und der Technik).

König, J., and Whitmarsh, T. (eds.) (2007) *Ordering Knowledge in the Roman Empire* (Cambridge: Cambridge University Press).

Kraemer, A. (1904) 'Ort und Zeit der Abfassung der Astronomica des Manilius', *Programm des Wöhler-Realgymnasiums in Frankfurt am Main*, 3–27.

Krautter, K. (1971) *Philologische Methode und humanistische Existenz: Filippo Beroaldo und sein Kommentar zum Goldenen Esel des Apuleius* (Munich: Fink).

Kristeller, P. O. (1972) *Renaissance Concepts of Man, and Other Essays* (New York: Harper & Row).

Kroll, W. (1924) *Studien zum Verständnis der römischen Literatur* (Stuttgart: Metzler).

Kronk, G. W. (1999) *Cometography: A Catalog of Comets. Vol. 1: Ancient–1799* (Cambridge: Cambridge University Press).

Kuhn, T. S. (1957) *The Copernican Revolution: Planetary Astronomy in the Development of Western Thought* (Cambridge, Mass.: Harvard University Press).

Lachmann, K. (1815) *Observationun criticarum capita tria* (Göttingen: Baier).

——(1876) *Kleinere Schriften zur classischen Philologie*, ed. J. Vahlen, 2 (Berlin: Reimer).

Laks, A. (2006) *Introduction à la philosophie présocratique* (Paris: Presses Universitaires de France).

Landfester, R. (1972) *Historia magistra vitae: Untersuchungen zur humanistischen Geschichtstheorie des 14. bis 16. Jahrhunderts* (Geneva: Droz).

Landolfi, L. (1990*a*) 'Manilio e gli eroi della Via Lattea: Tra doctrina e ideologia', *GIF* 42: 87–98.

—— (1990*b*) '*Numquam futtilibus excanduit ignibus aether* (Man. *Astr.* I, 876): Comete, pesti e guerre civili', *SIFC* 8: 229–49.

—— (1993) 'Andromeda: intreccio di modelli e punti di vista in Manilio', *GIF* 45: 171–94.

—— (1996) '*Concitat aerios cursus* (Man. *Astr.* 5, 577): Nascita e significato di una clausola', *RCCM* 1: 83–9.

—— (1999) 'OYRANOBATEIN: Manilio, il volo e la poesia. Alcune precisiazioni', *Prometheus*, 25: 151–65.

—— (2003) Integra prata: *Manilio, i proemi* (Bologna: Pàtron).

Landucci Ruffo, P. (1965) 'Lorenzo Bonincontri e alcuni suoi scritti ignorati', *Rinascimento*, 5: 171–94.

Lang, H. (1998) *The Order of Nature in Aristotle's Physics: Place and the Elements* (Cambridge: Cambridge University Press).

Lanson, G. (1887) *De Manilio poeta eiusque ingenio* (Paris: Hachette).

Lapidge, M. (1989) 'Stoic Cosmology and Roman Literature, First to Third Centuries AD', *ANRW* 2.36.3: 1379–1429.

Lawrence, M. (2008) 'Hellenistic Astrology', in *Internet Encyclopedia of Philosophy*. (http://www.iep.utm.edu/a/astr-hel.htm; accessed July 2008).

Leatherdale, W. H. (1974) *The Role of Analogy, Model and Metaphor in Science* (Amsterdam: North-Holland).

Le Bœuffle, A. (1987) *Astronomie, astrologie: Lexique latin* (Paris: Picard).

Lefebure, H. (1991) *The Production of Space* (Oxford: Blackwell).

Lehoux, D. (2006) 'Laws of Nature and Natural Laws', *Studies in History and Philosophy of Science*, 37: 527–49.

Lemay, R. (1978) 'Origin and Success of the Kitāb Thamara of Abū Jaʿfar Aḥmad ibn Yūsuf ibn Ibrāhīm from the Tenth to the Seventeenth Century in the World of Islam and the Latin West', in Ahmad Y. Al-Hassan *et al.* (eds.), *Proceedings of the First International Symposium for the History of Arabic Science: Held at the University of Aleppo, 5–12 April 1976. Vol. 2: Papers in European Languages* (Aleppo: Institute for the History of Arabic Science), 91–107.

Lewis, A. M. (1992) 'The Popularity of the *Phaenomena* of Aratus: A Reevaluation', *Studies in Latin Literature and Roman History*, 6: 94–118.

Lhotsky, A., and Ferrari d'Occhieppo, K. (1960) 'Zwei Gutachten Georgs von Peuerbach über Kometen (1456 und 1457)', *Mitteilungen des Instituts für Österreichische Geschichtsforschung*, 68: 266–90.

Lindberg, D. (1992) *The Beginnings of Western Science* (Chicago: University of Chicago Press).

Liuzzi, D. (1979) 'Manilio, Astronomica l. I: Destinatario ed epoca di composizione', *Quaderni*, 2 (*Miscellanea classico-medievale*), 127–39.

——(1983) *M. Manilio:* Astronomica. *Libro primo e secondo* (Lecce: Milella).

——(1986) '*Stella, Astrum, Signum, Sidus* negli *Astronomica* di Manilio', *CCC* 7: 43–51.

——(1991–7) *M. Manilio:* Astronomica, 5 vols. (Galatina: Congedo).

——(ed.) (1993) *Manilio fra poesia e scienza* (Galatina: Congedo).

Livingstone, D. N. (2003) *Putting Science in its Place: Geographies of Scientific Knowledge* (Chicago: University of Chicago Press).

Lloyd, G. E. R. (1966) *Polarity and Analogy: Two Types of Argumentation in Early Greek Thought* (Cambridge: Cambridge University Press).

——(1979) *Magic, Reason, and Experience: Studies in the Origin and Development of Greek Science* (Cambridge: Cambridge University Press).

Long, A. A. (1982) 'Astrology: Arguments Pro and Contra', in J. Barnes *et al.* (eds.), *Science and Speculation: Studies in Hellenistic Theory and Practice* (Cambridge: Cambridge University Press), 165–92.

——and Sedley, D. N. (1987) *The Hellenistic Philosophers*, 2 vols. (Cambridge: Cambridge University Press).

Lovatt, H. (2007) 'Statius, Orpheus, and the Post-Augustan *Vates*', *Arethusa*, 40: 145–63.

Lowe, D. (2004) 'Monsters in the Roman Sky: Heaven and Earth in Manilius' *Astronomica*', in P. L. Yoder and P. M. Kreuter (eds), *Monsters and the Monstrous: Metaphors of Enduring Evil* (Interdisciplinary Press), 143–56. (E-book; available at http://www.inter-disciplinary.net/publishing/id-press/ebooks/monsters-and-the-monstrous/; accessed Mar. 2010).

Luce, T. J. (1990) 'Livy, Augustus, and the Forum Romanum', in K. A. Raaflaub and M. Toher (eds.), *Between Republic and Empire: Interpretations of Augustus and his Principate* (Berkeley, Calif.: University of California Press), 123–38.

Luck, G. (1984) 'A Stoic Cosmogony in Manilius (I, 149–172)', in E. Lucchesi and H. D. Saffrey (eds.), *Mémorial André-Jean Festugière: Antiquité païnne et chrétienne* (Geneva: Cramer), 27–32.

Lühr, F.-F. (1969) *Ratio und Fatum: Dichtung und Lehre bei Manilius*. Diss. Frankfurt.

——(1973) 'Kometen und Pest: Exegetisches zu Manilius 1,874–895', *WS* 86: 113–25.

Lunelli, A. (1969) Aerius, *storia di una parola poetica (varia neoterica)* (Rome: Ateneo).

Lyne, R. O. A. M. (1978) 'The Neoteric Poets', *CQ* 28: 167–87.

MacGregor, A. P. (2004) 'Which Art in Heaven: The Sphere of Manilius', *ICS* 29: 143–57.

——(2005) 'Was Manilius Really a Stoic?', *ICS* 30: 41–65.

MacIntyre, A. (1988) *Whose Justice? Which Rationality?* (London: Duckworth).

Mansfeld, J. (1999) 'Theology', in Algra *et al.* (eds.), *The Cambridge History of Hellenistic Philosophy* (Cambridge: Cambridge University Press), 452–78.

Maranini, A. (1994) *Filologia fantastica: Manilio e i suoi* Astronomica (Bologna: Il Mulino).

Martindale, C. (1993) 'Descent into Hell: Reading Ambiguity, or Virgil and the Critics', *PVS* 21: 111–50.

Mastronarde, D. J. (2002) *Euripides: Medea* (Cambridge: Cambridge University Press).

Mauro, A. (1955) 'La data di nascita del Sannazaro', *GIF* 8: 1–13.

Meinwald, C. (2005) 'Ignorance and Opinion in Stoic Epistemology', *Phronesis*, 50: 215–31.

Merriam, C. U. (2001) *The Development of the Epyllion Genre through the Hellenistic and Roman Periods* (Lewiston, NY: Mellen).

Meserve, M. (2000) 'Medieval Sources for Renaissance Theories on the Origins of the Ottoman Turks', in B. Guthmüller and W. Kühlmann (eds.), *Europa und die Türken in der Renaissance* (Tübingen: Niemeyer), 409–36.

Minogue, K. (2007) *Kylie X*. EMI Records.

Montanari Caldini, R. (1989) 'Manilio tra scienza e filosofia: La dottrina delle comete', *Prometheus*, 15: 1–30.

Moorton, R. (1987) 'Euripides' *Andromeda* in Aristophanes' *Frogs*', *AJP* 108: 434–6.

Morales, H. (2004) *Vision and Narrative in Achilles Tatius'* Leucippe and Clitophon. (Cambridge: Cambridge University Press).

Moretti, G. (1994*a*) *Gli antipodi: Avventure letterarie di un mito scientifico* (Parma: Pratiche).

——(1994*b*) 'The Other World and the "Antipodes": The Myth of the Unknown Countries between Antiquity and the Renaissance', in W. Haase and M. Reinhold (eds.), *The Classical Tradition and the Americas*, 1.1 (Berlin: De Gruyter), 241–84.

Morgan, K. (2000) *Myth and Philosophy from the Presocratics to Plato* (Cambridge: Cambridge University Press).

Müller, E. (1901) *De Posidonio Manilii auctore*. Diss. Leipzig.

——(1903) 'Zur Charakteristik des Manilius', *Philologus*, 62: 64–86.

Munich, A. (1989) *Andromeda's Chains: Gender and Interpretation in Victorian Literature and Art* (New York: Columbia University Press).

Muratori, L. A. (1732) 'Laurentii Bonincontri Annales ab anno MCCCLX usque ad MCCCCLVIII', in id. (ed.), *Rerum Italicarum Scriptores*, 21 (Milan: Typographia Societatis Palatinae, 1–162; repr. Città di Castello: S. Lapi, 1981).

Murgatroyd, P. (1994) 'Narrative Techniques in Manilius, *Astronomica* 5, 538–618', *Studies in Latin Literature and Roman History*, 7: 416–29.

Naddaf, G. (2005) *The Greek Concept of Nature* (Albany, NY: SUNY Press).

Nancy, J.-L. (1978) 'Mundus est fabula', *MLN* 93: 635–53.

Netz, R. (1999) *The Shaping of Deduction in Greek Mathematics: A Study in Cognitive History* (Cambridge: Cambridge University Press).

Neuburg, M. (1993) 'Hitch your Wagon to a Star: Manilius and his Two Addressees', in A. Schiesaro, P. Mitsis, and J. S. Clay (eds.), *Mega nepios: Il destinatario nell'epos didascalico/The Addressee in Didactic Epic* (= *MD* 31) (Pisa: Giardini), 243–82.

Neugebauer, O. (1975) *A History of Ancient Mathematical Astronomy*, 3 vols. (Berlin: Springer)

Newlands, C. E. (1995) *Playing with Time: Ovid and the* Fasti (Ithaca, NY: Cornell University Press).

Newman, J. K. (1967) *The Concept of Vates in Augustan Poetry* (Brussels: Latomus).

Nicolet, C. (1991) *Space, Geography, and Politics in the Early Roman Empire* (Ann Arbor: University of Michigan Press).

Noonan, J. D. (1991) 'Propertius 1.3.3–4: Andromeda is Missing', *CJ* 86: 330–6.

North, J. (2008) *Cosmos: An Illustrated History of Astronomy and Cosmology* (Chicago: University of Chicago Press).

Obbink, D. (1999) 'The Stoic Sage in the Cosmic City', in K. Ierodiakonou (ed.), *Topics in Stoic Philosophy* (Oxford: Clarendon Press), 178–95.

Ogden, D. (2008) *Perseus* (London: Routledge).

Ogilvie, R. M. (1971) 'Monastic Corruption', *G&R* 18: 32–4.

O'Hara, J. J. (2005) 'Trying Not to Cheat: Responses to Inconsistency in Roman Epic', *TAPA* 135: 15–33.

——(2007) *Inconsistency in Roman Epic: Studies in Catullus, Lucretius, Vergil, Ovid and Lucan* (Cambridge: Cambridge University Press).

Otto, A. (1890) *Die Sprichwörter und sprichwörtlichen Redensarten der Römer* (Leipzig: Teubner).

Paschoud, F. (1982) 'Deux Études sur Manilius', in G. Wirth (ed.), *Romanitas, Christianitas: Untersuchungen zur Geschichte und Literatur der römischen Kaiserzeit* (Berlin: De Gruyter), 125–53.

Pauer, M. (1951) *Zur Frage der Datierung des astrologischen Lehrgedichts des Manilius*. Diss. Munich.

Pendergraft, M. L. B. (1990) 'On the Nature of the Constellations: Aratus, *Ph.* 367–85', *Eranos*, 88: 99–106.

Penrose, R. (1989) *The Emperor's New Mind* (Oxford: Oxford University Press).

Pertusi, A. (1976) *La caduta di Costantinopoli*, 2 vols. (Milan: Mondadori).

Perutelli, A. (2001) 'Il disagio del poeta didascalico: Sui proemi II e III di Manilio', *MD* 47: 67–84.

Pfeiffer, R. (1932) 'Βερενίκης Πλόκαμος', *Philologus*, 87: 179–228.

Phillips, K. M. (1968) 'Perseus and Andromeda', *AJA* 72: 1–23.

Pingré, A. G. (1786) *M. Manilii* Astronomicon *libri quinque* (Paris: De Chardon; repr. Paris: Bibliotheca Hermetica, 1970).

Platnauer, M. (1922) *Claudian: Works*, 2 vols. (Cambridge, Mass.: Harvard University Press).

Pöhlmann, E. (1973) 'Charakteristika des römischen Lehrgedichts', *ANRW* 1.3: 813–901.

Pontano, G. (1519) *Centum Ptolemaei sententiae ad Syrum fratrem à Pontano è Graeco in Latinum tralatae atque expositae* (Venice: Aldus).

Poppi, A. (1988) 'Fate, Fortune, Providence and Human Freedom', in C. B. Schmitt *et al.* (eds.), *The Cambridge History of Renaissance Philosophy* (Cambridge: Cambridge University Press), 641–67.

Porter, J. I. (2007) 'Lucretius and the Sublime', in S. Gillespie and P. R. Hardie (eds), *The Cambridge Companion to Lucretius* (Cambridge: Cambridge University Press), 167–84.

Powell, J. U. (1919) 'Fragments of Greek Poetry from Papyri in the Library of the University of Chicago', *Journal of Philology*, 34: 106–34.

Prenner, A. (2007) *Claudiano:* In Rufinum. *Libro I* (Naples: Loffredo).

Prinz, K. (1912) 'Die zeitlichen Indizien in den Astronomica des Manilius', *Zeitschrift für die österreichischen Gymnasien*, 63: 673–93.

Putnam, M. C. J. (1986) *Artifices of Eternity: Horace's Fourth Book of Odes* (Ithaca, NY: Cornell University Press).

Rabin, S. J. (2008) 'Pico on Magic and Astrology', in M. V. Dougherty (ed.), *Pico della Mirandola: New Essays* (Cambridge: Cambridge University Press), 152–78.

Ramorino, F. (1898) 'Quo annorum spatio Manilius Astronomicon libros composuerit', *SIFC* 6: 323–52.

Ramsey, J. T. (2006) *A Descriptive Catalogue of Greco-Roman Comets from 500 BC to AD 400* (= *SyllClass*17) (Iowa City: University of Iowa; repr. with corr. 2008).

——and Licht, A. L. (1997) *The Comet of 44 BC and Caesar's Funeral Games* (Atlanta, Ga.: Scholars Press).

Reed, B. (2002) 'The Stoics' Account of the Cognitive Impression', *OSAPh* 23: 147–80.

Reeh, A. (1973) *Interpretationen zu den Astronomica des Manilius mit besonderer Berücksichtigung der philosophischen Partien.* Diss. Marburg.

Reeve, M. D. (1980*a*) 'Some Astronomical Manuscripts', *CQ* 30: 508–22.

——(1980*b*) 'The Italian Tradition of Lucretius', *Italia Medioevale e Umanistica*, 23: 27–48.

Reeve, M. D. (1983) 'Manilius', in L. D. Reynolds (ed.), *Texts and Transmission: A Survey of the Latin Classics* (Oxford: Clarendon Press), 235–8.

—— (2005) 'The Italian Tradition of Lucretius Revisited', *Aevum*, 79: 115–64.

—— (2006) 'Lucretius from the 1460s to the 17th Century: Seven Questions of Attribution', *Aevum*, 80: 165–84.

—— (2007) 'Lucretius in the Middle Ages and Early Renaissance: Transmission and Scholarship', in S. Gillespie and P. R. Hardie (eds.), *The Cambridge Companion to Lucretius* (Cambridge: Cambridge University Press), 205–13.

Rehak, P. (2006) *Imperium and Cosmos: Augustus and the Northern Campus Martius* (Madison: University of Wisconsin Press).

Riess, E. (1891–3) 'Nechepsonis et Petosiridis fragmenta magica', *Philologus*, suppl. 6: 325–94.

Rinaldi, M. (1999) 'Pontano, Trapezunzio ed il *Graecus Interpres* del *Centiloquio* pseudo-tolemaico', *Atti della Accademia Pontaniana*, 48: 125–71.

—— (2004) 'Un sodalizio poetico-astrologico nella Napoli del Quattrocento: Lorenzo Bonincontri e Giovanni Pontano', *MHNH* 4: 221–43.

Robbins, F. E. (1912) *The Hexaemeral Literature: A Study of the Greek and Latin Commentaries on Genesis* (Chicago: University of Chicago Press).

Roellenbleck, G. (1975) *Das epische Lehrgedicht Italiens im fünfzehnten und sechzehnten Jahrhundert: Ein Beitrag zur Literaturgeschichte des Humanismus und der Renaissance* (Munich: Fink).

Romano, E. (1979*a*) *Struttura degli* Astronomica *di Manilio* (Palermo: Accademia di Scienze, Lettere e Arti di Palermo).

—— (1979*b*) 'Teoria del progresso ed età dell'oro in Manilio (1, 66–112)', *RFIC* 107: 394–408.

—— (1980) 'Andromeda: l'epillio retorico (Manil. 5, 540–618)', *Atti della Accademia di Scienze, Lettere e Arti di Palermo*, 38: 213–35.

Rösch, H. (1911) *Manilius und Lucrez*. Diss. Kiel.

Salemme, C. (1983) *Introduzione agli* Astronomica *di Manilio* (Naples: Società Editrice Napoletana).

—— (2000) *Introduzione agli* Astronomica *di Manilio*, 2nd edn. (Naples: Loffredo).

Samburzky, S. (1959) *Physics of the Stoics* (London: Routledge & Paul).

Santini, C. (1981) 'Il salto delle costellazioni: Da Germanico ai glossatori', *GIF* 33: 177–91.

—— (1993) 'Connotazioni sociologiche in margine ai *paranatellonta* maniliani', in D. Liuzzi (ed.), *Manilio fra poesia e scienza* (Galatina: Congedo), 109–25.

Scaliger, J. (1579) *In Manili Quinque Libros Astronomicon Commentarius et Castigationes* (Paris: Stephanus).

—— (1600) *M. Manili Astronomicon* (Leiden: Raphelengius).

—— (1655) *Marci Manilii* Astronomicon (Strasburg: Bockenhoffer).

Scaramella, G. (1905–16) 'Matthei Palmerii Annales, conosciuti sotto il nome di Historia Florentina'. As an appendix in L. A. Muratori (ed.), *Rerum Italicarum Scriptores*, 26.1 (Città di Castello: S. Lapi).

Scarcia, R. (1993) '*Intelligendi aditus*: Aspetti dello studio virgiliano di Manilio', in D. Liuzzi (ed.), *Manilio fra poesia e scienza* (Galatina: Congedo), 127–45.

Scarsi, M. (1987) 'Metafora e ideologica negli *Astronomica* di Manilio', *Analysis*, 1: 93–126.

Schadewaldt, W. (1952) 'Die Homerische Gleichniswelt und die Kretisch-Mykenische Kunst', in *Hermeneia: Festschrift Otto Regenbogen* (Heidelberg: Winter), 9–27 (repr. in id., *Von Homers Welt und Werk*, 3rd edn. (Stuttgart: Kohler), 1959, 130–54).

Schauenburg, K. (1960) *Perseus in der Kunst des Altertums* (Bonn: Habelt).

Schiesaro, A. (1990) *Simulacrum et imago: Gli argomenti analogici nel* De rerum natura (Pisa: Giardini).

——(1996) 'Aratus' Myth of Dike', *MD* 37: 9–26.

Schievenin, R. (2009). Nugis ignosce lectitians: *Studi su Marziano Capella* (Trieste: Edizioni Università di Trieste).

Schindler, C. (2000) *Untersuchungen zu den Gleichnissen im römischen Lehrgedicht (Lucrez, Vergil, Manilius)* (Göttingen: Vandenhoeck & Ruprecht).

Schrijvers, P. H. (1978) 'Le Regard sur l'invisible: Étude sur l'emploi de l'analogie dans l'œuvre de Lucrèce', in O. Gigon (ed.), *Lucrèce* (= *Entretiens Hardt*, 24; Vandœuvres-Geneva: Fondation Hardt), 77–121 (English version in Gale (ed.), *Oxford Readings in Classical Studies: Lucretius* (Oxford: Oxford University Press, 2007), 255–88).

——(1983) 'Le Chant du monde: Remarques sur *Astronomica* I 1–24 de Manilius', *Mnemosyne*, 36: 143–50.

Schütz, M. (1990) 'Zur Sonnenuhr des Augustus auf dem Marsfeld', *Gymnasium*, 97: 432–57.

Schwarz, W. (1972) '*Praecordia mundi*: Zur Grundlegung der Bedeutung des Zodiak bei Manilius', *Hermes*, 100: 601–14.

Schwemmler, F. (1916) *De Lucano Manilii imitatore*. Diss. Giessen.

Schwoebel, R. (1967) *The Shadow of the Crescent: The Renaissance Image of the Turk (1453–1517)* (New York: St. Martin's Press).

Scodel, R. (1999) *Credible Impossibilities: Conventions and Strategies of Verisimilitude in Homer and Greek Tragedy* (Stuttgart: Teubner).

Sedley, D. (1998) 'The Sequence of Argument in Lucretius I', in C. Atherton (ed.), *Form and Content in Didactic Poetry* (Bari: Levanti), 37–55.

——(2007) *Creationism and its Critics in Antiquity* (Berkeley, Calif.: University of California Press).

Sfyroeras, P. (2008) '*Pothos Euripidou*: Reading *Andromeda* in Aristophanes' *Frogs*', *AJP* 129: 299–317.

Shackleton Bailey, D. R. (1956) 'Maniliana', *CQ* 50: 81–6.

334   *Bibliography*

Shackleton Bailey, D. R. (1979) 'Review Article: The Loeb Manilius', *CP* 74: 158–69.

Sharrock, A. R. (1994) 'Ovid and the Politics of Reading', *MD* 33: 97–122.

Shaw, B. (1985) 'The Divine Economy: Stoicism as Ideology', *Latomus*, 64: 16–54.

Sikes, E. E. (1923) *Roman Poetry* (London: Methuen & Co.).

Skutsch, F. (1910) 'Firmiciana', *RhM* 65: 627–34.

Smith, M. S. (1975) *Cena Trimalchionis Petroni Arbitri* (Oxford: Clarendon Press).

Snell, B. (1952) *Leben und Meinungen der Sieben Weisen* (Munich: Heimeran).

Snyder, J. M. (1980) *Puns and Poetry in Lucretius' De Rerum Natura* (Amsterdam: Grüner).

Soldati, B. (1902) *Ioannis Ioviani Pontani* Carmina, 2 vols. (Florence: Barbèra).

——(1906) *La poesia astrologica nel Quattrocento: Richerche e studi* (Florence: Sansoni).

Spannagel, M. (1999) *Exemplaria Principis: Untersuchungen zu Entstehung und Ausstattung des Augustusforums* (Heidelberg: Verlag Archäologie und Geschichte).

Spencer, T. (1952) 'Turks and Trojans in the Renaissance', *Modern Language Review*, 47: 330–3.

Spivey, M. (2007) *The Continuity of Mind* (New York: Oxford University Press).

Stahl, H.-P. (1985) *Propertius 'Love' and 'War': Individual and State under Augustus.* (Berkeley, Calif.: University of California Press).

Tateo, F. (1960) *Astrologia e moralità in Giovanni Pontano* (Bari: Adriatica Editrice).

Taub, L. (2008) *Aetna and the Moon: Explaining Nature in Ancient Greece and Rome* (Eugene, Or.: Oregon State University Press).

Thielscher, P. (1956) 'Ist "M. Manilii Astronomicon Libri V" richtig?', *Hermes*, 84: 353–72.

Thomas, R. F. (1988) *Virgil:* Georgics, 2 vols. (Cambridge: Cambridge University Press).

Thorndike, L. (1923–58) *A History of Magic and Experimental Science*, 8 vols. (New York: Macmillan).

——(1958) 'Some Tracts on Comets, 1456–1500', *Archives Internationales d'Histoire des Sciences*, 11: 225–50.

Timpanaro, S. (1988) *Marcus Tullis Cicero:* Della divinazione, 2nd edn. (Milan: Garzanti).

Toffanin, G. (1938) *Pontano fra l'uomo e natura* (Bologna: Nicola Zanichelli).

Toohey, P. (1996) *Epic Lessons: An Introduction to Ancient Didactic Poetry* (London: Routledge).

Topitsch, E. (1972) *Vom Ursprung und Ende der Metaphysik: Eine Studie zur Weltanschauungskritik*, 2nd edn. (Munich: Deutscher Taschenbuchverlag).

Tournoy-Thoen, G. (1972) 'La laurea poetica del 1484 all'Accademia romana', *BIBR* 42: 211–35.

Trinkaus, C. E. (1970) *In Our Image and Likeness: Humanity and Divinity in Italian Humanist Thought* (London: Constable).

——(1973) 'The Renaissance Idea of the Dignity of Man', in P. P. Wiener (ed.), *Dictionary of the History of Ideas*, 4 (New York: Scribner), 136–47.

——(1983) *The Scope of Renaissance Humanism* (Ann Arbor: University of Michigan Press).

——(1985) 'The Astrological Cosmos and Rhetorical Culture of Giovanni Gioviano Pontano', *Renaissance Quarterly*, 38: 446–72.

——(1989) 'Coluccio Salutati's Critique of Astrology in the Context of his Natural Philosophy', *Speculum*, 64: 46–68.

Trousset, P. (1993) 'La "Carte d'Agrippa": Nouvelle Proposition de lecture', *Dialogue d'Historie Ancienne*, 19: 137–57.

Vallauri, G. (1954) 'Gli *Astronomica* di Manilio e le fonti ermetiche', *RFIC* 32: 133–67.

Valvo, M. (1956) 'Considerazioni su Manilio e l'ermetismo', *SicGymn* 9: 108–17.

——(1978) '*Tu princeps auctorque sacri, Cyllenie, tanti*...: La rivincita dell'uomo maniliano nel segno di Hermes', *Sileno*, 4: 111–28.

van Nouhuys, T. (1998) *The Age of Two-Faced Janus: The Comets of 1577 and 1618 and the Decline of the Aristotelian World View in the Netherlands* (Leiden: Brill).

van Wageningen, J. (1915) *M. Manilii Astronomica* (Leipzig: Teubner).

——(1920) 'De Manilii aetate', *Mnemosyne*, 48: 189–92.

——(1921) *Commentarius in M. Manilii Astronomica* (= *Verhandel. Nederl. Akad. van Wet. Afd. Letterk.* 22.4) (Amsterdam: Müller).

——(1928) 'Manilius 6', *Pauly-Wissowa*, 14.1: 1115–33.

Verde, A. F. (1974) 'Giovanni Argiropolo e Lorenzo Buonincontri professori nello studio fiorentino', *Rinascimento*, 14: 279–87.

Veyne, P. (1983) *Les Grecs, ont-ils cru à leurs mythes? Essai sur l'imagination constituante* (Paris: Éditions du Seuil; English trans. 1988, *Did the Greeks Believe in their Myths?*).

Vogt, K. (2008) *Law, Reason, and the Cosmic City: Political Philosophy in the Early Stoa* (Oxford: Oxford University Press).

Volk, K. (2001) 'Pious and Impious Approaches to Cosmology in Manilius', *MD* 47: 85–117.

——(2002) *The Poetics of Latin Didactic: Lucretius, Vergil, Ovid, Manilius* (Oxford: Oxford University Press).

——(2009) *Manilius and his Intellectual Background* (Oxford: Oxford University Press).

——(forthcoming). 'Marcus Manilius'. *Oxford Bibliographies Online*.

von Albrecht, M. (1994) *Geschichte der römischen Literatur von Andronicus bis Boëthius*, 2 vols. 2nd edn. (Munich: Saur).

von Hendy, A. (2002) *The Modern Construction of Myth* (Bloomington, Ind.: University of Indiana Press).

von Staden, H. (1992) 'Affinities and Elisions: Helen and Hellenocentrism', *Isis*, 83: 578–95.

von Stuckrad, K. (2003) *Geschichte der Astrologie: Von den Anfängen bis zur Gegenwart* (Munich: Beck).

Voss, B. R. (1972) 'Der Andromeda-Episode des Manilius', *Hermes*, 100: 413–34.

Vossius, G. J. (1662) *De veterum poetarum temporibus libri duo, qui sunt de poetis Graecis et Latinis* (Amsterdam: Blaeu).

Wallace-Hadrill, A. (2005) '*Mutatas Formas*: The Augustan Transformation of Roman Knowledge', in Karl Galinsky (ed.), *The Cambridge Companion to the Age of Augustus* (Cambridge: Cambridge University Press), 55–84.

Wallach, B. P. (1976) *Lucretius and the Diatribe against the Fear of Death:* De Rerum Natura *III.830–1094* (Leiden: Brill).

Waszink, J. (1956) 'Maniliana I', *SIFC* 27/8: 588–98.

Watt, W. S. (1994) 'Maniliana', *CQ* 44: 451–7.

Wempe, H. (1935) 'Die literarischen Beziehungen und das chronologische Verhältnis zwischen Germanicus und Manilius', *RhM* 84: 89–96.

White, M. (1992) *The Continuous and the Discrete: Ancient Physical Theories from a Contemporary Perspective* (Oxford: Oxford University Press).

——(2003) 'Stoic Natural Philosophy (Physics and Cosmology)', in B. Inwood (ed.), *The Cambridge Companion to the Stoics* (Cambridge: Cambridge University Press), 124–52.

Wilkinson, L. P. (1969) *The Georgics of Virgil: A Critical Survey* (London: Cambridge University Press).

Williams, G. D. (2008) 'Cold Science: Seneca on Hail and Snow in *NQ* 4B', *CCJ* 54: 209–36.

Williams, I. P. *et al.* (2004) 'The Parent of the Quadrantid Meteoroid Stream and Asteroid 2003 EH1', *Monthly Notes of the Royal Astronomical Society*, 355: 1171–81.

Wilson, A. M. (1985) 'The Prologue to Manilius 1', *Papers of the Liverpool Latin Seminar*, 5: 283–98.

——(1996) 'Manilius, Marcus', *OCD* 3rd edn.: 917–18.

Yamamoto, K. and Burnett, Ch. (2000) *Abū Ma'šar, On Historical Astrology: The Book of Religions and Dynasties (On the Great Conjunctions)*, 2 vols. (Leiden: Brill).

Yeomans, D. K. (1991) *Comets: A Chronological History of Observation, Science, Myth, and Folklore* (New York: Wiley).

Zanker, P. (1988) *The Power of Images in the Age of Augustus*, tr. A. Shapiro (Ann Arbor: University of Michigan).

Zeitlin, F. I. (1996) 'Signifying Difference: The Case of Hesiod's Pandora', in ead., *Playing the Other: Gender and Society in Classical Greek Literature* (Chicago: University of Chicago Press), 53–86.

Zhou, H. *et al.* (1997) 'New Reductions of Orbits Based upon Chinese Ancient Cometary Records', *Planetary and Space Science*, 45: 1551–5.

Zwierlein, O. (1987) 'Weihe und Entrückung der Locke der Berenike', *RhM* 130: 274–90.

Index Locorum

AUGUSTINE
City of God
12.19: 176–7

CICERO
Aratea
223-31: 20–1

De Consulatu Suo
6-10: 21

De Divinatione
2.89: 23

De Natura Deorum
1.41: 50
2.22: 90
2.37-9: 90–1
2.43: 102
2.49: 18
2.54-5: 18–19
2.60: 19–20
2.64: 50–1
2.104: 20
2.140: 29

Republic
6.15: 14

Timaeus
36: 21–2
43: 22

CLAUDIAN
In Rufinum
1.363-6: 257
1.372-3: 259–60
1.374-5: 259

DIOGENES LAERTIUS
7.147: 91

EUSEBIUS
Praeparatio Evangelica 15.15.3-5: 92

HESIOD
Works and Days
50-1: 207
80-2: 207

LUCAN
9.5-9: 16–17
9.11-14: 16–17

LUCRETIUS
1.803-8: 125–6
1.897-903: 125–6
5.609-30: 17–18

MANILIUS
1: 122–3
1.1-10: 59–60
1.1-4: 171
1.1-2: 8
1.1-4: 35
1.8-9: 189
1.10-11: 173
1.11-12: 189
1.16-19: 35–6
1.20-4: 179
1.25-33: 207
1.25-9: 263
1.30-1: 263
1.30: 7
1.79-80: 210
1.95: 210
1.96-8: 114, 178
1.104: 114
1.106-8: 178
1.108-9: 38–9
1.149-70: 82–3
1.185: 25
1.202-13: 179–80
1.215-46: 59–84
1.215-20: 73–4
1.221-35: 70–3
1.236-46: 65
1.239-40: 182
1.242-5: 109–10
1.247-54: 65–7
1.306: 153
1.331-2: 153
1.354-60: 237
1.377: 182
1.413: 160–1
1.453-5: 119

MANILIUS (*cont.*)
1.476-7: 25
1.532-8: 181
1.541-3: 181
1.758-61: 224
1.761-804: 223–8
1.809-926: 279–82
1.896-913: 215
1.898-903: 4
1.922-6: 217

2.25-7: 117
2.37-8: 49, 117, 235
2.38: 141–2
2.49-52: 187
2.67-71: 24–5, 193–4
2.73: 24–5
2.82-6: 115
2.105-36: 87
2.105-25: 110
2.105-8: 128
2.115-25: 112–13
2.115-16: 25, 93, 264
2.122-5: 194
2.125: 199
2.127-8: 194
2.136-49: 87, 110
2.141-6: 199
2.203-4: 179
2.340-2: 196
2.345-6: 196
2.358-9: 197
2.382: 197
2.414-15: 160
2.466-7: 197
2.485ff.: 52
2.579-82: 115
2.603-7: 115
2.823-5: 190

3.1-4: 186
3.3-4: 193
3.23-6: 183
3.203-509: 105–6
3.443-82: 228–31
3.625-65: 218–20

4.11: 200
4.121: 164
4.124-291: 123
4.158-60: 174
4.169: 154
4.176-88: 116

4.294-386: 124
4.294-6: 198
4.351: 153
4.380-6: 124
4.387-407: 125–7, 200–1
4.390-2: 113
4.406-7: 201
4.409-10: 127
4.430-8: 175
4.439-42: 176
4.542-50: 258
4.585-743: 231–4
4.742-3: 37
4.773-7: 258–9
4.807-9: 198
4.866-935: 110
4.866-72: 127
4.869-72: 185
4.873-7: 192
4.878: 39
4.883-5: 39, 192
4.903-8: 113
4.915-17: 38
4.916-35: 87
4.927: 38

5.21: 158
5.42: 157
5.50: 157
5.142-3: 36
5.276-7: 191
5.296: 163
5.298-310: 145
5.309: 159
5.390: 144
5.395: 160
5.398-400: 161–3
5.405: 158
5.407: 157
5.411-13: 162
5.431: 158
5.443: 161
5.449-85: 249
5.472-3: 145
5.476: 155
5.504-37: 248
5.518-19: 248
5.538-618: 150–1, 159, 163, 237–52
5.543: 157
5.558-66: 242–7
5.569-72: 240
5.575: 157

5.587-92: 241
5.607: 162
5.617-18: 159
5.619-30: 249
5.640-1: 149
5.655: 164
5.656-92: 249–50
5.734-45: 92, 118
5.743-5: 42

OVID
Ars Amatoria
1.55-6: 184
1.59: 184
3: 136–7
3.549: 195

Fasti
1.295-310: 134
1.314: 134

PETRONIUS
35-6: 123–4
39-40: 123–4

PLAUTUS
Rudens
1-15: 13–14

PLINY THE ELDER
2.28-9: 30

PROPERTIUS
4.1.71-150: 132–3

SENECA THE YOUNGER
Ad Helviam
8.5-6: 16
Ad Marciam
25.1-2: 15–16
26.1: 15–16
26.6: 43–4

Ad Polybium
1: 44

De Beneficiis
4.23.4: 26

Epistles
88.14-16: 28
93.9: 28–9
94.56: 29–30

Quaestiones Naturales
2.32.6: 27
6.16.2: 27
7.28.1: 28

SERVIUS
Commentary on Aeneid
6.714: 147–8

SEXTUS EMPIRICUS
Adversus Mathematicos
9.104: 89

SUETONIUS
Life of Augustus
94.12: 169

TACITUS
Histories
1.22: 131

VIRGIL
Georgics
1.32-5: 258
1.123-4: 210
1.145-6: 210
1.336-7: 28
1.464-5: 215–16
1.487-8: 215–16
1.491-2: 215–16
1.501-6: 217
1.509-11: 215–16
1.511-14: 217

VITRUVIUS
9.6.2: 133

General Index

Agrippa, Map of 231–4
Andromeda, myth of 238–41, 243–5
Arius Didymus 92–3
Astrology, *see also Astronomica*,
    astrological figures in
  ancient 8–9, 141–64
  and Augustus 130–1
  determinism v. (Christian) free will
    261–77
  early modern era 173–4
  popular modern vii
  Roman 130–1, 168–70
  and Tiberius 131
Augustus *see* Manilius and Augustus;
    Astrology and Augustus
Astronomica
  absence of planets from 3, 20–1, 121
  addressee/student of 122–8
  anthropology in 263–7
  astrological figures in 141–64
  catasterism in 116–19
  contradictions/inconsistencies in 7–8,
    85–119, 267
  date of 4–5, 255–6
  as didactic 7–8, 120–38
  digressions in 204–21, 222–34, 235–52
  framing technique in 52–3
  incompleteness of text of 3
  pedagogy v. determinism in 110, 121
  reception of 261–2, 267–77,
    278–310

Bonincontri, Lorenzo 10, 267–72, 277,
    278–310
  Commentary *Ad Astr.* 1.809-926:
    289–96
  De Rebus Naturalibus et Divinis
    I.1.474-591: 282–6, 298–300
  Commentary *Ad De Rebus*
    Naturalibus et Divinis I.1.474-591:
    301–10

census 173, 187, 188–194
comets 278–310
commercium 194–201

deducere 177–9
Descartes, René 55–6
didactic 136–7; *see also Astronomica*,
    as didactic
digressions *see Astronomica*, digressions
    in

Forum Romanum 223–8

Hermetism, *see* Manilius and
    Hermetism
Horologium Augusti 228–31
Housman, A.E. viii, 2, 105–6, 165–6, 171

Lucretius 107–8

Manilius
  and Aratus 8, 211–12, 216–18
  and astrology 6–7
  and Augustus 5, 129–38, 184, 212–13,
    217, 220, 222–34, 259–60
  decision to write about astrology 5
  and Firmicus Maternus 9
  and Germanicus 9
  and Hermetism 7
  and Hesiod 207–8, 218
  the historical figure 5
  and Lucretius 8–9, 208, 214, 219
  and Stoicism 6–7, 32–44, 88, 103, 195,
    247
  and Virgil 8–9, 170–1, 210, 214–18,
    219, 271
myth, relation with science 45–56

planets, *see Astronomica*, absence of
    planets from
Pontano, Giovanni 10, 272–7

ratio 172–3, 181–2, 186
Renaissance, Italian 9–10, 261–2,
    267–77, 278–310

Stoicism 88–103; *see also* Manilius and
    Stoicism
urbs/orbis conceit 183–4